CHICHESTER ARCHDEACONRY DEPOSITIONS

CHICHESTER ARCHDEACONRY DEPOSITIONS

1603 - 1608

EDITED BY

PETER M WILKINSON

SUSSEX RECORD SOCIETY
VOLUME 97

Issued to members of the Society for the year 2015

Published 2017 by
Sussex Record Society
Barbican House,
High Street,
Lewes,
East Sussex, BN7 1YE.

ISBN 978 0 85445 079 4

Printed by Hobbs the Printers Ltd., Totton, Hampshire.

VOLUMES ISSUED BY THE SUSSEX RECORD SOCIETY

Vol. 1 *Marriage Licences at Lewes, 1586-1642*
Vol. 2 *Sussex Fines, 1190-1248*
Vol. 3 *Post Mortem Inquisitions, 1558-1583*
Vol. 4 *Ecclesiastical Returns for East Sussex, 1603; Sussex Poll Book, 1705; Sussex MSS in the Harleian MSS; Bishop Praty's Register, 1438-1445.*
Vol. 5 *West Sussex Protestation Returns, 1641-1642*
Vol. 6 *Marriage Licences at Lewes, 1670-1732*
Vol. 7 *Sussex Fines, 1249-1307*
Vol. 8 *Bishop Rede's Register, 1397-1415* (Pt. 1)
Vol. 9 *Marriage Licences at Chichester 1575-1730*
Vol. 10 *Subsidy Rolls, 1296, 1327 and 1332*
Vol. 11 *Bishop Rede's Register, 1397-1415* (Pt. 2)
Vol. 12 *Marriage Licences at Chichester* (peculiars), 1579-1730
Vol. 13 *Cuckfield Parish Register, 1598-1699*
Vol. 14 *Post Mortem Inquisitions, 1485-1649*
Vol. 15 *Bolney Parish Register, 1541-1812*
Vol. 16 *Star Chamber Proceedings, 1500-1558*
Vol. 17 *Ardingly Parish Register, 1558-1812*
* Vol. 18 *Angmering Parish Register, 1562-1687*
Vol. 19 *Sussex Manors and Advowsons, etc., 1509-1833*, A-L
Vol. 20 *Sussex Manors and Advowsons, etc., 1509-1833*, M-Z
Vol. 21 *Horsham Parish Register, 1541-1635*
Vol. 22 *Cowfold Parish Register, 1558-1812*
Vol. 23 *Sussex Fines, 1308-1509*
Vol. 24 *East Grinstead Parish Register, 1558-1661*
Vol. 25 *Marriage Licences at Lewes, 1771-1837*, A-L
Vol. 26 *Marriage Licences at Lewes, 1772-1837*, M-Z
Vol. 27 *Preston Manor Court Rolls, 1562-1702*
Vol. 28 *Sussex Apprentices and Masters, 1710-1752*
Vol. 29 *Abstracts of Documents relating to the Dobell family*, 16th-18th cents.
Vol. 30 *Glynde Parish Register, 1558-1812*
Vol. 31 *Custumals of the Sussex Manors of the Bishop of Chichester, c.1256-1374*
Vol. 32 *Sussex Marriage Licences at Chichester, 1731-1774*
Vol. 33 *Sussex Inquisitions (from Bodleian Library), 1541-1616*
Vol. 34 *The Book of John Rowe, Steward to Lord Bergavenny, 1622*
Vol. 35 *Marriage Licences at Chichester, 1775-1800*, with Index 1731-1800
Vol. 36 *Sussex Chantry Records, 1535-1652*
Vol. 37 *Hastings Rape Records, 1387-1474*
Vol. 38 *Chartulary of Lewes Priory* (Pt. I), 11th-14th cents.
* Vol. 39 *The Buckhurst Terrier, 1597-1598*
Vol. 40 *Chartulary of Lewes Priory* (Pt. II), 12th-14th cents.
Vol. 41 *Transcripts of Sussex Wills up to 1560* Vol. 1 Albourne - Chichester
Vol. 42 *Transcripts of Sussex Wills up to 1560* Vol. 2 Chiddingly - Horsham
Vol. 43 *Transcripts of Sussex Wills up to 1560* Vol. 3 Horsted Keynes - Pyecombe
Vol. 44 *Records of the Barony and Honour of the Rape of Lewes, 1265-1466*
Vol. 45 *Transcripts of Sussex Wills up to 1560* Vol. 4 Racton - Yapton
Vol. 46 *Chichester Cathedral Chartulary*, 13th-16th cents.
Vol. 47 *Survey of Robertsbridge Manor, 1567-1570*
* Vol. 48 *The Town Book of Lewes, 1542-1701*

Vol. 49 *Churchwardens' Presentments*, (Pt. I), *Archdeaconry of Chichester, 1621-28, 1664-70*
Vol. 50 *Churchwardens' Presentments*, (Pt. II), *Archdeaconry of Lewes, 1674-1677*
Vol. 51 *Record of Deputations of Gamekeepers, 1781-1928*
Jubilee Volume *Sussex Views from the Burrell Collection*
Vol. 52 *Chapter Acts, Chichester, 1472-1544* (The White Act Book)
Vol. 53 *The Manor of Etchingham cum Salehurst, 1597-1865*
Vol. 54 *Quarter Sessions Order Book, 1642-1649*
Vol. 55 *Ministers' Accounts of the Manor of Petworth, 1347-1353*
Vol. 56 *Lay Subsidy Rolls, 1524-1525*
Vol. 57 *Custumals of Sussex Manors of the Archbishop of Canterbury, 1285-1330*
Vol. 58 *Chapter Acts, Chichester, 1545-1642*
Vol. 59 *Chartulary of Boxgrove Priory*, 12th-14th cents.
Vol. 60 *Custumals of the Manors of Laughton, Willingdon and Goring, 1292-1338*
* Vol. 61 *A Catalogue of Sussex Estate and Tithe Award Maps* (Pt. I), 1606-1884
Vol. 62 *Minutes of the Common Council of the City of Chichester, 1783-1826*
Vol. 63 *The Book of Bartholomew Bolney*, 15th cent.
Vol. 64 *Rye Shipping Records, 1566-1590*
Vol. 65 *Cellarers' Rolls of Battle Abbey, 1275-1513*
Vol. 66 *A Catalogue of Sussex Maps*, (Pt. II) 1597-1958
Vol. 67 *Estate Surveys of the Fitzalan Earls of Arundel*, 14th cent.
Vol. 68 *The Journal of Giles Moore of Horsted Keynes, 1655-1679*
Vol. 69 *The Town Book of Lewes, 1702-1837*
Vol. 70 *The Town Book of Lewes, 1837-1901*
* Vol. 71 *Accounts of the Roberts Family of Boarzell, 1568-1582*
Vol. 72 *Printed Maps of Sussex, 1575-1900*
* Vol. 73 *Correspondence of the Dukes of Richmond and Newcastle, 1724-1750*
Vol. 74 *Sussex Coroners' Inquests, 1485-1558*
* Vol. 75 *The Religious Census of Sussex, 1851*
Vol. 76 *The Fuller Letters, 1728-1755*
Vol. 77 *East Sussex Land Tax, 1785*
* Vol. 78 *Chichester Diocesan Surveys, 1686 and 1724*
* Vol. 79 *Saint Richard of Chichester*
Vol. 80 *The Ashdown Forest Dispute, 1876-1882*
Vol. 81 *Sussex Schools in the 18th century*
* Vol. 82 *West Sussex Land Tax, 1785*
Vol. 83 *Mid Sussex Poor Law Records, 1601-1835*
Vol. 84 *Sussex in the First World War*
Vol. 85 *Sussex Depicted: Views and Descriptions 1600-1800*
* Vol. 86 *Sussex Shore to Flanders Fields: E. Heron–Allen's Journal of the Great War*
* Vol. 87 *East Sussex Parliamentary Deposited Plans, 1799-1970*
Vol. 88 *Sussex Cricket in the 18th century*
* Vol. 89 *East Sussex Coroners' Records, 1688-1838*
* Vol. 90 *The Durford Cartulary*
* Vol. 91 *Sussex Clergy Inventories, 1600-1750*
* Vol. 92 *Accounts and Records of the Manor of Mote in Iden, 1461-1551, 1673*
* Vol. 93 *East Sussex Church Monuments, 1530-1830*
* Vol. 94 *Winchelsea Poor Law Records, 1790-1841*
* Vol. 95 *Littlehampton School Logbook, 1871-1911*
* Vol. 96 *Letters of John Collier of Hastings, 1731-1746*
* Vol. 97 *Chichester Archdeaconry Depositions, 1603-1608*

In print volumes marked with an asterisk can be obtained from the Sussex Record Society, Barbican House, Lewes, East Sussex, BN7 1YE or through the Society's website: www.sussexrecordsociety.org

CONTENTS

	Page
Acknowledgements	ix
Introduction	xi
Background information from unpublished sources	xlvi
A note on the editing and presentation	xlvii
Chichester Archdeaconry Depositions 1603-1608	1
Appendix 1: Deposition of Alice Dash concerning John Lilliatt and Alice Smyth 1607	267
Appendix 2: Account for the case of Coote v Brydye	270
Appendix 3: Example of the transcription method	275
Endnotes	280
Index of Persons	287
Index of Places	302
Index of Subjects	306

ILLUSTRATIONS

Chichester Consistory Court and Chapter	Frontispiece
House Tithe Barn, Sullington	xxv
Consistory Court, Chester Cathedral	xxxiii
Deposition of John Baylye	207

ACKNOWLEDGEMENTS

My first thanks must go to the Bishop of Chichester, the owner of the episcopal archive, and to the County and Diocesan Archivist, Wendy Walker, its custodian, for allowing me to publish the deposition book which provides the content of this volume.

When I drew up my first tentative plans for publication I was enormously reassured by Dr Felicity Heal who generously found time to look at my proposal and to encourage me to go ahead. Subsequently I have received continuing help and encouragement throughout the whole project from Wendy Walker as Chairman of the Sussex Record Society. The Council members of the Society have been a valuable source of assistance, especially in providing guidance on presentation. In particular I am grateful to Andrew Foster, whose critique of the introduction has provided valuable suggestions for its improvement, and to Brian Short for advice on agricultural matters and background material, and to Roger Davey for guidance on transcription.

In the four years since I started on the transcription and editing, the Searchroom staff at the West Sussex Record Office have borne my visits and requests with unfailing courtesy and patience. In my struggles with legal Latin, Tim Hudson has been a ready source of help; Christopher Whittick has tackled not only Latin and the palaeography problems but also, by his knowledge of the secular courts, illuminated my understanding of the church court procedures. Hugh Wilkinson and Jessica Stoll have read the varying stages of the book with patience and even enthusiasm, and have provided advice and valuable insights throughout.

I owe a great debt to Roger Pearce whose eagle eye and digital expertise achieved impossibilities in the preparation of the printers' copy – skills which he has fully matched by the analytical and miraculous speed with which he has produced the indexes.

From the very beginning, before she had even seen a deposition, Ruth Brown has encouraged the project. She has helped and advised at every stage from transcription to introduction, even to the extent of guiding me through walks along the disputed boundaries of tithe cases. Without her enthusiasm and support this book would never have reached completion. Nor would it without the determination of my wife, Jane, who has inspired me to undertake and persevere with the project, despite the domestic disruptions it has involved; and has patiently endured the regurgitation and discussion of centuries-old domesticities. Above all she has helped to guide me towards presenting the stories for the eyes of a modern reader – and has continued to reassure me of the value of the project.

It is a pleasure to record the assistance I have received from so many people and institutions on the different aspects of the book. Richard Saville has helped me find contemporary and modern printed material; Michael Moriarty and Colin Clark guided me through the possible courtroom sites in the Cathedral; the staff of Lambeth Palace Library, the Borthwick Institute at York, and the Chester Record Office and the Chester County Library have all answered my queries on different aspects.

For permission to reproduce illustrations I am grateful to the County Archivist, and to Mrs G Kitell and Stephen Craven; Clare Snoad of the West Sussex Record Office has provided the expertise to prepare the illustrations for printing. Martin Trigell of Hobbs the Printers has seen the production through with unfailing courtesy and efficiency.

Perhaps my final thanks should be to the one hundred and twenty two witnesses whose depositions have opened their own unique windows into scenes of everyday life four centuries ago. If their stories give pleasure or illumination to modern readers I hope this may be some compensation for the ordeals the deponents may have undergone when they gave their testimony.

Peter Wilkinson
April 2017

The Chapter House and Consistory Court, engraved by R H Nibbs, 1860. (West Sussex Record Office PD 1975).

CHURCH COURT DEPOSITIONS IN THE CONSISTORY COURT FOR THE ARCHDEACONRY OF CHICHESTER 1603-1607

INTRODUCTION

It is more than a century since the belligerent scholar Frederick J Furnivall, editor of Chaucer and founder of the *Oxford English Dictionary* and of the Early English Text Society, dedicated his collection of extracts from depositions, *Child Marriages, Divorce and Ratification in the Diocese of Chester 1561-66,* to:

The Antiquarians of Chester
In the hope
That they will hang one of their number
To encourage the rest
Forthwith to print all the depositions and other valuable material
In the diocesan registry at Chester
Which they have so long and so culpably left in MSS only.[1]

Perhaps this present edition may be seen as an attempt to save the members of the Sussex Record Society from the same fate. Marginalia[2] in the Chichester diocesan records show that Furnivall had also sampled them. But he failed to print any; and he does not seem to have expanded his threat.

Despite his fulminatory tone and dramatic title, Furnivall made a serious and important demand. The records of many English dioceses provide a unique and largely unexploited source to illuminate local life in the sixteenth and seventeenth centuries. What had particularly attracted him were the depositions of witnesses in church court cases; and in his brief forays at Chichester he was the first researcher to discover the diocese's rich collection.

For almost a century Furnivall's exhortation went unheeded. Historians remained largely unaware that there were church courts and that they had preserved such a legacy. Admittedly, most of the records lay inaccessibly in the strongrooms of the diocesan registrar. It was only with the growth of county and diocesan record offices after the Second World War that they could begin to discover the stories the witnesses had told.

And even when the records became easily available, they may have seemed inaccessible to many of their potential users. Even the depositions of the early modern period could deter readers faced with the difficult legal hand of the clerks. Additionally the patches of Latin – particularly those in the titling and the initial paragraph of each deposition – could frighten off those without a basic knowledge of the language. The final and most forbidding obstacle could be the act books, which are the only means of discovering the progress and outcome of the cases. Written entirely in Latin, and in

---

[1] F.J. Furnivall, *Child Marriages, Divorces and Ratifications in the Diocese of Chester, 1561-66. (1897).*
[2] The Chichester deposition books contain a several annotations with the initials FJF.

heavily abbreviated legal phraseology, they could seem impenetrable - famously evoking Elton's despairing condemnation:

> The act books of church courts are among the more strikingly repulsive of all the relics of the past - written in cramped and hurried hands, in very abbreviated and technical Latin, often preserved (if that is the right word) in fairly noisome conditions, ill-sorted and mostly unlisted, unindexed and sometimes broken in pieces ... Only young scholars, still enthusiastic, physically strong, and possessed of a sound digestion, are advised to tackle these materials.[3]

But church court records are too valuable to be left in obscurity; and it is the main purpose of this book to help to make them accessible. By publishing an edited transcript of the content of an entire volume of depositions, I hope to provide a clear understanding of the type of information they offer, and of the form in which it is presented, the range and variety of the different cases, and of the dynamics between litigant, lawyer and witness which shaped the content and phrasing of the testimony. I hope it will enable readers to discover that they are not faced with a sealed book. The obstacles I have described are not insuperable. The clerks' secretary hand is usually carefully written (as is necessary for a legal record). The Latin in the depositions is largely formulaic and repetitive. And, (after several decades of care and cataloguing in local authority repositories) even the act books and their unrelenting Latin will allow a cursory examination to yield up the chronology of each case and to indicate whether it achieved a sentence. To mine the depositions demands some labour, but it is not an unreasonable amount when set against the value of the information they can give.

In Sussex, the episcopal archives of Chichester diocese contain valuable records of the work of the bishop's two courts. As described more fully below, his office court exercised moral discipline while the instance court set out to resolve disputes between individuals. The latter has left behind a series of deposition books for the period between the Reformation and the Civil War. A particularly important and almost unbroken run of 16 volumes survives for the Archdeaconry of Chichester, 1557-1642.

The earlier exploration of church court records focused mainly on those of the office court. Scholars used them to discover the religious tensions in local communities in the wake of the Reformation and the Elizabethan Settlement. The Sussex Record Society was one of the first county publishing societies to do so when it published in 1950 Hilda Johnstone's *Churchwardens' Presentments, 17th century: Archdeaconry of Chichester*.[4] Later historians have turned to depositions in a number of dioceses as a means of illuminating wider issues of social history. Peter Clark demonstrated their value in his ground-breaking analysis of population movement and migration, age, occupation and literacy.[5] Laura Gowing[6] and others have used them to reveal the attitudes of women to marriage

---

[3] G R Elton, *England 1200-1640. The Sources of History: Studies in the Uses of Historical Evidence,* 1969, 104-5. I am grateful to Andrew Foster for supplying this quotation.

[4] Sussex Record Society, Volume 49.

[5] P Clark, *English Provincial Society from the Reformation to the Revolution: Religion, Politics and Society in Kent, 1500-1640.* 1977.

[6] L Gowing, *Domestic Dangers, Women, Words and Sex in Early Modern London,* 1996.

and gender. Most recently, for Alexandra Shepard they have produced a wide-ranging account of the financial resources of the lower social groups.[7]

Now that the wider use of depositions has established their value, it is important to make available a comprehensive and contextualised series to display their qualities as a historical source. They lend themselves to vivid and selective quotation, and the results are valuable. But no publication has yet shown them within the framework of the cases that produced them. Parallel depositions in the same case modify the information that each presents. The questions behind them, posed by the parties in their libels and interrogatories, reveal differing attitudes, and suggest changes in the reader's perceptions. Depositions from opposing parties add a further dimension. The court's decisions on publication and sentence, the parties' decision on settlement or lapse, can suggest the value they found in them. All these factors make it important to see them in their full context. A single deposition book will tell stories from a wide range of different types of case in differing localities; and with supporting information from the related court proceedings it will help us to attempt to understand the society which produced them.

If the text of this volume can illuminate the claims and questions that generated the depositions, can demonstrate the relationships among the witnesses and the disputing parties, and can provide a measure of the effect of the depositions on the outcome of their case, then I hope it will have achieved a worthwhile purpose.

From the Chichester Archdeaconry records I have chosen to make an edited transcript of the volume spanning the years 1603 to 1607. The period was a time of important developments in the national church. In 1603 the Puritans greeted the accession of James I with the radical Millenary Petition (which included a complaint on 'the long-someness of suites in Ecclesiasticall courts which hang sometimes two, three, foure, five, six or seaven yeares'). A year later the King summoned the Hampton Court Conference to face the threats posed by Puritanism. In the same year the church promulgated new Canons to reform its governance (and its courts). A new and reforming Archbishop of Canterbury, Richard Bancroft, was appointed and commenced his Metropolitical Visitation in 1605. Within the diocese of Chichester, the diocesan bishop was faced by a variety of problems. Puritanism in the east of the county was active and increasing, and difficult to control. In the west the old Catholic loyalties among the aristocracy and gentry provided equal difficulties. The disciplinary process based on visitations and presentments by parish officials was proving inadequate. Diocesan finance was equally inadequate to maintain the clergy – and even the bishop's residences.[8]

Whilst it might be tempting to expect such changes, both national and local, to be reflected in the records of the Chichester instance courts, they leave no mark. Such matters did not impinge on their task of resolving personal disputes. Even during Bancroft's Visitation, when the Archbishop's representatives took over the management of diocesan courts, the day to day business of the instance courts

---

[7] A Shepard, *Accounting for Oneself: Worth, Status and the Social order in Early Modern England*, 2015.

[8] The local scene has been described by Andrew Foster in 'Chichester Diocese in the early 17th Century' (*SAC* **123** (1985) 187-194).

continued undisturbed and under the direction of their usual local officials. The depositions that were produced in their proceedings were created as the result of a rôle which was relatively remote from contentious issues of doctrine or moral discipline. Instead, their records continued to provide their vivid and unique pictures of everyday life in rural Sussex.

The source material for this volume

The chosen document covers the period from December 1603 to April 1607.[9] It is a substantial volume containing 291 folios and provides a typical range of cases in the Chichester Archdeaconry court. My transcription covers the entire volume and, for completeness, where a case overlaps from an earlier volume or into a later one, I have included additional depositions. The earliest come from a single case and commences in May 1603; the latest come from four cases and end in July 1608.[10] To discover the progress of the cases I have used the court act books covering the period April 1603 to June 1609.[11] Frustratingly, one act book, covering the period between March and October 1607, has not survived, leaving the conclusion of several later cases unknown. Occasionally the act books contain statements by the parties which supplement the information given in the depositions, and I have included these where relevant. Some additional material has also been found in the separate series of Miscellaneous Court Papers.[12] These consist of papers accumulated by the registrar in the course of proceedings, but must represent only a fraction of those originally produced. The most valuable items they contain are the personal responses made by the parties; and these have been included whenever they have survived. Occasionally libels or allegations have survived and provide supplementary information which I have extracted where relevant.

Because such publication has not been attempted before, I have tried to present the depositions in a reasonably full form. I have resisted the temptation of drastic editing and I have attempted to set out in an introductory note the narrative of the proceedings in each case and, where relevant, some of its technicalities. I hope this will provide sufficient detail to evaluate them – and to contribute to more extensive use of such material in Sussex and beyond.[13]

The value of depositions

The depositions made in the ecclesiastical courts preserve the voices of a sector of the population, which was for the most part unheard and for the most part illiterate. The witnesses provide, ostensibly in their own words, descriptions of relatively mundane incidents within their community. Although they are testifying in court, they are not

---

[9] West Sussex Record Office (hereafter WSRO) Ep I/11/10.

[10] WSRO Ep I/10/9, 11.

[11] WSRO Ep I/10/21-28.

[12] WSRO Ep I/15/1, 3.

[13] The principles are set out in the note on editorial conventions; and as a sample of the original I have provided a complete transcript of one deposition, together with its edited version (Appendix 3).

describing dramatic scenes of violence or crime: the stories they tell arise from disagreements between (for the most part) law-abiding individuals, which would otherwise have remained unrecorded. Few personal writings such as diaries and letters survive from the first decade of the seventeenth century and those which do are almost entirely from the upper social strata.

The depositions give us scenes from the everyday life of a lowlier world in rural Sussex. And as well as offering entertaining snatches of salacious gossip and drunken outbursts they provide factual information, in consistent and comparable form, on life and work in the local community. The range of their stories is wide: tensions among the members of the congregation as they gathered for Sunday worship; religious customs and memories surviving from pre-Reformation, or at least pre-Elizabethan, years; the reputations and interrelationships of individuals within their community; the bargaining, rituals and uncertainties as couples made declarations and promises of marriage; the mixture of grief and practicality for the widow, family and neighbours around the bed of a dying man; the vulnerability of apparently respectable wives to whispers of sexual immorality, with the accompanying stigma of cuckoldry for their husbands; and, perhaps more unexpectedly, changes in farming customs (particularly agricultural innovations), and ensuing disputes between tithe payers and tithe owners.

The deponents tell their stories within legally imposed constraints. They respond to questions and statements presented to them by lawyers. They speak under oath; and they are examined in private to prevent collusion. But they are not lone voices. Because the court required at least two witnesses (and there were usually more) we can build up a credibly factual account of the events behind the disputes. Within this framework they can give us their narratives of local incidents with unique detail; they can paint a vivid picture of their community and the relationships and tensions within it, of life and activities within the home, the alehouse, the parish church and on the land.

The courts and their procedure.

The cases formed regular items of business in the work of the busy legal machine which operated in the bishop of Chichester's diocesan headquarters. While the county's secular courts continued to enforce the traditional legal framework dealing with felonies and misdemeanours through the Assizes, Quarter Sessions and the local magistracy, the ecclesiastical courts had become particularly active during the period 1570-1640 when the maintenance of religious orthodoxy of the newly established church needed to be reflected by the personal morality of its members. The courts were now expected to bring legal discipline into areas of life where the secular law had no jurisdiction.

Their legal process was based on civil[14] and canon law; and despite the Reformation their lawyers followed a medieval body of jurisprudence, practice and documentation. The secular courts, of course, looked to common and statute law. The Reformation had, however, added a new dimension to the practice of the church courts. Church

---

[14] The term civil can be confusing for a modern reader. In the mediaeval and early modern period it refers to ecclesiastical law as opposed to common and statute law.

attendance had been enforced by an Edwardian statute of 1552; the reformed Elizabethan church had been established by the 1559 Act of Uniformity; and a succession of other statutes and ordinances attempted to control religious life. These secular laws were incorporated into the existing civil law practice;[15] but the courts still reflected Queen Elizabeth's desire not to make windows into men's souls. It was behaviour rather than thought that they sought to control.

But in addition to the enforcement of religious conformity, the church courts took on the monumental task of enforcing personal morality. The potential for this had been available in pre-Reformation times; but in the period from the 1570s onwards it became a major part of the courts' activity. Its growth stems largely from changes in moral attitudes which may loosely be called Puritan, and perhaps also from changes in church customs. Before the Reformation, the practice of confession perhaps provided a means for the church to deal with what one might call private (and particularly sexual) transgressions. After the Reformation and the virtual abolition of auricular confession, such offences were 'detected' by churchwardens and clergy and presented publicly through the church's visitation procedure. They were dealt with in the church courts, earning them their nickname of the 'Bawdy Courts'. Presentments also ranged less pruriently over a wide range of other offences. They were not confined to religious issues such as Catholic recusancy, shortcomings in church and Sunday observance or in the maintenance of church fabric and fittings, but also dealt with failure to prove wills, and a range of anti-social behaviour such as drunkenness, brawling and even witchcraft.

Every Saturday saw sessions of the bishop's two Consistory courts in the Cathedral. They dealt with the western half of the county, the Archdeaconry of Chichester: 134 parishes running from Rusper in the north to Lancing in the south. They were paralleled by sessions on Friday of two courts with separate but smaller jurisdictions: the Dean of Chichester's peculiar jurisdiction (ten parishes in the City) and the Archbishop of Canterbury's peculiar jurisdiction of Pagham and Tarring (ten parishes scattered within the Archdeaconry). The latter court sat in the nearby church of All Saints in the Pallant but was timetabled to fit with the Dean's. The three courts were staffed by a professional team of judges, lawyers and registrars, most of whom would act in all the courts. The interlocking sittings of all the courts were therefore essential.

The eastern half of the diocese had a similar machinery. The Archdeaconry of Lewes had its own court, which usually sat on Tuesdays in the church of St Michael, conveniently sited in the centre of the town. It was staffed in a similar way to the Chichester Archdeaconry court, with local clergy providing surrogate judges, served by two notaries to act as registrars, and two proctors to act in the instance cases.

The scope of the courts was remarkably wide. One consistory court, which can, for simplicity, be termed the office court,[16] dealt with cases brought forward by the 'office of the judge'. It operated by a kind of summary jurisdiction, which dealt mainly with offences which had been reported by local churchwardens and clergy: matters of

[15] The civil and canon law practice of the church courts has been lucidly described in R H Helmholz's *Roman Canon Law in Reformation England* (1996).

[16] There are other titles in other dioceses and publications, of which the most frequent are correction court and detection court.

personal morality and church discipline produced by the presentment system described above. The process did not normally involve the summoning of witnesses or taking of written statements. People cited (summoned) to appear had to confess their fault or provide a defence, normally based on providing local 'compurgators', neighbours who would vouch for their innocence. The judges could impose a range of punishments (usually penance or excommunication). Sessions must have been busy, often dealing with 20 or 30 cases in a half-day sitting, while a steady stream of defendants and parish officials made their way in and out of the court.

Less in the public eye were the activities of the second consistory court, which can be termed the instance court. It was the process of this court which generated written depositions and thus provided the content of this book. Though quieter than the office court, its half day sittings were equally busy, but with fewer people present, mainly lawyers and officials. Cases were brought *instancia partium*, at the instance (and expense) of parties: roughly equivalent to a modern civil suit between individuals. In the courtroom, however, these parties were normally absent, as were the witnesses, who would have been examined elsewhere. Because the process focused on written material it has ensured a rich archival legacy. The business was conducted by proctors - the civil law equivalent of barristers - who acted for the plaintiffs and defendants. The core evidence came in the form of the lengthy depositions from witnesses, and was recorded verbatim in an impressive series of registers. In their depositions the witnesses responded to an elaborate series of statements and questions posed by one party - usually supplemented by interrogatories posed by the other.

There is a clear difference between the issues that were dealt with in the office and instance courts. In the office court the church authority attempted to control religious behaviour and personal morality; in the instance court the concerns were largely secular. Its main purpose was to provide an arbitration process for personal disputes, which we would consider unconnected with religion. Even its regular fare of tithe disputes was regarded as a matter of local taxation rather than a religious duty.[17]

There was little overlap between the work of the two courts. It was possible, however, to move a summary proceeding of the office court to the plenary process of the instance court. On such occasions the instance case would be presented *ex officio*, on behalf of the judge of the office court. This happened infrequently and there is only one example in this volume. Such a transfer would be most likely to happen when the presentment in the office court meant that a party could allege they had suffered measurable harm: case 30 relates to possible misappropriation of testamentary bequests. The most frequent ex officio cases at this period arose when adultery led to a suit for divorce (separation).

The proceedings in the instance courts had not been significantly changed by the Reformation and it was here that the lawyers worked most closely within traditional civil and canon law practices. But although they could truthfully point out that the civil and canon law within which they worked was the law of the land, they still had to accept the overall supremacy of the common and statute law and of the secular courts.

[17] It was the jurist John Selden, the definitive authority on tithe and former pupil of the Chichester proctor Hugh Barker, who pronounced that tithe was required *legum terrae* rather than *jure divino*.

Where any issue in ecclesiastical proceedings could be shown to impinge on common law then the case could be formally inhibited and moved to a secular court. But at the period under consideration, the boundaries were well understood: only one case in our series (case 33 Earle v Page) may have been transferred in this way.

Instance proceedings dealt mainly with four principal types of case, where the civil law had long held (and jealously guarded) its jurisdiction: tithe, testamentary, defamation and matrimonial. The Reformation had, however, significantly expanded the volume of business in two areas. The emphasis on sexual crimes in the office cases had led to a surge in instance cases of defamation, where the majority of suits were now brought to defend the reputations of women who had been called 'whore' or had been subject to rumours of promiscuous or libidinous behaviour. Tithe cases multiplied with the expanding complexities of tithe ownership after the dissolution of the monasteries and the growth of lay ownership of tithe, and with the growth of arrangements for payments in cash rather than kind.

Although the business of the two courts was normally kept separate, it is clear that matters originating in the office court could often influence the litigants in instance proceedings. Their attitudes could reflect tensions within a community, most notably between clergy and tithe payers (or non-payers). A number of cases in this book may originate in earlier friction where one party had been presented in the office court for offences connected with their parish church, usually non-attendance or an altercation over the right to a seat. The clergyman's sense of grievance could be heightened by court rulings, which sometimes allowed a parishioner to worship in another place if the relationship with his incumbent had completely broken down. All this could embitter a tithe dispute which became unnecessarily protracted or acrimonious.

The procedure in instance cases.

At commencement the plaintiff submitted a libel or an allegation which set out the complaint against the defendant. When this was contested by the defendant, the plaintiff called witnesses to give evidence in order to prove it. In response, further witnesses might be called by either party. One party or both sought the sentence (i.e. verdict) of the judge; and this would condemn one of the parties, assigning a penalty, usually of costs, penance or excommunication. Each stage of the case gave scope for elaboration and complication. The defence would normally add interrogatories to the libel or allegation: questions intended to make plain the sympathies of the witness and to establish facts relevant to the defence. The process of obtaining the depositions often meant that reluctant witnesses had to be compelled to appear. Once the witnesses had been examined, their depositions could be 'published'; and at this point they could be read by the opposing party. If either side wished to contest the depositions they could demand 'exceptions', producing further depositions which attempted to damage the character of the witnesses or the truth of their statements. Even when sentence had been delivered there was scope for an appeal; and it also often proved difficult to make the condemned party pay costs, perform penance or seek absolution. The majority of cases lasted between four and eight months; seriously contested cases could continue for up to two years or even longer.

The sophistication of the court procedure is striking. The consistency of the processes documented countrywide in the records of the courts at Chichester, Winchester, Oxford, Canterbury and York is clear evidence that the judges, proctors and notaries had good training in canon and civil law. There was of course literature to guide them: notably Francis Clerke's *Praxis in Curiis Ecclesiasticis.*[18] The clerical judges had usually achieved a degree of Bachelor of Civil Law at Oxford or Cambridge. Not all the proctors and notaries, however, were university educated: they must have been thoroughly trained by their colleagues in the local courts and were able also to make use of precedent books compiled by the lawyers in their courts.[19] Knowledge of civil law was not confined to a legal clique. Many of the parochial clergy gained a basic knowledge at Oxford and Cambridge, both of which universities had Henrician professorships of civil law. Even after the Civil War, Thomas Barlow, Bodley's Librarian from 1652 to 1677, encouraged its study 'as far as it may be necessary for a divine.'[20] As the depositions reveal, it was customary for clergy to give advice on will making when they visited their dying parishioners; they were often also involved in betrothal ceremonies; they might attempt reconciliation in defamation suits; and it was very much in their interest to be acquainted with the law on tithe.

The complexity of the procedure, however, makes cases difficult to follow; and the difficulty is compounded because the method of recording their progress in the court's act books does not set out the final verdict. The end of proceedings is clearly marked in those cases where the judge gives his 'sentence' (i.e. verdict) – but even then the name of the winning party may not be specified and has to be deduced from the name of the proctor who has submitted the draft sentence, or the party who has been taxed with the costs. Further details of the terms of sentence are hardly ever to be found, except in rare instances when the actual document has survived in the Miscellaneous Court Papers series.[21] But only a minority of cases achieve sentence. In a few others the act book records agreement between the parties, often with the final entry as 'Pax'. The majority simply lapse and we are left to deduce the outcome. Deductions can be helped by the signposts which indicate the progress of the case. If the plaintiff never gets beyond the initial stage of delivering the libel or allegation, then it is likely that the case has been withdrawn. If it reaches the stage that depositions are 'published', then it is likely that the case is moving in favour of the party which produced them. If one party petitions for sentence and the other does not make significant opposition, then again it is likely that the petitioner is in the ascendant. But these can only be treated as indicators. When cases lapse without reaching these stages, we can only guess that one party simply gave up.

The recording process in instance cases seems curious to a modern reader. The actual result of the case seems to be of almost minor importance and certainly has to be

[18] Clerke completed this work in 1596 and it became the guidebook of civil lawyers for the next half century. It is a measure of its influence that, although it remained unpublished until 1666, manuscript copies survive among the archives of more than a dozen dioceses (Helmholz, *Roman Canon Law in Reformation England*, 196-197).

[19] It is significant that collections of precedent books have been preserved among the Chichester episcopal archives, and in those of many other dioceses.

[20] B P Levack, 'Law' in N Tyacke, *The History of the University of Oxford*, (vol. 4) 567.

[21] WSRO Ep I/15/1.

deduced from the act books (as also happens in Chancery proceedings). By contrast the act books of the office courts record succinctly the details of offences, offenders, verdicts and punishments. In instance cases, however, all the documentation is focused on the collection and presentation of the evidence. The importance of this function is demonstrated by the way that the deposition books have been jealously preserved as the major record in the court records of most dioceses. They contrast strongly with the records of local secular courts like Quarter Sessions, where witness statements rarely survive from this period.[22] The value placed on the church court depositions seems to be reflected in their physical make-up: in the four decades up to the beginning of the Civil War, the depositions are registered in substantial bound volumes of between 250 and 300 folios. The act books were not always accorded such respect: in the period 1604-1607, for example, they were entered in much smaller volumes, usually containing fewer than 100 folios, with only rudimentary binding.

The lawyers had an elaborate process for producing the depositions. Both parties were encouraged to bring forward witnesses, both were given opportunities to present them with detailed statements for comment, and to add further material in the course of the proceedings; and both had the option of completing the process with elaborate interrogatories, which may appear, superficially, to represent something like cross examination. The completion of the depositions marked a crucial point in the case. If the judge accepted them, they acquired the status of a final record. They were 'published' and copies are made and supplied to the opposing party. This frequently marked the point at which one party would apply to conclude the case – and the conclusion might be agreed without a formal verdict having been issued by the judge.

The laboriously produced deposition books are by far the most weighty records in every sense. In collecting and assembling facts, or at least perceptions of facts, they emphasise the court's rôle of arbitration and negotiation. The depositions are compilations of all the available local knowledge; and when 'published' they provide yardsticks against which the disputing parties could compare their arguments – and perhaps reach compromises, inside or outside the courtroom.[23]

One must avoid the temptation, however, to assume that the deposition books include material from all the instance cases. Surprisingly, only a small proportion of the cases reach the stage of publishing depositions. A summary based on the nine months between 25 March and 31 December 1605 can provide a snapshot of the court's business. During this period 63 cases were in progress, of which only 13 produced depositions.[24] Differing forms of litigation meant that some cases did not need witness statements. Certain matters which might now be considered as administrative took the form of court proceedings. Unpaid bills, for example, provided regular business: senior clergy pursued procuration charges (due from lower clergy at visitations); proctors

---

[22] The value of this comparison is of course limited since the bulk of the business in these secular courts arose from prosecution rather than disputes between parties. That the records of the church courts at this period are more extensive is also partly due to the common law practice of retaining parchment documents as archival records while destroying most paper items.

[23] That this was not a local Sussex peculiarity is demonstrated by E M K Jarman in her study of the Chester Consistory courts, *An edition of the depositions… of the consistory Court of Chester September 1559-March 1558/9*. University of Liverpool Dissertation 2010).

[24] Of the cases with depositions seven were commenced in the period, while six had started earlier.

pursued clients who had failed to pay them their fees. Such transactions accounted for 20 of the cases and were normally settled within a few sessions. Of the remaining cases, 27 fell within the four major categories described below; and more than two thirds of these were completed within five court sessions.

A common contemporary criticism of the church courts was that they were dilatory and created unnecessarily extended business for the sake of the fees. But it is clear that the Chichester instance courts could process a large number of relatively minor cases in a surprisingly short time. There is every indication that their dealings with more substantial cases were equally efficient. Throughout the first four decades of the seventeenth century the volume of activity recorded in the act books and the deposition books maintained a high and if anything increasing level. The instance process, with its system of impartial information gathering, served a need. Though the litigants were rarely from the wealthy classes, they were prepared to undertake the expense of proceedings in a judicial system they trusted.

The court's arbitration rôle

The office court, and of course the secular courts, dealt with those who had broken the rules laid down by the church and the state. In contrast, instance proceedings aimed at resolving disagreements between individuals. They dealt with civil disputes, in the modern sense of the word; and the issues involved fell into four specific categories: testamentary or probate, tithe, defamation and matrimonial. Their proceedings, despite their adversarial framework, attempted resolution, and ideally reconciliation, between people with different perceptions of a situation. Matrimonial cases arose from changes in emotional relationships; testamentary, from perceptions of the responsibilities of the dead to the living; defamation, on how words, rather than sticks and stones, might affect an individual's position in the community. Even tithe, the most seemingly measurable and accountable, would focus on unwritten customs and agreements and on unforeseen changes in farming practice.

To harmonise differing perceptions there was a need to create a common ground of agreed fact. Depositions were the essential tools in the process of arbitration or compromise: they represented the final gathering of information which could be accepted by both parties. The arbitrators who took on this information gathering were the proctors: and this rôle, rather than courtroom confrontation, was their key task. So the primary job of the plaintiff's proctor was to collect the elements of his client's grievance into a narrative of complaint, by drawing up the libel or the allegation. This must be presented to the defendant; and witnesses would subsequently be examined in order to justify it. Before their examination, the defendant's proctor would contribute his interrogatories.[25] These were aimed principally at detecting potential bias in a witness but also at highlighting questionable statements in the narrative. It must be emphasised, however, that interrogatories were a supplementary part of the witness's examination and not a cross examination of evidence given. They were framed before

---

[25] In a few cases the defendant was not represented by a proctor. All such examples in this volume are in testamentary cases aimed at proving wills 'in form of law', where the defendant often fails to appear.

the examination was made; and this demonstrates their crucial role in the arbitration process. They enabled each witness to respond to the narrative of both plaintiff and defendant so that the deposition could be held to provide a balanced account which could be accepted by both parties. The fact that in nearly half of our cases the publication of the depositions led to their conclusion without final sentence suggests that they achieved such a result.

The combined efforts of the proctors were intended to produce a balanced and truthful version of the matters under dispute. Once published, in the form of depositions, they formed the core of the case and provided the material upon which the parties could negotiate – the essential tools of arbitration. The recognition of their special, independent, value meant that depositions could bring about the agreed conclusion of a case even without a final sentence from the judge.

The main types of case

To understand fully the issues reflected in the depositions it is helpful to look in more detail at the four principal types of case I have mentioned. It should be remembered, however, that these categories were not exclusive: the courts dealt with a smaller range of other matters which could be termed 'church rights' and concerned local customs such as the payments of mortuaries and rites of passage.

1. Testamentary: Wills and probate

The majority of wills proved by the church courts did not involve litigation. They were proved 'in common form' which normally meant that the executors of the will would swear before the judge that it had been properly executed. Although recorded in the commissary's records, these actions were not suits of court because no dispute was involved. There were occasions, however, when executors - particularly if a substantial part of the property had been left to them - felt the need to guard against claims from near kinsfolk. They adopted the instance procedure of proving 'in form of law' (*in forma iuris*).

Its purpose was to produce a more legally robust form of probate, and was seen to provide a valuable assurance for women. An executrix widow, for example, might try to establish her rights to her husband's estate and block the demands from children of an earlier marriage. As plaintiff she would initiate the case and would cite as defendants near kinsfolk and interested parties 'in special and all others pretending interest in general' (*in specie ac omnes et singulos alios*) to appear at all future hearings of the case. The plaintiff would produce an allegation and the defendants had the option of making a response. The plaintiff would produce witnesses to depose as to the validity of the will; and in most cases the defendants would fail to appear at the court sessions. The judge would usually conclude by pronouncing the will proved, regardless of the appearance or non-appearance of the defendants. Where proceedings followed this format they would often be completed within three months – a short period when compared with the other cases. Occasionally, however, the kinsfolk would contest the case, and even appeal against the verdict. In at least one case (case 23) an appeal seems to have reached the Court of Arches. Although the relevant Court of Arches records have not survived; the result of the case must have been in the plaintiff's favour, as the executrix was able to prove the disputed will in the Archbishop's Prerogative Court of Canterbury.

Seven of the 13 testamentary cases in this volume sought proof in form of law. The plaintiffs in five were women; and four more women were plaintiffs in other testamentary cases. The figures suggest that a woman, and particularly an executrix widow, was, or was perceived to be, more likely to meet opposition than a man. A situation which could provide scope for such controversy was the administration of the estate after a husband's second marriage (cases 29, 30, 38). In such cases the dispute could descend to a surprisingly low financial level, as happened when Joan Johnson, a stepdaughter, demanded her legacy of 40s (case 38). The proceedings went on for two years and must have consumed all or most of the legacy.

The most substantial cases would involve disputes as to the distribution of specific property or whether the testator was mentally capable.

2. Defamation

Accusations at this date had to relate to 'spiritual' matters. If the accusation involved an activity that could be connected to a crime that would be tried at common law then the action could not be pursued in the church courts. Someone defamed as a thief, for example, would have to turn to the secular courts. In practice this meant that the majority of cases alleged sexual misbehaviour: fornication or adultery. The court's powers of punishment were equally 'spiritual' and were limited to excommunication, the imposition of penance (usually by confession before the church congregation) and the payments of the costs of the case.

'Good name in man or woman' as Shakespeare pointed out 'is the immediate jewel of their souls'. In close-knit seventeenth century society, he was not exaggerating. For a married woman, rumour of sexual immorality was highly damaging. It was almost equally damaging for her husband: if he failed to control his wife's behaviour he had failed both to rule his household and to preserve the proper order within the community. Predictably, therefore, the majority of our cases arise from imputations against women: eight of the 12 plaintiffs were married women. Most of these cases provide minimal detail, little beyond branding the victim with the epithet 'whore'. The only spinster plaintiff (case 25), however, had to face an ingenious defence from a man who claimed she had lain with him and that they had been contracted to marry. The three male plaintiffs contested more unusual allegations ranging from brothel keeping (case 4), to begetting a bastard (case 5) and witchcraft (case 44).

In instance suits for defamation recent historians have discovered a valuable source for women's public expressions of their attitudes on sexual matters, at a time when there was little other scope for them to be heard. This has been well demonstrated, particularly from material in the London courts by Laura Gowing, Eleanor Hubbard and Bernard Capp and also by Diana O'Hara from the Canterbury diocese.[26] In cases in the predominantly rural area that made up the Archdeaconry of Chichester, however, the witnesses tend to confine themselves to simple narratives of verbal abuse. Perhaps

[26] See Bibliography.

surprisingly, the majority of witnesses were male; and where women did testify, they did not necessarily do so willingly.[27]

3. Tithe

The majority of these cases were brought by an incumbent against a parishioner on grounds of withholding tithe payments. Sometimes they arose from differing interpretations of local customs peculiar to the parish; sometimes from land affected by a disputed parish boundary; sometimes they reflect changes in farming practice such as inclosure or conversion of heath land to arable. Where the latter happened at Kirdford (case 19) the depositions contain the earliest known use of the word 'devonshiring',[28] the process of clearing heathland by burning to create the arable. The process of payment could be contentious: payment in kind entailed laborious arrangements for collection and storage; while substituting money payments could lead to disputes over terms. Inclosure features in case 46, which also records the introduction of sluices to drain land where the hay crop was affected by tidal overflow. The customs described were not confined to farming: case 5 provides memories of cakes and ale distributed during the perambulation of Madehurst parish boundaries in years before the Reformation.

The records of the office court can sometimes reveal an earlier history of antagonism between tithe owner and the non-payer, which went far beyond the tithe issues – and the judge did not always side with the clergy. John Page of Eartham (case 33), for example, had been churchwarden but refused to receive communion during the course of his case, eventually being allowed by the court to receive in another parish. When he was later also accused of sharing his bedchamber with his servant, another man's wife, he received relatively lenient treatment from the court.

4. Matrimonial

Matrimonial cases focused on the validity of a marriage or on its breakdown. The majority (and all in this volume) can be described in modern terms as 'breach of promise.' One party, usually the woman, prosecuted the other for reneging on an intended marriage. Usually she asserted a contract to marry, established by a public declaration and betrothal ceremonies. If the defendant had now married another woman, however, the court could not overturn the marriage. It is difficult to see what legal remedy the plaintiff could expect; and most cases appear to be the expression of injured pride and an attempt to humiliate the betrayer. Rarer matrimonial cases might deal with divorce (i.e. separation) or annulment (usually on the grounds of bigamy, or kinship within the church's prohibited degrees of relationship).[29]

All three cases in the volume were brought by women claiming breach after betrothal. Case 11 describes an unusual ceremony intended to cancel the betrothal; in case 45 the defendant is supported by the intervention of a man who claimed have had an earlier relationship with the plaintiff.

---

27 The two witnesses in of Carden v Harber (case 25), for example, had to be compelled to appear.

28 At this period the term often appears in the form 'denshiring'.

29 For two unusual cases involving marriage under duress see my article 'The Courts of True Love' (*Sussex Archaeological Collections* **152** 79-94).

Sullington Tithe Barn. The size of this seventeenth century barn gives an indication of the storage space needed by the tithe owner in a relatively small parish. Photographed by permission of Mrs G Kitell.

The progress of the cases

The complexity and the length of time occupied by the suits was largely dictated by their type. Tithe and probate could produce the longest contests, which is hardly surprising since they involved property or money.[30] Both types could last from three or four months to three years. The longer tithe cases could require complicated depositions setting out local agreements (compositions) and customs - though the latter could result in transfer to the common law courts which claimed final authority in matters of custom. Less complicated issues could be settled within nine months or less. The timing of testamentary cases was affected by two factors. The longer cases usually arose from disputes about specific legacies or the administration of an intestate's goods. Shorter cases, however, could result when the executor was attempting to prove a will 'in form of law' (as described above). Most cases of this type would be completed in three to six months; but those involving actual disputes between legatees could drag on for a year or years.

The third type of case, defamation, tended to be completed slightly more quickly – perhaps because money was not involved. The majority were completed within six months; though a few continued for more than a year. Outside these three main categories our series includes only three matrimonial cases and two concerning church rights: it would be unhelpful to try to generalise about their timing.

The following table demonstrates the effects of the differing categories of cases.

Table 1

	Total cases	Plaintiff wins	Defendant wins	Agreement	Lapse	Inhibited	Not known
Testamentary	13	9			2	2	
Tithe	16	1	1	2	8	1	3
Defamation	12	4	1	1	5		1
Matrimonial	3	1			1		1
Other	2	2					

In testamentary cases, which would normally seek a simple and binding legal ruling, a formal sentence is the most likely – reinforced in our period by the practice of proving wills in form of law. Surprisingly, given their more subjective nature, the pattern for defamation cases is not dissimilar with seven of the twelve producing a sentence or at least a formal ending. The lapses in other defamation cases, however, may represent genuinely unresolved contests, where the parties felt it was not worth continuing the argument. Tithe cases produced the most unexpected figures. An action to pursue the payment of tithe would seem to lead logically to a sentence. As attempts to enforce payments, whether in cash or in kind, would be perceived as equivalent to a local tax demand: a court ruling would seem the proper solution. Yet the 13 completed cases produced only two sentences and two agreements. This is in spite of the fact that the

[30] It should be noted, however, that bequests of land or buildings do not figure in these cases and would normally be dealt with by the secular courts.

depositions recorded in meticulous detail accounts of local customs and compositions - and that in the majority of cases they were produced for one party only.

The fact that only 22 of our 46 cases reached a formal ending is a measure of the reliance placed on the depositions. To describe other cases which lacked a sentence or formal agreement as 'lapsed' provides a convenient label: but it will often conceal a victory for one of the parties. If a case had reached the point where the proctor for one of the parties had requested judgement without significant opposition from the other we have to assume that they had conceded defeat.

This could happen after the depositions had been published: either party could then apply to 'propound all acts' – in other words to conclude the case on the basis of all the material submitted up to that point. If the judge accepted this, the case could be considered to have ended, even without a sentence. This amounted to victory for the party which had requested the conclusion – usually the plaintiff. And to have reached such a conclusion was almost certainly a mark of the strength of the evidence provided in the depositions. The witnesses had been produced to provide accurate local information (of particular value in tithe cases); and their statements had been accepted by both sides. The acceptance may have perhaps been reinforced by the comforting knowledge that the parties had avoided the fee of 20s normally charged for obtaining a sentence.

Although it may seem surprising, a resolution of this kind could have the full force of law. This legal force can be strikingly demonstrated in the matrimonial case I have mentioned above, when the witnesses deposed that a marriage had been made under duress from the bride's father. The possibility of divorce in the modern sense of the term did not exist, but nevertheless – and without sentence or any formal statement of annulment – both wife and husband married new spouses.[31]

In occasional cases which had become particularly complicated or acrimonious, the proceedings were suspended (inhibited) and transferred to the Archbishop's Court of Audience (cases 3 and 29), as I have described above.

In cases where a sentence was delivered, the proctor for the losing party usually gave notice of appeal to the Archbishop's Court of Arches or Audience.[32] The appeal had to be activated by further notice given within a set period; but this rarely occurs and it must be assumed that most sentences were uncontested. As sentence was often given in the absence of the parties it is likely that the initial notice of appeal was simply a means to keep the option available if needed.

Creating the deposition: its purpose and its rôle

The format of the depositions stems from the procedure through which the witnesses were examined. The most frequent initial tool for examination was the libel. This set out in numbered articles a narrative of the 'facts of the case' as the plaintiff saw them.

---

31 In my article, cited earlier, I mistakenly assumed that there had been a sentence; but there was none and the case had appeared to lapse.

32 Unfortunately the records of neither court survive for the relevant period.

It was usually accompanied by a series of numbered questions submitted by the defence (the interrogatories). An alternative initial tool for examination could be provided by an allegation – and this was frequently used in probate cases. At later stages in the case either side could produce further articles for examination. As well as allegations, the most frequent are additional positions, while, rarely, there are exceptions against the testimony of witnesses.

Although exceptions were invoked only in rare cases (five of our 46), they can provide interesting and often entertaining reading, as the proceedings in the case of Lacker v Hobbes (case 3) demonstrate. They set out to discredit witnesses by alleging a range of illegal or immoral activities, often completely unrelated to the case and amounting to character assassination. They can provide an interesting measurement of local reputation (or perhaps gossip), and sometimes suggest the tensions between social classes. An exception does not seek to qualify or remove specific facts in the opponent's deposition: it seeks to nullify its entire content and effectively destroy the opponent's case by the discrediting of the witness. It is perhaps significant that in the two cases (3 Lacker v Hobbes and 29 West v Lane) which involved a large number of examinations for exceptions, the proceedings were eventually transferred to a higher level, the Archbishop's Court of Audience. When the credibility of the depositions had been comprehensively undermined, the acrimony between the parties had proved too difficult to resolve at a local level.

It is also a measure of their importance that the depositions were carefully framed to reduce the risk of bias in the witnesses. The principal tools were the interrogatories, which were submitted by the opposing party in order to make the witnesses reveal possible sympathies: whether they were related to the parties; whether they appeared voluntarily or by compulsion; what expenses they would receive; and which party they favoured. This last question was almost invariably and predictably answered with a declaration that they aimed for justice for the party in the right. Regardless of the party they represented, the deponents did not show obvious signs of prejudice; their statements even suggest a measure of impartiality. In tithe cases, for example, although the witness had usually been called by the clergyman, the deposition would sometimes disagree with details of his claims.

Because the depositions were accorded such importance in the process, great care was taken in the way they were recorded and meticulously entered in the Deposition Books. The witnesses were examined in private rather than in open court - and in English, despite the fact that the clerks often inserted Latin phraseology. Once an examination was completed it was read over before a judge (again in private) and the witness signed it or (more usually) added his or her mark. A deposition was not made available to the opposing side until it was produced at a court session (usually immediately following the reading over) and formally 'published'. At this point it acquired its status as a legal record.

As well as the deponents, the parties contesting the case could also be examined; but their responses (*responsa personalia*), through a quirk of filing, were recorded on loose papers. A few have survived among the series of Miscellaneous Court Papers;[33] but the

[33] As far as possible, surviving responses have been inserted chronologically among the depositions.

majority have been lost. That they were not entered in the deposition books suggests that they were not considered to have the independence and impartiality of the witnesses' statements.

Ostensibly, the deposition's purpose was simple. A deposition (or rather depositions, as a minimum of two witnesses were required) was a statement providing the proof of a complaint or accusation. Usually it was part of the plaintiff's attack on the defendant; more rarely it served the defendant's counter attack. Proof is a significant term. It reflects a procedure aimed at justifying the plaintiff's case, a system that tended to work in favour of the party which had felt confident enough to initiate the case. Amid uncertainties and contradictions the depositions were perceived as providing the best available account and once published they would be accepted by the judge as a record. If the plaintiff could produce depositions to substantiate his claims, his opponent was unlikely to get a favourable verdict: as is demonstrated by the success of plaintiffs in 34 of our 40 known results. These results are also matched by the higher number of depositions produced for the plaintiff: 149 as against 73 for the defendant.

Although the statistics appear to show consistent weighting in favour of the plaintiff, they need not reflect a bias in the proceedings. The plaintiff had little financial incentive to litigate when victory could produce nothing more than the recovery of costs and the humiliation of the opponent.[34] So it is hardly surprising that in a civil dispute between parties the plaintiff would be unlikely to risk the expense unless there was a strong likelihood that the defendant could be made to repay it.

This pattern, however, raises a question of the value or purpose of a deposition on behalf of the defendant. His witnesses will rarely offer a detailed refutation of the statements presented for the plaintiff. In some cases his depositions can represent a 'counter action'.[35] More frequently they can introduce new material which could weaken or at least modify the plaintiff's narrative. In two matrimonial cases (11 & 45), for instance, defendants' depositions revealed, in the first, a ceremony which attempted to cancel a betrothal and, in the second, an earlier marriage contract. In tithe cases the defendants could set out differing local customs. In their most damaging rôle the depositions would present exceptions, which, as described above, would attempt to discredit the opponent's witnesses and disqualify their statements.

Outside the courtroom: the impact of the cases

Although the issues which initiated the cases might often seem insignificant, the impact on a community could be substantial and even dramatic. Though the proceedings were held without the publicity that accompanied the assizes or quarter sessions, they were still in the public domain. Within the parish or parishes involved their ripples were often visible. Defamation, after all, concerned one's reputation among one's neighbours – as, in a different way, did the majority of matrimonial cases. The issues of

[34] It should be remembered that the church courts did not impose punitive fines but simply condemned the litigant to the payment of costs and varying forms of penance.

[35] In the act book the titling of case 1 varies between 'Daniell v Bishoppe' and 'Bishoppe v Daniell'.

tithe cases might affect the entire local farming community. Only testamentary cases might be limited to a small circle of family and connections.

One case can demonstrate just how deep a local impact litigation in the instance court could make. Lacker v Hobbes (case 3) concerned tithe in the small parish of Houghton. Out of the 25 participants (parties and witnesses) 16 were parishioners, almost half of the adult male population. In the course of the proceedings, ten were the subject of allegations of crime, immorality or misbehaviour, for the most part unconnected with the case.

It started from an apparently minor disagreement. James Lacker, farmer of the tithes, was in dispute with Richard Hobbes over the payment of tithes on wool. After initial attempts to settle matters personally and amicably (ironically, both wished to avoid the expense of court proceedings) a case was instigated and focused on an offer of 26s 4d which Hobbes had made. Summoned by Hobbes, two witnesses, John and Thomas Northe, father and son, made apparently uncontroversial depositions. The results are unexpected and difficult to interpret. They seem to spring from a personality clash between Hobbes and the vicar of Madehurst, James Pellett, who served as minister at Houghton. Pellett made himself the self-appointed protector and legal advisor of Lacker (whose rôle in the proceedings became relatively passive). A few months into the proceedings, several parishioners, in church on Easter Day, suggested that the parties should settle the dispute personally and privately; Pellett proclaimed that 'it should not be ended now; law should end it.'

To achieve this, the plaintiff, or almost certainly Pellett, set about producing exceptions against the depositions of the two Northes. By October 1604 he had gathered eleven deponents. Pellett himself began a comprehensive character assassination. Thomas Northe, he asserted, was 'a sower of discord and debate between neighbours and friends by carrying lies and tales from one to another; neither doth any man ... make any account of his saying.' He had broken a contract to one woman and married another; and his father considered him 'a fool and an idiot.' Another deponent added that Thomas's father 'did allege unto the Lieutenant and Justices of the Peace at a general muster that he was very ignorant, purblind and deaf and an innocent, in respect whereof he was struck out of the muster book as unfit for service.' There were further assertions that Thomas Northe had claimed that Lacker, the plaintiff, had cuckolded him, leaving him to bring up a bastard child. Against John Northe it was claimed that 'he had a bastard 30 years ago' and that 'small credit' should be given to his sayings and that 'he was a man of unhonest life, a sower of discord and a common swearer and taker of the name of God in vain'.

Pellett's own deposition also provided the first instance of the antagonism between him and Hobbes, describing an incident when Hobbes 'was ready to ride on him with his horse and swore, "God's blood or God's wounds, wilt thou not give the way. I am a better man than thou." ' Both men were determined to assert their social superiority. Pellett claimed that Hobbes 'long before was but a capmaker and therefore he needed not to compare himself with him' and also quoted an exchange when he demanded, 'Prithee Hobbes, hold thy tongue', on which Hobbes countered, 'What, plain Hobbes, I am as good a gentleman as you.'

Surprisingly quickly, in December 1604, Hobbes made his riposte with his exceptions to the plaintiff's exceptions: depositions by a further eleven witnesses. Unsurprisingly, they asserted the integrity and competence of the Northes, and in the process branded a selection of Lacker's witnesses with adultery and with thefts of geese and sheep. They provide striking additions to the saga of animosity between Pellett and Hobbes, particularly an incident in church when Hobbes misread a phrase in the Psalms. Pellett exclaimed, ' "How now Hobbes, how blasphemously do you read there" whereunto Mr Hobbes answered, "Go forward Mr Pellett, it is a good horse that never stumbleth." ' The tension produces an interesting ambivalence in the witnesses. Most recounted the incident but also responded to a separate article when they asserted that Pellett was 'a good preacher, a man of honest life and conversation, no brawler nor sower of discord but rather a peacemaker.' Only one, Thomas Hunte, a yeoman and the nearest in status to Hobbes, was prepared to suggest that Pellett 'beareth some evil will' towards him and that 'it is not a fit thing for a man of his coat to reprove any man publicly in service time … in respect of that he showed himself no peacemaker but rather to make strife.'

The two ranks of conflicting witnesses were firmly contradictory: they produced nothing that could be considered common ground, no scope for arbitration. Within weeks the proceedings terminated with a letter of inhibition, transferring the case to the Archbishop's Court of Audience. And there the story ends, for no further records survive. The abrupt termination perhaps emphasises the failure to achieve the court's goal of dispute resolution: there was no way forward. Whether any peace was achieved within the Houghton community, we shall never know.

The Courts and the Cathedral

All the sessions of the consistory court were held in the Cathedral; but it is frustrating that the records contain no clear statement of where in the building the court functioned. The only indicator in our period is the unhelpful phrase in the act books, 'the accustomed place' (*loco cons[ueto]*). It is tempting to locate the sittings in the south transept where the walls were adorned with Lambert Barnard's paintings. There the participants would have been under the stern gaze of King Henry VIII and Bishop Sherburne and the gallery of portraits of kings and bishops (all of which were in the south transept at this time) They all proclaimed that the law of the church was an integral part of the law of the realm. If the court did sit there it must have introduced a considerable amount of noise and disturbance. Office proceedings, particularly, could have involved the comings and goings of 20 or 30 defendants cited to appear, accompanied perhaps by some of the parish officials (churchwardens and clergy) involved in presenting them; instance proceedings would involve a smaller number of people and a quieter procedure. It is probable that both courts would have sat in the same place, as both were normally held on the same day and staffed by the same officials. But from a nineteenth century reference we know that the Consistory court was then located in the present Chapter House and choir school, above the south aisle.[36] Its arrangement and fittings would have made it the most suitable place, and it is reasonable to assume that the room had served for the court in the previous centuries.

36 M A Lower, *The Churches of Sussex*, 3 (1872); see frontispiece.

Saturdays would see the two courts sitting in succession. Present for instance proceedings would be the judge, the registrar, the two proctors and one or more of the apparitors; occasionally there might be litigants. An impression of the scene can be gained from the illustration of the consistory court room which still survives at Chester cathedral, complete with its early seventeenth century furniture. In Chichester, in this relatively intimate setting, the court would progress 20 to 40 cases at each sitting. For many of them, there would be no new business. For the rest, the acts might record the submission of a libel or allegation, the arrangements for witnesses and examinations, the publication of depositions accepted by the court, petitions for judge's rulings or final sentences. Each item would be introduced by one of the proctors, with the other often registering some form of dissent. But despite the formal and adversarial phrases of the proctors, the records leave the impression more of a team meeting of arbitrators than of hostile litigation. The sense of intimacy is heightened by other cases where one proctor is represented by the other as he tries to claim unpaid fees from litigants – and even more by the fact that on the previous weekday in the same place one of the proctors would have been sitting as judge of the Dean's court and hearing cases presented by his colleague.

Judges, lawyers and officials

The Chichester courts were staffed by a professional team, most of whom acted in them all. The interlocking sessions were therefore essential. The team was small, effectively consisting of two judges, two proctors and two registrars. The proctors and the registrars must have been fully employed: the former in the elaborate casework demanded by their causes; and the latter by the administrative work created by wills and probate business, marriage licences and the bishop's episcopal activities – all in addition to the organising and recording of the court sessions.

The rôle of the judges reflected that of the bishop. The main courts (those of the Archdeaconries) were his consistories[37] and it was his right to sit in judgement there. In practice, almost all this work was delegated. Occasionally Jacobean bishops would preside at sessions of the office court: Bishop Harsnett did so on several occasions in the following decade. But it would be surprising to find a bishop presiding on instance cases. While he could exercise moral discipline when sitting in the office court, there could be little to gain from exercising the lowly rôle of arbitrator in the instance court. The main authority over the courts, however, rested in the hands of the bishop's senior official, normally titled his Commissary or diocesan Chancellor.[38] He was a senior civil lawyer (usually a Doctor of Civil Law) whose career often extended beyond the diocese.

During the period of this volume two men served in this office. Anthony Blencowe was educated at Oriel College Oxford and was later Provost there from 1572 until his death in 1618. He was Commissary of Chichester from 1590 to 1606 and later served

---

[37] The medieval hierarchy of two courts with that of the archdeaconry subject to that of the bishop had given way to a single consistory more than a century earlier. The changes are described by S J Lander in 'Church Courts and the Reformation in the Diocese of Chichester', R O'Day & F Heal *Continuity and Change: Personnel and Adminstration of the Church in England 1500-1642*, 215-37

[38] The post should not be confused with that of the cathedral Chancellor.

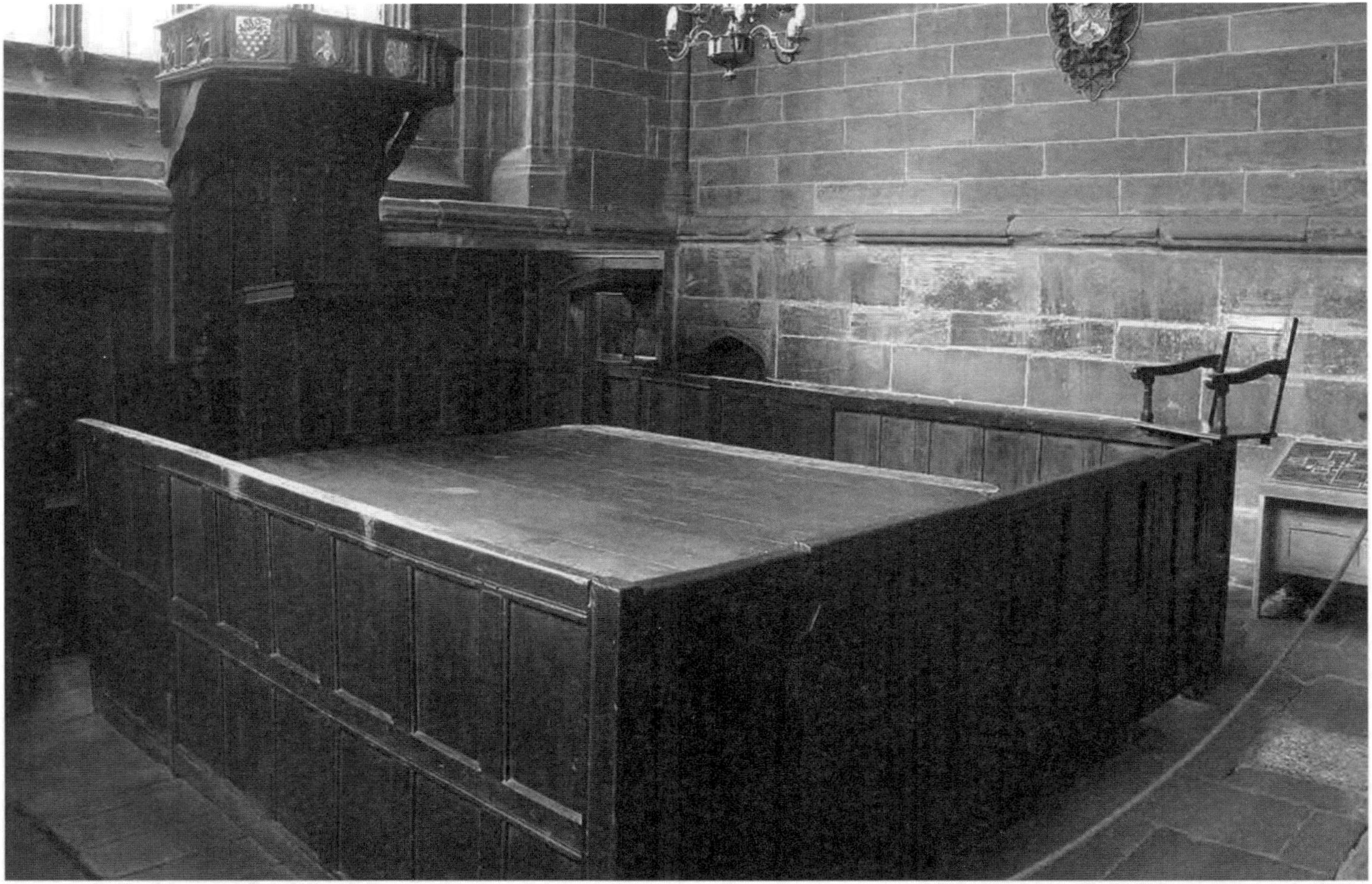

Consistory Court, Chester Cathedral. The furnishings date from 1636; those at the Chichester court would have been similar. Photograph copyright Stephen Craven; reproduced under the Creative Commons Licence.

as Commissary of Oxford diocese from 1614 to 1618. His successor, John Drury, had more local connection, having been appointed prebendary of Bishopshurst and vicar of Brighton in 1582 and rector of Pulborough by 1589. Both men delegated most of their duties to deputies or surrogates. Blencowe sat occasionally in the office court, while Drury presided there slightly more frequently and made a handful of appearances in the instance court.

For their surrogates, the commissaries looked to the residentiary canons of the Cathedral. Given the long tradition of friction between the bishops and the cathedral chapter, it may seem odd that the bishop should allow cathedral clergy to act for him in controlling his diocese. But the residentiaries (the most senior canons) provided the most readily available body of suitably educated clergy, often with legal training; and were of course conveniently sited to attend the courts.

The courts provided further important links between the cathedral and the bishop. Richard Juxon, as court registrar, was acting as bishop's registrar, an office which dealt with a full range of diocesan business; at the same time he served as registrar of the Dean and Chapter. One of the consistory proctors, Hugh Barker, had been the master of the cathedral's Prebendal School, holding the secular prebend of Highleigh; he also served as judge in the Dean's court. These arrangements suggest that at this time the relations between the bishop and the cathedral were reasonably harmonious. Comparisons at other dates might provide a useful indicator of the levels of trust between the two.

The day to day work for the commissary's surrogates during the first decade of the seventeenth century fell on two senior residentiaries. Henry Blaxton DD had become cathedral chancellor and a residentiary in 1573, having been brought in by Bishop Richard Curteys. Curteys's attempts to drag the diocese and the cathedral chapter towards a more radical Protestantism generated friction and confrontation throughout that decade; and Blaxton proved his active and public supporter. The other principal surrogate was Francis Coxe, slightly his senior among the residentiaries. Coxe had followed the approved route to seniority at Chichester via New College and the prebend of Wittering, a position appropriated to a teacher of theology. His allegiances were more traditional and he had been a prominent member of the faction which tried to block Curteys's attempts to gain control of the chapter. That, three decades later, these two former rivals should now be managing the bishop's consistory court in apparently harmonious fashion is an indication of the improved relations that had developed between diocese and cathedral.

The brunt of the instance court work was borne by the proctors and the registrar. The proctors were, in modern terms, the barristers, and acted in every instance case. Proctors were not usually ordained, but many had a university education – which could provide training in civil and canon law. Throughout our period the court was served by two proctors: Edward Cooke throughout, and Hugh Barker up to 1605 with Thomas Scales succeeding him. Cooke must have been the workhorse of the courts, acting there from about 1593 until his death in 1620. A man of that name graduated BA at Corpus Christi, Cambridge in 1591; but a degree is never attributed to him in the Chichester records, and he is normally described as 'gentleman'. He appears to have doubled his workload by acting in the Lewes consistory court, commuting to Tuesday sessions there in addition to his normal Saturdays at Chichester – to say nothing of occasional Friday appearances in the Dean's and Archbishop's courts. In the Chichester Archdeaconry court he seems to have been regarded as 'first call' in most cases: he acted for the plaintiff in a significant majority. It is interesting to note that although his wife was presented in the office court as a recusant on at least four occasions between 1601 and 1609, this does not seem to have affected his career.

Up to 1605 Cooke's opponent (though colleague would be a better term) was Hugh Barker. Barker (1565-1632) achieved eminence as a civil lawyer and merits an entry in the *ODNB*. He was educated at Winchester and New College, and during his spell as the master of the Prebendal School he earned the respect of perhaps its most famous pupil, John Selden, the lawyer and linguist. The award of his DCL in 1605 coincided with a move to London where he became a senior member of Doctors' Commons and eventually Treasurer and President. He practised in the highest civil courts and was appointed to the Court of High Commission; and he may have eventually reached the civil lawyer's pinnacle as Dean of Arches (though the records of this appointment are not entirely substantiated.). During his Chichester career he also served as the Dean's Commissary and in fact seems to have continued in this rôle for at least a year after he had ceased to act in the Archdeaconry court. In the Dean's court he would sit as judge over his fellow proctors – a situation that reflects the close relationship among the Chichester civil lawyers.

His successor in the instance court was Thomas Scales; but we can glean little personal detail from the records. He is described as MA but cannot be readily identified in the Oxford and Cambridge *Alumni*. Like Cooke, he is described as a gentleman and he took a full share of the workload of the Archdeaconry court, also acting occasionally as a judge in the Dean's.

It is tempting to look at the results of cases to measure the skill and success of the individual proctors. One might expect Barker, as the most talented, to produce the most successes – and perhaps Scales to produce the least – but there are no grounds to support this. The most essential rôle of a proctor was to appear for the plaintiff[39] (as I shall show later); and this rôle fell most frequently to Cooke. The results of the cases which ended in a formal sentence show that the plaintiffs were almost always the winners, regardless of which proctor might represent them.

A central figure in all the Chichester courts, both office and instance, and also in the Cathedral Chapter, was Richard Juxon, notary public and registrar. He served throughout our period and up to his death in 1612. It was the registrar's responsibility to manage the preparation of proceedings, the summoning of witnesses, the recording of acts and the taking of depositions. The workload must have been heavy and it appears that he was assisted by another notary, Christopher Theker, whose name appears regularly in the act books, often serving as Juxon's substitute. Juxon's claim to fame, of course, is to have been the father of William Juxon, who became Bishop of London, attended Charles I on the scaffold, and was appointed Archbishop of Canterbury after the Restoration. In 1612 on Richard's death, William had been

[39] Whilst the plaintiffs were always represented by a proctor, defendants occasionally acted without one.

admitted to his father's post as registrar, but by then was committed to academic life in Oxford.

The lowest in the tier of officials was the apparitor, who served as general factotum for the court. Always described as '*literatus*', his essential qualification was literacy. His main duty was to deliver citations (summonses) to parties and witnesses: a task which involved extensive travelling throughout the Archdeaconry. The most senior apparitor, Benjamin Freeman, who figures in the act books between 1606 and 1608, must have acquired enough basic legal knowledge to serve as an occasional proctor: he acted, for instance, in cases when three parties needed separate representation. From the time of Chaucer onwards apparitors held a dubious reputation; and the Chichester courts do not seem to have demanded high moral standards from them. Around January 1605/6 Freeman was involved in bastardy proceedings and married a Mary Base alias Martin, who had been excommunicated (though subsequently absolved). In March 1606/7 he was presented as a recusant, and later, in 1612, he was accused of withholding tithes.

The other apparitors most regularly employed in our period were the two Wadyes, Thomas, father and son. One of them was the subject of a letter of complaint sent to Richard Juxon by Michael Birkehead, the litigious vicar of Warnham.[40] He claimed that when attempting to prevent an unlicensed rival schoolmaster from teaching in his parish he 'left the presentment with Wadye the apparitor but … the party … hath not been cited … and indeed I do impute the whole fault upon the apparitor for I know him ready to receive a bribe'. Such accusations, however, do not seem to have damaged his career – or hindered a family tradition in office. A third Thomas Wadye was sworn as apparitor in 1663, which suggests that probably three generations occupied the post. Two other apparitors, Ellis and John Hames (presumably father and son) seem to have been of better character – or at least were not presented in the office courts. While the senior court officials normally resided in Chichester, the apparitors might live some distance away. Thomas Wadye senior lived in Thakeham, his son in Arundel; while Ellis Hames was in Midhurst. Given the travelling involved in delivering the citations throughout the Archdeaconry, residence around the centre of the area might have been an advantage.

The language of the deponents

For Furnivall, the scholar of mediaeval texts, perhaps the greatest attraction of depositions was the prospect of hearing vernacular speech. He must have found it a fascinating, if frustrating, exercise to guess at the extent that the written phrases reflected unmediated words uttered by the witnesses: the colloquial speech of (for the most part) uneducated people. The depositions were written down by the court officials, in tidy paragraphs which represent the responses to the separate and carefully phrased articles of a libel, allegation or similar document; and in making their examinations, the officials were attempting to create a definitive record. This had an effect: the language of the witnesses must often reflect the language of the lawyers, producing legal declaration more often than vernacular anecdote: it is hardly what we would expect of a tradesman or husbandman. Occasionally the language can be vivid

[40] WSRO Ep I/15/3/16 (122). See also cases 40-42.

when describing incidents at the core of matrimonial or defamation cases; but in contrast, descriptions of tithe customs or testamentary procedures often have a rigid legal style. At times these two extremes can be met in the same deposition.

But certainly the most characteristic and constant feature of the language is its legalistic and repetitious phraseology. Within the simplest of statements the examining official would insert an endless supply of legal phraseology. Its principal aims might be: to identify ('aforesaid', 'articulate'); to specify ('at the time and place aforesaid', 'and titheable places therein'); to locate ('in the parish of', 'in the county of'); to qualify ('as he remembereth', 'as he hath previously deposed'); and even to tautologise ('answered and said', 'verily believeth').

It is clear that the officials were determined to produce statements that were watertight against any accusation of ambiguity or inaccuracy. What is equally clear is that these elaborate and endlessly qualified phrases would not have been uttered by the deponents.

There is a further manifestation of the attempt to produce incontrovertible statements: the repetition or near repetition within the statements of different witnesses. This is particularly striking in the accounts of tithe customs or the phrasing of bequests. Even in matters where we might expect a more personal response, we can still find nearly identical phraseology uttered by different witnesses in responding to specific articles – which must reflect the fact that the witnesses were accepting descriptions composed by the lawyers or officials rather than recounting their personal recollections. The case of Lacker v Hobbes provides a good illustration of this, where the surviving set of interrogatories (case 3/16) can be compared with eleven depositions which answer them (case 3/17-27).

The goal of all this legal labour was publication. When the judge decreed that the depositions be published, they took on the quality of a public record: they were the proof of the libel or allegation that had engendered them. To attempt to controvert them required a major effort to force the case in a new direction. It is significant that only five cases produced exceptions against the depositions. Of these, two were the only cases to achieve sentences in favour of the defendants, and two of the remaining three were eventually transferred to higher courts.

The biographies of the witnesses

One feature of the established format of the depositions has particularly attracted the attention of modern researchers: the biographies which preface them. Written in formulaic Latin, they list the witnesses' status or occupation, age, the parish in which they live and those where they have lived previously, together with the length of residence; in many cases they also provide the witnesses' estimate of their personal financial value.[41] I have found no explicit reason for the compilation of this information. It may be intended to indicate the witness's position (and perhaps respectability) within the local community; perhaps also it might serve as a possible

[41] The information is normally given in the biography but in some cases it is provided in response to an interrogatory.

indicator of sympathy for one of the parties. Whatever their purpose, they were confined to the deponents. It is frustrating for modern readers that the plaintiff and defendant did not provide similar information when they made their statements of personal response.

As might be expected, these biographies are valued by family and local historians because they provide personal information in far greater detail than that obtainable from the more usual sources such as parish registers and probate records.[42]

It is noteworthy that within the four years covered by our cases, details of two witnesses, who each testify in two separate cases, provide an opportunity to compare the consistency of their biographical information. Edward Darkenall, a gentleman and possibly a lawyer who was examined in February 1603/4 and December 1604 (cases 7/2 and 3/17), presents a two or three year discrepancy when giving his age and substantially larger discrepancies when stating his length of residence in two parishes; and he totally omitted to mention another parish in one of his depositions. John Ellis, an Oxford educated clergyman, made two depositions separated by a two year interval (cases 6/3 and 29/14) but gave virtually identical figures for age and current residence in both. These two examples suggest that while the basic information is likely to be adequate, details of age and length of residence should be treated with some caution.

An interesting aspect of the biographies is the witnesses' estimate of their financial value. This appears in just over half of the depositions (122 out of 222).43 The figures they give must be entirely subjective but they are nevertheless valuable. The approximations provided in the table below give a useful indication of the perceived range of personal wealth in the main social classes.

Table 2

Summary of witnesses' self-valuations				
Status	Total	Range for majority	Total in majority range	Total range
Husbandman	69	£1 - £20	55	£1 - £100
Tradesman	11	£1 - £20	10	£1 - £40
Clergyman	7	£6 - £20	5	£2 - £40
Yeoman	18	£20 - £100	15	£2 - £200
Gentleman	3	£40 - £200	3	£40 - £200
Married woman	11	£0	11	
Widow	1	£6 13s 4d	1	
Spinster	2	£3 - £6 13s 4d	2	

[42] Thanks to a project by volunteers at the West Sussex Record Office, the biographies for the entire series of the Chichester Archdeaconry deposition books are now included in the online index on the WSRO website. East Sussex Record Office holds a card index of deponents in the court of the Lewes Archdeaconry.

[43] The information is normally given in the biography but in some cases it is provided in response to an interrogatory.

Married women, of course, consistently state that they are 'worth nothing' because they have a husband; but a widow and two spinsters align themselves with the lower social groups.

But, with all their inconsistencies, the value of the biographies is undeniable, as has been demonstrated in Clarke's groundbreaking analysis of migration and Shepard's valuable account of personal wealth.

The litigants and the witnesses

A machinery which attempted to solve disputes between individuals was bound to build up a special clientele – and one which differed from the more heterogeneous group of alleged offenders presented in the office court. In instance cases the parties, particularly the plaintiffs who initiated proceedings, were largely drawn from people capable of risking the court fees: respectable tradesmen, members of the middle classes and clergy. Labourers and even husbandmen are largely unrepresented. At a time when the daily wage was around 8d, this was hardly surprising.

For the potential costs were considerable. Regular charges for each court session were 1s for the proctor's fee and 4d for the recording of the court act. At various stages of the case there would be charges of 2s for procedural decrees by the judge; the fee for final sentence was £1. Additional charges were made for such items as the preparation and copying of documents, the serving of citations and the expenses of witnesses. Overall the Chichester fees were broadly similar to other contemporary scales such as those of the Salisbury diocese and the standard produced by Archbishop Whitgift in 1597.[44] The full account for the case of Coote v Brydye (case 11) which spanned the period from July 1604 to March 1606/7 has survived:[45] it demanded costs of £6 11s 8d from the defeated defendant.

We have seen that the results of cases tended to favour the complainants: before embarking, the majority must have taken the precaution of establishing that they had a strong case. Such reassurance might seem important in tithe and testamentary cases, which involved personal or real property. But plaintiffs also showed that they might be prepared to risk their money in actions which affected their status within the local community. In defamation cases they would seek to protect women (and particularly wives) from slurs about sexual behaviour; while matrimonial cases could reflect the social humiliation and wounded pride of a woman who had been rejected.

Appropriately for the church courts, the most frequent class of plaintiff is the clergyman – almost always in pursuit of his tithes or parochial dues. He is also the only litigant likely to undertake serial (or at least simultaneous) cases, usually in the context of local controversy over customs or the payment of specific types of tithe. In other cases, however, it may seem surprising that almost half the plaintiffs were women (21 in the 46 cases); but this does reinforce the view that, in a patriarchal society, the church courts could provide an avenue for women to litigate. That avenue, however, still lay

---

[44] A comparative table of these two scales is given by Martin Ingram, *Church Courts, Sex and Marriage in England, 1570-1640*, 56.

[45] WSRO Ep I/15/1 (1607); a summarised version is included in the Appendix.

within restricted boundaries, defined by the four principal types of action. Defamation produced nine female plaintiffs, compared with three male; and this reflects the fact that the vast majority of cases result from damaging imputations of adultery or fornication. Matrimonial cases, though small in number, did seem to provide a similar means for injured women to express themselves: all three of our plaintiffs are female. Testamentary cases produced a similar proportion: ten women compared with three men – although we must remember that this figure reflects the fact that the majority of testators were men and that frequently they appointed their widow as executrix. Nevertheless the device of proving a will in form of law was particularly valuable to an executrix as it provided a defence against the claims of male relations. The final gender balance is of course redressed by tithe cases, where 13 clergymen and three tithe farmers constitute the plaintiffs. As I show below, however, the involvement of women in rural Sussex is unlikely to match that in metropolitan London.

One might expect the deponents to mirror the social levels of the contesting parties; but they do not. The most striking difference between the two groups is the proportion of women. They provide only 10% of the witnesses (21 out of 222) - exactly equal to the total number of female plaintiffs - and often their testimony reflects a subordinate rôle as a servant or nurse. These figures are so extreme, however, that it is rash to treat them as a reliable norm without further research. The male deponents also tend to come from a slightly lower social class than their plaintiff counterparts. Of those whose status can be clearly identified, the largest group is the 105 husbandmen who provide almost exactly half the total. Next come 34 yeomen (15%), 11 clergy (5%) and six gentlemen (3%). Tradesmen are difficult to identify precisely but probably produce 10%.

We have a useful indication of the qualities expected in deponents: the exceptions in the Lacker v Hobbes case provide a detailed if exaggerated picture. A measure of social standing is desirable, such as the office of churchwarden, constable of the hundred or juryman, or at least categorisation as a 'substantial' man of the parish. High moral standards are assumed: they should be 'of honest behaviour', of credit among their neighbours; and they should tell the truth under oath. Basic capability is required: they need sufficient wit and understanding to transact business and competently to relate a narrative. The exceptions list a catalogue of moral, mental and physical deficiencies which will disqualify: lying, tale-carrying, swearing, brawling, quarrelling – and unsurprisingly, idiocy, blindness and deafness. More relevantly, the deponents must not be prejudiced by friendship or relationship with one of the parties. Few of the witnesses can have seen themselves as paragons and may have felt uncomfortably vulnerable to exposure.

The qualities of a deponent are more easily stated than assessed; but the prescriptions suggest an unstated assumption that he should be male. Perhaps, in a scattered and rural community, the traditional and biblical orthodoxy which maintained the patriarchal status of men's superior understanding remained unchallenged: thus male testimony might provide the best foundation for negotiation and arbitration. And perhaps the low proportion of women deponents can serve as evidence of this belief.

It is unlikely that many witnesses would have appeared of their own volition. Even the court's registrar, Richard Juxon, had to be compelled to depose in what would appear to be a relatively technical case about the will of his colleague, a surrogate judge of the court. For illiterate servants and husbandmen from rural parishes, to be faced by the officials and the incomprehensible procedures, usually within the forbidding surroundings of the Cathedral (where the majority of examinations were taken) must have been frightening and confusing.

It is remarkable that the witnesses give little sign of attempts to prevaricate or mislead. This is perhaps a tribute to the competence and professionalism of the proctors in maintaining a process aimed as much towards resolution as to condemnation. It is also remarkable that the deponents often show independence in delivering statements that do not conform to the expectations of the party which has called them, as for example in the case of Warde v French (case 2). In addition to answering material submitted by both parties (libel and interrogatories for example), occasionally a witness could be called twice, separately, and provide evidence for both plaintiff and defendant.

Sussex and beyond

To avoid treating the Chichester court in isolation it is worth trying to see its work in comparison with other dioceses. As I have shown, we can be confident that its actual procedures conformed to those adopted throughout England. What can be more significant is to discern whether there are variations between dioceses in the cases they dealt with. There is no easy means, unfortunately, of making accurate statistical comparisons from the printed sources currently available; but it is possible to gain a general impression from the publications derived from the records of the London and Oxford dioceses. *London Consistory Court Depositions, 1586-1611: List and Indexes*, edited by Loreen L Giese[46] provides a chronological list of the deponents, parties and types of case. *Oxford Church Courts' Depositions 1542-1639* by Jack Howard-Drake[47] is a monumental achievement which calendars a century's worth of the documents, and provides percentages for the different kinds of cases. To attempt a crude parallel I calculated similar percentages for the four main categories of Chichester cases in this volume (1603-1607), and for London 1607-1609 (London depositions for the period 1603-1606 were too physically fragile to be listed). The figures provide basic comparisons for the three jurisdictions. Unsurprisingly, the closest similarities are between the Chichester archdeaconry and the diocese of Oxford. In both, defamation cases created about 20% of the depositions and matrimonial about 10%. Testamentary cases fell within a wider band, between 25% and 35%. There was a striking divergence in tithe cases: around 20% in Oxford and over 40% in Chichester. This difference perhaps emphasises the rural nature of the Chichester Archdeaconry, which contained no urban community of significant size, as the city of Chichester had a separate jurisdiction. Oxford, by contrast, included not only its city but also towns like Banbury, Abingdon and Bicester. It is a reasonable assumption that tithe raised more serious issues in rural than urban areas.

This assumption is reinforced when comparison is made with London. Despite its rural hinterland in Middlesex, Essex and Hertfordshire, the figure for tithe falls below 15%.

---

[46] London Record Society, Vol 32 (1995)
[47] Oxfordshire County Council 1991-2008)

Testamentary figures are also low at around 10%. In striking contrast the figures for defamation and matrimonial cases produced respectively almost half and almost a quarter of the entire total. When we remember that these two categories involve a high proportion of women as parties and witnesses, it is understandable that the London records have provided a rich mine for gender historians.

The Chichester and Oxford figures emphasise the fact that Londoners lived in a very different world from their provincial contemporaries. Most strikingly, they suggest that there were major differences in the position of women. In London, as Laura Gowing and others have demonstrated, the courts, particularly in defamation and matrimonial cases, were seen to provide a platform in which women could express attitudes on social matters and the community in which they lived; and it is possible that they were prompted more by the opportunity for expression than for the judgements and legal resolutions which other litigants might be seeking. Rural Sussex may at first seem to show similarities: in the 46 cases there are 21 female plaintiffs – a figure which bears comparison with the London equivalent, 36. But the figures for female deponents (21 compared with 80) cannot compete. Much of this divergence must arise from London's high percentages of matrimonial and defamation cases. Not only are matrimonial cases much rarer in both Chichester and Oxford, but they are also confined almost entirely to disputes over the initial contract; in London over 40% deal with separation. There is a further divergence in testamentary cases. As we have seen, the proportion of such cases is much higher in Chichester than London; but so also is the proportion of female plaintiffs (10 in 13 cases). This may be partly due to the practice of executrices who protected themselves by proving the will in form of law; but there is no obvious reason why this device should not have been adopted elsewhere.

Conclusion

It must be emphasised that these figures cannot be treated as firm statistics; but at least they reinforce the impression that different understandings of the function of the courts could develop in different localities – understandings which reflect the prevailing attitudes of their local society. But in the first decade of the seventeenth century the increasing business transacted in these courts, in Chichester and in many English dioceses, shows that the role of instance proceedings in resolving local and personal disputes was respected and valued. Despite Puritan sneers they were generally perceived to act impartially, efficiently and reasonably quickly. They provided an affordable means of arbitration for the lower social groups: a service that was not available in the secular courts. They helped to resolve disagreements over everyday matters by collecting reliable facts that could be accepted by the parties in dispute.

In rural Sussex the proceedings reflected the established values of a firmly traditional, patriarchal, agricultural society. Litigants were pragmatic and practical: they sought facts not opinions. The witnesses they summoned rarely offered personal judgements; but they recorded with precision events, customs and expectations – amid the detail of everyday life in village and farm. The tradesmen and farmers (and their wives) who used the courts valued them particularly as an arbiter to resolve disputes over property – notably in tithe and testamentary matters – and to defend their standing within their community. They needed firm factual statements. The court officials, the litigants and the witnesses all saw the depositions as a means of delivering the facts.

On that basis (and even when cases were not resolved by a formal sentence), the proceedings could provide a legally framed and accepted record on the matters in dispute. Depositions provided the foundations, the vital arbitration tools which the parties sought. The problems they tried to resolve are remote from national issues and from the crimes dealt with by the secular courts. They arise from life in rural agricultural communities; they tell stories of everyday events which were too mundane to be recorded in other sources. Yet they have been largely neglected by historians, perhaps because of their ostensibly unspectacular content. But they have left us a vivid, varied and remarkably accurate legacy that preserves the events, customs and activities of their life in seventeenth century Sussex. I hope this volume may encourage historians to discover and share the world which the witnesses, often reluctantly, put on record.

BIBLIOGRAPHY

PRINTED SOURCES

Jura ecclesiastica: or a treatise on the ecclesiastical laws and courts. Shewing their origin (1742)
The clerk's instructor in the ecclesiastical courts: consisting of a variety of the best precedents (1740)
Burn, R, *Ecclesiastical Law* (7th ed. 1809)
Capp, B, *When Gossips Meet: Women, Family and Neighbourhood in early Modern* England (2003)
Chapman, C R., *Ecclesiastical courts, their officials and their records.* (1992)
Clark, P, *English Provincial Society from the Reformation to the Revolution: Religion Politics and Society in Kent 1500-1640* (1977)
Cockburn, W, *The clerk's assistant in the practice of the ecclesiastical courts* (3rd ed. 1760)
Consett, H, *The practice of the spiritual or ecclesiastical courts* (1708)
Coote, H C, *The practice of the ecclesiastical courts, with forms and tables of costs* (1847)
Cressy, D, *Birth, marriage, and death: ritual, religion, and the life-cycle in Tudor and Stuart England* (1997)
Elton, G R *England 1200-1640. The Sources of History: Studies in the Uses of Historical Evidence* (1969)
Floyer, P, *The proctor's practice in the ecclesiastical courts* (1746)
Foster A W, 'Chichester Diocese in the early 17th Century' in *Sussex Archaeological Collections* **123** (1985) 187-194.
Furnivall, F, *Child Marriages, Divorces and Ratifications etc. in the Diocese of Chester AD 1561-66* (1897)
Gibson, E, *Codex Iuris Ecclesiastici Anglicani* (1713)
Gowing, L, *Domestic Dangers, Women, Words and Sex in Early Modern London* (1996)
Giese, L L, *London Consistory Court Depositions, 1586-1611: List and* Indexes London Record Society, vol. 32 (1995)
Helmholz, R H, *Roman Canon Law in Reformation England* (1994)
Helmholz, R H, *The Canon Law and Ecclesiastical Jurisdiction from 1597 to the 1640s' in Oxford History of the Laws of* England (2003)
Houlbrooke, R A, *Church courts and the people during the English Reformation, 1520-1570.* (1979)
Howard Drake, J., *Oxford church courts : depositions, 1542-1634* (1995-2007)
Hubbard, E, *City Women: Money, Sex and the Social Order in Early Modern* London (2014)
Ingram, M, *Church Courts Sex and Marriage, 1570-1640* (1987)
Jarman, E K M, *An edition of the Depositions from EDC 2/6 deposition book of the Consistory Court of Chester, September 1558 - March 1558/9* (Dissertation, Master of Archives and Records Management, 2010)
Jacob, G, *A New Law Dictionary* (3rd ed. 1736)
Johnstone, H, *Churchwardens' Presentments (17th century). Part 1 : Archdeaconry of Chichester, 1621-28, 1664-70* Sussex Record Society, vol. 49 (1949)
Johnstone, H, *Churchwardens' Presentments (17th century). Part II : Archdeaconry of Lewes, 1674-77* Sussex Record Society, vol. 50 (1950)
Lander, S J, *Church Courts and the Reformation in the Diocese of Chichester, 1500-58'* in O'Day & Heal, *Continuity and Change: Personnel and Administration of the Church of England, 1500-1642* (1976)

Law, J T, *Forms of ecclesiastical law; or, The mode of Conducting Suits in the Consistory Courts : being a translation of the first part of Oughton's Ordo Judiciorum* (1831)
Levack, B P, *The Civil Lawyers in England, 1603-41* (1973)
Marchant, R A, *The Church under the Law: Justice, Administration and Discipline in the Diocese of York* (1969)
Outhwaite, R. B, *Clandestine Marriage in England, 1500-1850* (1995)
Outhwaite, R. B., *Marriage and Society: Studies in the Social History of Marriage* (1981)
Outhwaite, R. B., *The rise and fall of the English ecclesiastical courts, 1500-1860* (2006)
O'Day, R & Heal, F, *Continuity and Change, Personnel and Administration of the Church of England, 1500-1642* (1976)
O'Hara, D, *Courtship and Constraint: Rethinking the making of Marriage in Tudor* England (2000)
Probert, R, *Marriage Law and Practice in the Long Eighteenth Century: A* Reassessment (2009)
Rushton, K, A History of the Ecclesiastical Courts of the Diocese of Canterbury, 1566-86, based on the cause papers bound within Volume MS.F.4.12' in *Archaeologia Cantiana* Vol. 134 pp 263-281, 2014
Selden, J, *The Historie of Tithes* (1618)
Sharpe, J A, *Defamation and sexual slander in early modern England : the church courts at* York Borthwick Institute of Historical Research, (1980)
Shepard, A, *Accounting for Oneself: Worth, Status and the Social Order in Early Modern* England (2015)
SPCK, *The Canon Law of the Church of England* (1947)
Steer, F W & Kirby, I M, *Diocese of Chichester: Catalogue of the Records of the Bishop, Archdeacons and Former Exempt Jurisdictions* (1966)
Tarver, A, *Church Court Records* (1995)
Wilkinson, P M, 'The Courts of True Love', in *Sussex Archaeological Collections* **152** (2014) 79-94.
Willis, A J, *Winchester Consistory Court Depositions, 1561-1602* (1960)

WEBSITES

Cambridge Alumni up to 1751, https://archive.org/stream/alumnicantabrigipt1vol1univiala/alumnicantabrigipt1vol1univiala_djvu.txt, Accessed 5 March 2017.
CCED Clergy of the Church of England database, http://theclergydatabase.org.uk/, Accessed 5 March 2017.
Oxford Alumni 1500-1714, http://www.british-history.ac.uk/alumni-oxon/1500-1714, Accessed 5 March 2017.
Oxford Dictionary of National Biography, http://www.oxforddnb.com/search/people/index.jsp, Accessed 5 March 2017.
University of Nottingham MS Special Collections: Archdeaconry of Nottingham, http://www.nottingham.ac.uk/manuscriptsandspecialcollections/collectionsindepth/archdeaconry/introduction.aspx, Accessed 5 March 2017.
University of York: Borthwick Institute for Archives: York Diocese cause papers, https://www.hrionline.ac.uk/causepapers/, Accessed 5 March 2017.

BACKGROUND INFORMATION FROM UNPUBLISHED SOURCES

Much of the biographical information given in the introductory notes and footnotes is derived from parish registers. The search tools for unlocking them are now digital. The Sussex Family History Group's *Sussex Marriage Index* has proved invaluable, as have the *Find My Past* and *Family Search* websites. And the foundation beneath them is of course the collection of original registers and modern transcripts in the West Sussex Record Office.

Information about officials, parties and deponents in the Chichester city area has been mined from the WSRO Chichester Index compiled by Norma Pilbeam and Bernard Vick, which has extracted a vast range of material from a wide range of late 16th and early 17th century sources. To avoid overloading the text with annotations I have not usually cited specific references from these sources. Valuable information about the parties and deponents in the Chichester Consistory Office courts has been made accessible by the WSRO indexes to the act books for the period 1603-1609, compiled by John Bishop and Bernard Vick. This information can often add a new dimension to the instance proceedings. Without these indexes it would have been an impossible task to uncover such valuable facts. This volume would have been much poorer without the dedication and expertise of these three compilers, to whom I am heavily indebted.

A NOTE ON THE EDITING AND PRESENTATION

Although these depositions are intended to reproduce the oral statements made by the witnesses, they are recorded in a highly repetitive and formalised style. To overcome this I have omitted repetitious legal and formulaic phraseology such as 'aforesaid', 'as this examinate remembereth' and a host of others which can make the reading tedious and often confusing. I have set out these principles for omission in Appendix 3 together with sample versions of a deposition fully and literally transcribed as it appears in the original, followed by the form I have adopted for this edition.

I have prefaced each case with a summary setting out the central issues and procedure, and, where relevant, biographical details of the parties (mainly from the records of the act books of detection proceedings in the office court and from the Church of England Clergy Database). For each witness I have included the biographical details (as given in the statement at the start of each deposition, listing the places where the witness has lived and his or her age); to this I have added the personal financial value recorded in the deposition, have indicated whether he or she made a mark or a signature, and (where given) the date of examination.

In the depositions much of the information on non-controversial matters given by one witness will duplicate with that given by others. In this edition the statements of the first witness are given in full. To limit duplication the depositions of the subsequent witnesses are reduced to those statements which produce new or significantly different information. The task of making decisions as to what to omit is assisted by the regular form in which the libels and interrogatories (the most frequent tools of examination) are composed. In the libels the initial three or so statements set out formal and largely uncontroversial background facts; the final three or so are similarly uncontroversial and are confined to the formal status of the defendant and the witness. The initial four or so questions of the interrogatories are usually formal and deal with the relationship of the witness and the plaintiff – though they often produce a statement of the witness's financial status (which I have extracted and incorporated in the biographical statement). The intervening statements and questions are those most likely to differ significantly from the first witness's deposition – but they may still involve a significant amount of repetition.

Each paragraph within a deposition has been given an identifying number relating to the article to which it responds. This will identify which articles have been retained in the second and subsequent depositions. Where irrelevant matter within the individual paragraphs of the responses has been omitted this has been indicated by an ellipse. Similar procedure has been adopted for depositions responding to other forms of examination.

I have tried to adopt consistent conventions in transcribing. Place and Christian names are given in modern conventional form; surnames (whose spelling often varies within the same deposition) are normally given in the form used in the initial biography at the start of the deposition - or, exceptionally, the form used at the end of the deposition. Other spelling is modernised except where an archaic form is significant. Conventional abbreviations have been expanded to the modern form; roman numerals have been converted to Arabic; currency has been rendered in conventional £ s d form. For the titling of cases I have adopted the more familiar modern "v" (versus) rather than "contra" which normally appears in the original. Once a personal name has been given in full it has usually been represented by initials in subsequent references. As the original is largely unpunctuated, I have inserted minimal punctuation to make reading easier. Latin phrases are translated or more frequently paraphrased, and are printed in italics. Italics have also been used for editorial comment (including dating), notably for the descriptive paragraphs introducing each case and for indicating legal procedure.

The dates of the depositions are not recorded consistently, although many bear the precise date on which they were read over before the judge. Where this is not given, I have supplied (in square brackets) an estimated date from information in the court acts or from the position in the Deposition Book. For simplicity, all dates of depositions are given in italics.

Annotations consist either of editorial comment or citations giving the references for the documents transcribed. The former appear as footnotes and the latter as endnotes.

CHICHESTER ARCHDEACONRY DEPOSITIONS

1603 - 1608

THE CASES

1 Agnes Daniell of Selsey v Robert Bishoppe of Selsey: Defamation.	5
2 Richard Warde v John French: Tithe in Thakeham.	11
3 James Lacker v Richard Hobbes: Tithe in Houghton.	21
4 James Browne of Petworth v William Humfrey of Amberley. Defamation.	54
5 James Pellett, vicar of Madehurst, v Richard Coxe. Tithe.	56
6 Alice Standen of Yapton v John and Henry Standen. Testamentary.	66
7 Thomas Hunt of Houghton v Susan Hunt of Pulborough and William Hunt of Billingshurst. Testamentary.	71
8 Ralph Deare, vicar of Harting, v Thomas Hawsted, vicar of Rogate. Jactitation of tithe.	77
9 Robert Johnson, rector of West Chiltington v Henry Johnson of West Chiltington. Defamation.	87
10 Alice Stamer alias Greene v John Tickenor of Ferring. Testamentary.	90
11 Mary Coote of Singleton v John Brydye [of Boxgrove]. Matrimonial.	93
12 Raphael Widdowson, vicar of Oving, v Edward Rose. Tithe.	99
13 Mary Legate of Lodsworth v Julian Legate of Selham. Defamation.	101
14 Eleanor Butcher of Washington v Richard Lee of Washington. Defamation.	105
15 Peter Waters, rector of Wiston v John Willett and William Foster, and v John Parker, and v John Hatfeild. Tithe.	108
16 Thomas Goodwyn rector of Bepton v Edward Woldridge. Tithe.	112
17 Peter Betsworth v Edward Northe. Tithe in Kirdford.	115
18 Nicholas Diggens, vicar of Stoughton, v John Palmer. Church rights.	118
19 Thomas and Robert Hitchecocke v Thomas Goodwyn, rector of Bepton: Church rights.	122
20 Joan Gradell v William Gradell. Testamentary.	127
21 Charity Chandler of Midhurst v William and Ralph Chandler. Testamentary.	130
22 Katheryn Squier of Eastergate v Edward Duffeild of Aldingbourne. Defamation.	133
23 Margaret Palmer alias Lodger of Up Marden v Arthur Lodger. Testamentary.	136
24 Samuel Todd, rector of East Wittering, v John Newe. Tithe.	141
25 Mary Carden of Rustington v Nicholas Harber of Rustington. Defamation.	145

26 Samuel Todd, rector of East Wittering, v Richard Rablis. Tithe.	147
27 John Reade v William Lenn of Yapton. Testamentary.	149
28 Elizabeth Carpenter v Matilda Robinson and Joan Kneller. Testamentary.	151
29 Margaret West of Ford v Anne Lane. Testamentary.	154
30 Ex officio promoted by Thomas Baylye v William and Cicily Soane. Testamentary.	172
31 Alice Collye alias Parson alias Slater v Joan Slater. Testamentary.	177
32 Mary Robins of Shipley v Edward Hayler of Shipley. Defamation.	181
33 Ralph Earle, vicar of Eartham, v John Page. Tithe.	183
34 Agnes Nashe of Middleton, v William Holden of Middleton. Defamation.	189
35 Frances Tester v John Burdye alias Burdocke of Wisborough Green. Matrimonial.	192
36 Joan Blaxton, widow of Henry Blaxton, v Henry Blaxton, junior, of Chichester. Testamentary.	194
37 Margaret Tayler of Stoughton v Richard Tillboroughe of North Marden. Defamation.	197
38 Joan Johnson v Edward Woldridge of Woolbeding. Testamentary.	201
39 Rose Harris of Tortington v Edward Graye of Tortington. Defamation.	206
40 Michael Birkeheade, vicar of Warnham, v Richard Barttelot. Tithe.	210
41 Michael Birkeheade, vicar of Warnham, v William Perkyn. Tithe.	214
42 Michael Birkeheade, vicar of Warnham, v John Pancrasse. Tithe.	218
43 Hugh Roberts, vicar of Yapton, v Henry Standen of Felpham. Tithe.	221
44 Thomas Herold of Pulborough v Elizabeth Hitchcock. Defamation.	230
45 Joan Elliott alias Tapper of Bramshott v Richard Coote of Singleton. Matrimonial.	235
46 William Chatfeilde v John Whatley, and v Richard Knighte, and v Richard Aylinge. Tithe in Oving.	244

1/1 Agnes Daniell, wife of Richard Daniell of Selsey v Robert Bishoppe of Selsey: Defamation.[1]

Court acts: 16 April 1603 to 23 July 1604.

A complicated case and counter case. Agnes Daniell accused Bishoppe of calling her a whore and claiming that she had tried to steal his seat in Selsey church. After the depositions of her witnesses in May 1603, Bishoppe commenced a counter suit (probably as an attempt to avoid costs), producing witnesses who deposed in October 1603 followed by further depositions in January and February 1603/4. Eventually, in April 1604, Daniell was condemned to pay costs of 40s. On failing to do so she was excommunicated in July but sought and received absolution in November 1604.

The office court records do not include references to confirm Bishoppe's accusations of fornication. Bishoppe, however, had himself been presented and done penance in 1600 for the same crime.

Proctors: Barker for plaintiff; Cooke for defendant. Examinations: three depositions for plaintiff responding to libel of six articles; personal response of defendant responding to libel; personal response of plaintiff responding to two allegations; two depositions for defendant responding to allegation of one article and interrogatories of eight; two depositions for plaintiff responding to her additional positions of six articles to exceptions.

1/2 Robert Combes.[2] *Read over 25 May 1603.*

Of Selsey, fisherman; born there; aged about 40. Signs with mark.

To the libel:

L1 *Refers to oath.*

L2. That upon mid Lent Sunday last past after evening prayer in the parish church of Selsey Robert Bishoppe coming to Agnes Daniell sitting in the church porch said unto her, 'Now gentlewoman have you put me out of my seat?' And Agnes Daniell and Robert Bishoppe further questioning together, he called her whore and said, 'Now you whore, [*blank*] Stiles is gone', but did not call her Stiles whore. All which speeches were so spoken by him against her in the presence of Richard Eglie, Winifred Warner, Robert Combes and others.

L3. *Does not know beyond has already deposed.*

L4. That he verily believeth that by reason of the speeches the good name fame and credit of Agnes Daniell is much impaired and hurt.

L5. That Robert Bishoppe is of the parish of Selsey and subject to the jurisdiction of this court.

L6. *Deposition is true.*

1/3 Winifrid Warner.[3] *Read over 25 May 1603*

Wife of Thomas Warner of Selsey, fisherman; born there; aged about 40. Signs with mark.

L2. That about mid Lent Sunday last past Robert Bishoppe and Agnes Daniell being at some variance in the parish church of Selsey at evening prayer touching a seat in the church, he came unto her sitting in the church porch and after some speeches passed betwixt them he called her 'baggage and whore' and said, 'Now Stiles is dead and the men of war gone now thou canst have no more basters [*sic*],' meaning that she had played the whore with Stiles or some other man; but did not absolutely call her Stiles whore. All which speeches were spoken by Robert Bishoppe against her in the presence of Robert Combes, Richard Eglie, Winifrid Warner and others.

L4. That she verily believeth that the good name and fame of Agnes Daniell is nothing at all impaired because she hath always been accounted an honest woman ···.

1/4 Richard Eglie.[4] *Read over 25 May 1603*

Of Selsey, husbandman; born there; aged about 40. Signs with mark.

L2. That about mid Lent Sunday last Robert Bishoppe and Agnes Daniell being at some discord in the parish church of Selsey in time of evening prayer about a seat, he after evening prayer was done came unto her sitting in the church porch and reviled her in so much that he called her whore and arrant whore and said unto her that now when Stiles was dead and the men of war were gone she could have no more bastards; by reason of which speeches he believeth that he meant that she had played the whore with Stiles or some other But he did not absolutely say that she was the said Stiante's [*sic*] whore ···.

L4. That he verily believeth that the good name and fame and credit of Agnes Daniell is much impaired by reason of the speeches.

1/5 Robert Bishoppe.[5] *Read over 4 June 1603.*

Personal response. Signs with mark.

To libel ex parte Agnes Daniell

L1. *Refers to oath.*

L2. *Believes* that within the parish of Selsey and in some one of the months articulate Agnes Daniell abusing him, reviling and calling him whore master arrant villain and [dog]*, he in the presence of divers witnesses did tell her that she was a whore of her tongue. *Denies the rest.*

L3. [*Accepts that used the words specified*]

L4. [*Does not believe it to be true in anything beyond what he has admitted above*]

L5. *Believes it to be true.*

---

* Difficult reading.

L6. *Believes himself to be the party complained against on the part of Agnes Daniell, however unlawfully. Believes what he has stated above that he believes, and denies what he has denied.*

1/6 Agnes Daniell.[6] *8 October 1603.*

Personal response. Signs with mark.

To allegation ex parte Robert Bishoppe

Does not believe allegation to be true in anything.

To [2nd] Allegation ex parte Robert Bishoppe

Does not believe allegation to be true in anything.

1/7 Thomas Woodland.[7] [*October 1603*]

Of Selsey, yeoman; born there; aged about 44. Is worth £40. Signs with mark.

To the allegation ex parte Robert Bishoppe:

That about the first day of August last past he and Mr Henry Harrison vicar of Selsey coming along the highway from Selsey church not far from the churchyard, he heard Robert Bishoppe and Agnes Daniell in some talk touching a discord that was betwixt them and depending in this court about undiscreet [*sic*] words that had formerly passed betwixt them. In so much that Mr Harrison and Thomas Woodland wished Robert Bishoppe and Agnes Daniell to be at unity one with another and live together like neighbours, in so much that both were content to remit and forgive all offences and speech. And Robert Bishoppe and Agnes Daniell did then and there both of them in express words say that they did one forgive another and that hereafter they would become good friends and neighbours so that they were sorry that any such speeches that should happen betwixt them, meaning those speeches for which they went to suit to be the occasion of their falling out. And he further saith that upon their agreement Agnes Daniell did use some speeches touching upon the paying of the fees in this court, but Richard Daniell husband of Agnes Daniell being present answered, 'I pray thee wife take thee no care for that' meaning for paying the fees. All which speeches was so spoken and agreed upon in the place and time abovesaid and in the presence of Henry Harrison and Richard Daniell and Thomas Woodland. And he further saith that after the agreement, Agnes Daniell and Richard Daniell requested Robert Bishoppe and Thomas Woodland to go home with them and sup with them that night but Mr Harrison was not bid by reason he went from them a little before; neither did he, nor Robert Bishoppe, go with them to supper because he could not stay because there were cattle broke into certain crie* of his. By reason of all which speeches and agreements Agnes Daniell and Robert Bishoppe were fully and absolutely agreed.

To the interrogatories:

In 1. *Satisfactory.*

---

* Difficult reading.

In 2. *Negative* saving that Robert Bishoppe married with a woman who was Thomas Woodland's aunt's daughter but died about 6 years ago.

In 3. *Favours neither party. For the rest negative.*

In 4. That he came at the instant request of Robert Bishoppe and as he thinketh he will bear his charge; *for the rest negative.*

In 5. *Does not know beyond what has already deposed.*

In 6. That the composition or agreement was simply and absolutely made without any condition of paying any charges nor upon any other condition or cause not yet performed by Robert Bishoppe.

In 7. That Agnes Daniell did give her consent unto the agreement with* the special consent of her husband, for her husband at the same time stood by her and did not disagree nor dissent.

In 8. That he neither knoweth nor ever heard of any composition or agreement that was made between Robert Bishoppe and Agnes Daniell by Mr Dr Blaxton; *and for the rest does not know beyond what has already deposed.*

1/8 Henry Harrison.[8] *Read over 19 October 1603.*

Clerk, vicar of Selsey, where has lived for 27 years; before at Pagham for 4 years; before at Barnham; born there; aged about 64 years. Is worth £40. Signature.†

To the allegation:

That about the first day of August last past Henry Harrison and Thomas Woodland coming along from the church and going up Selsey street heard Robert Bishoppe and Agnes Daniell at some speeches touching a discord which happened betwixt them concerning some words of defamation for the which they are now in suit in this court, whereupon Henry Harrison and Thomas Woodland in the presence of Richard Daniell husband of Agnes Daniell requested Robert Bishoppe and Agnes Daniell to be friends and agree like neighbours and friends and forgive and forget all wrongs and injuries which had been betwixt them. Insomuch that after some communication Robert Bishoppe and Agnes Daniell consented to be friends and then and there became friends in so much that he said unto her he was very good friends with her and that he was sorry that there were any such cause of falling out. And she replied that she was and would be friends with him and she was sorry there was any such cause of falling out betwixt them. After which agreement she said that she would not loose [?lose] her charges; unto which speeches Richard Daniell replied, 'I pray thee wife hold thyself contented. Goodman Bishoppe and I are agreed for the charges'; whereupon she spoke no more touching the charge. And Richard Daniell and Agnes Daniell were desirous to have gone to drink with Robert Bishoppe, Thomas Woodland and Henry Harrison and

---

* unto with *in MS.*

† Vicar of Selsey in 1604 and vicar of Pagham from 1591 until his death in 1604.

so they had done, but that Henry Harrison, Thomas Woodland and Robert Bishoppe had then other business which letted them. And so he did hold Robert Bishoppe and Agnes Daniell to be lovers and friends and fully agreed touching the controversy.

To the interrogatories:

In 2. *Negative,* save that Joseph Harrison, his son, married with Alice Bishoppe daughter unto Robert Bishoppe.

In 4. That he came at the request of Robert Bishoppe without any charges only that he paid for his dinner.

In 7. That for the special words that Agnes Daniell did give her consent to the agreement he hath already answered; and for her husband's consent he saith Richard Daniell did further the agreement as much as he could. And she making this agreement with Robert Bishoppe, Richard Daniell standing by them did neither assent nor dissent from the same, but he was glad they were agreed.

In 8. That he knoweth of no other composition.

1/9 Thomas Woodlande.[9] *Read over 26 Jan 1603/4.*

[*Personal information as previous; gives age as 43. Mark perhaps crude version of TW*]

To the additional positions as to the exceptions ex parte Agnes Daniell to the deposition by Thomas Woodland and Henry Harrison:

ADE 1 & 2. That the agreement or transaction was simple pure and absolute and made upon no other condition than this examinate hath formerly deposed to the allegation made on the behalf of Robert Bishoppe against Agnes Daniell and to the interrogatories given on the behalf of Agnes Daniell.

ADE 3 & 4. That he never confessed neither before his production and examination that 'the greemente' was made upon any condition but simple pure and absolute as he formerly deposed; *and for Henry Harrison does not know.*

ADE 5. *Refers to oath.*

ADE 6. *Deposition is true.*

1/10 Henry Harrison.[10] *Read over 3 February 1603/4.*

[*Personal information as previous*]

APE 1 & 2. That the agreement was simple pure and absolute and made upon no other condition than Henry Harrison hath already deposed; for at that time he neither knew nor heard of any other transaction or agreement than he hath before recited. For Henry Harrison and Thomas Woodland had only respect unto the Christian reconciliation of Robert Bishoppe and Agnes Daniell and to bring both into Christian charity according to offices of Mr Harrison and Thomas Woodland, the one being vicar and the other churchwarden.

APE 3. That since his production and examination upon the allegation in the precedent article he hath partly understood by the speeches of Robert Bishoppe and Richard Daniell that they two were agreed that the transaction in the two precedent articles should be upon the conditions in the second article. But at the time of the agreement there were no other speeches used between Robert Bishoppe and Richard Daniell and Agnes his wife than he at the time of his former examination set down to his knowledge.

APE 4. That since his examination touching the transaction, he hath heard that Robert Bishoppe producted [*sic*] no witnesses to prove the defamation mentioned in the second article of these exceptions. But before his examination there were no speeches used of producting [*sic*] any witnesses of either side that he knew touching the proving of any defamation.

2/1 Mr Richard Warde v. John French: Tithe in Thakeham.[11]

Court acts: 1 October 1603 to 13 March 1603/4.

Warde, rector of Thakeham, accused French of failing to pay tithe on corn and livestock in the years 1602 and 1603. During this relatively short case Warde was able to obtain depositions from 12 witnesses. He alleged that the tithing of corn by setting it out in special stacks (heals, healings and fivings), and also payments for the birth of a foal, are established parish customs – to which John French failed to conform. The depositions look back over a period of up to 54 years and suggest that heals or healings were stacks of 10 sheaves of corn, and fivings stacks of five. More specifically the rector claimed a specific arrangement by which one fiving is set out as tithe for every five heals/healings. He objected to corn tithes being set out in single sheaves, but a number of deponents suggest that the latter arrangement had been accepted in the past. The case concluded by agreement between the parties.*

Warde was of St John's College, Oxford in and before 1566, curate of Thakeham from the 1580s and rector 1587-1605, succeeding Michael Warde, who was rector 1572-1587. He died in 1605. While John French served as churchwarden in the year before the case he was presented in the office court for reaping on a Sunday.

Proctors: Cooke for plaintiff; Barker for defendant. Examinations: 12 depositions for plaintiff responding to libel of 15 articles and interrogatories of 13.

2/2 Thomas Woodyer.[12] [*January 1603/4*]

Of Thakeham, weaver; born there; aged about 40. Is worth 20s. Signs with mark.

To the libel:

L 1. That Mr Richard Warde hath been parson of Thakeham for all the time libellate and long before.

L 2. That all the tithes within the parish of Thakeham have time out of mind been due unto the parson of Thakeham, as they are at this time due unto Mr Richard Warde, now parson, in the right of his parsonage.

L 3. That the parsons of Thakeham, predecessors of Richard Warde, hath or ought to have quietly and peaceably received the tithes for this 30 years last past, as he has until this suit began betwixt Richard Warde and John French, or otherwise except some other parishioners did give him or any of his predecessors occasion to sue them for detaining their tithes.

L 4. That for all the years in the article mentioned he hath known the parishioners, occupiers of lands, to set forth their tithes of wheat and oats yearly after this manner, viz to set forth by heales, sometimes by fivinges and sometimes by the tenth sheaf. And Thomas Woodyer for that small wheat and oats that he had of his lands hath for this ten or eleven years past set forth his tithes by the tenth sheaf, and the same tithe was never refused to be taken in the same manner until this last year. And then he set

* None of these three terms appear in the *OED*; but 'hale' is included as an obsolete word meaning a temporary shelter, a place roofed over but open at the sides.

forth his wheat by the fiving because Thomas Arcoll set up the tenth sheaf himself, which Thomas Arcoll is Richard Warde's man and taketh up all his tithes.

L 5. That he hath never heard any ancient old men within Thakeham nor any other say that the tithes were set up otherwise, viz sometimes by healinges, sometimes by fivinges and sometimes by the tenth sheaf.

L 6. That he doth not think that the parishioners are bound by any custom to set forth their tithe wheat or oats into heals or fivinges, but the parishioners sometimes of good will have set forth their tithes into heales or fivinges after the same were tithed by the sheaf, but not otherwise.

L 7. That he never heard of any parishioner, having had any colts fallen of their mares, ever paid anything in lieu of the fall of any colt until within this twelve month. Since which time he hath paid for the fall of a colt 4d; and whether any other of the parishioners paid the like he cannot depose.

L 8-9. That he cannot tell how many acres John French hath sown with wheat in the year libellate, neither what heales nor fivinges of wheat he had, nor what any were worth, neither how many acres he converted to meadow in 1602, nor how many cocks of hay, nor what any were worth, neither can he depose how many acres John French had sown with oats in the year 1603, neither what sheaves, fivinges or healinges he had of oats, nor what any were worth.

L 10. *Refers to statute and what has deposed.*

L 11. *Does not know beyond what has already deposed.*

L 12. *Does not know.*

L 13. That John French is of the parish of Thakeham and subject to the jurisdiction of this court.

L 14. *Refers to oath.*

L 15. *Deposition is true.*

To the interrogatories:

In 1. *Satisfactory.*

In 2. *Negative*; saving that he oweth Richard Warde 3s 4d or 3s 8d.

In 3. That he is worth in goods 20s.

In 4. *Negative,* saving that he came at the request of Richard Warde and he promised to bear his charge.

In 5. That Thomas Arcoll is appointed by Richard Warde to be his gatherer of tithes of hay corn and oats and so he hath been for one year, which he hath done saving the tithes now in contention.

In 6. That he hath known Richard Bushoppe, John Brooker and Thomas Jackett and many others for 30 years to set out their tithe wheat and oats in sheaves only at sometimes, and at other times in fivinges, and he hath heard that the like order hath been observed for 50 years, viz the parishioners have sometimes set out their tithe wheat and oats in sheaves and sometimes in healinges or fivinges, but he never knew that the parishioners did set out only in sheaves, but sometimes they did and sometimes they did not. He hath known Mr Lushar, who was farmer of the parsonage for 30 years, to take wheat and oats set forth in sheaves, and he hath known Christopher Hitcham, who was farmer of the parsonage for 24 years, to have the like.

In 7. That the parishioners are not bound to set forth their wheat or oats in heales or fivinges but that they may pay their tenth sheaf. Only sometimes the parishioners do sometimes out of courtesy, according as the weather falleth out, set wheat and oats in heales or fivinges.

In 8. *Does not know.*

In 9. *Does not know*, saving that he hath heard that John French in 1603 set out his tithe oats before two of his neighbours in sheaves and that Mr Warde did not fetch the same away.

In 10. *Does not know*, saving that he hath heard that Mr Warde did only find fault with John French for that he did not justly tithe his oats in 1603.

In 11 & 12. *Does not know.*

In 13. *Does not know*, saving that he hath heard that John French in 1603 set out some of his oats in fivinges and some in sheaves. And as he set up his own oats so he set up the tithe thereof.

2/3 Lambert Cayger.[13] [*January 1603/4*]

Of Thakeham, cooper, where has lived for 7 years; before at Barnham; born there; aged about 60. Is worth £20. Signs with mark.[*]

L 4. That for 30 years the parishioners have set out their wheat and oats in heales or fivinges at some times and at other times, if there happened to be any controversy, then the party which did disagree with the parson or with whom the parson was offended, did always set forth his wheat or oats by the tenth sheaf and not by the heale or fivinges because the parishioners did not think they were bound to set forth their tithes in heales or fivinges but only to set forth the tenth sheaf. But if the party with whom Richard Warde was not friends afterwards *became* to be friends then he would in courtesy set forth his tithe in heales or fivinges but not otherwise. And [*the same ?*][†] Lambert Cayger hath both known and seen for he hath seen old John Brooker do the like upon some controversy betwixt William Bennet who was farmer of the tithes under Richard Warde some years ago; and William Bennet took the same tithes away and Lambert Cayger hath heard said that it was but a little more trouble to him.

L 6. That he knoweth that if the tithes were set up in heales or fivinges it were more profitable to the church; yet the custom is not so.

---

[*] Later, in 1606, he was presented in the office court for haymaking on the Sabbath.
[†] Illegible.

L 7. That he never knew any of the parishioners pay anything in lieu of the fall of any colt until within this twelvemonth and then he paid 4d to Mrs Warde wife of Richard Warde in lieu of the tithe of his colt, conditionally that if the same 4d were not due Richard Warde should repay him.

In 6. That he hath seen old John Brooker about ten years ago set out his tithe wheat and oats in sheaves only and not in heales or fivinges, and William Bennett who was then farmer of the tithes did fetch the same tithes away. And he hath heard that many of the parishioners for 22 years past did set out their tithes in sheaves only and not in heales or fivinges and that the parsons or their farmers have so had their tithes.

2/4 John Brooker.[14] [*January 1603/4*]

Of Thakeham, husbandman, where he has lived for 12 years; before at Sullington 12 years; before at Thakeham; born there; aged about 60 years. Is worth £30. Signs with mark.

L 7. That he never knew that any thing was demanded or paid in lieu of any tithe colt fallen until within this twelve months since which time John Brooker hath heard that Lambert Cayger paid unto Richard Warde 4d in lieu of a tithe colt; and he had himself two colts fallen but he never paid any thing neither did he ever hear anything demanded.

In 6. That he hath known John Brooker* for some ten years did set forth his tithe wheat and oats in sheaves only in respect there were some controversy between his father and one William Bennett who was the farmer of the tithes. And his father being then four score years and upwards told him that he had known the parishioners set forth their tithes by the tenth sheaf for forty years; and so if William Bennet would take his tithes by the tenth sheaf, so it were; if not he might let the same alone. Then William Bennet took his tithes by the sheaf and carried the same away. And he further saith he hath heard his father say that for fifty years he did carry in tithe corn for one Robert Edens then parson, and then he was glad to gather up the tithes by the sheaf for the most part, for there were but few that set forth their tithes in fivinges; and so Robert Edens was glad to receive his tithes by the sheaf .

2/5 Daniel Sole.[15] [*January 1603/4*]

Of Thakeham, husbandman; born there; aged about 43. Is worth 40s. Signature.†

L 5. That he hath heard Richard Sole, Daniel Sole's father say, who is about 70 years of age, that the parishioners were wont for this 50 years last past to set forth their tithe sometimes by the heale or fivinge and sometimes by the sheaf but for the most part by the heale or fivinge. And further saith that he about 20 years ago gathered the tithes for Christopher Hitcham for about one year who was then farmer of the parsonage and for Mr Michael Warde who was parson of Thakeham for six years about 20 years ago, during which time he received more tithes in heales and fivinges than in sheaves.

---

* i.e. John Booker senior, his father.

† Perhaps brother of Christopher Sole below.

L 6. That he thinketh that the setting forth of tithes is a thing reasonable and profitable to the church.

In 6. That he neither knoweth nor ever heard of any parishioner for 40 or 50 years that did ever set out his tithe in sheaves only and not in fivinges, neither doth he know of any of the parsons of Thakeham for 40 or 50 years that ever carried away such tithe set out in sheaves as is aforesaid.

In 7. That he cannot depose whether the parishioners may choose at their discretion whether they will set out their tithes in sheaves only or in fivinges, neither whether the same were left to the choice and discretion of the parishioners for 40 years last past. But when they set up their own in fivinges then they are wont also to set up in fivinges for the most part.

2/6 Thomas Arcoll.[16] *[January 1603/4]*

*Of Thakeham, husbandman; born there; aged about 35. Is worth 40s. Signs with mark.**

L 4. That for this 20 years Thomas Arcoll hath known the parishioners to accustom to set forth their tithe wheat and oats by the heale or fivinges and not by the tenth sheaf, except some one or two that were sometimes in haste and having but a little tithing wheat or oats did here and there cast the tithes out by the sheaf in respect the tithe was so small. But it were very seldom for where one set forth his tithe by the tenth sheaf forty set forth by the heales or fivinges.

L 5. That he knew John Arcoll his father pay tithe wheat and oats for 20 years before his death, and he died about four years ago, unto the parson, during which time he never knew him pay any but by the heales or fivinges. But he never heard any old men declare that the tithe were accustomed to be set out in heales or fivinges time out of mind because he never heard of any such controversy before; neither did he ever hear that the parishioners were accustomed to set forth their tithe by the tenth sheaf except before excepted.

L 6. That it is a profitable thing to the church for the parishioners to set up their tithe in heales or fivinge, for by casting the same tithes out by the tenth sheaf there cometh great loss; but whether the parishioners be bound by custom he cannot depose.

L 8. That John French in 1602 had five acres sown with wheat and on every acre he had heales of wheat and about every heale worth 2s; and in the same year he had 15 acres which he converted to meadow and on every acre he had 20 cocks of hay worth 2d. And he had in 1603 8 acres sown with oats and every acre had 5 heales, every heale worth 10d. And he had pasturing two mares and of them he had two colts and for the fall of each colt he to pay 4d.

---

* Not only a farmer, but brother-in-law of the rector, and resident at the rectory, and Warde's appointed and obedient tithe collector. An important witness, he confirms the statements of the libel more positively than the other deponents. The relevant paragraphs of his deposition have been set out in full. He was churchwarden in 1604.]

L 11. That if in any case John French did set forth any tithes of hay wheat and oats in 1603 in the name of his tithes to the use of the church of Thakeham or left the same tithes upon the ground where they did grow, yet he did not set forth his true and just tithes. For first he set up some part of his oats growing in one field of five acres in fivinges without giving any notice, and afterwards pulled from every two fivinges a sheaf and threw the same into the furrow of the field, and so carried away his own oats and left the sheaves for the tithe thereof in the furrow contrary to the custom. And in 1602 he had a plot to the value of five acres sown with wheat and he reaped some part and carried away the wheat and left no tithe, and, as he heard John Arcoll say, who is [his] brother John French's boy, 'There were ten sheaves of the wheat which John French carried away and left no tithe thereof.' And in 1602 John French had growing upon a certain plot 15 cocks of hay which he did in like manner carry away and leave no tithe.

L 12. That John French being demanded of the tithes which he oweth denied the payment.

In 2. That Richard Warde married with Thomas Arcoll's sister and he is in the house with Richard Warde and gathereth up his tithes; but otherwise is not his servant for he is as much his own man as Richard Warde's.

In 5. That he is appointed by Richard Warde to be his gatherer of tithes of hay corn and oats for this two years and he hath gathered every man's tithe saving those tithes which are yet behind and due by John French.

In 6. That within this two years Thomas Arcoll hath only known one John Clerke and John French and no more to set out their tithe wheat and oats in sheaves only and not in fivinges. And he hath fetched away John Clerke's tithes tithed in sheaves to the use of Richard Warde and he hath also fetched away some part of John French's tithe of wheat and oats which were only tithed in sheaves and not in fivinges; but when [he] told Richard Warde, he was offended with him because he took the tithes tithed only by the tenth sheaf. Then Thomas Arcoll told John French that he was commanded by Richard Warde that he should receive no more tithes except they were set forth and tithed by fivinges or heales.

In 7. That for the most part he always heard that the parishioners time out of mind set out their tithes of wheat and oats in heales or fivinges and he never heard that the same tithings were left at the choice of the parishioners whether they would set out their tithes in heales or fivinges or in sheaves; for always they have used for the most part to set up their tithes as they set up their own corn.

In 8. That John French in 1602 tithed his wheat by the fivinges and his oats he tithed likewise in fivinges. And in 1603 he did divide the tithe of his wheat and oats only in sheaves and the wheat so tithed in sheaves this last year 1603 Thomas Arcoll fetched away and Richard Warde was offended with him. And for the tithe of John French's oats in 1602 he fetched them away in respect they were set out by fivinges. And for the tithes of the oats which John French had in 1603 he fetched away the tithe thereof so much as were set out by the fivinges; and the rest, which were thrown out into the furrow by sheaves as is mentioned in the 11th article of the libel, he did not carry away.

And for the tithes of an acre and a half of oats in 1603 because the tithe were set forth by fivinges and not by the tenth sheaf. [*sic*]

In 9. That Richard Warde did send a cart and oxen to fetch such tithes as were due in divers fields. And one Christopher Sole was going to the four acres and a half belonging to John French to fetch the tithe of the oats but Thomas Arcoll meeting him returned him back again because he knew that the tithe were set out only by the tenth sheaf.

In 10. That Richard Wood and Thomas Field did end and determine all matter concerning the tithe oats due by John French in 1602; but for the tithe hay and wheat due in 1602 the same are yet due and therefore they are not agreed for.

In 11. That in 1602 Thomas Arcoll had certain sheaves of wheat and cocks of hay from the lands of John French which he had away to the use of Richard Warde for his tithes, in the presence of John Forder one of Richard Warde's servants; but how many sheaves he cannot now remember.

In 12. That there were 65 sheaves of oats upon the four acres and a half of land divided and set out for the tithe in 1603.

In 13. That John French in 1602 set up all the tithe oats and tithe wheat which Thomas Arcoll carried away in fivinges; and he set up his own wheat and oats also in fivinges. And in 1603 he set forth some of his tithe wheat in fivinges and some in the sheaves; and he set forth some of his tithe oats in fivinges in 1603 and other some by the tenth sheaf; for in the year 1603 he tithed by the sheaf and did not set up his own sheaves at all in fivinges but did laden them to the cart as they did lie.

2/7 Stephen Cradell.[17] [*January 1603/4*]

Of Thakeham husbandman, where has lived for 10 years; before at Pulborough 10 years; before at Thakeham; born there; aged about 35. Is worth 40s. Signs with mark.

L 4. That for this 20 years all the parishioners having wheat or oats have accustomed to set up their tithe wheat and oats by heales and fivinges and not by the tenth sheaf; except it were at unseasonable weather when the parishioners did carry away their own wheat and oats before they set up the same in heales and fivinges.

2/8 Christopher Sole.[18] [*January 1603/4*]

*Of Thakeham, husbandman; born there; aged about 28. Is worth £5. Signs with mark.**

L 4 & 5. That he never knew but that the parishioners have always used to set forth their tithe wheat and oats by heales and fivinges and not by the tenth sheaf, except it were at some times when the weather were like to change. And Christopher Sole hath heard Richard Sole his father say, who is 75 years of age and divers other aged men of

* Actively involved in the physical labour of tithe collection. Perhaps brother of Daniel Sole above.

the parish. that for 50 or 60 years the parishioners were wont to set forth their tithe wheat and oats by heales and fivinges and not by the tenth sheaf.

L 8 & 9. That in 1603 Christopher Sole did fetch away from the ground of John French tithe wheat and tithe oats for Richard Warde which were due to be paid to him, all which were set forth by heales and fivinges and not by the tenth sheaf, except it were three odd sheaves for the tithe of three hiles [*sic* or hiales] of wheat which did grow upon a little garden plot near the house of John French. But how many heales or fivinges of wheat and oats he carried from the ground of John French or what every [*sic*] of the heales or fivinges were worth he cannot depose, and also, except the tithe of oats upon a certain close in the occupation of John French, which tithe were not set forth by heales and fivinges but only thrown forth in sheaves for he did see divers sheaves of oats lie in the close here and there one [*sic*] which sheaves cast forth for the tithe of the oats growing in the close were not carried away by Richard Warde.

L 11. That when Christopher Sole came unto the ground of John French to fetch the tithe hay he would not suffer him to rack [*sic*] the stedle or bottom of the cock by reason whereof Richard Warde had not his just tithes. For a man cannot take a cock of hay away clean from the ground with a prong except he rake the bottom with a rake. And that John French did not tithe his oats mentioned in the next precedent article by heals or fivinges but by the tenth sheaf only.

In 8. That John French did set up all his tithe wheat and oats in heales and fivinges in the year 1603 except the oats formerly deposed in the 8 & 9 articles of the libel which were neither set up in heales nor fivinges nor fetched away by Thomas Arcoll.

In 9. That Christopher Sole and John Bancombe were going with a wain and oxen to fetch the tithes of the four acres and a half in 1603, but not by Richard Warde's appointment, and met Thomas Arcoll. Which Thomas Arcoll returned Christopher Sole and John Bancombe back again and would not let them fetch the oats because they were tithed only by the sheaf.

In 13. That John French in 1603 set up some of his oats and wheat in fivinges and some in heales and so did he set forth the tithe thereof. And the oats upon the 4 and a half acres he set up his own oats in heales or fivinges but he set forth the tithe thereof in sheaves only.

2/9 Robert Smith.[19] *25 Jan 1603/4.*

Of Washington, husbandman, where has lived for 2 years; before at Warminghurst 1 year; before at Thakeham 1 year; before at Warminghurst 7 years; before at Blendworth, Hants, 5 years; before at North Marden 5 years; and before at Didling; born there; aged about 38. Is worth £5 [*?*].[*] *Signs with mark.*[†]

---

[*] Difficult reading.

[†] A former tithe collector for the rector, immediately preceding Thomas Arcoll above. Later, in 1605, he was churchwarden.

L 4 & 5. That Robert Smith did serve Richard Warde the last harvest was four years and was appointed by Richard Warde to be his gatherer; that every parishioner did that year set out their tithe wheat and oats by heales and fivinges and not by the tenth sheaf; except at a plot where there were not ten fivinges and in that case the parishioners paid by the tenth sheaf.

2/10 John Hawarde.[20] [*January 1603/4*]

Of Thakeham, husbandman, where has lived for 26 years; before at Storrington; born there; aged about 55. Is worth £5. Signs with mark.

L 4. That for 23 years he hath been a parishioner during all which time he hath set forth his own tithes after this manner viz when he set up his wheat or oats by fivinges or healinge then he set the tithe thereof by fivinges or healings. And if he did not set up his own corn then he did not set up the tithe corn but sent word to the parson to fetch away the tithe thereof. And the parson received the tithes whether they were in fivinges heales or sheaves and found no fault.

L 8 and articles & schedule. That in 1603 John Hawarde was requested by John French to be at the tithing of some part of the 4 ½ acres of oats. At whose request John Hawarde, finding the oats bound up in sheaves and lying all along the row, did nicely tell all the sheaves and at every tenth sheaf cast out the tenth sheaf a little from the other sheaves for the tithe thereof. And some of the oats were set up by the healinges before he set forth the tithes of the other oats in sheaves, but for all the oats he tithed they were nicely set forth by the tenth sheaf, which were in all 53 sheaves and a half that is for 53 heales of oats and a half; and every heal was worth 12d. And that for the oats that were set up in healinges he did not meddle with the tithing of them at all.

In 6. That he cannot depose how other men did set out their tithes of wheat and oats 40 or 50 years ago because he taketh not regard of other men's matters; but for his own tithe for this 23 years he always set them forth in manner and form as he hath already deposed.

In 9. That he did hear of his own children that the servants of Richard Warde came almost to the 4 ½ acres to fetch the tithe with a wain and oxen; and they meeting with Thomas Arcoll, he returned them back again and would not suffer them to carry away the oats because they were tithed only by the sheaf.

2/11 John Comber.[21] [*January 1603/4*]

Of Thakeham, husbandman, where has lived for 23 years; before at Billingshurst 1 year; before at Burpham 3 years; before at Warningcamp 2 years; before at Billingshurst 2 years; before at Thakeham; born there; aged about 53. Is worth £5. Signs with mark.

L 7. That he hath had 4 or 5 colts fallen of his mares and he was not asked anything until this last year; neither did he ever hear that anything were due unto any parson save only that he hath heard that the parishioners ought to pay for the fall of every colt and no more.

2/12 Thomas Haywarde.[22] *Read over 26 Jan 1603/4.*

Of Thakeham, cooper, where has lived for 35 years; before at Storrington; born there; aged about 45. Is worth £20. Signs with mark.

L 4. That for all the time in the article mentioned he set forth his tithe wheat and oats sometimes by the fivinges and sometimes by the tenth sheaf, and the parsons did always fetch away the same tithes so set forth by the healinges or by the tenth sheaf as Richard Warde hath done and never find fault whether set forth either by healinges fivinges or the tenth sheaf.

2/13 Thomas Wadye.[23] *January 1603/4*]

Of Thakeham, yeoman, where has lived for 36 years; before at Saffron Walden, Essex; born there; aged about 50. Is worth £20. Signature.[*]

L 4. That for 30 years he hath known the parishioners to set forth their tithes of wheat and oats by heales and fivinges and not by the tenth sheaf; and he hath paid to the parsons his tithe of wheat and oats by heales and fivinges and not the tenth sheaf for all the time.

L 5. That he hath heard old John Brooker who is now departed say when he was alive, who was then about 90 years, and one John Scutt deceased, who was then of the age of 60 years, then say in his life time that all the parishioners were always accustomed to set forth their tithe wheat and oats by heales or fivinges for 44 years ago before their deceases; and they never knew any parishioner set forth their tithe wheat and oats but by heales or fivinges and not by the tenth sheaf. And he hath heard Henry Slater late deceased say in his life time who was four score years of age that he never knew the tithe of wheat and oats paid by the tenth sheaf but altogether by heales or fivinges.

In 5. That Thomas Arcoll is appointed by Richard Warde to be his gatherer of tithes of hay corn and oats and he hath gathered every man's tithes for this two years except the tithes now in controversy.

In 6. That he never knew any [of] the parishioners set out their tithe in sheaves only, but he heard that one John Monke of Ashington who occupied certain lands about 10 years ago set forth his tithe wheat by the sheaf only.

In 10. That all matters for tithe hay and tithe wheat due by John French in the year 1602 and in controversy was referred to the hearing and determining of Richard Wood and Thomas Feilde. But whether the controversy was ended and determined he cannot depose.

---

[*] An important witness as he also served as the apparitor, an officer of the consistory court.[*]

3/1 James Lacker, farmer of the rectorial tithes of Houghton v Richard Hobbes of Houghton: Tithe.[24]

Court acts: 9 July 1603 to 16 March 1604/5.

The busiest and most acrimonious case in the volume, producing 24 depositions from 23 witnesses, started over a relatively minor point over the tithing of wool. As the case is unusual and complicated it is worth setting out the major details.

Initially both parties appear to have tried to avoid court proceedings (with Hobbes offering a payment of 26s 4d); or such at least was the assertion of the first two witnesses, John and Thomas Northe, who were produced by the defendant in December 1603 (3/2,3). Thereafter the proceedings focussed almost entirely on the personalities of the parties and witnesses. Between October and November 1604, after nearly a year of legal wrangling, 11 witnesses were called by the plaintiff, James Lacker, to attack the reputations of the two initial witnesses (3/4-14). In December 1604 the plaintiff made a personal response defending the reputation of his witness James Pellett and denigrating that of John Northe (3/15) and at about the same time submitted interrogatories defending the reputations of his witnesses and attacking those of the defendant (3/16). Between December 1604 and January 1604/5 a further 11 witnesses were called by the defendant, Richard Hobbes, to attack the reputations of the previous eleven and to defend those of the Northes (3/17-27). A surprising feature of this group is that it included John Northe, one of the two original deponents: on his second appearance he refused to answer certain articles which might incriminate him. The final statements in the case are a second personal response by Lacker in February 1604/5 providing some relatively minor detail about the witnesses (3/28) and a courtroom statement by Hobbes in March 1604/5 reiterating his willingness to pay the tithes but not the legal costs (3/29).*

From this point it is not clear what the likely progress of the case could be. Each party had taken uncompromising stances based on substantial bodies of material which contradicted that of his opponent. There was no obvious ground for negotiation. On 16 March 1604/5 the proceedings terminated with a letter of inhibition, transferring the case to the Archbishop's Court of Audience. Whether this was instigated by one of the parties – or even by an official of the Chichester court – is not stated. It seems possible that the lawyers or the judges felt that the case had reached deadlock. As the records of the Court of Audience and the Court of Arches do not survive for the relevant period, we can never know the end of the story.

The defendant, Richard Hobbes, was a member of a local gentry family, brother of a Francis Hobbes who had property in Nuthurst and Cuckfield. Richard may have had some legal background: he took the unusual step of making personal interventions in the court procedures on several occasions. Lacker plays a less prominent role and beyond the fact that he was the farmer of the Houghton rectorial tithes we have no indication of his status – though we know he was illiterate. He seems to be overshadowed by the more vocal figure of James Pellett, vicar of Madehurst, despite the fact that Pellett had no connection with the tithes as he had no beneficed position in Houghton, beyond taking services there.

The case provides a striking picture of the tensions and scandals within a small community. Fourteen inhabitants of Houghton appear as witnesses: probably a third of the adult male population of the parish.† There is puzzling discrepancy between the opposing groups of witnesses however: of those called

---

* The name is also often spelled as Laker.

† The Protestation Return of 1642 (Sussex Record Society Vol. 5) lists 36 male inhabitants over the age of 18.

by the plaintiff all but two are parishioners of Houghton; of those called by the defendant all but four are from elsewhere. The depositions include allegations about the crimes or misdemeanours of nine inhabitants, including seven of the witnesses. None relates to the matter of the case, and they include thefts of geese and sheep, breach of promise, adultery and the begetting of a bastard child.

*The local undercurrents in this case may connect it with that of Pellett v Cox (5/1-7), where James Pellett is the central figure. The depositions in Lacker v Hobbes document in some detail the acrimonious relations between Pellett and the defendant Hobbes. The cases started within a month of each other, in June and July 1603 and it is something of a coincidence that the dispute in the Madehurst case was centred on Rewell Lodge, which had been occupied, at a relatively recent date, by Richard Hobbes's brother Francis. It is also worth noting that two witnesses in the Madehurst case (John Perley and Anthony Stradlinge) were produced under compulsion by Hobbes in the second.**

It is slightly surprising that the main participants in such acrimonious proceedings do not figure prominently in the office court. Hobbes seems to have kept clear of it; Pellett and John Northe were presented for shortcomings in their duties as minister and churchwarden respectively, and Lacker for failing to pay his share in the drinking at Ascensiontide.

The type of material produced by the case is unusual. The two large series of depositions produced by the plaintiff and defendant are in response to exceptions. These are effectively attempts to deny the validity of the opponent's depositions, usually through a personal attack on the character of the parties or deponents. Inevitably, with so many witnesses responding to the same articles, they contain a great deal of repetition; and this poses editorial problems untypical of the more usual 'factual' cases. Although many of these witnesses may duplicate the statements of others it is not always appropriate to omit all duplicate material: it is important to record each individual's agreement or disagreement. Therefore a substantial amount of repetitious material has been retained.

But to keep duplication to the minimum a slightly different style of editing has been adopted for this case. In conformity with the other cases the first deposition in each series is transcribed in full, while in the succeeding depositions statements of simple fact which substantially duplicate those in the first are omitted. Additionally, in this case, certain formal procedural information is omitted: notably the name of the party who has called the witness; the statements of impartiality (favouring neither side); and the confirmations that the deponent is speaking the truth. Significant variations or additions are recorded, however, either in the transcription or in the notes below.

Thus in the responses to the plaintiff's exceptions (3/4-14):

> *Responses to Additional Positions 1-5 have normally been included in order to show the variations in opinion or factual statement;*
>
> *In other responses to factual articles duplicating answers have been omitted (AP (1) 6, 7, In 5, 6, 8-10, 14, 15);*
>
> *Articles of purely formal or procedural nature have been omitted (AP (1) 8, In 1-3, 7, 16-18);*
>
> *All witnesses confirm they appear on behalf of the plaintiff; all confirm that Thomas Northe is married and also confirm his literacy (In 4, 11, 12).; the comments of three witnesses*

* Both vouched for the good character of all the plaintiff's witnesses (including Pellett), with the exception of John Austyn senior and junior about whom they provided accounts of a sheep stealing incident.

(William Gardyner, Oliver Markes and Nicholas Beache) on his intelligence have been retained.

The depositions in response to the defendant's exceptions (3/17-27) have been treated in similar fashion:

The first six articles of the Additional Positions provide varying accounts of varying incidents and have been retained; accounts of a separate incident (AP (2) 10) have also been retained;

A significant number of articles (many more than in the plaintiff's exceptions) produced personal opinions and so have been retained with minor omissions (AP (1) 7-9, AP (2) 1-9, In 8, 9, 11-16);

Procedural items or uninformative negatives have been omitted (AP (1)10, AP (2) 11-12, In 1, 5-7, 10);

All witnesses confirm they appear on behalf of the defendant (In 4), with William and Edward Beake, John Perley, Anthony Stradlinge and John Kyne having been compelled.

Details of witnesses' trade, status and value have been incorporated in their initial biography.

Proctors: Cooke for plaintiff; Barker for defendant. Examinations: two depositions for defendant responding to allegation and additional positions with interrogatories of 11 articles; plaintiff's personal response to exceptions of ten articles; eleven depositions for plaintiff responding to exceptions of eight additional positions and eighteen interrogatories against the defendant's witnesses; eleven depositions for defendant responding to exceptions of ten articles and twelve articles of additional positions, and sixteen of interrogatories against defendant's witnesses; second personal response of plaintiff responding to additional positions of twelve articles against witnesses.

Depositions for the defendant (3/2, 3)

3/2 John Northe.[25] *Read over 12 December 1603*

Of Houghton, yeoman, where lived for 55 years; before at Bury; born there; aged about 70. Is worth £20. Signs with mark.

To the allegation and additional positions ex parte Richard Hobbes:

That about May last past and before the beginning of the suit, James Lacker and Richard Hobbes talking together at the barn door of Richard Hobbes in Houghton street about some matters then betwixt them, he, John Northe, coming along the street see [*sic*] the departure of the one from the other and met James Lacker. At which James Lacker told him that he had been in some talk with Mr Hobbes about such tithes which were due unto him by Richard Hobbes and, said James Lacker, 'I find him to offer me very friendly and well.' For Richard Hobbes and he conferring together touching the tithe wool of certain sheep which he sold to Mr Kempe of Slindon, Richard Hobbes said he would not deny him any tithes which were due unto him but would pay him all. And James Lacker further told that he and Richard Hobbes were determined to ride to Chichester together and ask counsel of one of the procurators whether he were to pay tithe wool for those sheep which he had sold; and if either of the procurators would say that Richard Hobbes ought to pay tithe wool then, said James Lacker, he said he would pay all. In so much that James Lacker said there should be no occasion of any suit betwixt them. And James Lacker further said, 'Neighbour Northe, you sold some sheep too, and if it fall out that I have right to the tithe wool for those sheep which Richard Hobbes sold, then, neighbour Northe, you shall pay tithe wool for those sheep which you sold away; otherwise not'. By reason of which speeches Richard Hobbes offered all his tithes and denied the payment of none before the going forth of the citation. And that after some time, he and James Lacker meeting again, he told him that he had been at Chichester and Richard Hobbes and he were in suit of law, and Richard Hobbes had tendered so much money in court to the use of James Lacker for tithes due as in the conscience of him [James Lacker] were due unto him; only he would not pay the charge due to be paid in the court. And touching the custom articulated in the *additional positions* he saith that the same is true.

Concerning the allegation and the additional positions, his deposition is true.

To the interrogatories:

In 1. *To the first article of danger of perjury by himself – denies; by his co-witnesses does not know.*

In 2. That he is worth £20; that he is a husbandman; that he liveth by his lands.

In 3. That he came at the request and charge of Richard Hobbes and without compulsion.

In 4. *Negative.*

In 5. *For himself, denies; for his co-witnesses does not know.*

In 6. *Negative.*

In 7 & 8. *Does not know.*

In 9. That Richard Hobbes sold unto Mr Kempe 300 sheep about Michaelmas in 1602, which was before shear time was twelvemonth, and that in 1602 the sheep did pasture within Houghton from and after shear time until Christmas.

In 10. *Does not know.*

In 11. Satisfactory.

3/3 Thomas Northe.[26] *Read over 13 December 1603*

Of Houghton, husbandman; born there; aged about 26.
Is worth £20. Signs with mark.

To the allegation and additional positions:

A1 That before midsummer last, he coming along the high street of Houghton, heard Mr Richard Hobbes request James Lacker to go home with him and receive his petty tithes as pig, wool and suchlike, Richard Hobbes and James Lacker then being in the middle of Houghton street. And he answered he would with a good will and so they walked along together towards the house of Richard Hobbes. By reason of all which

Thomas Northe certainly knoweth that Richard Hobbes did kindly and lovingly offer to pay unto James Lacker such tithes as were due unto him before the beginning of this suit. And touching the custom articulated in the *additional positions*, he saith the same is true.

In 3. That he came at the request and charge of Richard Hobbes and without compulsion.

In 9. That he heard that Richard Hobbes sold some sheep to Mr Kempe but how many he cannot depose, neither about what time nor how long they pastured within Houghton, neither whether he did pay James Lacker any consideration for the wool iuxta ratum temporis for the pasturing.

Depositions ex parte plaintiff concerning exceptions to the witnesses John and Thomas Northe (3/4-14).

To the additional positions or declarations to exceptions ex parte James Lacker.

3/4 James Pellett.[27] 18 October 1604

Clerk, vicar of Madehurst, where he has lived 11 years; before at Yapton 3 years; before at University of Oxford 5 years; before at Steyning; born there; aged about 38 years. Signature: 'Mr Jacobus Pellett Clericum - Vicarium - ac ministrum de Madehurst'.

To the additional positions:

AP (1)1-5. That about the 20th day of November before the production and examination of Thomas Northe, he being in the barn of James Lacker, Thomas Northe being also there said that he would go to the house of Mr Richard Hobbes for some money which he ought him for threshing, which he did accordingly; and at his return thence, which was within one hour, he came again to the barn. At which his return either James Lacker or one Robert Finch said unto him, 'Now Thomas Northe you have good store of money, and no doubt but Mr Hobbes hath given you good store of sauce and bacon.' Whereunto Thomas Northe answered no, he would give him none of his sauce nor bacon for Mr Hobbes fell out with him and would have had him to have gone to Chichester with him and for him to be sworn about the tithes which then were in question in this court before the beginning of the suit. And further Thomas Northe said that by his troth he could not tell what to say for he was never brought into any court to be sworn, neither could he tell whether the matter in question touching the tithes were offered unto James Lacker in the lifetime of Mr Francis Hobbes or since his death by Richard Hobbes; and by God he would not go for him, let him do what he could. All which speeches Thomas Northe used in the presence of James Lacker and Elizabeth his wife, Robert Finch and James Pellett. And he further saith that Thomas Northe before the beginning of this suit was, as at this present he is, a sower of discord and debate between neighbours and friends by carrying of lies and tales from one to another; neither is he a man of any credit amongst his neighbours; neither doth any man of honest conversation almost make any account of his saying; and for such a man he is and was before the beginning of this suit commonly reputed within the parish of Houghton. And he further saith that when the contract was supposed to be made betwixt Thomas Northe and Elizabeth Winsomme he afterwards married to another. James Pellett told John Northe, father unto Thomas Northe, that his son had done evil and contrary to the laws of God, whereunto he answered, 'Why, what would you have a fool and an idiot to do; you know what he is well enough.' And he further saith that since the examination of Thomas Northe on the behalf of Mr Hobbes, and since Mr Hobbes was chosen churchwarden in the parish of Houghton, it is credibly reported by William Gardener, John Austyn the younger and James Lacker that Mr Hobbes did will him to leave his lying and tale carrying up and down or else he would present him for his so doing. *For the rest does not know.*

AP (1) 6 & 7. *Does not know.*

AP (1) 8. *Deposition is true.*

To the interrogatories:

In 1. *Satisfactory.*

In 2 & 3. *Negative.*

In 4. *Favours parties indifferently; and wishes victory for the party in the right; for the rest negative* saving that he came to testify at the request of James Lacker.

In 5. That at some times when James Lacker did signify unto him what wrong and injury he did sustain by the suit through the depositions of Thomas Northe and John Northe, he said that he thought they would not be admitted witnesses against him in this court. And James Lacker did also blame him for that he, about a year ago before the beginning of this suit when there had like to have been some question in law betwixt Richard Hobbes and James Lacker, did at the request of Richard Hobbes determine the matter betwixt them without suit. In respect whereof James Lacker, as he said, was much hindered for he might have begun suit as well then as at another time; whereunto he said, 'You may do what you will then.' And otherwise *negative.*

In 6. *Does not know*, saving that Richard Hobbes about a twelvemonth [ago]* meeting him coming up at Houghton Hill near a gate there, Richard Hobbes being on horseback and James Pellett on foot, he was ready to ride on him with his horse and swore, 'God's blood or God's wounds, will thou not give me the way. I am a better man than thou.' Then James Pellett asked him how long he had been a better man than he; before, he heard that he not long before was but a capmaker and therefore he needed not to compare himself with him; he was brought up in the liberal† sciences of art. And at other times Richard Hobbes did quarrel and wrangle with him; but James Pellett never quarrelled with him.

In 7. *Negative.*

In 8. That for near as he can remember, he going along the high street at Houghton and hearing Thomas Northe and John Stempe and Oliver Cobbye to be at variance and Thomas Northe using some moutheye [*sic*] and unseemly words, he willed him to hold his peace for he was afraid that he would bring himself to some trouble for his lying and

---

* 'of go' in MS.

† Difficult reading.

tale carrying. And he continuing his unseemly speeches and following James and others along the street he called to James Lacker in railing sort and bad him pay him that he ought him, and withal bid a turd or a fart for him. *For the rest negative.*

In 9. That James Lacker hath often times spoken unto him of matters touching this suit but he never spoke to any for him touching this suit, saving that he, from James Lacker, requested Mr Cooke to remember his suit, and saving that he was requested by James Lacker to write down in writing what John Thornden, William Gardyner, Oliver Markes, John Austyn the elder, John Austyn the younger, Oliver Cobbye and others could say touching the insufficiency of Thomas Northe and whether he was a fit man to testify a truth in law or no, for the better instruction of Mr Cooke to draw articles; because otherwise, if it were not in writing, he might forget. Which note was sent to Mr Cooke and he said it was nothing worth because it was general; but what the words were he cannot now well remember, saving that they accounted Thomas Northe to be a man not fit to be a witness because of his tale carrying. *For the rest does not know.*

In 10. *Does not know.*

In 11. That Thomas Northe hath been married this three or four years; but touching the ordering of his house and family, he cannot depose.

In 12. That he knoweth not whether Thomas Northe can write and read English, but he verily believeth that he hath not wit and understanding sufficient to relate and deliver any matter of moment upon his oath, that he hath heard or seen, except some body help or prompt him.

In 13. That for his own part he doth not take them, John Northe and Thomas Northe, to be men of honest life and conversation in respect they be not men that are in charity with their neighbours. Neither doth he believe that there is credit to be given unto their sayings for the reasons beforementioned. And also for that Mr Hobbes himself hath reported unto him that John Northe is and hath been a very wicked man and that there was no credit to be given unto them; and for men of small credit they are commonly reputed.

In 14. *Does not know.*

In 15. That some speeches being used to Mr Hobbes by William Gardyner, clerk of the parish church of Houghton, for wages due unto him by Richard Hobbes of his Cooteslande and also to others, he said, 'Well these be but base shifts.' Then Richard Hobbes and others going along towards his own house, he said, 'These base shifts will not serve the turn.' Then James Pellett said 'base' in his face, for he could be content to quarrel with his neighbours in the churchyard and afterwards go into the street and break one Stakers's head and shed blood. And Richard Hobbes using many more words, he said, 'Prithee Hobbes, hold thy tongue,' and then Richard Hobbes said, 'What? Plain Hobbes? I am as good a gentleman as you'. Then he said he doubted that, for his bringing up hath been better than his; and so they departed. *For the rest negative.*

In 16-18. *Negative.*

3/5 William Gardyner.[28] [*October 1604*]

Of Houghton, husbandman; born there; aged about 71. Signs with mark.

AP (1) 1-5. That upon the 14th day of October 1604 Thomas Northe came unto the house of William Gardyner in Houghton and asked him whether he did see James Lacker of late and he said, 'No'. Then Thomas Northe said that he had arrested [*sic*] James Lacker the Saturday before and he was come to agree with him for it was not his own doing. And Thomas Northe, being in further communication, said that, touching the suit now betwixt James Lacker and Mr Hobbes, he [Mr Hobbes], when Thomas Northe was about to tell him one thing or other touching the words that he could depose, did still take the words out of his mouth and made him depose that which he himself could not tell or say what against James Lacker; and he wished that at the time of his examination he had been 40 miles from home for he did him wrong in his examination, in the presence of John Austyn the younger, Joan Gardyner, William Gardyner's wife, and William Gardyner. And he further saith that Thomas Northe at another time said that that which he could or should say for Mr Hobbes touching this suit could not be certainly declared by him whether it was done in the lifetime of Mr Francis Hobbes or since his death by Mr Richard Hobbes; but who heard the same else at that time he cannot depose. And he further saith that Thomas Northe said that his father and mother called him cuckold, and said that James Lacker had to do with his wife and the child that was born of the body of his wife was James Lacker's child, and that he kept another man's child. And his father and mother denieth that ever they spoke any such words and saith that he is a liar, and for a liar and tale carrier between neighbour and neighbour he is commonly reputed and taken and there is no credit to be given to his speeches; and for such a one he is accounted within the parish. And he further saith that since Mr Hobbes was chosen churchwarden he himself told Thomas Northe that if he would not leave his lying and tale carrying he would present him, *For the rest does not know.*

AP (1) 6. That John Northe had a bastard by one Jane Browne or Browneinge some 30 years ago; for which fault he did public penance.

AP (1) 7. *Does not know*, saving that there was such a suit between James Lacker and John Northe some three or four years ago.

In 6. That there are no such quarrels or suits betwixt any of the parties named in this article as is therein mentioned.

In 10. *Does not know beyond what has already deposed*, saving that he hath not heard that John Northe hath been suspected of any such crime this four or five years.

In 12. … That he thinketh him [Thomas Northe] not to have wit and understand sufficient to relate and deliver that which he hath heard and seen especially if it be any matter of moment ….

In 13. That for anything he knoweth or hath heard there is small credit to be given to the sayings or depositions of either John Northe or Thomas Northe. ···

In 14. That he heard John Stempe say that Thomas Northe fell forth with him at Arundel and gave him foul words. ···

In 15. That upon Sunday last he heard Mr James Pellet say that his father was a better gentleman than Mr Hobbes. *For the rest does not know.*

3/6 Oliver Cobbye.[29] [*October 1604*]

Of Houghton, shoemaker; born there; aged 40. Signs with mark.

AP (1) 1-5. That within a small time after the beginning of this suit Thomas Northe came unto Oliver Cobbye's shop in Houghton and asked him when he [Oliver Cobbye] went to Chichester, and told him that he must go to Chichester the next Saturday, which was the Saturday next after his then coming to his shop. For he said that he heard some words betwixt Mr Hobbes and James Lacker touching tithes due unto him, and he repeating them in Mr Hobbes's barn, Mr Hobbes took witness thereof and therefore he would make him go to Chichester and swear unto them. And Oliver Cobbye further saith that Thomas Northe is a liar and tale bearer between neighbour and neighbour and by reason thereof a sower of discord and debate between neighbour and neighbour. He is also … a man of no credit nor estimation … And he further saith that John Northe, father of Thomas, did allege and say unto the Lieutenant and Justices of the Shire at a general muster that he was very ignorant, purblind and deaf, and an innocent; in respect whereof he was struck out of the muster book as unfit for service.

In 13. That John Northe hath been a man of such life and conversation that men will credit him upon his sayings; but for Thomas Northe he cannot depose.

3/7 Robert Finch.[30] [*October 1604*]

Of Littleton, Sussex, husbandman, where lived for one month; before at Houghton for about six months; before at Petworth for about 9 years; before at Billingshurst; born there; aged about 24. Signs with mark.*

AP (1) 1-5. That a little before Christmas last Thomas Northe came unto the barn of James Lacker and said that he talking of some words that was betwixt Mr Richard Hobbes and James Lacker touching tithes as they walked along Houghton street and walked towards Richard Hobbes's house, Richard Hobbes coming into his own barn, Thomas Northe being then threshing within, and hearing him say that he heard them talk of tithes in the street, Richard Hobbes took witness of his words and said that he would depose the same at the court at Chichester the next Saturday. But Thomas Northe in the barn of James Lacker did say that he was never sworn in any court, neither could he depose anything for he could not tell what to depose; for he heard them talking of tithes but whether they were in Mr Francis Hobbes his lifetime or since his death they were due by Mr Richard Hobbes he could not tell. All which speeches he used in the presence of Mr James Pellett, James Lacker and Elizabeth his wife, and Robert Finch. And that Thomas Northe is accounted to be liar and a tale carrier from neighbour to neighbour and by reason thereof he is no credit nor estimation amongst his neighbours …

* Perhaps Littlehampton, or less probably Litlington.

In 13. That for John Northe his words will be credited. And touching Thomas Northe *does not know.*

3/8 John Austyn, junior.[31] *Read over 18 October 1604.*

Of Houghton, husbandman, where lived about 10 years; before at Madehurst; born there; aged about 30. Signs with mark.

AP (1) 1-5. That upon Sunday last past Thomas Northe came unto the house of one William Gardyner in Houghton and fell in talk with him; and John Austyn also coming into William Gardyner's house, he heard Thomas Northe say that he speaking of some words which he heard betwixt Mr Hobbes and James Lacker as they walked along Houghton high street touching tithes due by Mr Hobbes unto James Lacker, Mr Hobbes came into his own barn where Thomas Northe was threshing, and hearing him talk of the tithes Mr Hobbes took the words out of his mouth before he could speak and caused him to depose and speak he could not tell himself what. For the which he was sorry for he had done James Lacker wrong by means thereof and he wished that at this time he had been 40 miles from home (in the presence of William Gardyner and the wife of William Gardyner and John Austyn). And that Mr Hobbes, since he was chosen churchwarden, did say unto Thomas Northe that except he would leave his lying and carrying of tales he would present him. And that he is a sower of discord and debate between neighbours and friends by carrying of lies and tales from one to another and he is a man of no credit nor estimation among his neighbours ···. And that John Northe, father unto Thomas Northe, did allege before the Leif Tennante [*sic*] and justices of the shire at a general muster that he was deaf, purblind and an innocent; in respect whereof he was discharged and strucken out of the muster book. ···

In 13. That for John Northe he will be credited upon his oath but for Thomas Northe few or none will give credit to his speeches.

3/9 Oliver Markes.[32] [*October 1604*]

Of Houghton, husbandman, where lived about 4 years; before at Walberton about 40 years; before at Chichester about 2 years; before at Hawkley, Hampshire; born there; aged about 74. Signs with mark.

AP (1) 1-5. That Thomas Northe within the parish of Houghton hath been (long before his production or examination in this suit), as at this present he is, commonly reputed to be a liar, a sower of discord and debate between neighbours and friends, by carrying of lies and tales from one to another. In respect whereof he is a man of no credit nor estimation amongst his neighbours; neither doth any man of honest conversation and ability account of him or give any credit unto any of his sayings … within the parish of Houghton and other places thereunto adjoining. And he hath heard that John Northe did report of his son as in the fifth article is mentioned; but whether it was so he cannot depose.

In12. … He doth not believe that Thomas Northe can relate or deliver a speech or saying after any man except it be to make three times* more of it than it is, and contrary to the speech delivered by the party who spoke the same speeches.

In 13. That for John Northe he never heard but that there was credit given to his speeches in all things; and as for Thomas Northe he answereth as before.

3/10 John Austyn.[33] *Read over 23 October 1604.*

Of Houghton [no occupation given] where lived about 5 months; before at Greatham about 6 years; before at Houghton about 3 years; before at Madehurst about 20 years; before at Falmer; born there; aged about 73. Signs with mark.

AP (1) 1-5. That Thomas Northe ever since John Austyn hath known him to be of remembrance hath been, as at this present he is, a sower of discord and debate between neighbours and friends by carrying of lies and tales from one to another. In respect whereof he is a man of no credit amongst his neighbours, neither is there any credit to be given unto any of his speeches although it be upon his oath, for John Austyn believeth he knoweth not what an oath is. And he further sayeth that Mr Hobbes himself said, since he was chosen churchwarden unto Thomas Northe that if he would not leave his lying and tale carrying abroad from house to house he would present him, in the presence of John Austyn and divers other whose names he cannot now remember.

In 6. That Richard Hobbes and John Austyn were in suit in Bury court but one court day, and so agreed because Richard Hobbes was his tenant and broke covenant with him, for the which breach he sued him as is aforesaid.

In 13. That he never heard but that John Northe was always such a man as there was credit given to his speeches. And for Thomas Northe he answereth as before he hath answered.

3/11 John Thorneden.[34] *[October 1604]*

Of Houghton, husbandman, where lived about 20 years; before at Warnham; born there; aged about 50. Signature.

AP (1) 1-5. That Thomas Northe is commonly reputed within Houghton to be a sower of discord between neighbours and friends by carrying of lies and tales from one to another, by reason whereof there is small credit to be given to any of his sayings; neither doth almost any man of credit and good estimation give any credit to his sayings. And that John Northe father of Thomas Northe did allege before the Lieutenant and justices of the shire at a general muster that he was an innocent and a fool and deaf that he could not well hear, and therefore not fit for any service. In respect whereof his name was taken out of the muster book as unfit at any time after to be called to any muster. All which speeches were so spoken by John Northe against

* Difficult reading.

Thomas Northe in the presence and hearing of John Stempe and John Thorneden and divers others which he now remembereth not.

In 2. *Negative*, saving that his mother and James Lacker's wife did call one another cousin; but whether they were of kin one to another he cannot depose.

In 11. *Does not know* because he taketh very small regard or none at all of his affairs and business.

In 13. That for the time articulate and long before, the words and sayings of John Northe have been credited and believed. And for the words and sayings of Thomas Northe he cannot depose otherwise than he hath already deposed.

3/12 John Stempe.[35] *Read over 24 October 1604.*

Of Houghton [no occupation given]; born there; aged about 40. Signs with mark.

AP (1) 1-5. That Thomas Northe is sower of discord and debate between neighbours and friends by carrying of lies and tales from one to another, and in respect thereof a man of no credit nor estimation ···. And that John Northe father of Thomas Northe did allege before the Lieutenant and justices of the shire at a general muster about five or six years ago that his son was a fool, an idiot and an innocent, and somewhat deaf of hearing and therefore not fit to serve in that service. In respect whereof he was discharged and stricken out of the muster book ···. All which speeches were so spoken by John Northe against Thomas Northe in the presence of John Stempe, John Thorneden and divers others whose names he cannot now remember.

In 11. *Does not know* because he neither maketh nor meddleth with the affairs of Thomas Northe.

In 13. *Affirms concerning John Northe; concerning Thomas Northe cannot depose beyond what has already deposed.*

In 14. That there was some speeches used betwixt him and Thomas Northe about 3 weeks ago touching a matter, viz Thomas Northe ought 3d unto one Thomas Moone of Arundel for mending of his shoes and afterwards denied the same and said he had paid him and that he had witness of it, naming John Stempe. Then John Stempe being at Arundel Thomas Moone asked him whether he could testify that Thomas Northe paid him 3d for mending of a pair of shoes and he answered no, he knew no such matter. Then Thomas Moone said that Thomas Northe told him that John Stempe would testify that he had paid, which he utterly denied. Whereupon John Stempe the next time that he met with Thomas Northe told him that he had wronged him and willed him to leave his lying.

3/13 Edward Gardyner.[36] [*October-November 1604*]

Of Houghton, tailor, where lived about 15 years; before at Amberley about 7 years; before at Bury; born there; aged about 35. Signs with mark.

AP (1) 1-5. That he hath heard Nicholas Bunche say, who is now departed, that Thomas Northe and he being threshing together in the barn of Mr Richard Hobbes since the beginning of this suit, Thomas Northe, falling in some talk about tithes then in question betwixt Richard Hobbes and James Lacker, said (as Nicholas Bunche told Edward Gardyner) that he heard some speeches betwixt them touching tithes. Then Richard Hobbes being present bid him remember the time when the same speeches were used and asked him whether he would be sworn thereunto or no, for he must produce him as a witness to testify upon his oath at Chichester. Then Thomas Northe made answer that he could not well remember whether the same speeches were used in the lifetime of Mr Francis Hobbes or since his death. But who was then present more than Nicholas Bunche and Richard Hobbes and Thomas Northe, he cannot depose. And he further saith that Thomas Northe is accounted to be a liar, a sower of discord and debate between neighbours and friends by carrying of lies and tales from one to another. In respect whereof he is a man of small credit or estimation … And that John Northe father of Thomas Northe did allege before the lieutenant and justices of the shire at a general muster that he was a fool and an idiot and purblind and deaf and in respect thereof not able nor fit to do any service, whereupon he was discharged from doing any service at that time or since, in the presence of Edward Gardyner and divers others. …

In 6. That there is some controversy now depending betwixt Thomas Giberidge and John Beeke, who are something of kin to John Northe and Thomas Northe; but the controversy is put to compromise and not yet determined. And Thomas Giberidge and John Beeke were the cause thereof, as he thinketh, for they fetched away some certain sheep and cattle from Edward Gardyner by virtue of a pretended administration granted of the goods not administered by Susan Beeke, which were late the goods of Thomas Beeke. Which goods he did hold by virtue of an administration of the goods of Nicholas Bunche deceased to him granted to the use of Anthony and Denise* Gardyner his children.

In 13. That he believeth that touching John Northe's sayings for all the time articulate there hath been credit given unto them. *And concerning Thomas Northe cannot depose beyond what has already deposed.*

In 15. That some speeches being used betwixt Mr Hobbes and Mr Pellett about the time articulate, Mr Hobbes called Mr Pellett, 'Mr Pellett', and Mr Pellett upon some speeches called Mr Hobbes plain 'Hobbes' without any 'Mr'. Whereupon Mr Hobbes said unto Mr Pellett that he called him 'Mr' and he did think himself as well worthy of that title as Mr Pellett for he was as good a gentleman as he. Whereunto Mr Pellett answered he denied that, for he had some of his kindred that kept men that was [*sic*] as good men as Mr Hobbes that waited at their tables.

---

* Difficult reading.

3/14 Nicholas Beache.[37] [*October-November 1604*]

Of Houghton [occupation not given] where lived about 2 years; before at Cranleigh, Surrey, about 2 years; before at Wells, Somerset, about 8 years; before at Chiltington, Sussex; born there; aged about 32. Signature.

AP (1) 1-5. That Thomas Northe is holden to be a man of no truth touching his sayings within the parish of Houghton, for he will tell one tale as it might be today or any other day and deny the same words the next day following. In respect whereof there is no credit to be given to his sayings ···. And that he hath heard that he did contract matrimony together with Elizabeth Wynnsom and afterwards, not regarding his faithful and former promises made to Elizabeth, without any just cause did forsake Elizabeth and marry with one Mary Cobby … And that John Northe did allege before the Lieutenant and justices of the shire that his son was a fool and an idiot and therefore not fit for any such service; whereupon the Lieutenant and other the justices discharged him from the service. …

In 11. … He is not acquainted with the ordering of his [Thomas Northe's] house nor his other business. *For the rest does not know.*

In 12. That he thinketh that Thomas Northe sufficient wit and understanding to relate and deliver upon his oath that which he hath heard or seen.

In 13. That he thinketh that credit hath been given to the sayings of John Northe as well without his oath as upon his oath; *and as far as Thomas Northe is concerned he cannot depose.*

Personal response of the plaintiff.

3/15 James Lacker.[38] *Read over 5 Dec 1604.*

Personal response. Signs with mark.

To additional positions to exceptions ex parte Richard Hobbes against witnesses of Lacker:

AP (1) 1. *Believes all witnesses on his part to be true and faithful; also believes them true in giving testimony and so reputed. For rest of the matter contained in the article refers himself to the depositions of the witnesses. For rest does not believe article to be true in anything.*

AP (1) 2-5 [*sic*]. *Believes Mr James Pellett to be true and faithful and reputed as such and also true in giving testimony. For rest does not believe articles to be true in anything.*

AP (1) 7 & 8. *Does not believe articles to be true in anything.*

AP (1) 9. Believes that John Northe was and is a man of sufficient understanding to know how to order his house and how to dispose of his business, and how to relate a tale or otherwise to declare his mind as commonly country men are able and use to do. But he also believeth John Northe at the time of his production and examination, and also before and since, was and is a man of unhonest life and conversation, contentious, a sower of discord and a common swearer and taker of the name of God in vain; and that by reason thereof no credit was or is given to any of his sayings though he testify upon his oath. *For rest does not believe article to be true in anything.*

AP (1) 10. *Believes what is to be believed and denies what is to be denied.*

Interrogatories ex parte James Lacker against witnesses produced ex parte Richard Hobbes concerning his corroborative materials and exceptions.[39]

3/16

In 1. *Re perjury or false witnesses. Whether connected to defendant or witnesses or through trade or office, or domestic service or employment. Whether having improper financial dealings with parties or witnesses. What level of kinship or indebtedness.*

In 2. *What is his trade or skill, and how he makes his living.*

In 3. *Where lives and what he is worth.*

In 4. *Whether appears voluntarily or under compulsion. Who produced him and who pays expenses. To ask Edward Darkenall whether he appears ex parte Richard Hobbes or at request of Thomas Hunte, and whether they are related and in what degree..*

In 5. *Whether have been instructed as to their evidence. What were the instructions and who gave them.*

In 6. *Whether there is any reward given or promised or hoped for.*

In 7. *Which party he favours and would help if he had the power.*

In 8. Whether he do know Mr James Pellet, vicar of Madehurst, one of James Lacker's witnesses, and how long time he hath known him. Whether he be a good and learned preacher, a man of honest life and conversation, no brawler nor sower of discord, but a peacemaker and persuader of his neighbours and of those over whom he hath charge to love and quietness. Whether he be so reputed of those who know.

In 9. Whether James Pellett be a man that doth love and serve God, no foresworn person but such an one as will testify a truth especially being sworn so to do. Whether he be commonly reputed and taken for such an one.

In 10. Whether James Pellett hath uttered any angry words unto Richard Hobbes. Whether he were exasperated and urged thereunto through reviling and unseemly speeches used unto him by Richard Hobbes.

In 11. Whether he do know William Gardyner, Oliver Cobbye, John Austyn the younger, Oliver Markes, John Austyn the elder, John Thorneden, John Stempe, Edward Gardyner and Nicholas Beache, all of Houghton, and Robert Finch of Littleton, witnesses producted and examined on behalf of James Lacker. How long he hath known them and whether they be men of good estimation and credit, and of honest life and conversation, no foresworn persons but such as will depose and testify a truth especially upon their oath. Whether they be for such reputed .

In 12. Whether Thomas Northe, one of the witnesses on behalf of Richard Hobbes, be an idiot, a fool and one that wanteth the use of reason and common understanding. Whether he be so reputed of the inhabitants of Houghton where he dwelleth.

In 13. Whether John Northe, one other witness on the behalf of Richard Hobbes, be an adulterer or fornicator, and whether he did public penance in Houghton church. Whether there be a public fame thereof.

In 14. Whether John Northe and Thomas Northe be common swearers and takers of the name of God in vain, common liars, tale carriers, sowers of discord and debate between party and party, persons as to whose sayings no faith is to be given though they be sworn to speak the truth. And whether they are so commonly reputed of the inhabitants of Houghton who daily conversed with them and did observe their evil qualities and the manner of their bad life and conversation.

In 15. Whether he doth believe that if John Northe and Thomas Northe were not lewd persons and such as to whose sayings no credit is to be given that so many of the inhabitants of Houghton, being persons of good credit and estimation as are producted for witnesses in this cause on the behalf of James Lacker, would have testified their bad qualities and misdemeanours by virtue of their oath unless they had perfectly* known the same .

In 16. Whether all or most or some of the witnesses on behalf of James Lacker be of the most substantial men within the parish of Houghton and such as have borne the offices of churchwarden and high constable of the hundred; and whether all or some of them be commonly reputed and taken for such persons .

Examination of witnesses produced by Mr Richard Hobbes concerning additional positions and exceptions made against the witnesses against James Lacker examined at the first place (3/17-27).

3/17 Edward Darkenall.[40] *Read over 10 December 1604.*

Of Billingshurst, gentleman, where lived about 5 years; before at Ockley, Surrey, about 4 years; before at Slinfold about 2 years; before at Warminghurst; born there; aged about 35. Signature. Is worth 200 marks.

To the additional positions to the exceptions in the first place:

AP (1) 1. That upon the second day of December last, Mr James Pellett reading the Psalms used in the book of Common Prayer now allowed, Richard Hobbes answering him in the Psalms for that day contained in the Book of Common Prayer and for that day being Sunday prescribed, mistaking one word contained and specified in the 18th verse of the 9th Psalm, viz 'For the poor shall not always be forgotten: the patient abiding of the meek shall perish for ever'. Whereas he should in verity and truth have said, 'The patient abiding of the meek shall not perish for ever'. All which speeches and reading so spoke and read by him were so spoken and read in the parish church of Houghton against the meaning and intention of Richard Hobbes, as Edward Darkenall was informed by him. Notwithstanding, Mr Pellett in time of divine service in the open church of Houghton and before all the audience and persons there present, as namely William Gardyner, Thomas Hunte, Edward Darkenall and divers others, said unto him, 'How blasphemingly did you read there,' meaning that he did read blasphemy in leaving

* Difficult reading.

the word 'not' out of the verse, which was only by oversight and not otherwise, as he was credibly informed by Richard Hobbes. And for his own part, he then being present, he did hear and see that Richard Hobbes did not voluntarily or with any intention to disannul the Book of Common Prayer leave out in his reading the word 'not'. *For the rest does not know beyond what has already deposed.*

AP (1) 2-9. *Cannot depose beyond what has already deposed.*

AP (1) 10. *Deposition is true.*

AP (2) 1-12 *And concerning the exceptions given in the last* [*] *place ex parte Mr Hobbes cannot depose beyond what has already deposed*, saving that he believeth that all the witnesses in this cause are honest men, for he cannot detect any of them for any thing.

To the interrogatories:

In 1. *Satisfactory and responds in the negative.*

In 2. That he is a gentleman and liveth by the profit of his stock.

In 3. That at this present he dwelleth at Billingshurst and for 10 years last past he dwelt at Billingshurst and Ockley; and that he is worth of his own proper goods 200 marks.

In 4. That he came to testify at the request and charges of Mr Richard Hobbes without compulsion. And *for the rest negative*, saving that he is first cousin unto Thomas Hunte, viz Thomas Hunte his mother and Edward Darkenall's mother were sisters.

In 5. *For self negative; for fellow witnesses does not know.*

In 6. *Negative.*

In 7. *Favours parties indifferently and wishes victory for the party in the right.*

In 8. *Does not know*, saving that he never heard nor knew Mr James Pellett suspected or detected of any crime in this article contained otherwise than he hath formerly deposed; yet he hath known Mr Pellett for one whole year during all which time he never heard but that he was a good preacher, a man of honest life and conversation, neither any brawler nor sower of discord otherwise than he hath formerly deposed. *For the rest does not know.*

In 9. That in his conscience he thinketh James Pellett to have been and now is a man that feareth God. And that he would not nor did not forswear himself, being sworn in this cause, touching this matter for or concerning anything whereupon he was deposed. *For the rest does not know.*

In 10. *Cannot depose beyond what has already deposed.*

In 11. That for all the witnesses in this article contained he never heard nor knew but that they were, as at this present they are, men of good life and conversation and, according to their ability of good estimation, and never forsworn neither in this cause nor any other, saving Robert Finch of Littleton of whom he can depose nothing because he knoweth him not. But all the other he knoweth and touching them he answereth as afore is said and by him answered. *For the rest does not know.*

---

[*] i.e.second place.

In 12-14. *Does not know.*

In 15. *Does not know beyond what has already deposed.*

In 16. *Does not know beyond what has already deposed*, saving that he verily believeth that the witnesses articulate, or the most part or some of them, have borne the offices of churchwarden because they or some of them could not otherwise choose in respect of their small parish of Houghton and the inhabitants dwelling in the parish. *For the rest does not know.*

3/18 Gideon White.[41] [*December 1604*]

Of Barnham, husbandman; born there; aged about 50. Signs with mark. Is worth 40s.

AP (1) 1-7. That he never heard nor knew but that John and Thomas Northe have been accounted to be men of good name and fame and that credit was always given to their sayings. And for Thomas Northe especially, he did bargain once with him and sold unto him 20 bushels of wheat about 2 years ago and as much as [*sic*] since harvest last; and, for anything he could perceive, he did make his bargain well and sufficiently and as well as any other man could do, and according to his bargain paid unto Gideon White justly and truly the just price and no more. And he never heard but that he always dealt well and honestly with every man. *For the rest does not know.*

AP (1) 8. That he never knew but that both John Northe and Thomas Northe did live soberly quietly and peaceably amongst their neighbours and in good fashion for John Northe kept for him two colts and four hogs for the space of one half year; and for the keeping of them he used him well and honestly. *For the rest does not know beyond what has already deposed.*

AP (1) 9. That he could never find but that Thomas Northe and John Northe were of reasonable wit, disposition and understanding to relate a tale formerly spoken by another; and that they and either of them could and did order their business in such manner as other of their neighbours did. *For the rest does not know.*

To the additional positions in the second place:

AP (2) 1-5. That he never heard but that Mr James Pellett was always, as he is at this present, a man of good fame and name and such a one as credit always was given unto his sayings; and for such a one he is commonly reputed. And touching others in this article he cannot depose because he knoweth them not, saving Oliver Markes who is a man of good life and conversation.

AP (2) 6-8. *Cannot depose beyond what has already deposed.*

AP (2) 9-11. *Does not know.*

AP (2) 12. *Deposition is true.*

In 8. That he hath known Mr James Pellett for this 12 years last past, during all which time he never heard but that he was a man of honest life and conversation, no brawler nor sower of discord but rather a peacemaker and a good preacher; and for such a one he is commonly reputed within Houghton and other places.

In 11. That he knoweth none of the parties in this article saving Oliver Markes whom he hath known for this 20 years last past, during all which time he never heard but that Oliver Markes was a man of good estimation, credit and of honest life and conversation and no forsworn person. *For the rest does not know beyond what has already deposed.*

In 12. *Does not know beyond what has already deposed.*

In 13. *Does not know.*

In 14. *Does not know beyond what has already deposed.*

In 15. *Does not know.*

In 16. *Does not know beyond what has already deposed*, saving that he hath known Oliver Markes chosen to be churchwarden of the parish of Walberton once or twice before he came to dwell at Houghton. *For the rest does not know.*

3/19 John Etherton.[42] [*December 1604*]

Of Barnham, husbandman, where lived about 30 years; before at Walberton; born there; aged about 60. Signs with mark. Is worth £20.

AP (1) 1-7. That he never heard but that John Northe and Thomas Northe were men of good fame name estimation and credit … for anything that he ever heard to the contrary. …

AP (1) 8. *Affirms* for any thing that he ever heard.

AP (1) 9. That Thomas Northe did about some two years ago buy some certain of wheat of John Etherton; and for anything that he could discern he could make his bargain well enough. And according to his bargain Thomas Northe at the days appointed did send for the wheat and sent money justly and truly and no more than he should justly send. And he thinketh that he can order and guide his house well and relate a truth of such things as he hath heard told by any others. And touching John Northe he verily believeth that he is a man of good wit and understanding to perform anything in this article contained and for such a man he is commonly reputed. And touching Thomas Northe he cannot depose further than he hath already deposed.

AP (2) 1. *Does not know*, saving that he never heard but that Mr James Pellett always was an honest quiet and sober man and a good preacher. …

AP (2) 2. *Does not know* because he knoweth not William Gardyner.

AP (2) 3 & 4. *Does not know* because he knows neither of the parties.

AP (2) 5. That he never heard but that Oliver Markes was always a man of good fame and name and of honest life and conversation. …

AP (2) 6. *Does not know*, saving that he never heard but that John Northe was always accounted to be man of good fame and name and such a one as to whose sayings credit always was given. …

AP (2) 7 & 8. *Affirms*, for anything that he ever heard.

In 8. That he hath known Mr James Pellett this 10 years during all which time he never heard but that he was always accounted to be a good and learned preacher, a man of honest life and conversation and no brawler nor sower of discord but rather a peacemaker. …

In 11. That he knoweth none of the parties in this article saving Oliver Markes, whom he hath known this 30 years, during all which time he never knew but that he always was a man of good estimation, credit and honest life and conversation and no forsworn person. …

In 12. *Cannot depose beyond what has already deposed.*

In 13 & 14. *Does not know*

In 15 &16. *Cannot depose beyond what has already deposed.*

3/20 Thomas Stiant.[43] *Read over 13 December 1604.*

Of Walberton, husbandman, where lived about 20 years; before at Yapton; born there; aged about 50. Signature. Is worth £20.

AP (1) 1-7. That he never heard but that John Northe and Thomas Northe were always accounted to be men of good name and fame and also of good credit and estimation amongst their neighbours, and such men as credit was always given to their sayings. …

AP (1) 8. *Affirms* for anything he ever heard or knew to the contrary.

AP (1) 9. That he verily believeth that Thomas Northe is of a good and reasonable wit, discretion and understanding, able to guide his house and family and order his business in reasonable good sort. For about Michaelmas last was two years he bought 20 bushels of wheat of Thomas Stiant, at which time he did not only make his bargain well and in good sort but also performed his bargain according to his promise. And for anything that he then could discern Thomas Northe was able to relate and declare a sensible and reasonable tale formerly spoken by any other. And for John Northe he deposeth affirmatively for, because he is a sensible man and one that knoweth what he speaketh; and for such a one he is commonly reputed.

AP (2) 1. That he never heard but that James Pellett was always an honest man and a man of quiet life and conversation and no brawler nor quarreller. *For the rest does not know.*

AP (2) 2. That he never heard that William Gardyner was ever accounted to be such a manner of man as is specified in this article, but that always he was accounted to be an honest man.

AP (2) 3. That he never knew any such thing objected against either John Austyn the elder or John Austyn the younger as is contained in this article.

AP (2) 4. *Does not know* because he knoweth not Robert Finch.

AP (2) 5. That he never heard of any such thing or any such report that should go of or by Oliver Markes as is contained in this article.

AP (2) 6. That he never heard but that John Northe always was accounted to be an honest man and of good and honest reputation and credit. And he is now high constable of the hundred where he dwelleth.

AP (2) 7. That he never heard but that John Northe and Thomas Northe did always well and sufficiently and with good discretion order their affairs and business in good order and sort, and as other husbandmen near unto them doth with honesty and discretion

AP (2) 8. *Affirms* for anything that he ever heard.

In 8. That he hath known Mr James Pellett this 10 years during all which time he was always accounted to be a man of good life and conversation, no brawler nor sower of discord but rather a peacemaker, for anything he ever heard; and now he is a good preacher.

In 9 & 10. *Does not know beyond what has already deposed.*

In 11. That he doth very well know all the parties in this article mentioned except Nicholas Beache and Robert Finch, and he never knew but that they were always accounted to be men of credit and of honest life and conversation and no forsworn persons. *For the rest does not know.*

In 12 & 13. *Cannot depose beyond what has already deposed.*

In 14. *Negative* for anything he ever heard.

In 15. *Does not know* but referreth every man to his own conscience.

In 16. *Cannot depose beyond what has already deposed.*

3/21 William Beake.[44] *[December 1604 - January 1604/5]*

Of Houghton, husbandman; born there; aged about 44. Signs with mark. Is worth £20.

AP (1) 1-5. That upon Easter Sunday he heard Mr Pellett and Mr Hobbes reason upon some things as they were going towards the Communion table in the parish church of Houghton. But what they said or did he cannot depose because presently after service was done he departed thence before Mr Pellett began to administer the communion. …

AP (1) 7. That for John Northe he never knew but that he was an honest man and a man of credit and of good estimation … saving that there is now a speech of late within the parish of Houghton that he did commit adultery or fornication with a woman many years ago, and that for that fault he did public penance; but whether it was so he cannot depose. And for Thomas Northe he deposeth that he hath many times dealt with him and sold unto him as much corn every year for this two years last past as Thomas Northe paid either year for the corn £13 13s 4d. And for anything that he could discern Thomas Northe dealt honestly justly discreetly sensibly and well with him in all things. …

AP (1) 8 & 9. *Affirms.*

AP (2) 1. That since the beginning of this suit he heard James Pellett say unto Richard Hobbes in the church litten of Houghton, 'Hobbes, go thy way' and no more. Then Richard Hobbes said, 'What, plain Hobbes. I called you Mr Pellett.' And at another time since the beginning of this suit which was about three weeks ago, at the reckoning or account making in the church of Houghton for the buying of a new Bible, a Prayer Book and other things, Richard Hobbes, being one of the churchwardens, asked him for money towards the buying according to his [as]sessment or part; and he answered that he called for money apace but he see [*sic*] nothing coming in for it. Then Richard Hobbes answered that he would make account for all at the years end and William Beake laid down his money and said, 'There is the money,' and that his money was as ready as Mr Hobbes was; and so departed quietly and friendly. And afterwards he met with Mr Pellett the same day in the street of Houghton, who was present in the church when he did pay unto Richard Hobbes (and James Lacker was then present with James Pellett in the street). At which their meeting Mr Pellett said unto him, 'Now William Beake no man dare speak to the gentleman but you,' meaning unto Mr Hobbes ...

AP (2) 2. That he never knew but that William Gardyner was always an honest man and of good name fame and credit. ...

AP (2) 3. That he hath heard that John Austyn the elder and John Austyn the younger were suspected to have committed such crimes as in this article is specified, but whether it was so he cannot depose. But there goeth a public fame thereof within the parish of Houghton now of late. *For the rest does not know* because he never heard of any such thing before.

AP (2) 4. That Robert Finch was household servant unto James Lacker until midsummer last and that he did work with him since that time. ...

AP (2) 5. That such a report and public fame is spread abroad within the parish against Oliver Markes as in this article is contained, since the beginning of this suit; but he never heard of any such thing before.

AP (2) 6. That John Northe hath been chosen churchwarden of Houghton three or four times and is now high constable of the hundred of Bury; and hath and doth well sufficiently and honestly discharge his office therein and doth as good credit and fashion as other men do.

AP (2) 7. *Cannot depose beyond what has already deposed.*

AP (2) 8. *Affirms*, saving that since the beginning of this suit he hath heard within the parish of divers that Thomas Northe was a liar, a tale carrier and a sower of discord; but he never heard any such thing by him before. ...

AP (2) 9. *Does not know.*

AP (2) 10. *Does not know* because he was not at his parish church that day. But such a speech he hath heard that James Pellett should say in service time unto Mr Hobbes, 'How now, how blasphemously do you read there.'

In 8. That he hath known Mr James Pellett this seven or eight years, during all which time he never knew nor heard but that he was a learned preacher, a man of honest life and conversation and no brawler nor sower of discord but rather a peacemaker amongst his neighbours. …

In 9. *Affirms*

In 11. That he hath known all the witnesses in this article for this seven years, saving Robert Finch who he hath known for this three years, during all which time they and every of them were and be men of good estimation and credit … for he never heard nor knew any other by them or any of them otherwise than he hath formerly deposed.

In 12. *Negative.*

In 13. *Cannot depose beyond what has already deposed.*

In 14. *Negative concerning John Northe.* And for Thomas Northe he hath heard, since the beginning of this suit but never before, that he is a liar, a tale carrier, a sower of discord and debate betwixt party and party. But whether he be so or no he cannot depose.

In 15. *Does not know.*

In 16. That William Gardyner, John Austyn the elder and John Austyn the younger, Oliver Markes, John Thorneden, John Stempe, Edward Gardyner and Nicholas Beache have of his knowledge borne the office of churchwarden within Houghton. And they are substantial men and men of good name and fame within the parish. And in like manner so is Oliver Cobbye and Robert Finch men of good name and fame but he doth not remember that either of them did ever bear any office in the parish; and for such men they and every one of them are commonly reputed and taken.

3/22 Edward Beake.[45] [*December 1604 - January 1604/5*]

Of North Stoke, husbandman, where lived about 15 years; before at Houghton; born there; aged about 50. Signs with mark. Is worth £20.

AP (1) 1-6. That about some 14 years ago William Gardyner of Houghton, one of the witnesses on the behalf of James Lacker, charged Edward Beake that he did steal geese, but from whom he did not specify. Whereupon being wrongfully slandered, he procured a warrant to fetch him before Mr William Goringe, a justice of peace, to answer the slanderous speeches by him spoken against him. At which his coming before Mr Goringe, Gardyner did affirm that he said that Edward Beake stole geese; but in respect he could make no proof thereof Edward Beake was determined to have prosecuted law against him for slandering of him, until Mr Goringe did entreat him not to do so. So as at the last at the request of Mr Goring, he was content to forgive Gardyner for that time so that he would be content to ask him forgiveness in the parish church of Houghton in slandering of him, in time of divine service; which Gardyner consented unto and performed accordingly in the presence of all the parishioners there present.

AP (1) 7. That he had dealt, bargained and sold divers and sundry times any time this 7 years with John Northe and Thomas Northe for wheat and barley, 20 quarters or 30 quarters at one time; and he could never find nor learn but that they were honest dealing men, men of good credit and estimation and of good wit and discretion; and that both were at all times as good as their word and promise in all things. …

AP (1) 8. *Affirms.*

AP (1) 9. That Thomas Northe can read English and relate a speech after another, and he is also a man able to make a bargain well and discreetly, and of sufficient wit to guide and order his house as other country men are wont to do. And for such a one he is commonly reputed.

AP (2) 1. That he never knew but that James Pellett was a quiet man and no quarreller nor brawler.

AP (2) 2. *Cannot depose beyond what has already deposed.*

AP (2) 3-5. *Does not know.*

AP (2) 6. That he never heard but John Northe was always an honest man and a man of good name and fame … And that he is now high constable of the hundred where he dwelleth, and he hath been chosen churchwarden of Houghton divers times, and he hath been of divers juries. And he hath always performed the part of an honest man in all those offices for all he ever heard to the contrary.

AP (2) 7. *Affirms.*

AP (2) 8. *Affirms* for anything that he ever heard.

AP (2) 9-11. *Does not know.*

In 8. That he hath known James Pellett this 12 years, during all which time he never knew but that he was a good preacher and a man of honest life and conversation. *For the rest does not know.*

In 9. *Affirms*

In 11. That he hath known Oliver Cobby, John Austyn the younger and John Austyn the elder, Oliver Markes, John Thorneden, John Stempe, Edward Gardyner and Nicholas Beache this 3 or 4 years, during all which time he never heard nor knew but that they and every one of them were honest men and of good life and conversation and such as upon their oaths will testify a truth. And for William Gardyner he answereth as before; and Robert Finch he knoweth not.

In 12. That he could never perceive by Thomas Northe but that he was a man of sufficient wit and reason to buy and sell and order his affairs as other men do. *For the rest does not know.*

In 13. *Does not know.*

In 14. *Negative*, for anything that he ever heard or knew.

In 15. *Does not know.*

In 16. *Cannot depose beyond what has already deposed.*

3/23 John Perley, senior.[46] [*December 1604 - January 1604/5*]

Of Madehurst, yeoman; born there; aged about 70. Signs with mark. Is worth £20.

AP (1) 1-6. That for anything he ever heard Mr Pellet was always a quiet and discreet man and such a one as disposeth his parishioners at Madehurst to unity and brotherly love rather than otherwise … *and for the rest does not know.*

AP (1) 7. *Affirms*, for anything that he hath ever heard.

AP (1) 8. *Cannot depose beyond what has already deposed.*

AP (1) 9. *Affirms* as he thinketh, for he never heard nor knew but both of them John and Thomas Northe did order their affairs and business as other country men of their fashion ordinarily use to do, both orderly sensibly and discreetly. *For the rest does not know.*

AP (2) 2. That he never heard but that William Gardyner always was and now is an honest man, no quarreller, brawler nor sower of sedition, debate or discord but a quiet man; *and for the rest does not know.*

AP (2) 3. That about 17 or 18 years ago John Austyn the elder, having certain sheep of his own pasturing and feeding upon the south downs of Madehurst where he then dwelt, he sent one of his sons to fetch one of his own sheep home to be killed (as he then said); but howsoever it fell out his son brought home a wether sheep of John Lenn's of Lyminster. Which being missing by one Anthony Stradlinge, who then kept the sheep of John Lenn, Anthony Stradlinge caused the officers there to make search for the sheep. Which done, one Thomas Perley, then officer there lawfully authorised, Anthony Stradlinge and John Perley found the sheep at the house of John Austyn the elder, killed and ready dressed. Whereupon the parties beforenamed examined him how he came by the sheep and said that that sheep was John Lenn's of Lyminster. Then he answered that it was more than he did know before, for he sent his son for one of his own wethers; but, as it seemed, the boy that fetched the wether heard something of the searching beforehand, for the boy was not to be found but went or ran away for a good while after that. In respect whereof John Austyn the elder was carried before Mr Bartlett of Stopham, a justice of the peace, and there bound over to appear at the assizes next following to answer; but what end was there made he cannot depose. His said son was but young and, as John Perley verily believeth, it was John Austyn the younger that did fetch the sheep and no other of his sons. *For the rest does not know.*

AP (2) 4. *Does not know* because he knoweth not Robert Finch.

AP (2) 5. That he never heard any such thing by Oliver Markes as is contained in this article. *For the rest does not know.*

AP (2) 6. That he never knew but that John and Thomas Northe were, as at this present they are, men of good name fame and credit. *For the rest does not know beyond what has already deposed.*

AP (2) 7. *Cannot depose beyond what has already deposed.*

AP (2) 8. *Affirms* for anything he ever heard.

AP (2) 9-11. *Does not know.*

In 8. That he hath known Mr James Pellett this ten years, during all which time he hath been and now is a good and learned preacher, a man of honest life and conversation, no brawler nor sower of discord, but rather a peacemaker and a persuader of his neighbours over whom he hath charge to love and quietness … *For the rest does not know.*

In 9. *Affirms*

In 11. That he never heard but that William Gardyner, Oliver Cobbye, John Austyn the younger, Oliver Markes, John Austyn the elder, John Thorneden, John Stempe and Edward Gardyner were and are men of good estimation and credit and of good life and conversation. Neither did he ever know any of them were ever detected of any evil crime except John Austyn the younger and John Austyn the elder as he hath formerly deposed. And for Nicholas Beache and Robert Finch, he knoweth them not. *For the rest does not know.*

In 12. That he verily thinketh Thomas Northe hath sufficient wit understanding and use of reason to buy and sell and govern his house and family and other affairs as well as other plain country men do, for he hath heard of divers that hath bought and sold with him so report of him. *For the rest does not know.*

In 13. *For the rest does not know beyond what has already deposed.*

In 14. *Negative* for any thing that he ever knew; *and for the rest does not know.*

In 15. *Does not know.*

In 16. *Cannot depose beyond what has already deposed.*

3/24 Anthony Stradlinge.[47] [*December 1604 - January 1604/5*]

Of Madehurst, husbandman; born there; aged about 56. Signs with mark. Is worth 40s.

AP (1) 1-6. That he never head but that Mr James Pellett always was, as at this present he is, a man of honest life and conversation, a good preacher and one that followeth his function orderly, quietly and discreetly …. *For the rest does not know.*

AP (1) 7 & 8. *Affirms* for anything he knoweth.

AP (1) 9. *Affirms* for anything that he ever knew.

AP (2) 1. That Mr James Pellett is commonly reputed within the parish of Madehurst to be no quarreller, brawler, sower of discord and dissention amongst his neighbours, but rather a peacemaker. *For the rest does not know.*

AP (2) 2. *Negative* for any thing that he ever heard and he hath known William Gardyner this 40 years.

AP (2) 3. That about 17 or 18 years ago, he being then shepherd unto one John Lenn of Lyminster and keeping his sheep upon the south downs of Madehurst, he did miss one of his wether sheep that he kept for John Lenn. Whereupon he caused one

Thomas Perley of Madehurst, who was then officer there, to go with him and John Perley, Thomas Perley's brother, to go and make search for the sheep, which he did accordingly. At which their going to search amongst other places they went to the house of John Austyn the elder, and there they found the sheep which they looked for, killed and ready dressed. Whereupon Anthony Stradlinge and the parties aforementioned that was with him asked John Austyn the elder where he had the sheep; whereunto John Austyn said he sent his son John to fetch one of his own wethers, which did pasture upon the same downs, so to be killed as is aforesaid; and John his son mistook, and as it did fall out brought the sheep which was missing of John Lenn's. But his son was but then young and did then keep himself aside and could not be found. In so much that Thomas Perley and others carried John Austyn the elder before one Mr Bartlett of Stopham, a justice of the peace, and there he was bound over to appear at the next assizes following and answer the matter. And there the matter was ended, but how or after what manner he cannot depose.

AP (2) 4. *Does not know* because he knoweth not Robert Finch.

AP (2) 5. *Negative* for any anything that he ever heard, for he never heard Oliver Markes to be such a manner of man as is contained in this article.

AP (2) 6. That he never heard but John Northe was an honest man. *And for the rest does not know* because he is not of Madehurst parish, in respect whereof he hath little to do with him.

AP (2) 7. *Does not know*, saving that he thinketh John and Thomas Northe are men of ordinary understanding and can order their affairs as other ordinary men of the country do.

AP (2) 8. *Cannot depose beyond what has already deposed.*

AP (2) 9-11. *Does not know.*

In 8. That he hath known Mr James Pellett this ten years, during all which time he hath been accounted within the parish of Madehurst ... to be man of honest life and conversation, a good preacher, no brawler nor sower of discord but a peacemaker and a persuader of his neighbours and of those over whom he had and hath charge to love and quietness. *For the rest does not know.*

In 9. *Affirms*

In 11. That he hath known all the parties named in this interrogatory, saving Nicholas Beache and Robert Finch, or the most of them this 20 years; and he never heard but that either and every one of them were and are honest men, saving John Austyn the elder and John Austyn the younger which were in some trouble as he hath formerly deposed; but he never knew them nor either of them suspected of any evil crime neither before that time nor since. And for Nicholas Beache and Robert Finch he knoweth them not, saving that he hath seen Nicholas Beache once or twice. *For the rest does not know.*

In 12-15. *Cannot depose beyond what has already deposed.*

In 16. *Does not know*, saving that some of the witnesses are substantial and sufficient men of ability.

3/25 Thomas Hunte.[48] [*December 1604 - January 1604/5*]

Of Houghton, yeoman, where lived about 2 years; before at Selsey about 6 months; before at Ore about 4 years; before at Billingshurst; born there; aged about 34. Signature. Is worth £100.

AP (1) 1 & 2. That upon Easter day last, motion being made by Oliver Markes of Houghton in the church of Houghton when the most of the parishioners and Richard Hobbes and James Lacker were present, that whereas there was a controversy depending in this court for tithes betwixt Richard Hobbes and James Lacker, the same by some of the parishioners there present might be friendly ended without further suit in law. Unto which motion neither Richard Hobbes nor James Lacker answered nothing, but James Pellett in the presence of Oliver Markes, William Beake, John Thorneden, William Gardyner, John Northe, Thomas Hunte and divers others whose names he cannot now remember, said if he was as James Lacker it should not be ended now, law should end it. And that he verily believeth that James Pellett beareth some evil will towards Richard Hobbes, for upon the second day of this month of December being Sunday so near as he can remember, Richard Hobbes answering Mr Pellett in the psalms of David, as the order is, in the parish church of Houghton in time of divine service and Mr Pellett reading very fast, he answering him as is aforesaid did only against his will overstrip one word. Whereupon Mr Pellett publicly in the hearing of all the auditory there present in time of divine service reproved him and said, 'How now,' meaning 'How now Hobbes how blasphemously do you read there.' Whereunto Mr Hobbes answered, 'Go forward Mr Pellett. It is a good horse that never stumbleth', in the presence of William Gardyner, Edward Darkenall, Thomas Hunte and divers others whose names he cannot now remember.

AP (1) 5 & 6. *Cannot depose beyond what has already deposed*, saving that he verily thinketh James Pellett did either dissuade, counsel and advise James Lacker to stand in law with Richard Hobbes than otherwise, for the reasons before mentioned, and for that, in the presence of the witnesses before mentioned, viz Oliver Markes, William Beake, John Thorneden, William Gardyner and Thomas Hunte, he further said upon Easter Day last as aforesaid in Houghton church that if he might advise James Lacker this suit now depending should not be ended but by suit of law. *For the rest does not know.*

AP (1) 7 & 8. *Affirms* for anything that he ever heard.

AP (1) 9. *Affirms.**

In 8. That he hath known Mr Pellett this two years, during all which time he hath been a good preacher. But yet he thinketh that it was not a fit thing for a man of his coat to reprove any man publicly in service time and before such an audience as he reproved Mr Hobbes in Houghton church; and in respect of that he showed himself no peacemaker but rather to make strife. *For the rest does not know.*

In 9. *Affirms* for he maketh show as that he doth fear God.

---

* The deposition does not include the second series of additional positions.

In 11. That he hath known all or the most part of the parties nominated in this interrogatory almost this two years, during all which time they were and have been men of good estimation and credit and of honest life and conversation for anything that he ever head or knew. *For the rest does not know.*

In 12. *Negative* to his judgement, for Thomas Northe can buy and sell and make any bargain either of corn or any other thing in such manner and sort as that he with whom he bargaineth shall hardly deceive him.

In 13. *Negative* for any thing that he ever heard, saving that he hath heard since the beginning of this suit that John Northe a great while ago (as he thinketh before he was born) did do public penance in Houghton church; but wherefore he cannot depose.

In 14. *Negative* for any thing that he ever heard.

In 15. *Does not know* because he cannot search into other men's consciences. But for his own part he never found them nor either of them to be otherwise than honest men and no swearers nor liars.

In 16. That the witnesses in this article are honest men for anything he ever heard. *And for the rest does not know* because he hath been but a while a dweller at Houghton.

3/26 John Northe.[49] *Read over 28 January 1604/5.*

*Of Houghton, yeoman, where lived about 61 years; before at Bury; born there; aged about 71. Signs with mark.**

AP (1) 1 & 2. That upon Easter Sunday last openly in the parish church of Houghton, a motion being made by Oliver Markes, one of the witnesses formerly producted in this cause, that a friendly and neighbourly end of this suit and controversy might be made betwixt Richard Hobbes and James Lacker, Mr James Pellett answered that James Lacker should not by his will make any end of the suit otherwise than by law seeing the suit was so far proceeded, in the presence and hearing of John Northe and divers others whose names he cannot now call to memory.

AP (1) 5. *Negative.*

AP (1) 6. *Cannot depose beyond what has already deposed.* And touching the 7th 8th and 9th articles he answereth nothing because he is not producted upon them.

AP (2) 2. *Negative* for any thing that he ever heard, saving that William Gardyner about 18 years ago did charge one Edward Beake, then of Houghton, that he should steal some certain number of geese, but named not from whom he should or did steal the geese. Upon which speeches Edward Beake called William Gardyner into question before Mr William Goring esquire and one of our late majesty's justices of the peace, in so much that William Gardyner, being not able to make any just proof of the premises abovementioned pretended to be committed and done, was content there to submit himself unto Edward Beake; and further did before William Goringe promise to ask him forgiveness in the parish church of Houghton. Which promise was made in the

* No value given.

presence of Edward Beake, John Northe and others whose names he cannot now remember; and, as he hath heard, William Gardyner did ask him forgiveness as is aforesaid.

AP (2) 3. That, as he hath heard this article is true, but for his own part of his certain knowledge he cannot detect either of them, John Austyn the elder and John Austyn the younger, of any thing.

AP (2) 4. That Robert Finch did work with James Lacker about the time articulate. *For the rest does not know.*

AP (2) 5. That about two years ago here was a common speech within the parish of Houghton that Oliver Markes was vehemently suspected to commit adultery or fornication with Jane Roman. Which speech or common fame was only raised at the first by the wife of Oliver Markes; but there never was any proof made nor of any part thereof to this examinate's knowledge or hearsay.

AP (2) 6-8. He answereth nothing because he is not producted upon them.

AP (2) 9. *Cannot depose beyond what has already deposed to the first and second articles of the additional positions ex parte Richard Hobbes in the first place.*

AP (2) 10. That upon the second day of December Mr Pellett in time of divine service, hearing Mr Richard Hobbes answer him in the psalms of David as the order is in churches, Mr Pellett then saying service in the parish church of Houghton and Richard Hobbes mistaking only one word against his will, James Pellett presently in time of divine service said unto him, 'How now, how blasphemously do you read there', meaning that Richard Hobbes did read blasphemy. Whereunto he answered, 'Mr Pellett, I pray you read forward,' and no more, in the presence of Thomas Hunte, Edward Darkenell, John Northe and all others the parishioners of Houghton there present.

In 8. That he hath known Mr James Pellett this six years, during all which time he hath been, as at this present he is, a good and learned preacher and a man of honest life and conversation to John Northe's knowledge and no brawler nor sower of discord. *And for the rest does not know beyond what has already deposed.*

In 9. That he verily believeth James Pellett is a man that doth love and fear God and for such a one he is commonly reputed. *And for the rest does not know.*

In 11. That he hath known all the parties in the interrogatory for a long time, saving Nicholas Beache only who hath dwelt at Houghton some two years or thereabouts and no more and Robert Finch hath dwelt there about one year. Both which Nicholas Beache and Robert Finch and the other parties in the interrogatory mentioned he knoweth well; and for anything he can depose they are honest men and of good estimation and credit. And further he cannot depose otherwise than he hath already deposed.

In 12. That his son Thomas Northe is a man of such sort and carriage and of such wit and understanding as that he can perform and do anything touching the getting of his living as well as other plain meaning countrymen use to do. And for a plain dealing man and a man of good dealing in buying and selling of anything he is commonly reputed and taken within the parish of Houghton and other places.

In 13. That by law he is not bound to answer to this interrogatory for he will not depose against himself except by law he be compelled.

In 14. *Negative*

In 15.* *Deposes as to the 13th article of the interrogatories and not otherwise.*

In 16.† That some of the witnesses have been churchwardens of the parish of Houghton but none of them were ever constable of the hundred to his knowledge. And for their and every of their ability and sufficiency he cannot depose, saving that they and all of them are accounted to be men able to live of themselves by their labour and industry and not otherwise.

3/27 John Kyne.[50] *14 February 1604/5*

Of Bury, husbandman, where lived about 30 years; before at Wonersh in Surrey; born there; aged about 45. Signs with mark. Is worth £6 13s 4d.

AP (1) 7. *Affirms* for anything that he ever heard to the contrary.

AP (1) 8. *Deposes as previously and for the rest does not know.*

AP (1) 9. That Thomas Northe can read English, and for anything that he could ever perceive he was always a wary man and of a reasonable wit, discretion and understanding to order his business in such sort as ordinarily country men are able and use to do. For John Kyne did buy some certain quantity of malt of him two years together amounting to the value of £30, and for anything that he could perceive he had wit and discretion sufficient to make his bargain touching the sale as well as any other plain countryman may of his fashion; and according to his bargain, sale and promise made unto John Kyne did by himself or others justly and truly deliver the malt unto him or his deputy. In respect whereof he verily believeth Thomas Northe is a man of sufficient wit and understanding as other plain countrymen are to follow his affairs for his maintenance and living in this world. As touching John Northe, *affirmative* for anything that he ever heard or knew to the contrary or otherwise he thinketh he should not [*sic*] have been chosen high constable of the hundred where he dwelleth, as now at this present he is. *For the rest does not know.*

AP (2) 1. *Cannot depose beyond what has already deposed.*

AP (2) 2. *Negative* for any thing he ever heard.

AP (2) 3. *Cannot depose beyond what has already deposed.*

AP (2) 4 & 5. *Does not know.*

AP (2) 6-8. *Cannot depose beyond what has already deposed.*

---

* Misnumbered 14 in MS.

† Misnumbered 15 in MS.

AP (2) 9-11. *Does not know.*

In 4. That he was compelled by process out of this court to come and testify. Yet since that time he was requested to come by Mr Hobbes, who will bear his charges at this time as heretofore he hath done.

In 8. That he hath known Mr James Pellett this seven years, during all which time he never knew nor heard but that he was a good and learned preacher and no brawler nor sower of discord, but a man of good life and conversation. *For the rest does not know.*

In 9. *Cannot depose beyond what has already deposed.*

In 11. That he hath known all the parties in this interrogatory mentioned saving Robert Finch for this two or three years. And for anything he ever heard they nor any of them were detected of any crime but always they were accounted to be honest men and of good life and conversation.

In 12. *Cannot depose beyond what has already deposed.*

In 13-15. *Does not know.*

In 16. *Does not know* because he is not of the parish of Houghton. In respect whereof, although he hath known all the parties before by him confessed for all the time by him also specified, yet he knoweth not what office or offices they have borne in Houghton.

Personal response of the plaintiff

3/28 James Lacker.[51] *Read over 15 Feb 1604/5.*

Personal response. Signs with mark.

To additional positions [to the exceptions at the second place] ex parte Richard Hobbes against witnesses of Lacker.

AP (2) 1. *Believes it is as he has deposed previously. For the rest does not believe article to be true in anything.*

AP (2) 2 & 3. *Does not believe articles to be true in anything.*

AP (2) 4. Believes that Robert Finch about half a year before his examination was a day labourer with James Lacker and received of him for his work both meat drink lodging and wages. And he believeth that Robert Finch before his coming to James Lacker to work was household servant with Mr Richard Hobbes. *For the rest does not believe article to be true in anything.*

AP (2) 5. *Does not believe article to be true in anything..*

AP (2) 6-8. Believes that John Northe within five years last past hath been once chosen churchwarden of Houghton. And he also believeth that John Northe by the procurement of Richard Hobbes was chosen one of the constables of the hundred and is constable at this present. *Further believes it to be as his response to positions and articles of exceptive and corroborative material of Richard Hobbes. For rest does not believe articles to be true in anything.*

AP (2) 9. *Refers himself to the responses to interrogatories which believes to be true. For rest does not believe article to be true in anything.*

AP (2) 10. Believes that on a Sunday since the beginning of this suit when Mr Pellett was saying divine service in Houghton church, Richard Hobbes reading over loud said 'banish the lord out of the land'. Whereupon Mr Pellett reproving him said that he did read blasphemously. *For rest does not believe article to be true in anything.*

AP (2) 11. *Does not believe article to be true in anything.*

AP (2) 12. *Believes what is to be believed and denies what is to be denied.*

Extract from act book, 2 March 1604/5.[52]

3/29 [*Richard Hobbes protests in person*]

That about midsummer last past was twelvemonth and before the beginning of this suit, he did meet with James Lacker in the parish of Houghton and told him that he had certain small tithes to pay him, viz pig, wool, pigeons and such like; and did offer to pay him the tithes and intreated James Lacker to go home with him and receive his tithes or compound with him for them. All which speeches he uttered and offered to pay the tithes in the presence of Thomas Northe of Houghton being a witness examined for him in this cause.

Signature: ' per me Ric Hobbes'.

[*Hobbes offers 17s and demands Lacker meet costs of the case. Judge to rule.*]

4/1 James Browne of Petworth v William Humfrey of Amberley. Defamation.[1]

Court acts: 23 July 1603 to 26 May 1604.

The case arises from a gambling dispute over a game of backgammon in a Fittleworth inn. The random accusations of whoremongery appear to reflect a drunken outburst, but were considered sufficiently damaging to institute a defamation case. After the depositions were published, Browne's proctor demanded sentence, but the case lapsed after three months of indeterminate formal acts.

Proctors: Cooke for plaintiff; Barker for defendant. Examinations: two depositions for plaintiff responding to libel of eight articles.

4/2 Thomas Cooke.[2] [*January 1603/4*]

Of Fittleworth, gentleman where has lived for 33 years; before at West Burton 5 years; Thakeham 3 years; born at Slaughter, Gloucestershire.; aged about 73. Signature

To the libel.

L1. *Refers to oath.*

L2. That in July James Browne came to the house of Thomas Cooke in Fittleworth and requested him to accompany him to the house of one William Blundell who keepeth an inn in Lower Fittleworth, 'For', said James Browne, 'there is a reckoning' betwixt William Blundell and him. At which request he went with him to the house of William Blundell, at which their coming into the house [they] found there Richard Rooke, William Blundell, John Lewar, Richard Tolpott of Petworth, a tailor, and William Humfrey drinking together in a parlour. And after some communication first had among the parties William Humfrey challenged James Browne to play at tables with him for 6d a game. Then he answered, 'No,' that was too much he would play with him for 2d a game. Then William Humfrey said, 'No,' he would not play under 6d for one game only. Then William Blundell said to him, 'James play with him for 6d two games' and he would bear his half; then James Browne agreed and so he and William Humfrey went to play and William Humfrey won the first game and James Browne won the next two; by reason whereof he won the 6d. Then William Humfrey would have played again and James Browne said, 'No,' he would play no more. Then William Humfrey began to revile him in the most shameful manner and amongst other speeches said that James Browne and William Blundell were 'a couple of Ayledrapers'; whereupon Thomas Cooke answered, 'No William you are deceived. James keepeth no Alehouse.' Whereupon he answered, 'No, for he keepeth a whorehouse.' And William Humfrey* said that he knew many James to be cuckolds, but named no more but 'many James'. Then Thomas Cooke willed him to take heed of what he said; then William Humfrey replied that he knew what he said and he would speak the same words again for he had a brother that was twenty marks the worse for that house, meaning James Browne's house. All which speeches were used by William Humfrey in the presence and hearing of Richard Rooke, William Blundell, Richard Tolpott, Thomas Cooke and divers others.

---

* 'Browne' in error in text.

L3. *Does not know beyond what has already deposed.*

L4. That the common speech of people interpreteth such a one as keepeth a whorehouse to be a bawd, and for lucre and reward suffer the evil disposed persons to commit adultery and fornication in their house or houses and concealeth their offences.

L5. That in respect of the premises he deposed in the second article, the good name and fame of James Browne amongst his neighbours is much impaired.

L6. That William Humfrey was of the parish of Amberley and subject to the jurisdiction of this court.

L7 *Refers to oath.*

L8. *Deposition is true.*

4/3 Richard Rooke.[55] [*January 1603/4*]

Of Coates, husbandman; born there; aged about 26. Signs with mark.

L2. That in July he and others, being drinking of a pot of beer or two in the house of William Blundell, there came Thomas Cooke gentleman and James Browne, at which their coming William Blundell said, 'Mr Cooke you are welcome' and so after some communication came into the parlour where Thomas Cooke and James Browne were drinking together with William Humfrey, Thomas Pyper of Coates, Richard Rooke and others. And after a while William Humfrey challenged James Browne to play a game at tables for 6d a game. Then James Browne said he would not play so much a game; then William Blundell the host of the house bid him to play with him and he would bear his half; in so much that he went to tables with William Humfrey for 6d and said that he who first won two games should have the 6d; and as James Browne and William Humfrey were playing William Blundell spoke in so much that William Humfrey was angry and said it was hard for two to be against one yet won the first game; and then James Browne won the two next games so that he won the 6d. Then William Humfrey would have played again and James Browne would play no more; then William Humfrey railed against him and amongst other speeches said, 'Thus it is to play against a couple of aledrapers'; whereupon Thomas Cooke answered, 'No James Browne keepeth no alehouse.' Then William Humfrey said, 'No perhaps he keepeth worse house for he keepeth a whorehouse'; and he said he had known many James cuckolds. All which speeches and many more were used by William Humfrey against James Browne in the presence and hearing of Thomas Cooke, William Blundell, Richard Tolpott, Richard Rooke and others. And William Humfrey further said he had a brother was 20 marks the worse for such houses ···.

L5. He thinks that the good name and fame of James Browne amongst his neighbours for or in respect of the words of defamation is nothing at all impaired by reason his neighbours know what he is.

5/1 James Pellett, vicar of Madehurst v Richard Coxe alias Cockes of Madehurst. Tithe in Madehurst.[56]

Court acts: 25 June 1603 to 22 September 1604.

The case centred on whether tithe was payable on a relatively small area of land around Rewell Lodge, which lay in the south west corner of the parish at the north west edge of the extensive Rewell Wood. The depositions produced a consensus that the land lay within the parish of Madehurst but not within the manor, and that it had been open common until a recent date. After the plaintiff's depositions were completed, the defendant sought to produce witnesses but none were examined. From April the plaintiff pressed for sentence and the case eventually lapsed in September 1604.*

The case provides valuable details of perambulations and parish customs dating back to the reign of Queen Mary. It appears to have links with that of Lacker v Hobbes (3/1-29); Rewell lodge had in earlier years been occupied by the Hobbes family.

Proctors: Cooke for plaintiff; Barker for defendant. Process: six depositions for plaintiff responding to libel of ten articles, additional positions of eleven with interrogatories of thirteen.

Pellett was ordained in 1592 and was vicar of Madehurst from that year until his death in 1625.

5/2 John Perley, senior.[57] [*21-28 January 1603/4*]

Of Madehurst, husbandman; born there, aged about 72. Signs with mark.

To the libel

L1. That Mr James Pellet hath been vicar of Madehurst for all the time libellate and six years before; and so he hath been commonly reputed and taken within the parish of Madehurst for all the time. *For the rest refers to oath.*

L2. That for this 52 years last past and since, he hath known the vicars of Madehurst to have right to have and receive all the small tithes within the parish of Madehurst, as Mr Pellett now hath and receiveth. And he hath known Sir Robert Glaciter, clerk, who was vicar of Madehurst for about some 46 years ago receive from one [*blank*] Avery who then dwelt in the Rewell lodge such small tithes as were growing within the grounds belonging to the lodge called Rewell lodge, as namely pigs and other small tithes as belonging unto him in the right of the vicarage of Madehurst, as this examinate now thinketh Mr Pellett now vicar of Madehurst ought to have and receive.

L3. That for this 46 years ago he believeth the vicars of Madehurst have and ought to have had and enjoyed the small tithes coming growing and renewing within the Rewell quietly and peaceably, and in all other places within the parish of Madehurst and titheable places thereof, time out of mind.

L4. That for all the time libellate and long before, every parishioner of Madehurst having any milch kine and mares pasturing and feeding within the parish and titheable places thereof hath used and accustomed to pay yearly unto the vicar or to his farmer or lawful deputy 6d for the white or milk of every cow in lieu and in discharge of tithe in

* The name is consistently spelt Rwell throughout.

milk in kind, and 1d for the fall of every colt of mares pastured within the parish and titheable places thereof.

L5 & 6. *Does not know.*

L7. That the said Coxe is a layman and in respect thereof he hath no right to any tithes belonging to the vicar of Madehurst. *For the rest does not know.*

L8. That the said Coxe late was of the parish of Madehurst and now is of the parish of Binsted, as this examinate thinketh. By reason of both which the said Coxe then was and now is subject to the jurisdiction of this court.

L9. *Refers to oath.*

L10. *Deposition is true.*

To the additional positions

AP1. That for this 52 years ago he hath known the parcel of land commonly called the Rewell to be commonly reputed and taken to be as part and parcel of the parish of Madehurst, as now amongst all the parishioners it is commonly reputed and taken to be.

AP2. That for all the time in the next precedent article he hath know [*sic*] a certain house or building commonly called the Rewell lodge to be built and situate upon the parcel of ground called the Rewell, as at this present time there is.

AP3. That for all the time libellate and for two years before, Richard Coxe alias Cocke was an inhabiter and dweller in the house; and so he was commonly reputed and taken.

AP4. That for 52 years ago last past there were another little house built upon the parcel commonly called the Rewell, which was called the Rewell lodge.

AP5. That for 52 years past and since, he hath known all the inhabitant, dwellers in two houses, and their servants and family to have accustomed to come upon Sundays and holydays to the parish church of Madehurst to hear divine service and to receive the holy Communion and to bury their dead and to christen their children, church their wives, as being parishioners of Madehurst. And the inhabitants within Rewell lodge always pay unto the vicar their offerings due at Easter as being of the parish of Madehurst. And that Richard Coxe for all the time he dwelt in the house was wont to come upon Sundays and holydays to the parish church of Madehurst to hear divine service, and did christen his child there, and paid for the repairing of a seat for himself or his wife in the church; and both he and his wife received the Communion and paid their offerings at Easter as being parishioners of Madehurst.

AP6. That in Queen Mary's time he hath known that the parish clerk or sexton of the church of Madehurst did use and accustom to carry holy water from the church unto every house within the parish and titheable places thereof, and not unto any house not being situate within the parish or titheable places thereof.

AP7. That he hath heard that the parish clerk or sexton of Madehurst did used to carry holy water to the Rewell lodge as in this article is mentioned. *For the rest does not know.*

AP8. *Does not know.*

AP9. That he never heard but that it was a common speech within Madehurst that the parcel of ground commonly called the Rewell was situate within Madehurst; and further saith that he, himself being tithing man within Madehurst for 41 years ago last past, received a warrant from the justices of the peace to search for such things as were then lost within Madehurst & no further. He made search within the Rewell lodge as being within the parish of Madehurst and titheable places for those things which were lost at the same time

AP10. *Cannot depose beyond what has already deposed.*

AP11. *Deposition is true.*

To the interrogatories

In 1. *Satisfactory*

In 2. *Negative.*

In 3. *Favours parties indifferently and wishes victory for the party in the right; for the rest negative.*

In 4. That he came at the charges of Mr Pellett to testify what he doth know in this matter without compulsion; and that nothing is neither given nor promised unto him for his testimony herein; only his charge is borne by Mr Pellett and he hath promised him 6d for his day's journey when he was produced.

In 5. That 52 years last past he hath gone with the rest of the parishioners of Madehurst the perambulations and processions of the parish.

In 6. That when the parishioners of Madehurst walked their yearly perambulations of the bounds, circuits and limits of Madehurst, they have not fetched in the Rewell lodge in their perambulations because they accounted the Rewell lodge not to be of the manor of Madehurst; neither in their perambulations did they fetch in the lands called Heberden land because the same land is not of the manor of Madehurst. Yet both Rewell lodge and Heberden land were always accounted to be of the parish, and that the dwellers and inhabitants in the house situate and builded upon the land called Heberden lands did always come to the parish church of Madehurst upon Sundays and holydays, and received the Communion in the same church, and did christen and bury in the same church and pay all duties belonging unto the church as parishioners of Madehurst.

In 7. That there is some three or four parishioners of Madehurst which are not wont to be chosen churchwardens, sidemen or constables in their courses because they only occupy a cottage and about some six or seven acres of lands. But they contribute with the rest of the parishioners towards the reparations of the church, steeple, bell, book, surplice and other charges and burdens belonging to the church of Madehurst as occasion requireth.

In 8. That he hath known one [*blank*] Wilbye, one Averye, Randall Whallye and William Fuller, one [*blank*] Greene, Mr Francis Hobbes and Richard Coxe alias Cocke to be dwellers and inhabitants in the Rewell lodge. All which were commonly reputed to be men of discretion and ability sufficient to be churchwardens, sidemen, constables or other officers to be chosen within Madehurst.

In 9. *Negative.*

In 10. That he hath known forty landscots, taxations or collections made in the parish of Madehurst to and for uses mentioned in this article or some of them.

In 11. That he never knew nor heard that any dwellers in the Rewell lodge or occupiers of the ground called the Rewell was ever taxed or sessed or did pay or contribute any thing towards any of the charges and burdens in the next precedent interrogatory mentioned happening within the parish of Madehurst other than this examinate hath formerly deposed, viz they have paid tithe pigs and their offering at Easter to the vicar of Madehurst and that Cocke alias Coxe repaired a seat in the church either for himself or his wife and paid for the same which others did in the like case.

In 12. *Does not know beyond what has already deposed.*

In 13. *Negative*

5/3 John Coote.[58] *[21-28 January 1603/4]*

Of Felpham, husbandman, where he has lived for about 3 years; before at Madehurst for 6 months; before at Eartham about 7 years; before at Madehurst about 4 years; before at Bignor; born there; aged about 74 years. Signs with mark.

L2. That for this 48 years ago the right of small tithes within Madehurst did always belong unto the vicar as at this present they do unto Mr Pellett. And that for 48 years ago divers of the parish had cattle and sheep pasturing and feeding sometimes upon the south common within Madehurst, sometimes in the lands commonly called the Rewell, without the disturbance of any person whatever. For pasturing of which sheep and cattle, sometimes upon the common and sometimes upon the Rewell, the said parishioners paid small tithes or petty tithes unto the vicar as in the right of his vicarage, viz tithe wool and tithe lamb as being within the parish of Madehurst and titheable places. For at that time the said ground called the Rewell lie open to the common.

L4. That for all the time libellate and long before, every person having any milch kine and mares pasturing within Madehurst hath used and accustomed to pay yearly unto the vicar … 6d for the white or milk of every cow and 1d for the fall of every colt. Which was agreed upon by the parishioners of Madehurst about 20 years ago, as this examinate hath heard; but the same was not so much when this examinate dwelt at Madehurst.

AP1 That for 48 years ago he knew the said parcel of land commonly called the Rewell to be commonly reputed to be within the parish of Madehurst, for the parishioners put their cattle and sheep upon the common adjoining unto the Rewell, and their cattle and sheep did at their pleasure pasture as well within Rewell as upon the downs or common thereunto adjoining; for the Rewell did then lie open to the said Common. And the parishioners having their cattle and sheep pasturing as well upon the Rewell as upon the down did pay their tithe wool and lamb milk, cash* or money in lieu of tithe milk, unto the vicar of Madehurst as being within the parish. By reason of all which this examinate believeth the land called the Rewell is part or parcel of Madehurst.

* Calsh in MS.

AP2. That for 48 years ago there was a certain house situated upon the Rewell lodge, so it was commonly reputed.

AP5. That for 48 years ago all the inhabitants and dwellers within the house or lodge and their families used on Sundays and holydays to come unto the parish church of Madehurst to hear divine service; and did receive communion there and christen there and had seats appointed there, as being parishioners. But what dues they paid he cannot depose because he took no regard of any man's business.

In 4. That he came at charge and request of Mr Pellett to testify without compulsion. *For the rest negative*, saving that Mr Pellett beareth his charge and giveth him 6d for either day journey.

In 5. That he dwelt within the parish of Madehurst four years and a half; and as he remembereth he went the perambulations with the rest of the parishioners three times at the least.

In 6. That at the time when the parishioners of Madehurst and this examinate did walk the perambulations of their parish they did not fetch in all the bounds and circuits, limits of their parish, but only crossed through the fields where crosses were and stone heaps, and sometimes came to one of the bounds of their parish and then turned back again, and here and there read an epistle and gospel and some prayers, and stayed and drunk in many places, but not otherwise.

In 7. That all the parishioners of Madehurst are not all chosen in their courses to be churchwardens, sideman or constables for they omit the poorer sort …

In 8. That he never knew any inhabitant or dweller in the Rewell lodge save one; and what his name was he doth not now remember.

In 12. That Sir Robert Lanciter [*sic*] who was vicar of Madehurst 48 years ago received tithe wool, tithe lamb, and money for and in lieu of tithe milk, for such kine and sheep as any parishioner had pasturing within the Rewell.

5/4 John Page.[59] *Read over 20 Jan 1603/4.*

Of Madehurst, husbandman; born there; aged about 75. Signs with mark.

L4. For about 34 years every person having milch kine and mares pasturing hath used to pay yearly, according as the parishioners did agree amongst themselves, 6d for the white or milk of every cow and 1d for the fall of every colt. But they were not accustomed to pay so much before.

AP1. That for 55 years he knew the parcel of ground called the Rewell to lie open to the common next adjoining; and every one of the parishioners of Madehurst that had any kine or sheep put [them] upon the common; and did pasture upon the Rewell as being within the parish. And every parishioner having any kine or sheep pasturing upon the Rewell did pay yearly tithe wool and lamb and tithe milk or money in lieu; and so the same land was always commonly reputed to be within the parish.

AP4. That for 55 years ago and long before there were another house called the Rewell lodge.

AP5. That all the inhabitants dwelling within the two houses called the Rewell lodge for 55 years and upwards accustomed upon Sundays and holy days to come unto the church of Madehurst … and the inhabitants in the Rewell lodge had seats appointed in the church, as Richard Coxe had a seat appointed as being a parishioner. And he further saith that Richard Coxe did repair a seat either for himself or his wife.

AP6 &7. That for 55 years ago he, being clerk of the parish church, was commanded by Sir Robert Glaciter vicar of Madehurst to carry holy water unto every house within Madehurst and to no other house out of Madehurst. Amongst which houses, he was commanded to carry holy water from the church to Rewell lodge, which was first built and afterwards pulled down and re-edified; which he did for six years.

AP9. That for 55 years before and since it hath been a common speech that the Rewell and the two houses called the Rewell lodge were always within Madehurst. For 45 years he had 100 sheep pasturing within the Rewell for 22 years together next after the said 45 years [*sic*]; during which he and others who had sheep pasturing in the Rewell did always pay their tithe wool and lamb.

AP10. That for 55 years the vicars of Madehurst did receive all the small tithes in the Rewell.

In 4. That he came at the request and charge of Mr Pellett without compulsion; and nothing is given for his testimony save only 12d for his two days journey.

In 5. That he hath been a dweller in Madehurst 75 years and that he hath gone the perambulations and processions 50 times.

In 7. That all the parishioners of Madehurst are wont to be chosen churchwardens, sideman and constables, except four or five of the poorer sort and the keeper of Rewell lodge or underkeeper. But all the parishioners do contribute towards the repair of the church except Edward Stradlinge, Nicholas Aylinge and Thomas Shepparde who payeth no such duties.

In 8. That he hath known one [*blank*] Averye, Randoll Whalley, Richard Skynner, John Arnolde, William Fuller, one [*blank*] Badcocke, Duke, Ludgater, Mr Francis Hobbes and Richard Coxe alias Cocke dwell in Rewell lodge. But whether they were commonly reputed to be men of discretion and ability sufficient to be churchwardens or other officers usually to be chosen, he cannot depose; but the parishioners did never choose any of them.

In 10. That he hath known many landscots, taxations or collections towards the reparations of the premises; but the certain number he cannot depose.

In 11. That he hath never known the dwellers of Rewell lodge was ever taxed any of the charges, saving Richard Coxe for the repairing of a seat in the church of Madehurst.

In 12. That he hath known Sir Robert Glociter, who was vicar of Madehurst 55 years ago, to have received of Thomas Page, this examinate's father, and of all others that had any sheep pasturing within the Rewell, the tithe wool and lamb of their sheep.

5/5 Edward Stradlinge.[60] [*21-28 January 1603/4*]

Of Madehurst, tailor, where has lived 30 years; before at Singleton five years; before at Madehurst; born there; aged about 58. Signs with mark.

AP1. That for 46 years he hath known the land called the Rewell reputed to be within the parish of Madehurst (notwithstanding some part hath for this 10 years been inclosed and fenced in).

AP3. That Richard Coxe for 4 or 5 years before the beginning of this suit was an inhabiter in Rewell lodge.

AP5. That for 46 years the inhabitants within the two houses called Rewell lodge and their servants upon Sundays and holydays were wont to come unto the parish church to hear divine service … And that Richard Coxe did come to the parish church and had a new seat built in the church and paid his offering at every Easter; and all the inhabitants in the house had seats in the church and were always reputed to be parishioners.

AP9. That for 46 years it was a common speech that the Rewell was of Madehurst, for then and before and since the Rewell did lie open to the common; and the parishioners pastured their cattle and sheep in the Rewell and paid their small tithes upon their cattle and sheep always to the vicar.

In 4. That he came at the instant request and charge of Mr Pellett without compulsion. *For the rest negative.*

In 5. That he hath dwelt in the parish of Madehurst for 53 years first and last; and he hath gone on the perambulations and precessions [*sic*] for the most part every year when he was within the parish, after he came to understanding.

In 6. That the parishioners of Madehurst did never in their perambulations bound out the Rewell from their parish as being no part of their parish, neither did they fetch the same into their circuit; neither did they fetch in or bound the lands called Heberdens, nor the lands called William Gobles. Because the parishioners did at that time keep the highway for the most part and walked only to crosses and some other places. Yet notwithstanding the lands Heberdens and William Gobles are both of the parish of Madehurst and always paid their small tithes (as the dwellers and occupiers of Rewell lodge) as parishioners.

In 8. That he hath known one Wassher, Simon Shorte, one Elson, one Chaundler, one Randoll Whalley, one Vaffin, John Arnolde, one Ludgater, one Orgalles, one Richard Greene, Mr Francis Hobbes, Richard Coxe and divers others to dwell in the Rewell lodge. And some were of discretion and ability to be chosen churchwardens and none of them were ever chosen to be in any of the offices because they were all ways employed about other business touching their place.

In 10 &11. That he hath known many landscots, taxations or collections towards the defects but he never know [*sic*] nor heard that any the dwellers in the Rewell lodge was ever taxed or sessed towards the charges.

In 12. That John Page, John Perley, Adam Racton, Anthony Stradlinge, William Ludgater and divers others for 46 years had their sheep and their cattle pasturing on the

Rewell; and paid their small tithes unto Robert Glociter clerk who was then vicar, and paid the like unto one Mr Miles and Mr Francis Doell who were all vicars of Madehurst.

5/6 Thomas Northe.[61] *[21 January 1603/4]*

Of Bignor, husbandman, where he lived for 60 years; before at North Stoke for 3 years; before at Madehurst for 7 years; before at Bury; born there; aged 83. Signs with [elaborate] mark

L3. That for 50 years and time out of mind the vicars did enjoy the small tithes until this suit began.

L4. That he cannot well depose how the parishioners of Madehurst paid their tithes in none of the years mentioned, because he hath not dwelt within the parish this 60 years and two. But when he dwelt there the parishioners paid their tithes orderly and well to the vicar's contentment.

AP1. That the lands called the Rewell, for 78 years to this examinant's knowledge, did lie upon* to the common, so much that if any of the parishioners of Madehurst put their cattle or sheep upon the common they might pasture on the land called the Rewell; and by reason thereof he believeth was within the parish.

AP2. That for 74 years there was a house built upon the Rewell and the house was commonly called the Rewell lodge; and he has heard that this house was taken down and another built instead.

AP5. That for 74 years he did know one Wilbye, who then dwelt at the Rewell lodge, and his wife and children and servants usually accustom to come to the church of Madehurst upon Sundays and festival days to hear divine service and did receive the holy communion and did christen there. And Wilbye and his wife had either of them a seat in the church, viz the two uppermost seats; and Wilbye did pay hollybread to the church and clerk's wages and (for Thomas Northe's father was clerk) he see [*sic*] these two duties paid himself. And he saith that Wilbye built a cross in the highway betwixt Crescroftgate and Wickenscorner and made seats about the cross; and every gangemonday for 6 or 7 years, when the parishioners went their perambulations and procession, Wilbye brought from the lodge two great spiced cakes and drink to the cross for the parishioners to eat and drink; which cross was called Wilbye's Cross. By reason of all which he believeth Rewell lodge was within the parish.

AP6 & 7. That he, being the clerk's son, did carry holy water from the church for his father for 74 years ago for 6 or 7 years together to every house within the parish, and not to any house situate out of the parish; during all which 6 or 7 years he carried holy water to the Rewell lodge as being within the parish.

In 4. That he came at the instant request and charge of Mr Pellett; and he gave him 6d for his day's journey and 6d more for his son to be a guide to him being old.

In 5. That he dwelt 7 years in Madehurst and went the perambulations and processions with the parishioners 6 years.

---

* ?open.

In 6. That at the time when he went with the parishioners in their yearly perambulations, the parishioners did then (which is about 74 years ago) only walk their stations, as it was then called; and did not fetch in all the circuit and bounds; neither did they bound out the Rewell lodge and the lands called the Rewell as being none of their parish.

In 7. That he cannot depose whether all the parishioners of Madehurst were chosen churchwardens, sidemen or constables in their courses, neither whether all of them did contribute towards the reparations of the church ....

In 8. That he never knew any man dwell in the Rewell lodge save Wilbye. Which Wilbye was of discretion and ability sufficient to be churchwarden .

In 9. That he cannot depose whether Wilbye was ever chosen into any of the offices.

In 10. That he doth not remember of any landscot, taxation or collection that was made whilst he dwelt in the parish; neither can he depose whether Wilbye did ever pay any of the duties.

In 11. *Cannot depose beyond what he already has deposed*, for he never knew any dwell in the Rewell lodge save only Wilbye.

In 12. That one Sir Robert was vicar when Thomas Northe dwelt at Madehurst, which was about 60 and 14 years ago, and then Wilbye dwelt in the Rewell lodge. But what tithes he paid he cannot depose, for the said Rewell did then lie open to the common.

5/7 Anthony Stradlinge.[62] *Read over 27 January 1603/4.*

Of Madehurst, husbandman; born there; aged about 56. Signs with mark.

L5 & 6. That Richard Coxe had pasturing in the Rewell in the years 1602 and 1603 11 or 12 ewes in the summer time; but what lambs he had of the ewes he cannot depose because Richard Coxe put his ewes to pasture at Tortington from Michaelmas in either year until Lady Day in either year; and there the ewes ewed [*sic*]. And he had in 1602 and 1603 about 12 li of wool in the whole about 24 pound of wool, every pound of wool worth 10d. But he cannot depose whether Richard Coxe had any wethers or tegs pasturing within the Rewell. And he further saith that Richard Coxe had in either of the years two kine and a heifer pasturing more upon the Rewell; but what calves he had he cannot depose. For which two kine and a heifer, as he believeth, the tithe milk or white of every such cow pastured there one year with thother [*sic*] was worth 6d by the year. And he further saith that Richard Coxe had pasturing in either of 1602 and 1603 one mare; but whether she brought forth a colt or no he cannot depose. And touching other things he cannot depose saving that the parishioners did always pay for the fall of every colt 1d.

AP1. That there is a piece of land called the Rewell which hath for 44 years been commonly reputed to be of the parish of Madehurst.

AP5. That for this 44 years he hath known all the inhabitants in the Rewell lodge accustom to come to the church upon Sundays and festival days to hear divine service ... And the inhabitants in the Rewell lodge have had seats belonging unto them in the church. And Richard Coxe did come to Madehurst church to hear divine service and did christen two children and caused his wife to be churched and both he and his wife did receive the communion there; and he did pay towards the building of a new seat for himself .

AP9. That there for 44 years he hath known that it is common speech that the Rewell was always in the parish of Madehurst, and he hath heard old ancient men who departed this life many years ago say that the Rewell was accounted to be within the parish. And he further saith that for 46 years [he] did know that the parishioners put their cattle and sheep to Madehurst common. And cattle and sheep did pasture all over the Rewell upon such pasture as there were as well as upon the common as being within Madehurst, for the Rewell lie [*sic*] open to the common time out of mind until now of late.

In 5. That he hath dwelt within the parish all his lifetime and he hath gone about 30 times the perambulations and processions.

In 6. That the parishioners never in their yearly perambulations bound out the Rewell as being no part of their parish; neither did they fetch in the same in their circuits because the same ground is not of the manor. Neither did they fetch in the land called Heberdens nor the land of William Goble because the lands are not of the manor. Yet the lands called the Rewell and the lands called Heberdens and William Gobles are all situate within the parish.

In 7. That all the parishioners except the poorer sort are wont to be chosen churchwardens, sidemen and constables in their courses. And he further saith that the parishioners of the poorer sort that occupieth but half a dozen acres of ground did not contribute towards any of the charges in the article.

In 8. That he hath known one Averell, William Fuller, one Duke, Elson, Ludgater and Edward Chaundler, Randall Whalley, William Orgalls, Mr Frauncis Hobbs, Richard Coxe alias Cockes, and others which now he doth not remember, to be dwellers in the Rewell lodge. And some of them were of discretion and ability sufficient to be chosen churchwardens in any parish and some of them were not.

In 9. *Negative*, for the parishioners spared them in respect all of them or the most part were but underkeepers and they were most commonly busied other ways.

In 11. That he never knew any dweller in the Rewell lodge was ever taxed or sessed any thing towards the charges in the 10th Interrogatory mentioned.

6/1 Alice Standen, relict and executrix of Thomas Standen of Yapton v John and Henry Standen, nephews. Testamentary.[63]

Court acts: 28 January 1603/4 to 28 July 1604.

A transaction to prove Thomas Standen's will 'in form of law' * *rather than 'common form', as a means of protecting the executrix against objections from other near members of kin, There was a potential area for dispute: Thomas Standen had left a life interest in land to his wife, with reversion to his nephews, John and Henry. Unlike most other probate cases of this type, it was firmly contested; and even when the judge gave sentence for Alice, the defendants threatened an appeal to the Court of Arches. Despite the judgement, Thomas Standen's will does not appear to have been proved in the Chichester diocesan courts or in the Prerogative Court of Canterbury.*

Standen had married Alice at Yapton on 25 May 1569. She was a widow, having married John Dammer twelve years earlier. Her will, which was proved in 1616,† *left personal property to a plethora of Dammer children and grandchildren. It can be assumed that Standen's real property passed to male Standen relatives.*

Proctors: Cooke for plaintiff; Barker for defendant. Examinations: five depositions for plaintiff responding to allegation of five articles with will annexed, and interrogatories of twelve.

6/2 William Reames.[64] *Read over 15 February 1603/4*

Of Yapton, husbandman, where has lived for about 22 years; before at Blatchington; born there; aged about 48. Is worth £40. Signs with mark.

To the allegation and the testament

A1-4 That upon the 9th day of January last past John Dammer son in law‡ unto Thomas Standen, the testator, came unto the house of William Reames to speak with him. And William Reames being then from home, at his coming home which was presently after the departure of John Dammer, his daughter told him that John Dammer was at his house to speak with him. Upon which he went unto the house of Thomas Standen to know what the matter was, at which he found Mr John Elise writing of the testator['s] will. And Thomas Standen being of perfect mind and memory did make and ordain his last will and testament as is contained in the will exhibited in this court, and did give, will and dispose every legacy unto such persons as are therein given, saving where it is set down in the will that after the decease of his wife he gave all his free land in Yapton and Walberton to his kinsmen John Standen and Henry Standen. The testator willed his freelands after the decease of his wife to his two kinsmen to be equally divided betwixt them. And he did constitute Alice Standen his wife sole executrix and did will every other thing of his own accord and without compulsion as is set down except before excepted. And he further saith that after the will was written, Mr Elise did openly read the will twice over and Thomas Standen did acknowledge the will to be his, in the presence of John Lawrence, John Standen, Henry Standen, John Elise, Thomas Furlonger, William Belchamber and William Reames.

---

* See Introduction: Testamentary, Wills and Probate.

† STC II 1616 Arundel Deanery No. 25

‡ Stepson.

And he further saith that Thomas Standen was of perfect mind and memory, for he spoke very sensibly and well and knew every man there present, and made no show of anything whereby he should hold him to be otherwise than of perfect mind and memory

A5. *Deposition is true.*

To the interrogatories

In 1. *Satisfactory.*

In 2 & 3. *Negative*

In 4. *That he is worth £40. For the rest negative.*

In 5. That he came to testify what he doth know at the request of Alice Standen and she will bear his charges. *For the rest negative.*

In 6. *Does not know* saving that he believeth the will hath not been altered but that it now is as it was before.

In 7. *Does not know beyond what has already deposed.*

In 8. *Does not know beyond what has already deposed.*

In 9. *Negative.*

In 10. *Does not know beyond what already deposed* saving that Mr Elise did forget to insert the words 'equally to be divided' into the will.

In 11. That Mr Elise, asking the testator when the will was made, 'Goodman Standen what say you for stripping or wasting of the woods?' and he answered, 'I think she' meaning Alice his wife 'will not do so.' *For the rest does not know.*

In 12. *Does not know.*

6/3 John Elise.[65] *Read over 15 February 1603/4*

*LLB, rector of Ford where has lived 16 years; before at University of Oxford about 7 years; before at Denbigh in Denbighshire; born there; aged about 44. Is worth £40. Signature.**

A1-3. That upon the 9th day of January last past the testator sent for him to come unto him to speak with him. At which his coming unto the house he found Thomas Standen sick in his bed; and he seeing him to be somewhat sick fell in some talk touching his soul's health; and after some communication Thomas Standen requested him to write his will. At whose request he writ the will exhibited, and Thomas Standen being of perfect mind and memory did of his own accord and without compulsion make and declare his last will and testament in all points as is set down. And he did make Alice his wife his sole executrix. And after the writing he did read the same will twice unto

* The signature uses this form of the surname. Elsewhere it appears in a variety of spellings. Elise was ordained in 1580; rector of Ford from 1585 and vicar of Poling from 1594 until his death in 1619.

him openly in the presence of John Lawrence, William Reames, John Standen, Henry Standen, Thomas Furlonger, William Belchamber and John Elise. And after the reading Thomas Standen acknowledged the same and revoked all former wills and in testimony set his mark. And John Elise saith he was of perfect mind and memory, for he was able to deliver his will plainly and knew every person there present, and could give a reasonable answer in matters touching the health of his soul and could repeat after this examinant the Lord's Prayer, the Creed and anything else that was spoken to him. By reason of all which he believeth Thomas Standen was of perfect mind and memory.

In 5. That he came at the request of Alice Standen without compulsion and she will bear his charges. *For the rest negative.*

In 6. That the will exhibited in this court hath remained in the custody of John Elise ever since the death of Thomas Standen until such time as he delivered the same will unto Mr Cooke the relict's procurator. But he neither interlined, razed, added or detracted, changed or altered anything, saving that after the publishing and after the decease of Thomas Standen, he did only set down his own name unto the will as a witness.

In 11. That he asked Thomas Standen at the making of the will whether his wife should occupy the lands making no strip nor waste and said the lands were largely given; whereunto he answered she was no such unreasonable woman.

In 12. That he could not find by the testator that his meaning was that the words mentioned in the next preceding article should be inserted into his will; for he used no such words and therefore he left the same words out of the will.

6/4 William Belchamber.[66] *Read over 15 February 1603/4*

Of Yapton, husbandman, where has lived for about 7 years; before at Fishbourne for one year; before at Flansham for one year; before at Angmering for 8 years; before at Wepham in Burpham ; born there; aged about 32. Is worth 40s. Signs with mark.

A 1-3. That upon the 9th day of January last past William Belchamber hearing that Thomas Standen lie sick he took occasion to visit him. And coming unto the house of Thomas Standen in Yapton and conferring with him about some matters, after a while Mr John Elise of Ford came likewise; and after some press of time Thomas Standen requested Mr Elise to write his will which he did. And Thomas Standen being of perfect mind and memory did make his will as is set down and exhibited into this court, seen and read unto William Belchamber at the time of his examination in all points, saving where it is set down that he gave all his lands in Yapton and Walberton after the decease of Alice his wife unto two kinsmen John Standen and Henry Standen and to their heirs for ever, to be equally divided betwixt them. And he further saith that Thomas Standen did constitute Alice sole executrix ··· .

In 5. That he came at the request of Alice Standen without compulsion and at the charges of her, and she payeth 6d for his two days journeys.

In 6. *Does not know* saving that he believeth that there is nothing altered in the will.

In 11. That at the time of the making of the will John Elise asked what he would have done that his wife should make no strip nor waste of the woods growing upon his lands and Thomas Standen answered, 'For that I hope she will not'

6/5 Thomas Furlonger.[67] *Read over 15 February 1603/4*

Of Yapton, husbandman, where has lived about 30 years; before at West Marden about 4 years; before at Kirdford ; born there; aged about 53. Is worth 40s. Signs with mark.

A1-3. That upon the 9th day of January last past Thomas Furlonger going to the house of Thomas Standen to visit him in his sickness, after a while Mr John Elise of Ford came in like manner and after he, John Elise and others had continued with him some certain time, Thomas Standen requested John Elise to write his will which he did accordingly. And Thomas Standen, being of perfect mind and memory, did make his last will and testament in manner and form in all things as is specified in the will exhibited into this court, saving that after the decease of Alice his wife he did give all his freeland in Yapton and Walberton unto his two kinsmen John Standen and Henry Standen equally to be divided and to their heirs for ever, which words might be left out of the will by error only. And he did constitute Alice his sole executrix ….

In 5. That he came to testify at the request of Alice Standen at her charge and she giveth 6d for his two days journeys and no more.

In 6. *Does not know,* saving he thinketh there is nothing altered in the will.

In 11. That John Elise put forth a question to know what order Thomas Standen would take that his wife should make no strip nor waste of the woods, and he said he hoped she would make no strip nor waste.

In 12. That he verily believeth the words in the next precedent article mentioned was left out of the will because Thomas Standen would not have the same inserted.

6/6 John Lawrence.[68] *Read over 15 February 1603/4*

Of Walberton, husbandman, where has lived about 10 years; before at Sullington about 12 years; before at Storrington about 8 years; before at Wiggonholt about 8 years; before at Stopham ; born there; aged about 60. Is worth £20. Signs with mark.

A1-3. That John Lawrence coming unto the house Thomas Standen upon the 9th day of January last past to visit him hearing that he was sick and being sent for by him, he found him sick in his bed. And Thomas Standen told him that he had sent for Mr Elise to make his will unto which speeches he said, 'It is well brother that you have done so.' Then Thomas Standen willed him to stay with him still and that he would make him one of his overseers and that he would request him to be a witness. Then John Elise came and Thomas Standen requested him to write his will which he did accordingly. And he did make his last will as is set down in the will exhibited and did will every legacy. Only where it is mentioned that he gave all his freeland in Yapton and Walberton after the decease of Alice his wife unto his kinsmen John Standen and Henry

Standen to be equally divided betwixt them and their heirs (for [such?]* his will was and he did give them the same lands), but how the words after the decease of his wife to be equally divided were left out he cannot depose ···.

In 2. That he is the natural brother of Alice Standen and uncle unto John Dammer who hath a house given unto him by the will. *For the rest negative.*

In 5. That he came to testify at the request of Alice Standen and at her charge but nothing is neither given nor promised.

In 6. *Does not know,* saving that he verily believeth there is nothing interlined, razed, added or detracted, changed or altered in the will since Thomas Standen's death.

In 11. That John Elise put out a question to know what he would do that his wife should make no waste of the woods and Thomas Standen answered, 'No I hope she will make no waste.'

In 12. That Thomas Standen did not will that there should be any such thing inserted into his will.

* Difficult reading

7/1 Thomas Hunt, brother and executor of George Hunt of Houghton deceased, v Susan Hunt, of Pulborough, relict of George Hunt, and William Hunt of Billingshurst, senior, brother. Testamentary.[69]

Court acts: 11 February 1603/4 to 21 April 1604.

A transaction to prove George Hunt's will 'in form of law' * *rather than 'common form', as a means of protecting the executor against objections from other near members of kin. After the defendants were pronounced contumacious, sentence was given in favour of the plaintiff. Although the defendants threatened an appeal to the Court of Arches, the appeal does not appear to have been pursued.*

Hunt had married Susan Apsley in May or June 1603.† *His will was proved on 21 April 1604, the day the case was concluded. The complicated will suggests that Edward Darkenalle, its writer, had legal training or experience. Hunt's real and leasehold property is bequeathed to his brothers, but with an exception in favour of a son if his wife should be pregnant with a male child. Susan Hunt is to receive all that was settled on her at marriage, plus four gowns, but was 'not to meddle' with other apparel. No baptism record for a child of Susan Hunt in 1604 has been found.*

Proctors: Barker for plaintiff; Cooke for defendant. Examinations: three depositions for plaintiff responding to allegation of five articles with will annexed, and interrogatories of nineteen.

7/2 Edward Darkenalle.[70] [*February 1603/4*]

Of Billingshurst, gentleman, where has lived about 4 years; before at Ockley, Surrey, about 7 years; before at Slinfold about 10 years; before at Billingshurst about 3 years; before at Warminghurst; born there; aged 38. Is worth 200 marks. Signature ‡*[with notary's mark?].*

To the allegation and the testament

A1. That George Hunt being of perfect mind and memory made his last will in writing in manner and form as in the will exhibited; and he constituted Thomas Hunt his brother his executor; and he did give every legacy in such manner and form as in the will is contained.

A2. That the will was by the commandment of George Hunt put in writing by Edward Darkenalle, for he sent for him upon St Stephen's day in the morning last past to come to him. At whose coming George Hunt requested him to write the will exhibited; at whose request he writ the will by the direction of George Hunt in manner and form as in the same will is set down. And after the writing thereof he read the will unto him publicly and openly in the presence of Susan Hunt the relict, William Hunt, the testator's brother, Daniell Jackson, Francis Cobbye and Edward Darkenalle; and others might be present at the reading which he now remembereth not.

---

* See Introduction: Testamentary, Wills and Probate.

† Marriage licence granted 28 May 1603.

‡ The same Edward Darkenalle makes a deposition later in the year on 10 December (f 112r). The signature here and at f 112r is accompanied by an elaborate flourish which may be a notary's mark. The discrepancies between his two biographies provide a useful caution as to the reliability of these statements. His residence at Ockley is given here as 7 years but as 4 in the later version; his residence at Slinfold is given here as 10 years but as 2 later; his residence at Billingshurst is omitted later; his age is given here as 38 but as 35 later.

A3. That George Hunt after the reading acknowledged the same for his last will in the presence of the witnesses. And Edward Darkenalle when he read the will did say unto him at the reading of every legacy, 'Cousin is this to your liking and as you will have it?' and he answered, 'Yea it is well.' And for the greater testimony to be given to the will George Hunt did write his name thereunto and set his seal upon the label which fixeth the sheets of paper together. And he saith George Hunt was of perfect mind and memory both at the writing of the will and at the reading, acknowledging, subscribing and sealing for he was able to deliver his mind for the framing very plainly and spoke plainly and sensibly. And when he writ his name to the first sheet of paper he would have writ his name to every one, and Edward Darkenalle told him he should not need to write his name to any more of the sheets save only the first and last sheets, then George Hunt asked him whether that were sufficient or no and he answered yes. By reason of all which he believeth he was of perfect mind and memory.

A4. *Does not know beyond what has already deposed.*

A5. *Deposition is true.*

To the interrogatories

In 1. That he is first cousin by the sister's side unto George Hunt; *for the rest negative; for fellow witnesses does not know.*

In 2. *Is worth 200 marks;* and that he is a gentleman and lives by his lands and the benefit of his stock; and for the rest of the article he answereth as before to the preface of his examination.

In 3. That he came at the request of Thomas Hunt to testify and at his charge without compulsion.

In 4. *Favours parties indifferently and wishes victory for the party in the right*; but he is more conversant with Thomas Hunt than with Susan Hunt.

In 5. *Negative.*

In 6. *Negative* saving that he delivered the will to Mr Barker one of the procurators of the Court to exhibit, and excepting that he did inform Mr Barker how and in what manner the will was written, acknowledged, subscribed, sealed and delivered.

In 7. That the will exhibited was fully written and finished the 29th day of December last past about 8 of the clock in the forenoon in an upper chamber of the house of George Hunt where he did lie, and by him acknowledged in the presence of Susan Hunt, Thomas Hunt, William Hunt, Daniell Jaxon, Francis Cobby and Edward Darkenalle.

In 8. That the will was put in writing by Edward Darkenalle by the appointment of George Hunt and by his directions; and the will was written by him the most part in a parlour and the rest in the testator's chamber. Which was all that he did bequeath unto Susan his wife. And he was writing of the will part of the 27th, 28th, and 29th days of December last past.

In 9. *Deposes as to the previous article*

In 10. That the will was only written once, for when he had taken instructions of George Hunt for writing* of two or three legacies, he still went down into a parlour to write the same down because there were still some company of women with George Hunt that he could not write the will in his chamber. And the will was read unto George Hunt in his chamber once only after the finishing thereof; but Edward Darkenalle read every legacy as he writ the same unto him once or twice. And George Hunt did subscribe seal and approve the same for his last will and testament by these words: 'I acknowledge and make this for my last will and testament.'

In 11. That George Hunt did well understand what manner of legacies he did give; and Edward Darkenalle saith he gave the legacies of his own accord without the persuasion of any person whatsoever.

In 12. That George Hunt did lie in his bed when the will was written, and when it was read unto him and by him subscribed unto, sealed and approved.

In 13. That George Hunt was of perfect mind and memory till the very last of his breath for he made no sign of imperfection of memory at all. For when his speech failed him, which was but a little before his death, Edward Darkenalle coming to unto him, he held up his finger as who should say his rings was [*sic*] gone, then Edward Darkenalle said unto Susan Hunt his wife, 'Cousin he wisheth his rings; you have them.' Then she said, 'Yea George, I have thy rings'; and so she put them upon his finger again.

In 14. *Negative; for fellow witnesses does not know.*

In 15. That the testament was written in six sheets of paper; and George Hunt and the witnesses only subscribe [*sic*] their names and set their marks unto two of the sheets, for the reasons in the third article of the allegation mentioned, viz George Hunt and Edward Darkenalle did write their own names, and th'other two witnesses set their marks because they could not write.

In 16. That the seal appended to the will was made and sealed with the proper and usual seal of George Hunt, and Edward Darkenalle set the same seal to the wax and George Hunt took the same off again. And he saith that the same seal hath remained ever since in the hand and custody of Thomas Hunt the executor for it† is made only upon the top of a pen and inkhorn.

In 17. *Refers to the will exhibited; and otherwise does not know.*

In 18. *Negative,* saving that he gave Mr Barker some instructions for framing the allegation as he hath formerly deposed.

In 19. That he had conference with Mr Cooke, procurator of the adverse party, what he being a witness should do in this matter and what course the executor should take for the proving of the will; and did ask Mr Cooke whereupon he and his contestes‡ should be examined because Thomas Hunt the executor was desirous to retain Mr Cooke of his counsel for the proving of the will. But Mr Cooke being not desirous to

---

* written *in MS.*

† is *in MS.*

‡ Fellow witnesses.

be retained did neither instruct him nor none of his contestes nor tell them upon what matters or interrogatories or what questions they should be examined upon. *For the rest negative; for fellow witnesses does not know.*

7/3 Daniel Jaxon.[71] *[February 1603/4]*

*Of Bramley within the parish of Shaverd [Shalford], Surrey, husbandman, where has lived for one month or more; before at Houghton for about 7 months; before at Preston Candover, Hants, for about 4 * years; before at Odiham, Hants, for about 2 years; before at Wolsey [?],† Hants for about one year; before at Winnall, Hants, for about 5 ‡ years; before at Preston Candover, Hants, for about 4 years; before at Coldwaltham; born there; aged about 32. Is worth 20s. Signs with mark.*

A1. That he taking occasion to visit the testator divers and sundry days in his sickness at his house at Houghton, and upon the Thursday next after Christmas Day last past about 8 o'clock in the forenoon was called up into the chamber of George Hunt where he lie [*sic*] in his bed. At which his coming up Edward Darkenalle said unto him, 'My cousin wills that you should be called up to be a witness to this will.' After which speeches he presently began to read the will wherein Thomas Hunt is named executor. And when he did read any legacy George Hunt asked him, 'To whom?' meaning to whom that legacy was given then Edward Darkenalle said to such a one naming the person; unto which speeches the testator answered, 'It is well.' And in the end when the will was read, the testator being of perfect mind and memory and being first asked by Edward Darkenalle whether he did acknowledge the same for his last will, he answered, 'Yes, I acknowledge and mark this for my last will,' and thereunto set his hand and seal in the presence of Susan Hunt the testator's wife, William Hunt the testator's brother, Thomas Hunt, Francis Cobbye, Edward Darkenalle and Daniel Jaxon . And the testator was of perfect mind and memory, for when he subscribed his name to the first sheet of paper he would have subscribed to all rest and Edward Darkenalle said, 'Cousin, you shall not need to set your hand to every sheet because it is painful unto you, for it will be sufficient for you to set your hand only to the first and last sheets.' Then the testator said, 'Cousin, will that be sufficient?' and he answered, 'Yes.' And further the testator did speak plainly and sensibly although it did somewhat grieve him to speak, and knew every man there present; by reason of which he believeth the testator was of perfect mind and memory. And half an hour after the reading George Rose of Amberley coming unto the testator to see how he did, George Rose took him by the hand and said, 'How now fellow George?' and George Hunt said, 'I thank you not well' and pointed to his stomach. And the will was writ by Edward Darkenalle by the appointment of George Hunt and this is the very will which was read which Daniel Jaxon is examined upon for he knoweth his own mark set thereunto, and remembereth every legacy therein given.

In 2. ··· That he is a husbandman and touching the rest he answereth as before to the preface of his examination.

---

* '12' *deleted in MS.*

† Not identified.

‡ Difficult reading

In 3. That he came at the charge and request of Thomas Hunt without compulsion.

In 4. *Favours parties indifferently and wishes victory for the party in the right;* and that he is and was as much conversant with th'one as th'other.

In 11. That George Hunt did well understand what legacies he did give. *For the rest does not know.*

In 12. That George Hunt did lie in his bed when the will was read and that he had then upon his back a white cut doublet.

In 13. That George Hunt was of perfect mind and memory till his death, and showed no sign of ill remembrance but many of good remembrance more than he hath already set down.

7/4 Francis Cobbye.[72] *Read over 23 February 1603/4*

Of Houghton, husbandman, where has lived about 7 years; before at Amberley about 4 years; before at Felpham about 3 years; before at Coldwaltham about 2 years; before at Houghton born there; aged about 38 years. Is worth £16 3s 4d. Signs with mark.

A1. That upon the Thursday next after Christmas Day last past about eight of the clock in the forenoon, he being at work in the house of George Hunt in Houghton and George Hunt lying sick in his bed, he was called up into the bedchamber to be a witness unto the will. At which his coming into the chamber ··· after a while Edward Darkenalle read the will and almost at every legacy he said unto George Hunt, 'Is this your will and meaning?' and he answered and said yes it was as he would have it. And he is certain that the will exhibited is the very will which Edward Darkenalle read unto George Hunt in the presence of Susan Hunt, William Hunt and Thomas Hunt, the testator's brothers, Daniell Jaxon, Francis Cobbye and Edward Darkenalle, because he see [*sic*] his own mark set unto the first and last sheets which he very well knoweth; and he very well remembereth the legacies. And he further saith that after Edward Darkenalle had read the will the testator set his hand and seal thereunto. And being asked by Edward Darkenalle whether he did make and acknowledge the same for his will, George Hunt being of perfect mind and memory answered yes he did ···; and that he was of perfect mind and memory for at the reading of the will he made answer to every legacy and said that it was as he would have it, and he spoke plain to everyone. By reason of which he believeth he was of perfect mind and memory and did give everything set down, and that he named Thomas Hunt executor.

In 1. *To the danger of perjury, negative,* saving that now and then he worketh a day's work with Thomas Hunt and that he is to pay unto him for work done about some 18s.

In 3. That he came at the request and charge of Thomas Hunt without compulsion .

In 4. *Favours parties indifferently and wishes victory for the party in the right;* and that he is more conversant with Thomas Hunt than Susan Hunt because he doth now and then work with him.

In 11. That the testator did well understand what manner of legacies he did give and he gave the legacies of his own accord without the persuasion of any other or else he would not have confirmed the same.

In 12. That George Hunt did sit up in his bed when he subscribed the will and that he had a cut white doublet on.

8/1 Mr Ralph Deare, vicar of Harting, v Mr Thomas Hawsted, vicar of Rogate. Jactitation* of tithe.[73]

Court acts: 17 December 1603 to 12 May 1604 [with sporadic later entries up to 19 January 1604/5].

The case was brought to counter the claim of the vicar of Rogate to tithes on the recently enclosed area of common called New Wood (now Nyewood) in East Harting on boundary of the two parishes.

After the depositions were published on 21 April 1604 no significant further acts were recorded.

Proctors: Cooke for plaintiff; Barker for defendant. Examinations: seven depositions for plaintiff responding to libel of thirteen articles with interrogatories of twenty.

Deare was BA of Magdalen Hall, Oxford, 1585, was ordained in 1586 and was vicar of Harting from 1587 until his death in 1612. Hawsted was ordained in 1593 and was vicar of Rogate from 1597 until his death in 1612.

8/2 Mark Pitt.[74] *[March 1603/4]*

Of Harting, yeoman; born there; aged about 48. Is worth £40. Signs with mark.

To the libel

L1. That Ralph Deare hath been vicar of Harting for all the time libellate as he is now. *For the rest does not know.*

L2. That the vicars of Harting time out of mind hath hitherto had all the small tithes in the tithing of East Harting within the parish of Harting as belonging unto the vicars of Harting in the right of their vicarage or their farmers, as Ralph Deare hath or ought to have, and all the tithe corn[?]† growing within certain garden plots within the tithing by what names soever. *For the rest cannot depose.*

L3. That the predecessors of Ralph Deare have ever since Mark Pitt was of knowledge quietly and peaceably enjoyed the tithes as he now ought to receive.

L4. That the ground or field commonly called the New Wood for the 40 years last past have been fully situate within the parish of Harting; and so it is now commonly reputed as well within the parish of Harting as other parishes thereunto adjoining; and that no part of the ground was within the parish of Rogate to his knowledge, hearsay or remembrance. *For the rest does not know.*

L5. *Affirms from what has heard.*

L6. That he never heard but the parish of Harting was always separated and not united nor subject to the parish of Rogate, nor to any parish; and it is commonly reputed to be a parish of itself. *For the rest does not know.*

L7. That he never heard to the contrary that the small tithes of any cattle pasturing upon the said ground was always paid unto the predecessors of Ralph Deare, saving

* Wrongful claim

† Difficult reading

that he nor his predecessors did never have any tithes of wheat or any other grain growing within one parcel of ground now commonly called Mille Mershe containing 30 acres now in the occupation of Richard Braye and John Mersher, farmers of the said ground, which was enclosed 40 years ago by Edmund Ford esquire out of the corner* called New Wood. But Mr Deare and his predecessors for all the time above mentioned have had the tithe of pigs, geese and the fall of colts within the ground containing 30 acres. *Beyond that does not know.*

L8. That Thomas Hawsted vicar of Rogate did never receive any tithes upon the parcel of land called New Wood or any parcel thereof of any person especially of the tenants or inhabitants of Rogate. *For the rest does not know.*

L9.† *Does not know.*

L10. *Does not know.*

L11. That Thomas Hawsted is vicar of Rogate and of the archdeaconry and diocese of Chichester and subject to this court.

L12. *Refers to oath.*

L13. *Deposition is true.*

To the interrogatories

In 1. *Satisfactory.*

In 2. That he is bayley [*sic*] and servant unto Sir Edward Carrell for his hundred of Denford [*sic*] and weareth his cloth. And he is indebted unto him in some sum of money which he hath gathered for him for estreats, but how much he cannot depose because as yet he hath not made his last account. And touching Ralph Deare and Sir Thomas Carrell, *negative.*

In 3. *Negative.*

In 4. *He is worth £40*; that he cometh at the request and charge of Mr Deare to testify. *For the rest negative.*

In 5. That Sir Edward Carrell knight is patron of the parsonage of Harting and receiveth yearly all or the most part of the tithes belonging to the parsonage or disposeth at his pleasure, except the small tithes formerly set down. But what rent he payeth to Mr Shorter the parson of Harting he never heard; and further he cannot depose.

In 6. That for anything he knoweth Ralph Deare doth solicit the cause himself and payeth his own charge. *For the rest does not know.*

In 7. That certain of the parishioners of Rogate are free commoners or intercommoners with the parishioners of Harting upon the common called New Wood,

---

* Difficult reading.

† *Deleted*: 'That notwithstanding the premises, Thomas Hawsted in the years and months in the first article of this libel, before divers credible witnesses contrary to the truth, did boast preach and declare unto part or all of the parishioners of Harting that part of Newe Wood was within Rogate.'

paying 2s 6d by the year to the lord of Harting; but he never heard that any of the parishioners of Rogate did pay any tithes unto the vicar of Rogate for their cattle pasturing upon the ground called New Wood alias Nyewood, nor that the ground was accounted to be partly within Harting and partly within Rogate but always to be wholly within Harting. And that Robert Vallor of Rogate having one mare pasturing within the same ground and having one colt fallen there about 7 years ago, he requested him to carry 1d unto Ralph Deare for the fall of the colt as due unto him in the right of his vicarage. *For the rest does not know.*

In 8. That some of the parishioners of Rogate have been dutercommoners [*sic*] or free commoners and have had right to pasture their cattle upon New Wood ever since he can remember* [*and have paid*] a yearly sum of money called New Wood silver for the pasturing; but how much he cannot depose. *For the rest does not know.*

In 9. That he never knew any parishioner of Rogate which had common[*?*]† in New Wood and had pastured his cattle within the parish of Rogate and upon the said common and nowhere else did pay to the vicar of Rogate or his farmer only all the tithe for his cattle so fed. For he believeth that the vicar of Harting ought to have the tithe for all the fall of colts, pigs and geese in New Wood; and he about seven years past did bring from one Robert Vallor of Rogate unto Ralph Deare 1d for the fall of one colt. *For the rest does not know.*

In 10. That Robert Vallor occupied 10 acres. *Cannot depose beyond what has already deposed.*

In 11. That he cannot remember that he hath gone the perambulation of the parish at any time.

In 12. That he never heard that any part of the common of New Wood was within the parish of Rogate but he hath always heard it to be all within the parish of Harting. *For the rest does not know.*

In 13. That he never knew any perambulation made by the parishioners of Rogate. *For the rest does not know.*

In 14. *Deposes as before. For the rest does not know.*

In 15. That he knoweth no such parish nor no such tithes paid. *For the rest does not know.*

In 16-18. *Does not know.*

In 19. That he believeth that there lieth of these [*sic*] common called Nyewood alias New Wood between the said heap of stones and the highway northward towards the parish of Rogate 8 or 10 acres. *For the rest does not know.*

In 20. That he hath heard the parishioners of Rogate in their perambulations have included the said 8 or 10 acres; but he believeth they did wrongly for that the land is within the parish of Harting.

---

* Five lines deleted.
† Difficult reading.

8/3 Thomas Marner.[75] *Read over 15 March 1603/4*

Of Harting [no occupation given] where has lived for about 40 years; before at Linchmere; born there; aged about 78. Is worth 20s. Signs with mark.

L2. That for the space of 40 years he hath known that all the small tithes within the tithing of East Harting to belong unto the vicars of Harting, saving the tithe of wool, lamb, hay, milk and the fall of calves; and also that tithe corn and tithe hay upon certain garden plots are due to the vicar of Harting; and the vicars of Harting have received all the small tithes and all the corn and hay in the garden plots. ⋯.

L3. …That the vicars of Harting have this 45 years enjoyed all the small tithes until of late this examinate did hear say that* Mr Hawsted, vicar of Rogate, did take up a pig of one Prior of Rogate which was fallen in New Wood and within the parish of Harting. ⋯.

L5. That he hath gone the perambulations and processions of Harting twice since his abode within the parish, and that he and the rest of the parishioners did include all New Wood as parcel of Harting. ⋯.

L7. That he hath known the vicars of Harting or their farmers for these 40 years have had all the small tithes of all colts, pigs and geese fallen within New Wood as belonging to the vicarage of Harting. And that he knew one Thomas Champion dwelling in Rogate about 20 years ago did pay to Mr Colpas then vicar of Harting one pig for the tithe of certain pigs farrowed within New Wood; and Champion then willed Thomas Marner to remember that the tithe pigs, tithe colts and tithe geese fallen in New Wood belong to the vicar of Harting. And he never knew any controversy but that the vicars of Harting did enjoy all the tithes of colts, pig and tithe geese until now that Thomas Hawsted did take up a pig of one Prior. ⋯.

L8. That he never knew any vicar of Rogate had any tithe in New Wood until of late he heard that Mr Hawsted did take up a pig of Ralph Prior ⋯.

In 4 …*He comes at the expense and request of Mr Deare.* ⋯.

In 7. That some of the parishioners of Rogate do intercommon in New Wood and have paid amongst them to the lords of the manor of Harting yearly 2s 6d being called the New Wood silver. ⋯.

In 8. That some of the parishioners of Rogate have had common and cattle pasturing on New Wood for this 40 years and upward. ⋯.

In 9. That he never knew any of the parishioners of Rogate to pay any tithes of their cattle pasturing within New Wood to Mr Hawsted, save only Ralph Prior who paid a tithe pig farrowed in New Wood about a year ago, which tithe pig was due to Mr Deare. ⋯.

In 10. That Thomas Champion of Rogate about 20 years ago paid unto Mr John Colpas then vicar of Harting a tithe pig fallen within New Wood, and he doth not remember that he had any land within Harting. And that Ralph Prior paid a tithe pig likewise to Mr Deare about a year ago and he occupieth no ground within Harting. ⋯.

---

* Five words interlined: difficult reading.

In 11. That he hath gone the perambulations of Harting twice within this 40 years and they did include and fetch in all the common called New Wood as being part of Harting. ···.

In 12. That he never knew any part of New Wood to be within Rogate but always accounted to be within Harting. But he hath heard say that the inhabitants of Rogate have claimed part of New Wood to be within Rogate. ···.

In 13. That he hath heard that some of the parishioners of Rogate have included part of the common in some of their perambulations; but he thinketh they did wrong for all is situate within Harting. ···.

In 14. That he knoweth that the pigs of Thomas Campion [*sic*] and Ralph Prior, whereof Mr John Colpas and Mr Deare and Mr Hawsted had each of them a tithe pig, were pastured farrowed and fallen in New Wood; and he knoweth in what place the pigs were farrowed. ···.

In 15. That he knoweth not any other parish where the tithes of cattle feeding upon any common were paid to any other parson. ···.

In 16. That he went the perambulations twice, and he and the rest of the parishioners went along close by the hedge of New Wood and so included all the common called New Wood; further he saith that the other parishioners of Harting in all their perambulations have gone the same way. ···.

In 17. That the two times that he went the perambulations, which was once in Mr John Colpas his time and another time since Mr Deare was vicar, there was a gospel and other prayers said ···.

In 18. That he never knew any gospel or prayers said at the places mentioned in the interrogatory.

In 19. That between highway that cometh from Dumpford [*sic*] lane and the parish of Rogate there lieth 3 or 4 acres of ground of the common in his judgement. ···.

In 20. That the parishioners of Rogate have included in their perambulations the piece of common in the precedent article but they had no right so to do.

8/4 Richard Turner.[76] *Read over 15 March 1603/4.*

Of East Marden, mason, where has lived for about 40 years; before at Rogate for about one year; before at Harting; born there; aged 80. Is worth nothing. Signs with mark.

L2. That about 50 years ago as he dwelling in Harting did know that all the small tithes within the tithing of East Harting within the parish of Harting did belong unto the vicar of Harting, saving tithe lamb tithe wool tithe milk and the fall of calves ···.

L3. That about 50 years ago, he then dwelling in Harting, one Mr Keynishe or one Mr Colpas was then vicar of Harting did enjoy the small tithe of East Harting and so hath all the vicars since .

L4. That he hath known New Wood this 60 years to be within the tithing of East Harting within the parish of Harting and no part within the parish of Rogate ···.

L5. That about 58, 59 or 60 years ago he went with others of the parishioners of Harting the perambulations and processions of the parish of Harting twice or thrice and once did carry the banner called the Bell banner; and they did include all New Wood ···.

L7. That he hath known the vicars of Harting about 60 years ago have had all the small tithes of any cattle pastured within New Wood. And he believeth that the tithes do belong to the vicars of Harting for he being born in Harting did often hear his father and other of the parishioners say that New Wood was within the parish.

L8. That he never knew any of the vicars of Rogate to receive any tithes growing upon New Wood. But he, dwelling with one Thomas Salsberye in Rogate about 50 years ago, Thomas Salsberye having a sow farrowed in New Wood willed him then his servant to fetch the four [*?*]* pigs home for fear of the Varmen [sic]. And when he had brought them home Thomas Salsberye told him that the tithe did belong to the vicar of Harting. And further that while he dwelt with Thomas Salsberye he paid two or three tithe pigs of his sows farrowed in New Wood unto the vicar of Harting; for he saw when all the pigs were fett [*sic*] away by the vicar. And by reason thereof he verily believeth that no part of New Wood belongeth to the parish of Rogate, neither hath Mr Hawsted any right to receive any tithes of any cattle within New Wood ···.

In 4. ...He is a mason and thereby getteth his living, and came at the request and charge of Mr Deare. ···.

In 7. That some of the parishioners of Rogate did intercommon and have common within New Wood but that they of right ought to common there he believeth not.

In 8. That some of the parishioners of Rogate have been intercommoners and have commoned their cattle in Nyewood [*sic*] these 60 years. ···.

In 9 That he never knew any of the parishioners of Rogate to pay any tithes of their cattle pasturing within Nyewood to the vicars of Rogate, but only to the vicars of Harting. ···.

In 10. That Thomas Salsbery of Rogate paid three tithe pigs being fallen within New Wood to the vicar of Harting as being within the parish of Harting, and he doth not remember that he had any land in Harting ···.

In 11. That he hath gone the perambulations of Harting twice or thrice within this 60 years and in either did include all the common called New Wood and never left out any part of the common. ···.

In 13. That he never heard that the inhabitants of Rogate did include New Wood in their perambulations but always it was reputed to be within Harting. ···.

In 16. That when he went the perambulations of Harting they went from the house of [*blank*] Packe of Rogate all along by the hedge ends of the common to the lane called Huyedown lane and then into a grove; and so they did include the common. ···.

---

* Difficult reading

In 18. That at the times when he went the perambulations, the vicar of Harting then being at Heydownelane end, did say a gospel and certain prayers and laid his book upon some boys' heads and the clerk pulled some of them by the ears and bid them remember the bounds of the parish. But concerning the heap of stones he doth not remember any. ···.

In 19. That between the highway and the parish of Rogate there lieth some 3 or 4 acres of Nyewood. ···.

8/5 John Penn.[77] [*March-April 1604*]

Of East Harting, husbandman; born there; aged about 60. Is worth £13 13s 4d. Signs with mark.

L3. That the vicars of Harting did receive all the tithes within the tithing of East Harting as Mr Deare now doth until now of late that Mr Thomas Hawsted did take up a tithe pig of one Prior of Rogate which was fallen in New Wood ···.

L7. That the vicars of Harting for 50 years last past have received the small tithes within New Wood: viz pigs, geese and the fall of colts as grow in two garden plots within the field called New Wood, as Mr Deare ought to have until now of late that Mr Hawsted took up a tithe pig of one Prior .

In 4. He comes at the request and charge of Mr Deare ···.

In 8. That some of the parishioners of Rogate have been intercommoners and have had right to pasture their cattle upon New Wood paying 2s 6d .

In 10. That he cannot now well remember the names of the parishioners of Rogate that did pay tithes of New Wood nor the names of the vicars or parsons of Harting that did receive any such tithes except Mr Deare, Mr Shorter or his farmers and Sir Edward Carrell, because he meddleth little about other men's matters. But he never knew but that all the tithes in New Wood were always paid to the parson and vicars of Harting ···.

In 11. That he hath gone the perambulations of Harting three or more times for this 50 years last past but they never left out any part of the common called New Wood and never left out any part of the common.

In 14. That he is certain that the tithe due unto the vicars of Harting within New Wood is due to the vicar of Harting, for he himself being a free commoner hath paid the tithes himself. But what manner of cattle any of the parishioners of Rogate had in New Wood or how long in any one year he cannot depose, for he hath enough to do to look to his own cattle and his own business and not to look how long other men's cattle pasture here or there. But he himself hath paid to the vicar of Harting both tithe pig, tithe geese and 1d for the fall of a colt.

In 16. That the parishioners of Harting did always in their perambulations go first upon Rogation Monday directly from the church round about the ground called the New Wood to a place called Heydown lane end, and so to Trotton Park pale, and so to Harting Beacon, and then betwixt North Marden Common and Harting Common, and so to the church again; and so other days other circuits and bounds as the order of the parish is. ···.

In 17. That the vicar of Harting and the parishioners when they walked their perambulations do usually say a gospel or some other prayers at their utmost and furthest bounds and so go to some other bounds.

In 18. That he never knew no gospel read nor any other prayers said at any such heap of stones; neither did he ever know any such heap of stones at Dumpford Lane.

8/6 William Bradfolde.[78] *March-April 1604*]

Of East Harting, bricklayer; born there; aged about 54. Is worth £20. Signs with mark.

L2. That the vicars of Harting have had right to all the small tithes within the tithing of East Harting as Mr Deare hath viz: pigs, geese, 1d for the fall of every colt, tithe apples, hemp and all other small tithes; and that the vicars of Harting always had as Mr Deare now hath right to tithe corn, hay and all manner of tithes upon certain garden plots in New Wood in East Harting time out of mind.

L3. That the predecessors of Mr Deare have received the tithes as Mr Deare now hath ever since he was vicar till now of late that certain of the parishioners of Rogate having cattle pasturing in New Wood did pay unto the vicar of Rogate tithe pigs, geese and 1d for the fall of a colt which did all fall within New Wood viz: one Prior paid a tithe pig unto Mr Hawsted now vicar of Rogate, and one Packe paid a tithe goose and 1d for the fall of a colt all within New Wood.

L7. That the predecessors of Ralph Deare for 50 years have received the small tithes within the close called New Wood, as he did until the wrong was offered unto him.

In 4 …That he came at the request and charge of Ralph Deare ···.

In 10. That he hath heard that one Prior and one Robert Faller [*sic*] and divers others of the parish of Rogate have paid their tithes in New Wood unto the vicars of Harting and never unto the vicars of Rogate, except before excepted.

In 11. That he hath for the most part this 50 years gone the perambulations of Harting, and he remembereth well he hath gone them 3 or 4 times; but the parishioners never omitted New Wood.

In 14. *Cannot depose beyond what has already deposed* for he neither knoweth how long any men's cattle pastureth within New Wood nor what manner of cattle, but hath respect only to his own cattle and his own business.

In 16. That upon that day when the parishioners of Harting do go the perambulations to fetch in New Wood they go over by a place called Lipscombe, and so to Packe gate, and so along the hedge to Heydowne lane end and there the vicar readeth a gospel, and so to a place called Fronckes, and so over a brook to a place called Somer lane, and so up along to Harting Beacon. And so from place to place until they have fetched in all the bounds in so much that they do bound in all New Wood.

In 17. That the vicar and parishioners do read a gospel when they go their perambulations at the uttermost and furthest bounds, and so go onwards to some other bounds.

8/7 Nicholas Somer.[79] *March-April 1604*]

Of East Harting, husbandman; born there; aged about 56. Is worth £20. Signs with mark.

L7. That for 46 years the predecessors of Mr Deare did receive all the small tithes within New Wood as Mr Deare hath until a little before this suit began except tithe lamb tithe wool tithe milk and the fall of calves; and that the predecessors of Ralph Deare have received the tithe corn hay and all other kind upon certain garden plots within Newland.

In 4 ...That he came at the request and charge of Ralph Deare ⋯.

In 11. That he hath gone the perambulations of Harting about six times but did never omit any part of New Wood ⋯.

In 14. That he very well knoweth that one Faller did deliver 1d unto Mark Pitt to be delivered unto Ralph Deare for the fall of a colt in New Wood, and that one Prior of Rogate paid a tithe pig unto him ⋯.

In 16. That the parishioners of Harting use commonly when they walk their perambulations to go from Harting church down to Chawcroft, and so to Milne Marshe and then easterward to Haydowne lane and at Haydowne lane end the vicar of Harting readeth a gospel, and so down to Dumpford gate, and so into a piece of land called Fraunckes land, and so into Sommer lane, and so into the New Wood again and then into a certain piece of land called Woodhurste, and so along to Eastbrooke and there the vicar of Harting readeth another gospel and there the parishioners drink, and so up to Harting Beacon and there they tread the bounds down to Bramsteade corner, and so into the holt, and so fetch the holt round and then come up to East Harting park pale, and so go to the church again. And so they did compass all New Wood fully to be situate within the parish of Harting.

In 18. That he never knew of any such heap of stones lying in New Wood by any highway side; neither doth the vicar of Harting read any gospel at Dumpford lane.

8/8 Anthony Ware.[80] *March-April 1604*]

Of West Harting, tailor; born there; aged about 56. Is worth £20. Signature.

In 2. *Negative*, saving that that he is tenant to Sir Edward Carrel and payeth him 2d by the year for rent.

In 4 ⋯That he came at the request and charge of Mr Deare ⋯.

In 16. That the parishioners of Harting in their perambulations use commonly to go from the church to Richard Lipscombe's house, and then on to a piece of ground in the occupation of William Keyse of Rogate, and then into New Wood, and so along by the hedge until they come to Richard Parke's gate, and so keep the hedge till they come to Heydowne lane end and there the vicar readeth a gospel, and so fetch in four closes in the occupation of Richard Faller, and so return down to a lane that leads to Dumpford, and so into the ground called Frounckes, and so over to Dumpford park pale, and so to the grounds of East Harting, and then up to downs as far as Northmerke corner and so to the parish pale of Harting and then home.

In 19. That he never heard of any such heap of stones .

9/1 Mr Robert Johnson, rector of West Chiltington v Henry Johnson of West Chiltington. Defamation.[81]

Court acts: 28 April to 22 September 1604.

Robert Johnson alleged defamation after Henry Johnson had accused him of being the father of his [Henry Johnson's] wife's child. The West Chiltington registers record baptisms of Johnson children in 1600 and 1606 but none in between. Henry Johnson's lurid accusations did not materialise as presentments in the office court; and in 1608 he was presented on the grounds that 'he lieth daily at the alehouse and cometh not to his wife at all'.[82]

On 21 July 1604 (after the publication of the depositions) Henry Johnson's wife Joan initiated a counter case; both cases disappear from the court act book after two further acts.

Robert Johnson was ordained in 1560 and was rector of West Chiltington from 1571 until his death in 1611.

Proctors: Cooke for plaintiff; Barker for defendant. Examinations: two depositions for plaintiff responding to libel of ten articles and interrogatories of seven.

9/2 Thomas Wadye.[83] [*June 1604*]

Of [West] Chiltington, husbandman, * *where has lived for one year; before at Pulborough for about two years; before at Thakeham; born there; aged about 24. Is worth £6 13s 4d. Signature.*

To the libel.

L1. *Refers to libel and oath.*

L2. *Refers to libel and oath; for the rest does not know.*

L3. That about 8 weeks ago he, going to the parish church of Chiltington upon one Sunday to hear divine service, did openly see Henry Johnson come into the parish church and Joan Johnson alias Larkyn his wife with him having a child in her arms. After the service was read Joan laid down the child close by Mr Robert Johnson in the church in the presence of a great number of the parishioners. Then Henry Johnson said, 'Here is your child. Take it for it is none of mine.' Whereunto Mr Robert Johnson answered, 'No I defy thee,' it meaning the child was none of his. Nevertheless Henry Johnson and his wife departed and left the child in the church and charged Robert Johnson was his, notwithstanding the child was born of the body of Joan Johnson the wife of Henry Johnson in wedlock after they two were married together. And he further saith that Henry Johnson told him that Robert Johnson did promise to give him £40 (which was only in the presence of Thomas Wadye). And the same was spoken by Henry Johnson against Robert Johnson in the presence of Thomas Wadye, John Greenefeild, Robert Barnard, [*blank*] Johnson, son of Robert Johnson and [*blank*] Johnson and divers others.

L4. *Cannot depose beyond what has already deposed.*

L5. *Affirms.*

---

* Probably Thomas Wadye junior, an apparitor of the court.

L6. That after the solemnisation of the marriage between Henry Johnson and Joan his wife, Joan was conceived with child and the same child was born in wedlock; *for the rest does not know.*

L7. That he verily believeth that Mr Robert Johnson is nothing the worse thought of amongst his parishioners for the speeches of defamation, because he was always and now is taken to be an honest man.

L8. *Affirms.*

L9. *Refers to oath.*

L10. *Deposition is true.*

To the interrogatories

In 1. *Satisfactory.*

In 2. *Negative.*

In 3. *That he is worth £6 13s 4d; for the rest negative.*

In 4. *Does not know.*

In 5. *Does not know,* saving that he hath heard that Mr Robert Johnson should have been married unto Joan.

In 6. *Does not know,* saving that he hath heard Henry Johnson say that Robert Johnson promised him £40 if he would marry Joan; and of that sum of money he paid him £5.

In 7. *Cannot depose beyond what has already deposed.*

9/3 John Greenefeild.[84] *Read over 14 June 1604.*

Of [West] Chiltington, husbandman, where has lived about 7 years; before at Wiggonholt about 5 years; before at Chiltington about 4 years; before at Pulborough; born there; aged about 30. Is worth £6 13s 4d. Signs with mark.

L3. That about 8 weeks ago, he being at his parish church in Chiltington upon one Sunday to hear divine service, and Henry Johnson and Joan Johnson alias Larkyn wife of Henry Johnson having a young child there with her, Henry and Joan presently after service was done went both towards Mr Robert Johnson where he did sit. Which done, Joan Johnson laid the same child down close by Mr Robert Johnson and Henry Johnson said, 'Here take up thy child for it is thy child and none of mine.' Whereunto Mr Robert Johnson answered no, he defied him for it was none of his. Then Henry Johnson answered that the child was Robert Johnson's child and not his; and so they departed and left the young child in the church, which child was born of the body of Joan Johnson long after that she and Henry Johnson were married together. All which speeches were spoken in the presence of John Greenefeild, Thomas Wadye the younger, Robert Barnard the elder; and divers others were then present in the church and heard the same.

L5. That Henry Johnson and Joan Johnson were man and wife long before the words of defamation, as they are at this present.

L6. That before the uttering of the words and after Joan Johnson married unto Henry Johnson, she was delivered of a child. Which child is mentioned in the libel and was born in wedlock.

L7. That the good name and fame of Robert Johnson is nothing impaired by the speeches of defamation for anything that he ever heard.

In 5. *Negative,* for his knowledge.

In 6. *Does not know,* saving that he hath heard Henry Johnson say that Robert Johnson did promise him £40 if he would marry Joan .

10/1 Alice Stamer alias Greene v John Tickenor of Ferring. Testamentary re administration of Agnes Stamer widow of Kingston. [85]

Court acts: 31 March to 27 October 1604.

Administration of Agnes's goods, with those of her husband John, had been granted to the proctor Edward Cooke on behalf of her daughter Alice on 16 March 1603/4; confusingly, the administration was granted to John Tickenor the following day. The case concerned John Tickenor's right to corn belonging to Agnes. After Tickenor had been pronounced contumacious for failing to appear, the witnesses made their depositions but the case made no further progress and lapsed after 27 October.

Proctors: Cooke for plaintiff; Barker for defendant. Examinations: three depositions for plaintiff responding to thirteen articles and nine interrogatories.

10/2 Thomas Drewett.[86] [*July 1604*]

Of Kingston by Ferring, husbandman; born there; aged about 48. Is worth £13 13s 4d. Signs with mark.

To the articles

Art 1 & 2. *Affirms.*

Art 3. That Alice Greene alias Stamer was the natural and lawful daughter of Agnes Stamer deceased. *For the rest refers to oath.*

Art 4. *Affirms.*

Art 5. That in the lifetime of Agnes Stamer and very shortly after her decease he was requested by John Greene husband unto Alice Greene to view what corn was after the decease of Agnes Stamer left in the barn. At whose request he viewed and there were four quarters of wheat and four quarters of barley: every quarter of wheat worth 20s and every quarter of barley worth 10s. All which corn did grow upon a certain copyhold belonging unto Agnes Stamer and was carried into the barn, and by reason thereof her own proper goods and nobody's else's. *For the rest does not know.*

Art 6. *For the rest does not know beyond what has already deposed.*

Art 7. That John Tickenor had the corn but by what authority he cannot depose.

Art 8. *Does not know.*

Art 9. *Affirms.*

Art 10. *Refers to oath.*

Art 11. *Affirms.*

Art 12. *Refers to oath.*

Art 13. *Deposition is true.*

To the interrogatories.

In 1. *Satisfactory*

In 2. *Favours parties indifferently. For the rest negative* saving that he is indebted unto the party producent about 2s 6d and three half bushels of barley and three pecks of wheat.

In 3. *Is worth £13 13s 4d. For the rest negative.*

In 4. That he came to testify at the charge and request of John Greene husband of Agnes [*recte* Alice] Greene. *For the rest negative.*

In 5. That he very well knoweth that Agnes Stamer had the goods at the time of her death because he see [*sic*] the same in her barn, and for anything he knoweth the same were in her own right. But he must need say that Agnes Stamer did say one day when there was a court holden at her house, she then surrendering her copyhold, that then she had nothing to take to nor help herself seeing she had surrendered her copyhold. But upon what occasion she said so he cannot depose.

In 6. *Does not know* saving that he hath heard that the husband of Agnes Stamer did in his lifetime make a deed of gift of all his goods unto John Tickenor upon the condition articulate. *For the rest does not know.*

In 7. *Does not know.*

In 8. That he never heard that Agnes Stamer made any will but died intestate. *For the rest does not know.*

In 9. *Deposes as previously. For the rest does not know.*

10/3 John Esteade.[87] *Read over 1 July 1604.*

Of Kingston by Ferring, husbandman, where has lived for about 20 years; before at Amberley for about 20 years; before at Wonersh in Surrey; born there; aged about 65. Is worth £20. Signs with mark.

Art 5. That at a certain time a little after the decease of Agnes Stamer he went into the barn of Agnes Stamer and did see some certain of wheat and some certain of barley. And there was about some three quarters of wheat and 12 bushels of barley, every quarter of wheat worth 20s and every bushel of barley worth 14d. ··· And saith that he hath heard that there was in the lifetime of Agnes Stamer remaining in her barn 4 quarters of wheat and 4 quarters of barley, the wheat being worth 20s the quarter and the barley 10s the quarter *For the rest does not know.*

Art 7. That the wheat and barley came to the possession of John Tickenor for he see [*sic*] him and other of his servants both wynn and carry the same to the market to sell; but by what authority he cannot depose. *For the rest does not know.*

In 2. *Favours parties indifferently; for the rest negative* saving that his wife and John Greene is [sic] brother's and sister's children.

In 4. That he came at the charge and request of John Greene husband unto Alice Greene ···.

In 5. *Does not know beyond what has already deposed* saving that when she did surrender up her copyhold, when there was a court kept at her own house, unto John Tickenor she openly said that now when her copyhold was gone she had nothing to trust unto. But upon what occasion she said so he cannot depose.

In 6. That he hath heard that Agnes Stamer's husband did make such a deed. But whether it was so or no he cannot depose.

In 8. *Does not know beyond what has already deposed* saving that he did hear say that Agnes Stamer did give unto Agnes Tickenor one gown and a petticoat.

10/4 John Graye.[88] *Read over 8 September 1604.*

Of Kingston by Ferring, husbandman, where has lived about 40 years; before at Aldingbourne about 8 years; before at South Bersted; born there; aged about 52. Is worth £6 13s 4d. Signs with mark.

A5. That he, at a certain time a little after the decease of Agnes Stamer by chance going along by the barn of Agnes Stamer, did see some certain quantity of wheat and barley; but how much there was he cannot tell, neither whether it did pertain to her or not. And he knoweth that she had a gown, a hat, a petticoat and a smock and a neckencher [*sic*] and kercher at the time of her decease because he hath seen her go in these things; but what they were worth he knoweth not neither whether she gave them away at the time of her decease. ···.

A7. That the wheat and barley came to the possession of John Tickenor, for he see [*sic*] him carry some of the said wheat the same to Steyning market and there he sold it; but by what authority he cannot depose. ···.

In 4. That he came at the request and hath 6d for his dinner of John Greene husband unto Alice Greene. ···.

11/1 Mary Coote of Singleton v John Brydye [of Boxgrove]. Matrimonial (breach of betrothal contract).[89]

*Court acts: 28 July 1604 to 27 July 1605. Further business concerning costs 21 June 1606 to 14 March 1606/7 [and perhaps later]**

The couple were betrothed at a ceremony in Lent 1604. A further ceremony in June 1604 was intended by Brydye to end the betrothal, perhaps due to pressure from his father. Brydye arranged to marry Ann Barden, but Coote attempted to forbid the banns and then instituted proceedings against him on 28 July. Despite the judge's injunction that Brydye should not contract or marry during the case, he married Barden on 31 July 1604 at Linchmere. Eventually, on 27 July 1605, judgement was given in favour of Mary Coote; but it does not appear to have invalidated the marriage (perhaps having taken into account Brydye's formal ending of his contract with Coote). Curiously, in March 1606/7, at the very end of the proceedings, the court issued an order for the solemnization of a marriage; but its significance is unclear. Brydye was however taxed with the costs of the case amounting to £5 11s 8d. The full bill survives and is printed in the Appendix. A Mary Coote married Richard Woode at Singleton on 10 December 1610.

Proctors: Cooke for plaintiff; Barker (later Scales) for defendant. Examinations: two depositions for plaintiff responding to allegation of one article and interrogatories of ten; two depositions for defendant responding to allegation of six articles and interrogatories of ten.

11/2 Richard Gardener.[90] [*October-November 1604*]

Of Charlton in Singleton,[no occupation given], where has lived about 25 years; before at Eastergate about 3 years; before at Ford ; born there; aged about 33. Signs with mark.

To the allegation

That in Lent last past he, [Blaise] Brydye, father of John Brydye, Richard Smithe uncle unto Mary Coote, John Dowce of Tangmere, Edward Horne of Boxgrove, and John Blewett of Harting, being all together at the house of one [*blank*] Bolsham of Midhurst, innkeeper, and hearing Brydye the elder, John Brydye his son, Richard Smithe uncle unto Mary Coote and Mary Coote treat and talk of marriage to be had and solemnised between John Brydye and Mary Coote, John Brydye's father asked Richard Smithe what he would give unto Mary Coote to augment and amend her portion or stock; and he answered nothing saving that he would give her and John Brydye one sack of wheat and another of malt to make them merry together. Then Edward Horne and John Blewett, sons in law unto [Blaise] Brydye, said unto Brydye, 'Faith father give them your good will to marry together and never make more ado.' Then Brydye answered, 'Then let them marry together in the name of God for they shall have my good will so to do,' and so gave his consent thereunto. Then John Brydye said unto her, ' Mary give me thy hand for I will marry thee if I have not 2d with thee'; and Mary Coote giving him her hand, he took her by the hand and said, 'Mary, before this company I will marry thee as my wife and never depart from thee till God depart us.' Then John Brydye and Mary Coote departed hands and she took him by the hand again and said, 'John I will marry thee as my husband and never depart from thee until God depart us.' Whereupon he

* Court acts March-October 1607 do not survive.

called for a quart of claret wine to drink unto her and she drank unto John Brydye his father in the presence of the persons aforesaid. All which speeches were used in the presence of [Blaise] Brydye, John Brydye, Richard Smithe, John Dowce of Tangmere, Edward Horne of Boxgrove, John Blewett and Richard Gardener. And that in respect of the promises, John Brydye and Mary Coote in his judgement were and are man and wife before God, and also that there were public banns asked betwixt them three several Sundays, as well within the parish church of Singleton where Mary Coote dwelleth, as within the parish church of Boxgrove where John Brydye then dwelt. *For the rest does not know.*

To the interrogatories

In 1. *Satisfactory.*

In 2. *Favours parties indifferently and wishes victory for the party in the right;* and that he married with Mary Coote's own sister. *For the rest does not know.*

In 3. *Negative.*

In 4. That he cometh at the request of Mary Coote and she will bear his charges and give him 6d for his day's journey. *For the rest negative.*

In 5. That John Brydye's father and Richard Smithe were the only solicitors in this cause in making up the contract, for Richard Smithe and Mary Coote requested him to be present at Bolsham's house and John Brydye's father and John Brydye requested others to be present. But he is not in alliance nor any way indebted unto any of the parties save unto Mary Coote and Richard Smithe her uncle by marriage of his wife: that is Richard Smithe is uncle unto Mary Coote and Richard Gardener's wife. *For the rest does not know.*

In 6 & 7. *For the rest does not know.*

In 8. *Negative. For the rest cannot depose beyond what has already deposed.*

In 9. That he hath heard that John Brydye is married already and so was before the beginning of this suit; and that he is married to one Charles Barden's daughter; and Mary Coote did hear and had knowledge that he should be married some four or five days before he was married, in respect whereof she forbid the banns the Sunday before he was married. And he was married at Linchmere, where she forbid the banns, the Tuesday next following the Sunday, as he hath heard by Mr William Lacye.

In 10. That he verily believeth that Mary Coote would now willingly marry with John Brydye if in case [*sic*] the law would permit them to marry, in respect of her oath and promise formerly made unto him.

11/3 Richard Smithe.[91] [*October-November 1604*]

Of Durford in Rogate, yeoman, where has lived about 10 years; before at Sidlesham about 2 years; before at Westhampnett about 5 years; before at Cocking about 8 years; before at Amberley; born there; aged about 60. Signs with mark.

To the allegation.

That John Brydye and Mary Coote did many times treat and talk of marriage to be had and solemnised betwixt them, in so much that there was a day appointed when he and she together with other of their friends should meet at Midhurst to finish and determine the matter of marriage betwixt them two. Whereon he, at the request of Joan Coote mother of Mary Coote and sister unto him, did go to Midhurst upon the day appointed which was in Lent. And after some communication first had betwixt John Brydye and Mary Coote, [Blaise] Brydye the father of John Brydye demanded of him what portion Mary Coote should have to her marriage and he answered, '£10 for that was her father's gift' and it might be her mother would give her £10 more at her death but not before. Then [Blaise] Brydye asked him what he would give unto his kinswoman and he answered he would give her a sack of wheat and a sack of malt to make them merry. And upon further communication, John Blewett of Harting and Edward Horne of Boxgrove, sons in law unto [Blaise] Brydye, said unto [Blaise] Brydye, 'Father make no more ado, grant them your good will that they may marry.' Then [Blaise] Brydye answered, 'I grant them my good will. God send them well to do.' Whereupon John Brydye took Mary Coote by the hand and said, 'Mary I will never forsake thee whilst I live' and then they parted hands and took hands again and she, taking him by the hand again said, 'John I will never forsake thee whilst I live.' All which was done in the presence of [Blaise] Brydye, John Brydye, John Dowce, John Blewett, Edward Horne and Richard Smithe.

To the interrogatories

In 2. *Favours parties indifferently and wishes victory for the party in the right;* and that he is uncle unto Mary Coote for her mother is his sister ···.

In 4. That he came at the request of Mary Coote but at his own charges.

In 5. *Does not know* for, for his own part, he was not a solicitor in this matter and touching the rest he answereth as before.

In 7. *Does not know,* saving that John Brydye should have enjoyed a certain house and land at Shottermill, which is a copyhold paying £8 by the year in his father's lifetime; and he was to pay nothing after his father's decease .

In 9. That John Brydye is and was married before the beginning of this suit, as he hath heard, but unto whom or how long Mary Coote had knowledge before, he cannot depose.

In 10. That he verily believeth that Mary Coote would willingly solemnise matrimony with John Brydye if the laws of this realm will permit her in respect of her promise ···.

11/4 Daniel Court.[92] [*January 1604/5*]

Of Charlton, yeoman; born there; aged about 44. Is worth £200. Signature.

To the allegation.

A1-5. That in the month of June last past Richard Gardyner of Charlton came unto the house of Daniel Court and requested him to go with him unto the house of one Jane Coote, widow, in Charlton to bear witness of a matter which was betwixt one John

Brydye and Mary Coote, sister in law unto Richard Gardener. At whose request he went unto the house of widow Coote, at which his coming there were then present [*blank*] Horne of Boxgrove, Richard Cooles, Richard Gardyner, John Brydye and other two young men of Boxgrove whose names he doth not now remember. Whereupon John Brydye said unto him that he had made bold to send for him to be a witness in a matter betwixt him and Mary Coote; and upon those speeches presently they called for Mary Coote who was then in another room. And when she came in he said unto her, 'Mary, whereas there hath been some matter before this time betwixt you and me concerning marriage are you content to part and leave off as we came together?' Then she asked him whether he was content to part or leave off as they first came together, in so much that those words were repeated betwixt them twice or thrice that at length she urged unto him that he had foresworn to marry with her and so did not she foreswear to marry with him; and that his father had protested that if he did marry with her he should inherit none of his lands nor goods. Then upon other speeches John Brydye asked her once more whether she was content to leave him as she found him and one to give leave to the other to marry with whom they list. Then she asked him whether he would bear the burden of it and he answered, 'I hope in God, Mary, it will be no hurt to thee nor me, for if there be any hurt it will fall upon them that were the occasion of it'; but named no body. And at the last he said unto her, 'How sayeth thou Mary, art thou content to depart as we began?' and she said, 'Are you content?' as is aforesaid, and so they used the like words twice or thrice till at the last he said that he was content to depart from her and to leave all things as they were at the first. And she answered she was in like manner content, and so he took her by the hand and kissed her, and then one drunk to the other. And so she departed out of that room and went into the next room and fell to crying as high and as fast as ever she could. And but a little before her departure out of the room he said unto her, 'Mary, now art thou free thou mayest marry with any man and I may marry with any woman; and I pray God send thee a better husband than I should have been unto thee.' All which speeches were used in the presence of the witnesses before named.

A6. *Deposition is true.*

To the interrogatories

In 1. *Satisfactory. For himself, negative; for fellow witnesses, does not know.*

In 2. That he is a husbandman and thereby getteth his living.

In 3. *Is worth £200.*

In 4. That he came at the instant request of John Brydye without compulsion; and he will bear his charges; *for the rest does not know.*

In 5. *Negative.*

In 6. *Cannot depose beyond what has already deposed.*

In 7. *Does not know.*

In 8. That he heard John Brydye and Mary Coote publicly asked once, as the order is, in the parish church of Singleton in time of divine service; and the banns was there put in and they two asked by the appointment of John Brydye only without the privity of

Mary Coote. But whether the banns were publicly read betwixt them in the parish church of Boxgrove he cannot depose.

In 9 & 10. *Does not know.*

11/5 Edmund Horne.[93] [*January 1604/5*]

Of Boxgrove, mercer, where has lived about 5 years; before at Harting; born there; aged about 41. Is worth 20s. Signature.

To the allegation.

A1-3. That in Lent last past John Brydye and Mary Coote did contract matrimony together at Midhurst, in the presence of Blaise Brydye, father unto John Brydye, John Dowce, John Blewett, Richard Smithe, Richard Courte and Edmund Horne, after these words or the like viz (he said unto her that day being appointed for the meeting as well of the friends of him as also of her there assembled),* 'Mary, if you be as well content to spend thy life with me as my wife as I am content to spend my life with thee as thy husband, give me thy hand and I will give my hand to thee; and so before these witnesses we do acknowledge ourselves before God to be man and wife.' And then took hands and thereupon drunk the one to the other as man and wife before God. All which was done of either party in the presence of the parties abovenamed. And he further saith that about June next following he was requested by John Brydye to go along with him to Charlton, where Mary Coote dwelleth with her mother, to be a witness unto the departure of John Brydye from Mary Coote and the contract betwixt them touching matrimony. At whose request he went to the house of Mary Coote's mother, at which his coming there were present Daniel Courte, Richard Coote, Richard Gardyner, Nicholas Hamon of Boxgrove and others. In whose presence John Brydye said unto Mary Coote, 'Mary, you know there hath been something betwixt we two touching marriage but I will never marry thee whilst I live.' Whereunto she answered, 'John if you can so leave me with a safe conscience, so it is.' Whereunto he answered that he might; but showed no reason wherefore he might leave her and not make her his wife. Then she answered that if he could so leave her in respect of other matters formerly passed betwixt them two with a safe conscience, then God speed him well. And after many other speeches he and she departed; and she only departed into the next room and presently fell of [*sic*] crying so fast as ever she could. But a little before her departure John Brydye said unto her, 'Mary, now am I as free to marry with another as ever I was and so are you'; whereupon she answered, 'In the name of God, John, if you can so do with a safe conscience.' But he further deposeth that before the departure or giving leave the one to the other to marry with whom they list, if by law they may give leave, there was a man whose name he cannot nominate that met him, and John Brydye, and his wife, and told all of them that he was going to Boxgrove to Mr Hull vicar there to will him that the banns of matrimony should go forward in Boxgrove church, but by whose appointment he cannot depose, and said that the banns were stayed after the second asking because there went a speech that John Brydye should not enjoy the house and lands after his father's decease. But by whose

* Brackets as in MS.

appointment he knoweth not that the banns were stayed; but afterwards the banns were asked the third time and nobody forbid the same. ···

To the interrogatories

In 1. *Satisfactory;* and that he married with Rachel Brydye sister unto John Brydye and by reason thereof he is brother in law. ···

In 2. That he is a mercer and thereby getteth his living.

In 4. That he came at the request and charge of John Brydye.

In 8. That in the presence of Edmund Horne, John Brydye caused Thomas Browne parish clerk of Boxgrove to publish and proclaim the banns of matrimony between John Brydye and Mary Coote; and he paid his duty for proclaiming the banns.

In 9. That he hath heard that Mr William Lacye married John Brydye and Anne Barden within the parish church of Linchmere. ···

12/1 Mr Raphael Widdowson, vicar of Oving, v Edward Rose and his wife Agnes alias Westemill of Westhampnett. Tithe. [94]

Court acts: 7 July 1604 to 15 December 1604.

The dispute was over the payment of tithe on pastured stock. In the initial stages the parties agreed on payment, but the plaintiff demanded payment of the costs of the case. After the depositions were made and Rose was examined, no further acts are recorded.

Proctors: Barker for plaintiff; Cooke for defendant. Examinations: three depositions for plaintiff responding to libel of eight articles with interrogatories of nine; personal response of defendant to additional positions of libel.

Widdowson was ordained in 1588 and was vicar of Oving from 1600 until his death in 1610.

12/2 Richard Greenefeild.[95] [*2 November 1604*]

Of the city of Chichester, alderman, where has lived for about 50 years; before at Pulborough; born there; aged about 60. Is worth £200. Signs with mark.

To the libel

L1-6 and schedule. That for this 20 years last past he hath paid to the vicars of Oving, as he doth to Mr Widdowson at this present, for the pasturing of all manner of his cattle that did pasture in Oving, as oxen, kine, sheep, horses and other dry [*sic*] cattle, after the rate of 8d in every 6s 8d that he paid for the rent of any ground within Oving. And as he thinketh, all others of Oving occupiers of any lands do pay unto the vicar of Oving the like for pasturing or else he thinketh he hath great wrong.

L7. *Affirms.*

L8. *Deposition is true.*

To the interrogatories

In 1. *Satisfactory; for himself, negative; for fellow witnesses, does not know.*

In 2. That he is a butcher and thereby getteth his living and that he is worth £200.

In 3. *Favours parties indifferently and wishes victory for the party in the right.*

In 4. That he came to testify at the request of Mr Widdowson but at his own charges.

In 5. *Negative.*

In 6. *Does not know beyond what has already deposed.*

In 7. *Does not know,* saving that he believeth that he payeth his tithes according to the custom of the parish of Oving for the tithe herbage of barren and idle cattle fed and pastured within Oving.

In 8 & 9. *Cannot depose beyond what has already deposed.*

12/3 Henry Peachye.[96] [*2 November 1604*]

Of Oving, husbandman, where has lived for about 5 years; before at Bosham for about 2 years; before at Aldingbourne for about 10 years; before at Eartham; born there; aged about 39. Is worth £6 13s 4d. Signature.

L2-6 and schedule. That for this 5 years last past he hath paid to the vicar of Oving, for such cattle as he had pasturing in Oving being no fatting cattle, such tithes as did come for all the time abovementioned and long before, as he hath heard every person dwelling within Oving or occupying any lands which he kept for herbage and having any barren idle and fatting cattle hath paid yearly unto the vicar of Oving: 8d in every 6s 8d which they pay for rent. *For the rest does not know*

In 2. That he is a husbandman and thereby getteth his living ··· .

In 4. That he came to testify at the request of Mr Widdowson and at his charge.

In 7. That he cannot depose that any within the parish of Oving doth keep fatting cattle and other milch cattle together in one ground but that they do only pasture their fatting cattle by themselves. For which cattle as he hath heard they were always accustomed to pay 8d in the noble for tithe herbage only.

12/4 Richard Stronge.[97] *Read over 2 November 1604.*

Of Oving, [husbandman], where has lived about 7 years; before at Slindon about 10 years; before at Climping; born there; aged about 30. Is worth £10. Signature.

L2-6 and schedule. That for this 7 years last past he hath paid unto the vicar of Oving a certain stipendiary, which the vicar and he agreed upon quarterly every year in lieu of all his small tithes until now of late within this twelvemonth last; that he did occupy a certain piece of ground called Church Croft for the which he payeth 8d in the noble as the custom is for such cattle as he hath feeding. And he hath heard that it hath been a custom within the parish for many years ago that the parishioners have usually paid unto the vicar for the herbage of their cattle 8d in every noble of the rent due to the landlord. *For the rest does not know*

In 2. That he is a husbandman and thereby getteth his living ··· .

In 4. That he came to testify at the request of Mr Widdowson and at his charge.

In 7. That for the pasturing and feeding of barren and idle cattle the parishioners of Oving have always paid 8d in the noble for herbage.

12/5 Edward Rose.[98] *Read over 5 Dec 1604.*

Personal response. Signature.

To 3rd article of additional positions of libel ex parte Raphael Widdowson.

In responding more fully to the article confirms the rest of his response up to the words 'partim maiores at partim minores.' For rest does not believe article to be true in anything.

13/1 Mary Legate wife of Edward Legate of Lodsworth v Julian Legate wife of Edward Legate of Selham. Defamation.[99]

Court acts: 27 October 1604 – 16 February 1604/5.

Case and counter case. Mary accused Julian of calling her a baggage, which implied adultery. Later in the case Julian, who lived with Mary as a servant, countered by accusing her of scandalous late night behaviour outside her home. The cases lapsed in after formal and indeterminate acts in January and February 1604/5.

Julian Farnden married Edward Legate at Selham on 21 October 1599; a Mary Racton married Edward Legate at Walberton 7 August 1592. It is not clear whether the two husbands were related.

Proctors: Cooke for plaintiff; Barker for defendant. Examinations: two depositions for plaintiff responding to libel of seven articles and interrogatories of eight; two depositions for defendant responding to libel of eight articles and interrogatories of seven.

13/2 Thomas Page.[100] *16 November 1604*

Of Lodsworth, shearman; born there; aged about 50. Signs with mark.

To the libel

L1. *Refers to oath.*

L2. That about a month ago, he coming from divine service in his parish church of Lodsworth and going towards his own house, Mary Legate and Julian Legate were at some words going together near the church litten gate, so much that Julian Legate told Mary Legate that she was baggage and did lie abroad under a hedge, and that she, when she was her servant, did fetch her home or in at midnight. But what the meaning was he cannot depose, saving that he thinketh her meaning therein was not that Mary Legate did commit adultery or fornication with any man because she always was accounted to be an honest woman. All which speeches were so spoken by Julian Legate in the presence of Edward Long, Andrew Hover, Joan Chalcrofte the wife of Thomas Chalcrofte, Thomas Page and others.

L3. *Cannot depose beyond what has already deposed.*

L4. That for his own part he thinketh never the worse of Mary Legate for the speeches because he never knew anything by her but well and honest. *For the rest does not know.*

L5. *Affirms.*

L6. *Refers to oath.*

L7. *Deposition is true.*

To the interrogatories

In 1. *Satisfactory.*

In 2. *Negative.*

In 3. *Is indifferent to the parties and wishes victory for the party in the right. For the rest negative.*

In 4. That he came to testify at the request of Edward Legate husband of Mary Legate. *For the rest negative.*

In 5. That at the time and place before deposed Mary Legate did say unto Julian Legate that she was a thievish baggage. And being demanded then by Edward Legate husband of Julian Legate wherein she was a thievish baggage Mary Legate answered that she stole half a shirt from her, and that, as he remembereth, Mary Legate said unto her that she made her a couple of kerchers with the same half shirt. *For the rest does not know.*

In 6. That Julian Legate did say indeed that Mary Legate was a more or a greater baggage than she for because she lie [*sic*] under a hedge and was fetched into her house at midnight. *For the rest does not know.*

In 7. *Cannot depose beyond what has already deposed.*

In 8. *Does not know.*

13/3 Edward Longe.[101] *Read over 16 November 1604.*

Of Lodsworth, carpenter; born there; aged about 44. Signs with mark.

L2. That about a month ago, he coming from his parish church of Lodsworth upon a Sunday, he heard Julian Legate call Mary Legate baggage; and said that she did lie under a hedge whenas she, Julian Legate, then being her servant, was glad [*sic*] or did rise and did let her into her house at midnight. But whether her meaning was that she did commit adultery or fornication in her absence or no he cannot depose; but for his own part and by the report of her own neighbours, she is holden to be no such manner of woman.

In 4. That he came to testify at the request and charges of Edward Legate husband unto Mary Legate ⋯.

In 5. That at the time and place before deposed Mary Legate did call Julian Legate baggage and thievish baggage; and being demanded wherein she was thievish baggage Mary Legate answered she stole from her, when she was her servant, a shirt to make her a couple of kerchers. ⋯.

13/4 Robert Legate.[102] [*December 1604*]

Of Lodsworth, husbandman; born there; aged about 55 years. Is worth £100. Signs with mark.

To the libel

L1. *Refers to oath.*

L2. That about some five weeks ago he, being near unto the church litten gate, heard Mary Legate say unto Julian Legate that she was a thievish baggage, 'For', said she, 'thou did steal half a shirt from me to make thee a couple of kerchers.' Then upon further speeches Julian Legate said, 'Well I would be ashamed to use my husband as thou used thine: to go from him and to lie under a hedge whenas I fetched thee in at midnight.' All which speeches were used in the presence of divers witnesses. *For the rest does not know.*

L3. *Cannot depose beyond what has already deposed.*

L4. *Does not know.*

L5. That both the parties were angry and choleric. *For the rest does not know beyond what has already deposed.*

L6. *Negative,* for that he never knew any evil name nor fame of or by Julian Legate.

L7. *Affirms.*

L8. *Deposition is true.*

To the interrogatories

In 1. *Concerning risk of perjury:* that Julian Legate and Robert Legate are cousins of the third degree: viz she married with the said Edward Legate of Redland, which was son unto William Legate, which was son unto Everit Legate. *For the rest negative.*

In 2. *That he is worth £100*; and that he is a husbandman and thereby getteth his living.

In 3. That he was compelled to come to testify by process out of this court and that he came at the charge of Edward Legate.

In 4 & 5. *Negative.*

In 6 & 7. *Cannot depose beyond what has already deposed.*

13/5 Barbara Skinner.[103] [*December 1604*]

Wife of William Skinner of Lodsworth trugmaker, where she has lived for about 3 years; before at Lurgashall about 3 years; before at Haslemere, Surrey, about 4 years; before at Crundall, Hampshire; born there; aged about 40 years. Married and therefore worth nothing. Signs with mark.

L2. That about five weeks ago, she coming from her parish church of Lodsworth and going towards her own house, she heard Mary Legate say unto Julian Legate that she was a baggage and Julian Legate answered that Mary Legate was a baggage. And so there was baggage and baggage betwixt both of them in so much that Mary Legate said that Julian Legate was 'a baggage and a thievish baggage' for she, when she was her servant, did steal half a shirt to make a couple of kerchers. All which speeches were used in the presence of Robert Legate, Edward Longe Thomas Page, Andrew Hover, and divers others.

L4. *Does not know,* saving that, for anything that she ever heard, she that is named 'baggage' is accounted to be a woman of light or evil life or supposed to have committed adultery or fornication. ···.

L6. *Negative,* because Julian Legate always was and now is accounted amongst her neighbours to be an honest woman.

In 2. That of her own proper goods she is worth nothing because she hath a husband; and that she came at the charges of Edward Legate husband of Julian Legate without compulsion.

In 7. That Julian Legate called Mary Legate baggage and said that she would be ashamed to make her husband lie and cry as she did when Julian Legate was her servant and fetched her into her house at midnight to keep quietness.

14/1 Eleanor Butcher wife of Richard Butcher of Washington v Richard Lee of Washington. Defamation.[104]

Court acts: 20 October 1604 to 28 September 1605.

Eleanor Butcher accused Richard Lee of calling her a whore. Lee delayed proceedings by pleading poverty, then by refusing to respond to the libel and finally by making an unspecified allegation. The cases lapsed after formal and indeterminate acts between July and September 1605.

Proctors: Barker for plaintiff; Cooke for defendant. Examinations: three depositions for plaintiff responding to libel of six articles and interrogatories of ten; personal response of defendant responding to libel of six articles.

14/2 John Butcher alias Pyper.[105] [*November 1604*]

Of Washington, yeoman; born there; aged about 27. Is worth 40s. Signature (John Butcher alias Pyper).

To the libel

L1. *Refers to oath.*

L2. That about Bartholomew tide last past, he, being at the house of Richard Butcher alias Pyper in Washington where he did sojourn and make his abode as he hath done for this three years, he heard Richard Lee say unto Eleanor Butcher alias Pyper that she was as arrant a whore as any in England. All which speeches were used in the presence of Edward Parson, John Wells and John Butcher.

L3. *Cannot depose beyond what has already deposed.*

L4 & 5. *Affirms.*

L6.. *Deposition is true.*

To the interrogatories.

In 1. *Satisfactory,* and that Richard Butcher and John Butcher are brothers' children and as he thinketh Richard Butcher is indebted unto him about the sum of £6 13s 4d. *For the rest does not know.*

In 2. *For the rest does not know beyond what has already deposed,* saving that he liveth by his labour and service and at this time he selleth wood which before he bought standing or growing to amend and enlarge his ability as reason good he should.

In 3. *Is worth 40s.*

In 4. That he came to testify at request and charges of Richard Butcher, husband of Eleanor Butcher, without compulsion.

In 5. *Negative.*

In 6. That at the time and place before deposed he heard Eleanor Butcher say unto Richard Lee that she would not suffer such a cuckold,* meaning him, to come into her

* Difficult reading.

house and misuse her in such sort as he hath formerly deposed, in the presence of the witnesses before mentioned.

In 7. *Negative.*

In 8. That Richard Lee is accounted to be a poor man. *For the rest does not know.*

In 9. *Negative.*

In 10. That he hath been a sojourner in the house of Richard Butcher for this three years; and touching the rest of the article he never heard nor knew of any such thing.

14/3 Edward Parson.[106] *Read over 29 November 1604.*

Of Climping, tailor, where has lived one month; before at Washington about 1 year; before at Ashurst; born there; aged about 18. Is worth 40s. Signs with mark.

L2. That about Bartholomew tide last past, he being at the house of Richard Butcher alias Pyper in Washington, he heard Richard Lee call Eleanor Butcher alias Pyper whore, and said that she was as arrant a whore as any in England. All which speeches were used in the presence of John Wells, John Butcher and Edward Parson.

In 4. That he came to testify at the charges and request of Richard Butcher, husband of Eleanor Butcher, without compulsion.

In 6. That at the time and place before deposed Eleanor Butcher did say that she would not have such a cuckold, meaning Richard Lee, abuse her so in her own house.

In 8. That he thinketh Richard Lee is a poor man and for such he is commonly reported; but he verily believeth he is worth above 40s.

In 10. That John Butcher hath been a sojourner in the house of Eleanor Butcher ···.

14/4 John Wells.[107] [*December 1604*]

Of Washington, yeoman, where has lived about 1 year; before at Angmering about 3 years; before at Storrington; born there; aged about 24. Is worth £6 13s 4d. Signs with mark.

L2. That about one month before Michaelmas last, he being at the house of Richard Butcher upon some occasion, he heard Richard Lee call Eleanor Butcher alias Pyper 'whore' but whether he called her 'arrant whore' or 'as arrant a whore as any in England', he cannot depose. All which speech was spoken in the presence of John Butcher alias Pyper, Edward Parson who wrought then at Washington and John Wells.

In 2. Deposes as before to the preface of his examination; and that he is a serving man and by his service getteth his living; and he has as much land as is worth £5 by the year.

In 4. That he came to testify at request and charges of Richard Butcher, husband of Eleanor Butcher, but he was first compelled by process of this court.

In 6. That Eleanor Butcher said that Richard Lee's wife was a whore and an arrant whore and she would prove her a whore. But he did not hear her call Richard Lee a cuckold and whether John Butcher and Edward Parson heard the same words he cannot depose.

In 10. *Does not know* saving that John Butcher hath sojourned in one house together with the party producent ever since John Wells came to Washington which is about a year ago. ⋯.

14/5 Richard Lee.[108] *Read over 7 April 1605.*

Personal response. Signs with mark.

To the libel

L1. *Refers to canons and oath.*

L2-4. *Does not believe articles to be true in anything.*

L5. *Believes is of parish of Washington and subject to court.*

L6. *Believes himself to be the party complained against on the part of Elinor Butcher, however unlawfully. Believes what he has stated above that he believes, and denies what he has denied.*

15/1 Mr Peter Waters,* rector of Wiston v John Willett & William Foster of Wiston. Tithe.

The same v John Parker of Steyning. Tithe.

The same v John Hatfeild of Wiston. Tithe. [109]

Court acts: 22 September 1604 to 9 March 1604/5.

Three cases against separate defendants proceeded through a series of virtually identical acts. The plaintiff produced identical verbatim personal responses to material from two defendants; the two depositions serve both cases. The issue in dispute was tithe due to Waters in the period between the death of the previous incumbent and the termination, at Michaelmas 1604, of an agreement with Sir Thomas Sherley, owner of the Wiston estate and patron of the living. Both deponents had acted as agents for Sherley. Once their depositions had been taken, the case lapsed after a few formal acts.

Proctors: Cooke for plaintiff; Barker for defendant. Examinations: two personal responses of the plaintiff responding to material of six articles; two depositions for defendant responding to allegation of six articles and nine additional positions.

Peter Waters was instituted as rector of Wiston on 27 July 1603 on the death his predecessor John Byngham who had died by May 1603.† He held the living until his death in 1612.

15/2 Mr Peter Waters, rector of Wiston.[110] *Read over 23 November 1603.*

Personal response. Signature.

To material ex parte John Hatfeild.

M1-3. Believes that Sir Thomas Sherley, knight, by virtue of a grant by word or writing from Mr [*blank*] Bingham, the next immediate incumbent before Peter Waters of the parsonage of Wiston, was farmer of all the tithes within Wiston during the life of Bingham; and that the grant by the death of Mr Bingham did end. By reason whereof Sir Thomas Sherley, for that (as he said) he had in the lifetime of Mr Bingham entered into a composition with divers of the parishioners for all their tithes from the time of their agreement until the feast of St Michael the Archangel next following the death of Mr Bingham, about one fortnight after Mr Waters was instituted into the rectory, as he believeth, did desire him that he might continue his right to all the tithes from the time of the death of Mr Bingham until the feast of St Michael next following; and promised to pay the just value of the tithes to Mr Waters in lieu and consideration thereof. Whereupon Mr Waters did yield and agree that Sir Thomas Sherley should continue his right from the time of the death of Mr Bingham until the feast of St Michael and no longer time. *For rest does not believe articles to be true in anything.*

M4. Believes that before the beginning of this suit he hath received from Sir Thomas Sherley the sum of £24 in part of payment of his promise for the value of all the tithes

---

* The spelling Walters is also used frequently and apparently randomly.

† No burial entry has been found, but administration of his goods was granted on 13 May 1603 (WSRO STC III/E f 34).

from the time of the death of Mr Bingham until the feast of St Michael next following . *For rest does not believe article to be true in anything.*

M5. *Does not believe article to be true in anything.*

M6. *Believes what is to be believed and denies what is to be denied.*

15/3 Mr Peter Waters, rector of Wiston.[111] *Read over 23 November 1603.*

Personal response.

To material ex parte John Parker.

[*Identical to 15/2 above*]

15/4 Robert Slater.[112] *8 January 1604/5.*

Of Ashington cum Buncton, husbandman, where has lived about 2 years; before at Warminghurst about 12 years; before at Wiston about 9 years; before at West Grinstead; born there; aged about 47. Signature.

To the allegation

A1. That Mr Peter Waters is parson of Wiston before the beginning of this suit for he was present when he took possession of the church, which was about November last past. And he further saith that Mr John Woodcocke, clerk, was also present and did deliver him possession. *For the rest does not know.*

A2. That about Michaelmas in the year 1603, he being then receiver unto Sir Thomas Sherley, knight, of all his rents and tithes within Wiston for that year, Sir Thomas willed him to gather the tithes due unto the parson of Wiston according to a scroll which he gave unto him; which was only to receive of every man whose name was therein contained such sums of money as were also therein contained. And he willed him to pay unto Mr Waters £40 so soon as he could gather up the money specified in the scroll for tithes due for the year 1603. In so much that he gathered up so much money as he could gather* according to his master's command, which he did make up and pay unto Mr Waters £38; some part whereof he paid unto Mr Waters before the beginning of this suit and the residue hath paid unto Mr Waters since the beginning of this suit. And further saith that he hath known Sir Thomas Sherley to have received some tithe in kind as wheat, barley, peas, beans, oats, fatches [*sic*] or tares, hay and such like of Phillip Bennett, John Darkeing and John Bennett for their tithe corn and hay within the parish of Wiston where they occupied land for 16 years ago. And both they and some other [*sic*] hath paid the like tithe in kind ever since who have occupied the lands unto Sir Thomas; for he dwelling with Sir Thomas hath received the same tithes in kind to the use of Sir Thomas. And he further saith that one Thomas Willett of Wiston, upon some composition, did receive some tithes in kind, namely hay of one William Whitebreade of Ashurst who occupied one meadow or two about some 5 or 6 years ago. And

---

* *Deleted*: 'and made it up.'

Thomas Willett's father by virtue of the like agreement received the like tithe hay for 20 years ago last past. *For the rest does not know.*

A3. *Does not know.*

A4. *Does not know beyond what has already deposed.*

A5. *Does not know,* saving that John Willett in the year 1603 paid unto him tithe oats in kind viz two quarters, and in the same year he received of William Foster about some 12s for all his tithes. *For the rest does not know.*

A6. *Deposition is true.*

To the additional positions.

AP1. That Mr Byngham in his lifetime did covenant that Sir Thomas Sherley should enjoy the tithes of Wiston so long as he did pay yearly about 16 or 20 days after every quarter £5, and every year a quarter of wheat and a quarter of barley about Candlemas; and also that Sir Thomas should and might dispose of the tithes at his will and pleasure. *For the rest does not know.*

AP2-4. *Cannot depose beyond what has already deposed.*

AP4 [*recte* 5]. That he received all the tithes due unto Sir Thomas Sherley [of the said John]* Willett and William Foster due unto him at the feast of All Saints 1603.

AP6. *Does not know.*

AP7. *Does not know,* saving that he believeth Mr Waters doth or may enjoy the parsonage house of Wiston if he list.

AP8. *Cannot depose beyond what has already deposed.*

AP9. *Deposition is true*†.

15/5 John Styler.[113] *Read over 31 January 1604/5.*

Of Wiston, gentleman, where has lived about 8 years; before at Steyning about 12 years; before at Rusper; born there; aged about 60. Signature

A2. He knoweth not of any such demise or grant made unto Sir Thomas Sherley from Mr Waters and for his own part he utterly denieth that Mr Waters made any such grant, demise or composition unto him as is likewise specified in this article. And touching anything contained in this article he cannot depose because at that time and before he was out of Sir Thomas's favour; in respect whereof he hath never meddled with any of his business touching the parsonage of Wiston .

AP1. That Mr John Bingham did in his lifetime make some covenant or grant unto Sir Thomas Sherley for all or some of his tithes of Wiston; but what the covenant was he

---

* Crossed through but reinstated.

† After his deposition, the following two folios (ff 135-136v) are left blank, apparently for further depositions by Slater, who signs at the bottom of the blank f 136v.

cannot depose, for if there were any such made it was before he came to Wiston to dwell.

AP2 & 3. *Does not know,* saving that he hath heard some of the parishioners say as in this article is mentioned, and saving that some of the parishioners about some six or seven years ago did bring unto him some certain sums to the use of Sir Thomas Sherley, for the which he gave them acquittances as for tithes because they said the same money was for their tithes; but whether it was so he cannot depose. And further he saith that he was never authorised by Sir Thomas Sherley to receive the money, but when they paid he made them acquittances and paid him the money. And he further saith that some of the parishioners paid no money nor anything else in lieu of any tithes this nine or ten years last past. *For the rest does not know.*

AP5. *Cannot depose beyond what has already deposed,* saving that he is certain that he received no money of any of the parishioners this three years for any tithes due unto Sir Thomas Sherley nor in lieu of any tithes. Neither hath he ever since that dealt with them touching any such matter.*

* After his deposition, the following two folios (ff 144r-1145r) are left blank, apparently for further depositions by Styler, who signs at the bottom of f 144r and f 145r.

16/1 Thomas Goodwyn rector of Bepton v Edward Woldridge.* Tithe.[114]

Court acts: 27 September 1604 to 9 February 1604/5.

The rector of Bepton claimed payment in kind for honey from two hives sold by Woldridge to Robert Hitchecocke. The case probably has connections with case no. 19 below, where Thomas and Robert Hitchecocke were the plaintiffs, claiming parochial rights against the rector of Bepton. After Robert Hitchecocke had testified in Woldridge's case, Woldridge testified in the Hitchecockes'.

Hitchecocke made his deposition in this case shortly after the commencement of the second case. Although he had been called as a witness by Goodwyn, his deposition provided a forthright account of the disagreements between the two men. This may have effectively and rapidly ended the case: no other witness was called and the parties came to an agreement within ten days of Hitchecocke's appearance.

Goodwyn was rector of Bepton from 1602 until his death in 1607.

Proctors: Cooke for plaintiff; Barker for defendant. Examinations: personal response of defendant responding to additional positions of five articles; personal response of plaintiff responding to allegation of nine articles; one deposition for plaintiff responding to additional positions of six articles and interrogatories of twelve.

16/2 Edward Woldridge.[115] *Read over 24 January 1604/5.*

Personal response. Signs with mark.

To additional positions ex parte Mr Thomas Goodwyn

AP1. *That all his hives in parish of Bepton in years 1603 and 1604 mentioned in his reply to libel he sold to Robert Hitchecocke, and all in 1603 mentioned in his response he sold to Richard Wright of Elsted. For rest does not believe article to be true in anything.*

AP2. *That for the bees mentioned received sum of 6s. For rest does not believe article to be true in anything.*

AP3 & 4. *Does not believe article to be true in anything.*

AP5. *Believes what is to be believed and denies what is to be denied.*

16/3 Mr Thomas Goodwyn, rector of Bepton.[116] *Read over 26 Jan 1604/5.*

Personal response. Signature

To allegation ex parte Edward Weaver alias Woldridge

A1. That in 1602 he sold unto Edward Weaver alias Woldridge certain tithe corn within Bepton for £22. *For rest does not believe article to be true in anything other than he deposes below.*

A2. That he did take the £22 in full satisfaction of the tithe corn and grain. *For rest does not believe article to be true in anything.*

A3. *Believes it to be true.*

---

* The name occurs in several variants. This form has been adopted throughout.

A4. *Believes it to be true concerning small tithes. For rest does not believe article to be true in anything.*

A5. *That from the beginning up to the words* 'commonly reputed and taken' *he does not believe it to be true in anything. From thereon believes it to be true.*

A6. Believes that Robert Hitchecocke in 1604 did drive two of the beehives specified in some place within Bepton and had wax and honey. *For rest does not believe article to be true in anything.*

A7. Believes that before the beginning of this suit he was told by one of small credit that Edward Woldridge had sold unto Robert Hitchecocke certain stalls and hives of bees, and that he had driven the hives and had taken the honey and wax from them in 1604. *For rest does not believe article to be true in anything.*

A8. Believes that before the beginning of this suit Robert Hitchecocke did verbo tenus* tender unto him 16d for tithe honey and wax of two beehives which, as he said, he had bought of Edward Woldridge. *For rest does not believe article to be true in anything.*

A9. *Believes what is to be believed and denies what is to be denied.*

16/4 Robert Hitchecocke.[117] *Read over 30 January 1604/5.*

Of Linch Farm, yeoman, where has lived about 16 years; before at Farnham, Surrey; born there; aged about 45. Is worth £40. Signature.

To the additional positions to the libel.

AP1 & 2. That in harvest last past he did buy of Edward Woldridge two stalls of bees, for the which he did promise to pay 12s, and unto Mr Thomas Goodwyn the tithe of the two stalls of bees 16d; which Robert Hitchecocke according to his promise did tender unto Mr Goodwyn in lieu of his tithes. Which 16d Mr Goodwyn refused and said that he was to receive his tithes in honey and wax. Whereupon Robert Hitchecocke answered how could that be when he had bought the stalls of bees of Edward Woldridge for 13s 4d, viz either stall of bees 6s 8d, upon condition that he should pay unto Mr Goodwyn, out of the said 13s 4d, 16d in lieu of his tithes and no more in respect whether the property was altered and no tithes in kind was to be paid unto him. Then he answered that he was to have the same tithes in kind of Edward Woldridge. Whereunto Robert Hitchecocke answered as before, and further said unto Giles Bridger, John Sayer, Richard Martyn, Henry Packer, Edward Newton and others, all of Bepton, 'My masters, because Mr Goodwyn now being here present shall not object against me hereafter that I did not tender unto him 16d in the behalf of Edward Woldridge for his tithes of two stalls of bees which I bought, I pray now you bear witness that here is 16d in money in my hands ready for to deliver unto him for his tithes, which here before you all, being himself here present, he refuseth to receive.'

AP3. *Cannot depose beyond what has already deposed*, saving that he took away the two stalls of bees which he bought of Edward Woldridge rather after the usual time which men

* Orally

accustomably use to take away after the buying. In respect whereof the stall was not so good as he could have wished but that was his hindrance and no body's else.

AP4. That for the two stalls of bees he cannot depose what honey nor wax did come of them because he was not at the killing of the bees.

AP5. *Is not obliged to respond to the same* because that article is not yet admitted.

AP6. *Deposition is true.*

To the interrogatories

In 1. *Satisfactory.*

In 2 & 3. *Negative.*

In 4. *Favours parties indifferently and wishes victory for the party in the right;* and that he came to testify at the request of Mr Goodwyn and he will bear his charges; and that he is worth £40; *for the rest negative.*

In 5. *Does not know beyond what has already deposed.*

In 6 & 7. *Cannot depose beyond what has already deposed.*

In 8 & 9. *Affirms.*

In 10. *Cannot depose beyond what has already deposed,* saving that he verily believeth that Mr Goodwyn did refuse the 16d rather out of malice and evil will which he did bear towards Edward Woldridge.

In 11. *Does not know.*

In 12. That when Robert Hitchecocke bought the two hives or stalls of bees the bees were alive and better for store than to be killed; and might have been all the better kept all the next year after for store than killed. *And for the rest relating to Edward Woldridge, negative.*

17/1 Peter Betsworth of Kirdford v Edward Northe. Tithe.[118]

Court acts: 12 November 1604 – 8 June 1605, 5 October 1605.

Betsworth, probably the farmer of the Kirdford vicarial tithes, claimed tithe on crops on improved land. Waste or heath land had been 'devonshired', a process which involved clearing by burning followed by grubbing so that it converted to arable. The term here predates the earliest usage recorded in the OED. Unusually, the only witnesses were called by the defendant: they argued that no tithe could be claimed until seven years after the conversion.

The plaintiff petitioned for sentence in May 1605 but the court acts ceased in the following month, to be followed by a single but uninformative entry at Michaelmas.

Proctors: Barker (later Scales) for plaintiff; Cooke for defendant. Examinations: response by defendant to libel of eight articles; two depositions for defendant responding to allegation of six articles and interrogatories of nine.

17/2 Edward Northe.[119] 1 December 1604

Personal response. Signs with mark.

To libel ex parte Peter Betsworth

L1. *Believes article to be true as far as relates to 1604 and the month of that year. For rest does not believe article to be true in anything.*

L2 & 3. *Believes article to be true in respect of tithe in Kirdford,* saving tithe of all kind of corn upon barren waste as heath grounds until 7 years after the grubbing and first tillage. To which tithes excepted he doth not believe Peter Betsworth to have had any right to any of the tithe corn. *For rest does not believe articles to be true in anything.*

L4 & 5. Responds and believes that upon certain barren and heath grounds, which at Edward Northe's great cost and charges within these two or three years last past at the farthest, was devonshired, burned and grubbed in the year 1603, he had as much wheat as was worth 30s, as much rye as was worth 20s, and as many oats as was worth 10s. And in the year 1604 he had as much wheat as was worth 20s, as much rye as was worth 20s, and as many oats as was worth 10s. *For rest does not believe articles to be true in anything.*

L6. *Believes he was required to pay the tithes accepted by him in libel; and that he rightly refused to pay others for reasons given above.*

L7. *Believes he is of parish of Kirdford and subject to jurisdiction of court.*

L8. *Believes himself to be the party complained against on the part of Peter Betsworth, however unlawfully. Believes what he has stated above that he believes, and denies what he has denied.*

17/3 Richard Floate.[120] 15 February 1604/5

Of Kirdford, husbandman; born there; aged about 68 years. Is worth £6 13s 4d. Signs with mark

To the allegation ex parte Edward Northe.

A1-3. That Edward Northe hath for some six years occupied certain lands called Shillingly Park within the parish of Kirdford, which at his first occupation was only barren waste furres [furze] or heath grounds. But since about some three years ago Edward Northe, by his great charges and industry, hath grubbed and otherwise tilled the grounds that he hath brought the grounds to devonshiring, in so much that the same is now Upland ground and converted to sowing. And he further saith that he verily thinketh that some of the ground was converted to sowing about five or six years ago and not above; in respect thereof Mr Betsworth is not to have any tithe wheat, rye, oats or any other kind of grain upon the lands so grubbed and converted unto sowing ground until seven years after the first grubbing and sowing be expired. For he hath heard John Mills of Brahurste say, who occupieth the like lands under my lady of Arundel as well as Edward Northe, that he was in suit for the like tithes with the parson of Wisborough Green or his farmer; and the parson could not recover any tithes till seven years were first expired. And he further saith that John Lacker of Kirdford was likewise in suit with the parson of Kirdford not long since about the like tithes of corn upon the like barren heath and waste ground after the first grubbing and sowing thereof; and, as John Lacker told him, the parson could recover no tithe corn till seven years next after the grubbing.

A4. *Does not know beyond what has already deposed,* saving that he knoweth that Edward Northe had upon the grounds called Shillingly Park certain wheat, rye and oats in the years [*sic*] 1603 and he occupieth no lands elsewhere. *For the rest does not know.*

A5. *Refers to oath.*

A6. *Deposition is true.*

To the interrogatories.

In 1. *Satisfactory.*

In 2. *Negative.*

In 3. *Favours parties indifferently and wishes victory for the party in the right.*

In 4. *Is worth £6 13s 4d.* That he came to testify at the instant request of Edward Northe and he will bear his charges. *For the rest negative.*

In 5. That before the grubbing and sowing the occupiers did ordinarily and commonly feed and pasture upon the grounds their kine and bullocks and some sheep, the pasture of every cow being worth by the month 12d, every bullock 5d, and every score of sheep 6d and no more, by common estimation of men.

In 6. That he hath known Edward Northe mow some part of his ground as meadow ground every year since he occupied the same, which is about six years ago, and he had, one year with another, about some six loads of hay. *For the rest does not know.*

In 7. *Does not know,* saving that he thinketh the vicar of Kirdford receiveth the tithes.

In 8. That before the grubbing of the bushes, the bushes did grow very thick together, but now within this two years there groweth but few bushes, about half a score upon every acre one with another and a good way distant one from another, and they are but small bushes.

In 9. *Affirms* for this two or three years last past.

17/4 Robert Arnold.[121] [*February 1604/5*]

Of Kirdford, husbandman; where has lived about 20 years; before at Northchapel; born there; aged about 60. Is worth £40. Signs with mark.

A1-3. That at the first when Robert Arnold knew the lands called Shillingly Park the same was only a park and deer was pasturing there; but now of late within this 30 years last past the deer was took out and the wood thereupon growing cut down. In so much that afterwards the park was let to several men and so separated into fields. And some did grub their parts and converted to devonshireing and so ploughed and sowed the same with wheat, rye, oats and such like grain; and others employed their parts as themselves listed. In so much that Edward Northe, who hath occupied some part of the park this five or six years, hath devonshired, by little and little since he came to have some part of the lands, the most part of the said ground now in his occupation and grubbed the same. And afterwards he hath sown some part by his great industry, pains and charges with wheat rye, oats and such like kind of grain yearly; and he hath not occupied any of the said grounds above five or six years. In respect whereof he is not bound to pay unto Mr Betsworth anything for the tithe corn because the same was only barren waste or heath grounds before Edward Northe did devonshire, plough and sow the same with wheat, rye, oats and such like to his great charges.

In 4. …. That he came to testify at the instant request and charge of Edward Northe and he will bear his charges. *For the rest negative.*

In 5. That before the grubbing, devonshiring and ploughing there pastured ordinarily and commonly kine, bullocks and sheep, the pasture of every cow worth by the month 12d, and every bullock 6d, and every score of sheep 10d.

In 6. *Does not know,* saving that some part of the ground is here and there in some places mowed yearly. In so much that one or more of the occupiers may yearly mow and have, one year with another, as Edward Northe hath had, about four loads of hay upon the land in his occupation.

18/1 Nicholas Diggens, vicar of Stoughton v John Palmer. Church rights.[122]

Courts Acts: 28 July 1604 to 29 November 1605; 15 March 1605/6 to 17 May 1605; 29 September 1606 to 11 October 1606; 15 December 1607; 30 April 1608.

This lengthy case falls into several different stages. Up to November 1605 it followed a relatively normal course leading to sentence in favour of the plaintiff with the defendant ordered to pay costs. Between March and May 1606 further acts recorded an abortive attempt to appeal. Between September and October 1606 they recorded moves for the defendant's excommunication. December 1607 recorded his provisional absolution, but in April 1608 came the request for letters significatory for his arrest by the secular authorities as an excommunicate.

Palmer objected to the payment of mortuaries to the vicar on the death of a parishioner and to 'chrisom' payments associated with the churching of a mother after the birth of her child. In the first stage the plaintiff took the unusual steps of invoking records from the Dean and Chapter archives (extracted by the registrar, Richard Juxon) and of extracting wills of Stoughton residents named in the depositions.

Proctors: Barker (later Scales) for plaintiff; Cooke for defendant. Examinations: personal response by defendant to libel of 12 articles; depositions by five witnesses for plaintiff to articles 2, 3 and 10 of libel, with eight interrogatories.

Nicholas Diggens was ordained in 1574 and held the living of Stoughton from 1575 until his death in 1609. In March 1606 John Palmer was presented in the Office court for failure to receive communion.

18/2 John Palmer.[123] *Read over 15 December 1604.*

Personal response. Signs with mark.

To libel ex parte Nicholas Diggens.

L1. *Believes it to be true.*

L2 & 3. *Believes them to be true* saving only mortuaries or corse presents and excepting a chrisom, one loaf of bread and 2½d, for the churching of every woman after their childbirth. To which, tithes excepted, he does not believe Nicholas Diggens or any of his predecessors to have had due right or title or to have been in lawful possession of receiving, the said tithes excepted.

L4-7 *Believes them to be true.*

L8. *Refers to statute and for rest does not believe article to be true in anything.*

L9. *Believes it to be true.*

L10. *Does not believe article to be true in anything.*

L11. *Believes he is mere layman and has no rights in vicarage. Refuses to pay the mortuary or the chrisom 2½d and loaf of bread sought in the libel. For rest does not believe article to be true in anything.*

L12. *Believes himself to be the party complained against on the part of Nicholas Diggens, however unlawfully. Believes what he has stated above that he believes, and denies what he has denied.*

18/3 John Rasoll.[124] *[February 1604/5]*

Of Stoughton, husbandman; born there; aged about 60. Is worth £6 13s 4d. Signs with mark.

To the libel

L2. [*sic*] That he hath dwelt and been brought up in the parish of Stoughton all his life time, during all which he never heard nor knew that any parishioner did ever refuse to pay a mortuary or corse presents to the vicar of Stoughton. Neither did he ever know but that the vicar had always right to have and receive the mortuary according to the statute libellate as Mr Diggens hath at this present. And he further saith that he himself paid unto Mr Diggens 10s about 20 years ago for a mortuary due by the death of Julian Rasoll his mother. And as he thinketh every parishioner of Stoughton doth the like, for he never knew nor heard to the contrary all his lifetime till now John Palmer refuseth the payment thereof. And touching the rest of this article he cannot depose otherwise than he hath already deposed.

L3. *Affirms,* for anything he ever heard or knew to the contrary (except before excepted).

L10. [*sic*] *Does not know.*

To the interrogatories

In 1. *Satisfactory and responds negatively.*

In 2. *Is worth £6 13s 4d* and that he is a husbandman and thereby getteth his living.

In 3. That he came to testify at the charges and request of Mr Diggens without compulsion.

In 4. *Negative.*

In 5. *Cannot depose beyond what has already deposed.*

In 6. That the inventory of the goods of every party deceased, by reason of whose death any mortuary was paid to Mr Diggens or any of his predecessors, must extend unto £40 if they pay for the mortuary. And so consequently if the inventory extend to less they pay less.

In 7. *Does not know.*

In 8. That he never knew any householders deceased within the parish of Stoughton for whom no mortuaries have not been paid to Mr Diggens or his predecessors where mortuaries were due.

18/4 Joan Howcrofte.[125] *[February 1604/5]*

Of Stoughton, widow; born there; age 60 or more. Is worth £6 13s 4d. Signs with mark.

L2. That for all the time that she hath dwelt in the parish of Stoughton she never heard nor knew but that the vicars of Stoughton had always right to have all the small tithes and especially mortuaries or corse presents as Mr Diggens ought to have. She 34 years ago paid unto the vicar of Stoughton a mortuary due by the death of Francis Burrowe her husband; but who was then vicar of Stoughton she cannot now well remember. But she is sure that she paid either 10s or 6s 8d, but whether [*sic*] she cannot depose. And she thinketh that all the parishioners and householders within the parish doth pay the like, for she never heard that any refused till this time that John Palmer refused. And she further saith that she paid another mortuary due by the death of John Howcrofte her last husband for [*sic*] about four or five and twenty years ago; but whether she paid 10s or 6s 8d she cannot depose. And touching the chrisom, a loaf of bread and 2½d, she hath paid the same for 41 years ago and divers times since. And she never knew any woman within the parish but have paid the like at their churching or giving God thanks.

L3. *Affirms* that for any thing that she knew or heard until this suit begun.

L10. That the Chrisom cannot be less worth than 12d or some 8d or 6d and 2½d in money, and the loaf of bread was always accounted a halfpenny loaf. *For the rest does not know.*

In 1. *Satisfactory and responds negatively,* saving that Mr Diggens is indebted unto her some 2s.

In 2. *Is worth £6 13s 4d* and that she liveth by her lands.

In 3. That she came to testify at the instant request and charges of Mr Diggens without compulsion.

In 5. *Cannot depose beyond what has already deposed* because she taketh no great heed of other folks' matters.

18/5 Thomas Catcheler.[126] [*February 1604/5*]

Of Stoughton, husbandman; born there; aged 60 or more. Is worth £40. Signs with mark.

L2. That he never heard nor knew but that the vicars of Stoughton have always had right to have the small tithes and especially mortuaries as Mr Diggens ought to have. And he further saith that he for his own part about 25 years ago paid 6s 8d unto the farmer for a mortuary by the death of Julian Cathelove [*sic*] his mother. And all other householders payeth mortuaries unto the vicars of Stoughton for he never heard to the contrary till now that John Palmer refused to pay. And for the Chrisom, one loaf of bread and 2½d, he hath paid the sum himself or compounded eight several times at the churching or giving of thanks of his wife; and all other householders doth the like. And he further saith that the first Chrisom loaf of bread and 2½d that he paid is about 34 years ago.

L10. That every Chrisom one with another was worth 10d, and the loaf of bread was always accounted a halfpenny loaf.

In 3. That he came to testify at the instant request and charge of Mr Diggens without compulsion.

In 5. *Cannot depose beyond what has already deposed,* saving that Edward Catcheler, Thomas Catcheler's brother's son, paid a mortuary about 20 years ago due by the death of

William Catcheler, Thomas Catcheler's brother; but how much was paid he remembereth not.

18/6 Thomas Baylye.[127] [*February 1604/5*]

Of Stoughton, yeoman; born there; aged about 30. Is worth £40. Signs with mark.

L2. That he never heard nor knew but that the vicars of Stoughton had always right to have the small tithes and especially mortuaries or corse presents, for he about 12 years ago paid a mortuary by the death of Thomas Baylye his father, viz 10s. And touching the Chrisom, one loaf of bread and 2½d, he hath paid the same three times. And so, for anything that he hath heard to the contrary, the duties was never denied until this suit began. *For the rest does not know* because he never heard the like matter in question before; neither doth he use to look into other men's matters.

L10. That the Chrisom might be 6d and the loaf of bread was always accounted to be a halfpenny loaf.

In 1. *Satisfactory and responds negatively* saving that he renteth his own tithes that is due unto Mr Diggens.

In 3. That he came to testify at the request and charge of Nicholas Diggens without compulsion.

In 6. *Does not know,* saving that he thinketh his father's goods contained in his inventory did extend unto about 8 or 9 score pounds.

18/7 John Crowcher. [128] *Read over 21 February 1604/5*

Of Stoughton, husbandman; born there; aged about 46. Is worth £100. Signs with mark.

L2. That he never heard nor knew but that the vicars of Stoughton had always right to have the small tithes and especially mortuaries, for he hath heard his mother say, who is now living and four score years of age and upwards, that she paid a mortuary unto one Franckewelle, who was parson of Racton and had served the cure at Stoughton for one Mr Brighte who was then vicar of Stoughton for 30 years ago, due by the death of Thomas Crowcher his father, viz 10s. And he never heard to the contrary but every householder in the like case, or after the decease of any person by whose death a mortuary was due, did pay unto the vicar of Stoughton till this suit began. And otherwise he cannot depose because he neither maketh nor meddleth with other men's matters, saving that he heard his mother further say that she never heard nor knew but that mortuaries all her lifetime were always paid. And touching the Chrisom, one loaf of bread and 2½d, he cannot depose because he never had occasion to pay any.

L10. *Does not know* for the reasons aforementioned.

In 2. *Is worth £100* and that he is a husbandman and thereby getteth his living.

In 3. That he came to testify at the request and charge of Mr Diggens without compulsion.

19/1 Thomas and Robert Hitchecocke v Thomas Goodwyn, rector of Bepton: Rights to services and sacraments in Bepton church.[129]

Court acts: 8 December 1604 to 5 October 1605.

The case may be linked to no. 16 as Robert Hitchecocke (probably brother of Thomas) and Edward Woldridge appear as parties or deponents in both. The central issue was the state of the parish of Linch, which lies adjacent to Bepton. Throughout the 16th century no incumbent had been appointed; the parish church (which had stood close to Linch Farm) was in ruins, and so was the chapel of ease at Woodmans Green. The case reflects the antagonism between the inhabitants of Linch farm and the incumbent of Bepton. An arrangement, accepted in both places, had allowed the inhabitants of Linch Farm to regard Bepton as their parish church. Incidents in the office and instance courts, however, provide a confusing narrative of disagreement between the parties. In 1602, not long after Goodwyn's appointment to Bepton, Thomas Hitchecocke was presented for failing to attend service at Bepton. In December 1604 the Hitchecocke family, started instance proceedings after the rector of Bepton had presented them in the office court, on an unspecified complaint, earlier that month. Both parties accepted the fact that the inhabitants of Linch Farm had used Bepton church as their parish church; the grounds of Goodwyn's objections are not stated but it would appear that he was attempting to repudiate the arrangement. In the following month Robert Hitchecocke made his hostile deposition in the other case. The final proceedings in the present case seem to point in the Hitchecocke family's favour, despite the absence of a formal sentence; but surprisingly the office court, two years later in 1607, recorded Thomas Hitchecocke's unsuccessful attempt to avoid serving as churchwarden of Bepton - on the grounds that he was not 'of the parish'.*

In the proceedings the defendant did not make the normal personal response to the plaintiff's libel, but made two formal statements before the judge (recorded in the act book) – at the same time dispensing with the services of his proctor. Thereafter he failed to appear; the judge notified intention to sentence on behalf of the plaintiff; the defendant was pronounced contumacious; and the case expired in a few insignificant acts in the final two months.

Proctors: Barker for plaintiff; Cooke (briefly in February 1604/5) for defendant. Examinations and statements: two statements by defendant in response to libel; five depositions for plaintiff responding to libel of thirteen articles.

19/2 Thomas Goodwyn.[130] 16 Feb 1604/5

Response to libel made before the judge. Signature.

That the inhabitants of Linch Farm, time out of mind and exceeding the memory of man, have used to resort to Bepton Church to hear divine service and receive the sacraments of the parsons of Bepton; and that the parsons of Bepton have buried, christened and married in the church and churchyard the inhabitants of Linch Farm in such manner and form as they have used to bury, christen and marry their parishioners of Bepton. All which Thomas Goodwyn believeth to be true because he hath heard it reported by John Andrewe of Bepton who hath told him that his mother, being of the age of four score years at the time of her death, was born in Linch Farm and was christened in the church of Bepton; and told him moreover that the inhabitants of

---

* The situation did not alter until the church at Woodman's Green was rebuilt at the end of the 17th century.

Linch Farm time out of mind have resorted to the parish church of Bepton to hear divine service and receive the sacraments.

Statement accepted by proctor for plaintiff.

19/3 John Hull.[131] [*February 1604/5*]

Clerk, vicar of Boxgrove, where has lived about 23 years; before at West Dean about 7 years; before at East Marden about 7 years; before at Bepton about 20 years; before at Newton, Hampshire; born there; aged about 84. Signature.

To the libel.

L1. *Affirms.*

L2. That he hath known the inhabitants of the manor or farm commonly called Linch Farm for this 50 years last past to have right to hear divine service upon Sundays and festival days, and to receive the holy sacrament with their families and servants at the parish church of Bepton at the hands of the parson of Bepton together with the parishioners of Bepton (or at the hand of some other by his appointment because he was altogether absent and had the cure served by John Hull one while and by others at other times), as Thomas Hitchecocke, Robert Hitchecocke, Agnes Weller, Katheryn Hitchecocke and Martha Hitchecocke now inhabitants of the manor ought to resort to the church of Bepton. And he hath known one William White and Robert Clare who were inhabitants of Linch Farm for 37 years ago with their families and servants to do the like.

L3. *Affirms* for anything he knew to the contrary till now that this suit began.

L4. *Affirms,* saving that he cannot depose whether Mr Goodwyn hath buried or caused to be buried in the church or churchyard of Bepton all or some of the inhabitants in Linch Farm as often as they were brought unto him after their decease; nor for churching their wives, christening their children or administering the sacraments, because he doth not know Mr Goodwyn. But Mr Martin, who was parson there for 38 years ago [*sic*], and divers others before him, did perform all and everything mentioned in this article to the inhabitants of Linch Farm.

L5. *Does not know.*

L6. *Affirms* touching churching of their wives, receiving of the communion, christening of their children, burying their dead and paying their offerings as being parishioners of Bepton.

L7. *Article is true.*

L8. That he heard, when he was an inhabitant in Bepton, old and ancient men and women of Bepton say that time out of mind and exceeding the memory of man the inhabitants of Linch Farm have had right to hear divine service and receive the sacraments, and so have heard divine service and received the sacraments on Sundays and holy days and other days in the parish church of Bepton, and have had their wives churched, their children christened and their dead buried in the church and churchyard of Bepton, as namely one William Newton, late of Bepton deceased, and his wife, told the same to him (who was about three score years of age at John Hull's first coming to Bepton); and John Aylinge of hellon [*sic*] who was also three score years of age told him the like; and divers others.

L9. *Affirms from certain knowledge.*

L10. *Does not know* saving that he hath heard so since this suit began.

L11. *Does not know.*

L12. *Affirms.*

L13. *Deposition is true.*

19/4 Henry Voake.[132] [*February 1604/5*]

Of Harting, husbandman, where has lived about 4 months; before at Rogate about 11 years; before at Harting about 7 years; before at Bepton; born there; aged 60 or more. Signature.

L2. That for 42 years ago and before and since, he hath known the inhabitants of Linch Farm, as namely one Crowcher and others, commonly resort to the parish church of Bepton to hear divine service and receive the sacraments with their families and servants together with the parishioners of Bepton, as Thomas Hitchecocke, Robert Hitchecocke, Agnes Weller, Katheryn Hitchecocke and Martha Hitchecocke now inhabitants of the manor do at this present. But touching their right so to do he cannot depose. Yet he never knew nor heard but that the inhabitants of Linch Farm did always, time out of mind and exceeding the memory of man, hear divine service and receive the communion together with their family and servants at Bepton.

L3. *Affirms* touching their quiet possession of hearing divine service and receiving the sacraments; but touching their right cannot depose.

L4. *Affirms* till now that this suit began.

L8. *Does not know beyond what has already deposed,* saving that Crowcher who dwelt in Linch Farm about 42 years ago did always hear divine service and receive the sacraments, church his wife, christen his children, bury his dead and such like in the parish church and churchyard of Bepton. As one William White and Robert Clare being since inhabitants of Linch farm did since, and as Thomas Hitchecocke, Robert Hitchecocke, Agnes Weller, Katheryn Hitchecocke and Martha Hitchecocke now inhabitants in Linch farm do and did till the beginning of this suit. And he further saith he never heard nor knew to the contrary but that time out of mind and exceeding the memory of man the inhabitants of Linch farm did always resort to the parish church of Bepton.

19/5 William Newton.[133] [*February 1604/5*]

Of Midhurst, husbandman, where has lived about 3 years; before at Cocking about 8 years; before at Bepton; born there; aged about 60. Signs with mark.

L2. That he hath known the inhabitants of Linch Farm 50 years or thereabouts to use and resort to the parish church of Bepton to hear divine service with their families and servants and receive the holy communion together with the parishioners of Bepton, as namely the servants of one William Paye who about 50 years ago was farmer of Linch Farm; but Paye never dwelt there himself but occupied the said farm by his servants whereof William Newton was one. And he and his fellow servants, dwellers in the farm, did resort to the church of Bepton. And after William Paye left the farm, one Henry Byckley, gentleman, occupied the farm by his servants whereof William Newton was one; and he did likewise resort to the parish church of Bepton to hear divine service and receive the sacraments. And Mr John Hull now vicar of Boxgrove was curate in William Paye's days, and one [*blank*] Burton was after Mr Hull, and one Mr Martin was parson of Bepton afterwards, and one Mr James was parson of Bepton after him, and now Mr Goodwyn is parson. And he never heard nor knew never knew nor heard but the inhabitants of Linch Farm did always hear divine service and receive the communion at the hands of the parties aforenamed without contradiction till now that this suit began; and so always did time out of mind.

L8. That he hath heard Joan Andrewe say, who was wife unto John Andrewe who sometimes dwelt in Linch Farm, which Joan Andrewe was born in the farm and she was 75 years of age at her death, that the inhabitants of Linch Farm time out of mind did always resort to the parish church and did hear divine service and receive the sacraments upon Sundays and festival days and have their wives churched, their children christened and their dead buried. He hath also been told the like of his own father who was 60 years of age at his death, and also by his mother who was 80 years of age at her death. And he never heard of any man to the contrary.

19/6 Edward Woldridge.[134] 1 March 1604/5

Of Bepton, husbandman; born there; aged about 52. Signs with mark. *

L8. That he hath heard William Woldridge his father say, who was 87 years of age at his death, that he never heard nor knew but that inhabitants of Linch Farm ··· did always resort to the parish church of Bepton to hear divine service and receive the sacraments together with their families and servants, and have their wives churched, their children christened and their dead buried. And he never heard any of his forefathers or ancestors speak to the contrary.

19/7 John Andrewe.[135] *Read over 1 March 1604/5.*

Of Bepton, yeoman; born there; aged about 49. Signature.

---

* His name occurs in several variants. The form Woldridge has been adopted throughout.

L2. ··· that he hath known one William White who was an inhabitant in Linch Farm serve the office of churchwarden about 30 years ago, as other parishioners of Bepton did in like case. And Thomas Hitchecocke, Robert Hitchecocke, Agnes Weller, Katheryn Hitchecocke and Martha Hitchecocke now inhabitants in Linch Farm have right to hear divine service.

L8. That he hath heard Joan Andrewe his mother say, who was born at Linch Farm and was at her death 76 years of age, that she never knew any service said in the chapel at Linch but that always the inhabitants in Linch Farm time out of mind did resort to the parish church of Bepton ···; and he further saith that he hath heard his mother say that one William Crowcher her father, who was an inhabitant in Linch Farm about three score years ago, was chosen churchwarden of Bepton ···.

19/8 Thomas Goodwyn.[136] 2 March 1604/5

Response to libel made before the judge.

That time out of mind the inhabitants of Linch Farm have upon Sundays and holy days resorted to Bepton Church* ··· receive the sacraments and have their children ··· buried respectively in the church and ··· aforesaid in such manner and form as the parishioners ··· have used to do; and that he did complain to the judge ··· against Thomas Hitchecocke and others mentioned ··· resorting to the church of Bepton contrary to law.

Statement accepted by proctor for plaintiff.

---

* From this point in the deposition there are lacunae due to a damaged page.

20/1 Joan Gradell, widow and executrix of William Gradell decd. v William Gradell. Testamentary. [137]

Court acts: 23 March 1604/5 to 13 July 1605.

William Gradell, junior, the son of William Gradell, vicar of Binsted, disputed the making of his will. The will[138] *was proved on 7 March 1604/5 and left substantial bequests to his other children, Joan and Fortunatus. To William he left a cow, a calf and a mare 'provided that if he be not content with that he shall have nothing.' After the depositions were made, William objected to the witnesses but did not pursue his objections; the judge gave sentence for the plaintiff.*

Proctors: Cooke for plaintiff; Barker (later Scales) for defendant. Examinations: two depositions for plaintiff responding to allegation with will annexed of six articles, with interrogatories of nine.

20/2 David Prichard.[139] [*May-June 1605*]

Of Yapton, schoolmaster, where has lived one month; before at Tortington about 1½ years; before at Yapton about 1½ years; before at the University of Oxford 13 years; before at Anglesey in county of Anglesey; born there; aged about 40. Is worth £6 13s 4d. Signature.* †

To the allegation and testament

A 1. That Mr William Gradell the elder the 22 day of February last past, being then sick in body but perfect of remembrance, sent one Joseph his manservant unto David Prichard at Yapton to will him to come unto him to speak with him. And so soon as Joseph came he presently went along with him to the house of Mr Gradell at Binsted, at which his coming, he found Mr Gradell sick in his bed in an upper chamber. And seeing him sick in his bed he demanded of William Gradell the occasion why he sent for him. Then William Gradell said that he sent for him to make his will and then, his wife being present he willed his wife to reach unto David Prichard a book which did lie upon a close bench wherein there was some white paper. Which done there was not white paper enough whereupon to write his will; in so much that David Prichard was glad to go to Yapton to fetch a sheet of white paper. And at his return to Binsted William Gradell was gotten up and sitting in a wicker chair by the fireside in the chamber; and when David Prichard was with him, William Gradell took a testament or will by him formerly made and willed him to write after the same will word for word in manner and form as the same was written in the preface. And when he had written until he came to the first legacy then William Gradell, being of perfect mind and memory, willed him to write, from his own mouth and of his own accord without the persuasion of any other, every legacy contained and specified in the will now exhibited in this court whereupon he is now examined, seen and perused by him at the time of his examination. And William Gradell did of his own accord give and bequeath all the legacies as in the will exhibited; and he did constitute Joan Gradell his wife his sole executrix. All which he knoweth to be true because he writ the same will from the mouth of William Gradell. And he further saith that William Gradell was of perfect

---

* Anglice [*twice in MS*].

† Despite his time in Oxford he was not a graduate and was described as 'literatus'. (Ep I/17/10 ff 168v, 185v; STC III/E f 25v.) He was licensed to teach grammar and letters in Yapton in 1602.

mind and memory because he could speak plainly and sensibly and declare every gift mentioned in his will of himself; and for anything David Prichard could perceive he was then of as perfect memory as he ever see [*sic*] him.

A 2. That the testament was put in writing by the appointment of William Gradell and after the writing thereof publicly read unto him by David Prichard. And after the reading he said the will was well, and presently called David Prichard for pen and ink and set his hand thereunto as a witness and write himself the writer thereof; which he did. But when he read the will there were nobody present save David Prichard; only neither did William Gradell in express words acknowledge the same for his last will and testament save only he said when he set his hand thereunto, 'Well that's for me. I pray you set your hand unto it and write David Pritchard the writer hereof'; which he did accordingly. Then William Gradell said that that day soon at night he would send to Henry Page to put his hand unto the will and be a witness thereunto. *For the rest does not know.*

A 3-5. *Does not know beyond what has already deposed.*

A6. *Deposition is true.*

To the interrogatories

In 1. *Satisfactory.*

In 2. *Favours parties indifferently and wishes victory for the party in the right. For the rest negative,* saving that now and then that he did read prayers for William Gradell sometimes at Tortington and sometimes at Binsted

In 3. *Is worth £6 13s 4d. For the rest negative*

In 4. That he cometh to testify at the instant request and charge of Joan Gradell. F*or the rest negative.*

In 5. That William Gradell did make his last will and testament of his own accord without the persuasion or enticement of any other. *For the rest does not know.*

In 6. That he knoweth of no suggestion or report given by any against William Gradell.

In 7. That William Gradell lived 5 days after the making of the will; and he knoweth of no signs or tokens of lightness or distemper that he used at all, of light memory or understanding, in his lifetime.

In 8. That he did see William Gradell set his hand unto the will and did give him pen and ink so to do; and he did read all the will unto William Gradell before he set his hand thereunto.

In 9. *Does not know beyond what has already deposed.*

20/3 Henry Page.[140] [*May-June 1605*]

Of Binsted, husbandman, where has lived about 16 years; before at Tortington about 2 years; before at Madehurst; born there; aged about 40. Is worth £20. Signs with mark.

A 1-5. That in February last David Prichard of Yapton, schoolmaster, came unto the house of Henry Page in Binsted and told him that he should go up to William Gradell's house to be witness unto his will. Whereupon he the very same day went unto the house. At which his coming he found William Gradell sick in his bed in an upper chamber; and after some communication first he willed Joan his wife to reach him his will which was in a coffer in the room where he then did lie; which his wife did accordingly. Then William Gradell willed him to set his hand thereunto as a witness. Then he took the same will which is now exhibited into this court in his hands and set his hand thereunto; and after he began to read and before he had read about a twelve lines William Gradell said unto his wife, 'Joan, Goodman Page will see what money I have given', whereupon he left reading of the will any further; but he is sure that this will now exhibited, seen and perused by him at the time of his examination, is the very will which William Gradell willed him to set his hand unto. And he further saith that at that time William Gradell was of perfect mind and memory, for he spoke well and sensibly and bid his wife fetch his will and said Henry Page would see what money he had given. And by reason of all which he believeth he was of perfect mind and memory.

In 4. That he came to testify at the instant request and charges of Joan Gradell. *For the rest negative.*

In 5. *Does not know* saving that he thinketh that William Gradell did make his will of his own accord without the persuasion of any other. *For the rest does not know.*

In 6. That he knoweth not any that suggested any report given against William Gradell.

In 7. *Does not know beyond what has already deposed,* saving that William Gradell lived three or four days after the making of his will.

21/1 Charity Chandler, widow and executrix of William Chandler of Midhurst v William and Ralph Chandler, paternal uncles of William Chandler. Testamentary.[141]

Court acts: 8 June 1605 to 28 September 1605.

A transaction to prove William Chandler's will 'in form of law' * *rather than 'common form', as a means of protecting the executrix against objections from other near members of kin, represented by the uncles. The will left property to the executrix and her heirs; the testator had expressed fears 'lest any of his kindred should murmur'. The depositions established that the will was properly executed. The defendants failed to appear after the initial hearing, and probate was granted on 10 October 1605.*[142]

Proctors: Scales for plaintiff. Examinations: four depositions for plaintiff responding to allegation of five articles with will annexed.

21/2 Edward Mason.[143] *Read over 28 June 1605.*

Of Farnham [Fernhurst?] in Sussex, yeoman, where has lived for about 30 years; before at Sleaford, Lincolnshire about 9 years; before at Musgrave in Westmorland; born there; aged 55. Signature.

To the allegation

A1. That William Chandler, the testator, being of perfect mind and memory did upon the 4th day of May 1605 make and declare his last will and testament as is now exhibited seen and perused by Edward Mason at the time of his examination, and whereunto he set his hand. And William Chandler did bequeath every legacy in the will contained of his own accord without the persuasion of any other person whatsoever. And of the will he did appoint Charity Chandler his wife his sole executrix. And he further saith that William Chandler was at the making of the will of perfect mind and memory for he spoke perfectly well and was able to deliver everything from his own mouth of his own accord. And further William Chandler told him that about the very age that he the testator was his father deceased; and also William Chandler requested him to call Robert Billinghurst unto him for he would gladly have him present; and said that he knew that he could fetch him sooner than any of his servants. By reason of which speeches he verily believeth that he was of perfect mind and memory.

A2. That the will was put in writing by Mr Constantine Harman, clerk, by the appointment of William Chandler, and after the writing was publicly read unto him by Mr Harman in the presence of Constantine Harman, Robert Billinghurst, Ellis Hames and Edward Mason.

A3. That William Chandler after the reading of the will did acknowledge the same will now exhibited to be his last will and testament; and for the better proof thereof set to his hand and seal.

A4. *Does not know beyond what has already deposed.*

A5. *Deposition is true.*

---

* See Introduction: Testamentary, Wills and Probate.

21/3 Constantine Harman.[144] *Read over 28 June 1605.*

Clerk, of Midhurst, where has lived 12 years or more; before at Warminster, Wiltshire, about 4 years; before at Wimbledon, Surrey, about 20 years; before at Burton on Trent, Staffordshire; born there; aged about 60. Signature

A1. That William Chandler, the testator, upon the 4th day of May last being of perfect mind and memory did make and declare his last will and testament, as the will exhibited which is written with Constantine Harman's own hand, seen and perused by him at the time of his examination. And that William Chandler of his own accord without the persuasion of any other person whatsoever did bequeath every legacy unto such persons as is also specified. And of the will he did appoint Charity Chandler his wife his sole executrix. And he further deposeth that William Chandler at the writing and making of his will was of perfect mind and memory, for he spoke well and perfectly and was able to deliver every legacy from his own mouth; and at the reading thereof he willed him to read aloud with a good voice. By reason of which speeches he verily believeth that William Chandler was of perfect mind and memory.

21/4 Ellis Hames.[145] *Read over 10 July 1605.*

*Of Midhurst, yeoman, where has lived about 11 years; before at Chichester; born there; aged about 38. Signature.**

A1. That William Chandler the testator did make his last will and testament the 4th day of May, which is the very will now exhibited into this court whereunto Ellis Hames hath set his hand as a witness. And by the same he did give every legacy of his own accord without the persuasion of any other. And William Chandler was of perfect mind and memory for he spoke perfectly and well and called unto Ellis Hames for a glass of beer which he delivered unto him, and he drank thereof and took Ellis Hames the glass again to set up, and called him by his name and all others there present by their names. And he told everyone there present that he sent for them to be witnesses unto his will; and he further said unto the witnesses that he made full account that he should not escape his sickness, wherefore he requested that they would not disclose what was written in his will until after his departure lest any of his of his kindred should murmur at the same. In respect whereof he verily believeth that he was of perfect mind and memory.

21/5 Robert Billinghurst.[146] *Read over 11 July 1605.*

Of Midhurst, yeoman, where has lived about 25 years; before at Chiddingfold, Surrey; born there; aged about 55. Signature [Robert Billinghurst]†

A1. That the testator William Chandler being of perfect mind and memory did make and declare his last will and testament the 4th day of May last past ···. And that he was of perfect mind and memory at the making of the will for he said, 'Mr Billinghurst give

---

* Also an apparitor of the court.

† The signature uses this form of the surname. Elsewhere it often appears as Billingshurst(e).

me your hand, I have sent for you to see my will finished.' For he did then say he could not live long and further said that he had given the tenement wherein he dwelt to his wife. Whereupon he asked, 'What for term of her life?' and he answered, 'No to her heirs forever for she is the best worthy of it.' And further William Chandler said unto him that he would request him to be one of his overseers and that he should lose nothing thereby. And the will being all finished William Chandler bid Mr Harmon the writer thereof read out lustily. And William Chandler spoke very perfectly and well: by reason of all which he believeth he was of perfect mind and memory.

22/1 Katheryn Squier, wife of Richard Squier of Eastergate v Edward Duffeild of Aldingbourne. Defamation.[147]

Court acts: 8 June 1605 to 2 November 1605.

Although the case was brought to reject the assertion that Katheryn Squier was a whore, the depositions by the three male witnesses all focus on the statement that her husband was a cuckold. The case proceeded rapidly through an unusually small number of sessions; and the judge gave sentence for the plaintiff. Although the defendant gave notice of appeal, there is no indication that it was pursued. Duffeild probably had a poor local reputation: he was presented in the office court for failure to attend church and receive communion, and for failure to maintain the churchyard.

The close similarity of the witnesses' statements – especially in the near verbatim narratives of the incident – is striking. To demonstrate this, substantial portions have been retained below rather than omitted.

Proctors: Cooke for plaintiff; Scales for defendant. Examinations: three depositions for plaintiff responding to libel of nine articles and thirteen interrogatories.

22/2 John Dowse.[148] [*Read over 8 July 1605*]

Of Tangmere, husbandman, where has lived one year and six months; before at East Dean about 14 years; before at Boxgrove; born there; aged about 24. Is worth £30. Signs with mark.

To the libel.

L1. *Refers to oath.*

L2. That upon the 1st day of May last past being Sunday, he being upon some occasion of business together with divers others at the house of one [*blank*] Hubberde who keepeth a victualling house at Eastergate, he heard Edward Duffeild call Richard Squier 'A cuckoldy knave and a cuckoldy fool', and that he would prove him a cuckoldy fool: meaning thereby that Katheryn Squier wife of Richard Squier was and is a whore and hath committed adultery or fornication since she was married to him. And that after the words were so uttered Edward Duffeild went forth of the house and came in again; and then being demanded by Richard Squier whether he would stand to the words, he answered that Richard Squier was so and that he would justify the same to be true. All which speeches were so spoken by Edward Duffeild against Richard Squier in the presence of Thomas Floate, William Upfull, William Squier, Thomas Swayne, John Dowse, John Skerle, Richard Foake and divers others.

L3. That both at the uttering of the words of defamation and long before, Richard Squier and Katheryn Squier were man and wife and so commonly reputed and taken.

L4. That by the common interpretation of men he is called a cuckold, a cuckoldy knave or a cuckoldy fool whose wife has committed adultery or fornication and for such a one commonly reputed and taken and not otherwise.

L5. *Does not know beyond what has already deposed.*

L6. *Affirms,* for by reason of Edward Duffeild's speeches, the same speeches are now rehearsed and spoken by divers.

L7. *Affirms.*

L8. *Refers to oath.*

L9. *Deposition is true.*

To the interrogatories

In 1 & 2. *Does not know beyond what has already deposed.*

In 3. *Does not know beyond what has already deposed,* saving that the words were spoken about six or seven of the clock in the afternoon.

In 4. *Does not know beyond what has already deposed,* saving that the words were spoken in the hall of the house.

In 5 & 6. *Negative.*

In 7. *Wishes victory for the party in the right.*

In 8. That the words of defamation by him formerly deposed were spoken by Edward Duffeild in manner and form as he hath deposed; but he doth not believe them to be true.

In 9. By reason of the speeches there is a fame within the parish of Eastergate that Edward Duffeild uttered such words.

In 10. That he came to testify at the request of Richard Squier.

In 11. That he heard the words spoken *openly and not by hearsay.*

In 12. *Negative,* saving that he is a friend unto Richard Squier and Katheryn his wife, even as he is to Edward Duffield and all others that giveth him no other occasion but to be friends with them.

In 13 *Is worth £30.*

22/3 Thomas Floate.[149] [*Read over 8 July 1605*]

Of Tangmere, tailor, where has lived about 15 years; before at Boxgrove about 2 years; before at Oving about 7 years; before at Storrington; born there; aged about 46. Is worth £6 13s 4d. Signs with mark.

L2. That in May last past so near as he can remember, but the very day he cannot now remember saving that it was upon a Sunday, he being then in the house of one [*blank*] Hubberde who keepeth a victualling house at Eastergate together with others of his friends conferring together, he heard Edward Duffeild call Richard Squier 'a cuckoldy knave and a cuckoldy fool' and that he would prove him a cuckoldy fool meaning thereby that Katheryn Squier wife of Richard Squier was and is a whore and hath committed adultery or fornication since she was married to him. And afterwards Edward Duffeild, being asked by Richard Squier whether he would justify the words, said yes that he would approve them to be true. All which words were so spoken by Edward Duffeild against Richard Squier in the presence of William Upfull, William

Squier, Thomas Swayne, Richard Foake, John Skerle, John Dowse, Thomas Floate and divers others.

L3. *Affirms from his certain knowledge,* for he was present at their marriage.

In 2 & 3. *Does not know beyond what has already deposed,* saving that the words was uttered about the hour of six or seven of the clock in the afternoon.

In 4. That the words were uttered in the hall of the house and also without doors near the house of Hubberde.

In 8. *Does not know,* saving that the words of defamation are not true although Edward Duffeild said he would prove them to be true.

In 10. That he came to testify at the request of Richard Squier.

In 11. That he heard the words spoken *openly and not by hearsay.*

In 12. *Negative,* saving that he is a friend and wellwisher unto Richard Squier and Katheryn his wife, as he is to Edward Duffield and all others in matters of equity and right, as one neighbour should be to another.

22/4 William Upfull.[150] *Read over 8 July 1605.*

Of Tangmere, husbandman; born there; aged about 27. Is worth £6 13s 4d. Signs with mark.

L2. That upon the first day of May last past being Sunday, he being then in the house of one [*blank*] Hubberde who keepeth a victualling house in Eastergate with other his friends, he heard Edward Duffeild call Richard Squier 'Cuckold, cuckoldy knave and a cuckoldy fool' and that he would prove him a cuckoldy fool: meaning thereby that Katheryn Squier now wife of Richard Squier was and is a whore and hath committed adultery or fornication since she was married to him. And Edward Duffeild being asked by Richard Squier whether he would justify the words said yes he would justify them and approve them too. All which speeches were spoken by Edward Duffeild against Richard Squier in the presence of William Squier, Thomas Swayne, Richard Foake, Thomas Floate, John Skerle, John Dowse, William Upfull and divers others.

L3. *Affirms from his certain knowledge,* for he was present at their marriage.

In 1-4. *Does not know beyond what has already deposed,* saving that the words were uttered betwixt the hours of seven and eight of the clock in the afternoon both in the hall of the house and without doors near unto the house of Hubberde.

In 8. *Does not know beyond what has already deposed,* saving that he doth not believe the words of defamation are true although he said he would prove them to be true.

In 9. That there cannot but be a fame within the parish of Eastergate that Edward Duffeild did utter such words of defamation; but there is no fame that the same words are true.

In 10. That he came to testify at the request of Richard Squier.

In 11. That he heard the words spoken *openly.*

In 12. *Negative,* otherwise than he is a friend to any other.

23/1 Margaret Palmer alias Lodger, mother of William Lodger of Up Marden deceased, v Arthur Lodger brother of deceased. Testamentary. [151]

Court acts: 28 September 1605 to 29 November 1605.

A transaction probably intended to prove William Lodger's will 'in form of law' * *rather than 'common form', as a means of protecting the executrix, his mother, against objections from other near members of kin, represented by Lodger's brothers, who had been given only token bequests. The depositions established that the will was properly executed. Sentence was given for the plaintiff on 20 November 1605; and the defendants announced their intention to appeal.*

Office court proceedings against Arthur Lodger for living with another man's wife suggest that there may have been tensions between him and his brother and mother. The diocesan probate records include the will of a William Lodger of Up Marden, proved on 3 December 1605. It is undated and the content does not accord with the details contained in the depositions and court acts. † *At this period there were a number of Lodger families in the parishes of Up Marden, Stoughton and Compton; but the parish register entries are incomplete and no burial entry for a William Lodger around July 1605 has been found. However, a will of William Lodger was proved in the Prerogative Court of Canterbury on 6 February 1605/6 and matches the details given in the depositions.*[152] *It was proved by the executrix, his mother, Margaret Palmer. Although the relevant Court of Arches records have not survived, we must assume that the appeal went forward and that the sentence in favour of the executrix was upheld.*

Proctors: Scales for plaintiff; Cooke for defendant. Examinations: three depositions for plaintiff responding to allegation of five articles with will annexed, and interrogatories of seventeen.

23/2 Mark Apitt.[153] [*October 1605*]

Of Up Marden, yeoman, where has lived about 11 years; before at Harting; born there; aged about 43. Is worth £40. Signature 'Marke Pytte'.

To the allegation and the testament.

A1. That William Lodger being of perfect mind and memory did make and declare his last will and testament the 17th day of July last past, which is the very will exhibited into this court seen and perused by Mark Apitt. And by the will did give every legacy unto such person or persons as in the same will is specified of his own accord, without the persuasion of any person; and of the will he did appoint Margaret Palmer his mother his whole and sole executrix. And that William Lodger at the time of making his will was of perfect mind and memory for he did name every particular person unto whom he gave anything, and told Mr Diggens the writer of his will what he would give to everyone, and spoke plainly and well. And he gave no sign by idle talk nor otherwise of evil memory; by reason of all which he verily believeth that William Lodger was of perfect mind and memory at the time.

---

* See Introduction: Testamentary, Wills and Probate.

† The testator asks to be buried at Stoughton; the brothers Arthur and Richard are not mentioned as beneficiaries; Margaret, the executrix and prover, of the will is described as wife and relict; Diggens and the Apitts are not mentioned; there is no bequest to the poor; and the witnesses are John Smith and Richard Lodger. (WSRO STC I/15/225)

A2. That the will exhibited was put in writing by the commandment of William Lodger by Mr Nicholas Diggens, vicar of Stoughton, and by him publicly read unto him in the presence of Margaret Apitt (Mark Apitt's wife), Mr Diggens and Mark Apitt.

A3. That after the reading of the will unto William Lodger he did acknowledge the same for his last will and testament; and for the better proof thereof set his mark thereunto in the presence of Mr Nicholas Diggens, Mark Apitt and Margaret Apitt.

A4. *Does not know beyond what has already deposed.*

A5. *Deposition is true.*

To the interrogatories

In 1. *To the danger of perjury and the penalty of false witness, negative.*

In 2. *Is worth £40*; and that he is a husbandman and liveth by occupying a farm which he renteth.

In 3. That he came to testify at the request of Margaret Palmer.

In 4. *Favours parties indifferently and wishes victory for the party in the right.*

In 5. That William Lodger gave by the will unto Margaret Apitt 20s, and unto Nicholas Diggens a witness in this cause 3s 4d, and unto Mark Apitt 3s 4d. And that is all that he and his wife receive by the same will howsoever. But he would not depose an untruth touching this matter for all that William Lodger did give by his will.

In 6. *Negative.*

In 7. That the will was made and written the 17th day of July last past about nine of the clock at night in the hall of the house of William Lodger, in the presence of Nicholas Diggens the writer thereof, Mark Apitt and Margaret Apitt. *For the rest does not know*

In 8. That the will exhibited was made in writing in the lifetime of the testator and by his appointment and not after his decease; and the will was written by Mr Nicholas Diggens, clerk, by the direction and from the mouth of William Lodger.

In 9. That the testament was all written at one time and in one place.

In 10. That the will exhibited is the original will.

In 11. That the testament was read unto the testator by Mr Diggens only once, in the presence of Mark Apitt and Margaret Apitt and Nicholas Diggens; and after the reading he did ratify and confirm the same, and did subscribe his mark thereunto by saying that he did acknowledge the same for his last will and testament.

In 12. That William Lodger did make his will of his own accord without the persuasion of any other.

In 13. That William Lodger was lying in his bed when the will was writing, saving that at some times he did sit up in his bed. And he had a fustian doublet on when he did sit up. *For the rest does not know.*

In 14. That he verily believeth that William Lodger at the making of his will was of perfect memory because he spoke sensibly and as well as Mark Apitt can speak now at his examination, and because he showed no evil sign to the contrary, and because twice or thrice he willed Margaret Palmer his mother to be good to the poor over and above that which he had given them.

In 15. *For himself negative. For the others does not know.*

In 16. That he did not hear William Lodger in his last sickness once so much as name Arthur Lodger or his brother Richard Lodger or any other of his kindred to be sent for to come unto him in his sickness.

In 17. *Does not know.*

23/3 Nicholas Diggens.[154] [*October 1605*]

Clerk, vicar of Stoughton, , where has lived for about 26 years; before at Birdham for about one year; before at Elsted; born there; aged about 60. Is worth £6 13s 4d. Signature.

A1. That William Lodger sent for Nicholas Diggens the 17th day of July last past to come unto him, he being sick in body but of perfect mind and memory. At which his coming he requested Nicholas Diggens to make his will which he did accordingly; and, of his own accord and mere motion without the persuasion of any other, did make and ordain his last will and testament and did give every legacy unto such persons as in the same are specified. Which will is the very absolute and true will now exhibited, written by Nicholas Diggens with his own hand by the appointment of William Lodger and by him seen and perused. And of the will William Lodger did appoint Margaret Palmer his mother his sole and only executrix. And that William Lodger was of perfect mind and memory at the making his will for he was able to deliver of himself every legacy to every person and to name them; and he spoke sensibly and well and he did make no evil sign at all of light memory. In respect of all which he believeth that William Lodger was then of perfect memory as he Nicholas Diggens was and is at the time of his examination.

In 2. ··· he is a minister, and by the profit of his vicarage he liveth and maintaineth himself and his charge.

In 3. That he came to testify at the request of Margaret Palmer.

In 5. That this business doth not any way concern him directly nor indirectly, saving that the testator gave him 3s 4d by this will and saving that he writ the will; and for other profit or gain he shall reap none nor lose nothing howsoever this suit goeth. And for Mark Apitt the other witness there is 20s given unto his wife and 3s 4d unto him and that is all that they shall reap by the will howsoever. *For the rest does not know.*

In 7. That William Lodger did make his will the 17th day of July last past about nine of the clock at night in the hall of the house, and did give everything therein contained, in the presence of Mark Apitt and Margaret Apitt his wife and Nicholas Diggens.

In 11. That the will was once read unto the testator by Nicholas Diggens and no more; and after the reading thereof William Lodger did acknowledge the same by these words, 'I acknowledge this will to be my last will and testament.' And before the ratifying of the will and for the better proof thereof he set his mark thereunto. All which subscribing of his mark was done by William Lodger in the presence of Mark Apitt and Margaret Apitt his wife and Nicholas Diggens.

In 14. That the testator at the making of his will was of perfect memory for he was able to deliver his mind as sensibly and as well as Nicholas Diggens is now. For he gave no evil sign of light memory at all but gave all good signs of good memory; for twice or thrice he prayed his mother to be good unto the poor over and above that which he had given unto them.

In 16. That William Lodger in his last sickness and at the time of making his will did say that he would give, and so did give, unto Arthur Lodger and Richard Lodger both his brothers 12d apiece and no more. For, said William Lodger, they nor either of them ever came to see him in his sickness, and that they were better able to live than he. But Nicholas Diggens never heard that William Lodger did will that either or any other of his kindred were willed to be sent for in his sickness. *For the rest does not know.*

23/4 Margaret Apitt.[155] *Read over 19 October 1605.*

Wife of Mark Apitt of Up Marden, where has lived about 10 years; before at Westbourne; born there; aged about 50. Signs with mark.

A1. That Margaret Apitt divers times was sent for by William Lodger to come and visit him in his sickness, and that upon the 17th day of July last past she being at the house of William Lodger, the testator being sick in body but of good and perfect remembrance made his last will in the presence of Mr Nicholas Diggens, vicar of Stoughton, Mark Apitt, Margaret Apitt's husband, and Margaret Apitt, which is the very will now exhibited into this court seen and read unto her. By which he did will and bequeath every legacy unto such persons appointed of his own free will and without the compulsion of any other person; and of the will he did appoint Margaret Lodger alias Palmer his mother whole and sole executrix. And that he at the time of making his will was of perfect mind and memory for he spoke as plainly and sensibly as she can now speak, and he was able to render an answer of anything that was asked him well and sufficiently; and he made no sign of evil remembrance. By reason of all which she believeth he was of perfect mind and memory.

In 2. That she is worth nothing of her own proper goods because as yet she hath a husband.

In 3. That she came to testify at the request of Margaret Lodger alias Palmer without compulsion.

In 5. That there is given by this will unto her 20s; and to Mark Apitt 3s 4d; and to Mr Diggens 3s 4d; otherwise it doth neither directly nor indirectly concern her nor her husband nor Mr Diggens.

In 11. That the will was but once read unto the testator by Mr Diggens and then William Lodger did ratify the same and did subscribe his name and said that the same was his last will, and delivered the same to Margaret Lodger alias Palmer.

In 14. That William Lodger both at the making of his will and at the subscribing was of as perfect mind and memory as Margaret Apitt.

In 16. That she did never heard William Lodger make any motion in his last sickness that his brother Arthur or his brother Richard should be sent for; neither doth she know the reason why they were not sent for.

24/1 Mr Samuel Todd, rector of East Wittering v John Newe. Tithe. [156]

Court acts: 28 June 1605 to 22 March 1605/6.

The plaintiff claimed great tithes from Weekelands and Stubcrofte Farm as well as three minor customary items. Tithe on hay and coppice wood had been paid to Birdham parish. The claim initially extended to another property, Cunny's, but this was excluded after the defendant made a payment of 10s. The defendant produced three witnesses; after their examination the case continued but without significant acts for four months before it lapsed.

The case is paralleled by no 26, Todd v Rablis, below, where two of Newe's witnesses were called by the defendant. An unusual element in both cases was the fact that depositions were produced for the defendant but not for the plaintiff. This reinforces the impression that Todd was an unpopular incumbent: he was presented in the office court for adultery and for a number of failures in his parish duties. A further case, Todd v Busby started at the same time but lapsed almost immediately, producing no depositions.

Proctors: Scales for plaintiff; Cooke for defendant. Examinations: three depositions for defendant responding to allegation of one article and interrogatories of 12.

Samuel Todd, MA, was ordained in 1581 and held the living of East Wittering from 1600 until his death in 1613.

24/2 William Rumbridger.[157] [*November 1605*]

Of East Wittering, yeoman, where has lived about 50 years; before at Birdham; born there; aged about 54.

Signs with mark (initials).

To the allegation

A1 That for this 40 years ago last past William Rumbridger, going at that time to school with Sir Christopher Raye then parson of East Wittering and also dwelling with him, he heard Sir Christopher Raye say that he never had any tithes in kind upon Weekeland save only when the land was eared,* ploughed and sowed, at which time he had tithe corn; but otherwise he never received any other tithes upon Weekeland save only when the same was sowed. Saving also that Sir Christopher Raye then said that he received yearly out of the farm called Stubcrofte Farm one lamb at or after the feast of St Mark the Evangelist, one fleece of wool at Sheartide, and one cheese at Michaelmas or thereabouts in lieu of all tithe due unto him upon Stubcrofte Farm and Weekeland parcel thereof (except before excepted, viz when Weekeland happened to be eared ploughed and sowed: at which time the farmer of Weekeland did always pay the tithe corn and not otherwise). And if Weekeland were not eared ploughed or sowed in any year then the occupiers of Weekeland paid nothing save only the lamb, one fleece of wool and one cheese and no more. And for any tithes coming upon Stubcrofte Farm and Weekeland other than he hath deposed, Sir Christopher Raye then said that the other tithes were always paid to the farmer of Shamblebarne within the parish of Birdham as of right the same ought to be paid, and not to the parson of East Wittering.

---

* Till or plough.

And that about 26 years ago, he then dwelling with Mrs Stanney of Whetstoane who was farmer of the barn [*sic*] called Shamblebarne, he then received all the tithes upon Stubcrofte Farm and Weekeland himself to the use of his mistress (viz except the corn upon Weekeland when the same was sowed and also except the lamb, one fleece and one cheese yearly during the time that he dwelt with her which was due to the parson of East Wittering). And that for this 40 years he hath known Weekelande to be reputed to be part and parcel of Stubcrofte Farm for this reason following: first because for all the time abovementioned the farmer of Stubcrofte Farm did always lot and scot* with the parishioners of East Wittering towards all taxations, either to the church or otherwise, for the whole farm called Stubcrofte Farm, and not for Stubcrofte Farm and Weekelande as being several things but as being both joined together as one farm and never severed the one from the other; and secondly because the farmers of Stubcrofte Farm for all the time have paid their fifteenths† due to her late majesty, as they do now to his majesty, due out of Stubcrofte Farm and Weekeland as one thing and not as two things, but as one farm of itself. And so Weekeland hath always for 40 years been accounted within the parish of East Wittering to be part and parcel of Stubcrofte Farm; and so the same is now reputed to be by all the parishioners of East Wittering.

To the interrogatories

In 1. *Satisfactory.* And he answereth as to the preface of his examination and that he hath known Mr Todd this 10 years and John Newe 30 years.

In 2. That he oweth unto John Newe 50s for an ox which he bought of him the other day but the money is not to be paid until Christmas. *For the rest negative.*

In 3. *Favours parties indifferently and wishes victory for the party in the right. For the rest negative.*

In 4 & 5. *Does not know beyond what has already deposed.*

In 6. That the parson of East Wittering for this 40 years last past have [*sic*] been, as Mr Todd now parson there is, in possession of receiving tithe corn upon Weekeland when the land is sown. But for grass, hay, hazel, hornbeam, willow, thorns, bushes or other coppice wood whatsoever he knoweth not, believeth not, nor ever heard it reported that any such tithe were ever paid to the parson of East Wittering but always to the farmer of Shamblebarne. *For the rest does not know.*

In 7. *Does not know beyond what has already deposed,* for he never knew nor heard who purchased the same nor when it was joined to Stubcrofte Farm

In 8. That the land called Cunnyes was never reputed to be part of Stubcrofte Farm; neither doth he know any land within the parish of East Wittering which is part of the farm, except the land called Weekeland which both is and hath been accounted to be part of Stubcrofte Farm for this 40 years. *For the rest does not know.*

In 9. That the occupiers of Stubcrofte Farm have for this 30 years had four seats properly belonging unto them in the parish church of East Wittering: viz two seats for men and two seats for women. But whether any of them four seats did properly belong

---

* Pay local taxes.

† National taxes.

to Weekeland or no he cannot depose; but for all the time the occupiers did properly sit in the four seats. *For the rest does not know.*

In 10. That he cannot depose anything concerning the custom articulate more than he hath already deposed.

In 11. *Cannot depose beyond what has already deposed,* for he knoweth not that the parson of East Wittering did ever receive any wrong or injury by having the tithes mentioned, because those tithes are due to the parson of East Wittering this 40 years and no other tithes than he hath set down. *For the rest does not know.*

In 12. That he is of the parish of East Wittering and if the like matter do touch him hereafter he will answer the same without fear.

24/3 William Sutton.[158] [*November 1605*]

Of East Wittering, husbandman, where has lived about 50 years; before at Alsnill, Hampshire; born there; aged about 63. Signs with mark.*

A1 That for this 40 years last past he hath known Sir Christopher Raye, who was then parson of East Wittering, receive of one [*blank*] Branne, who was then farmer of Stubcrofte Farm, in lieu of all tithes upon Stubcrofte Farm and Weekelands only one lamb at St Mark's tide, one fleece at Sheartide and one cheese at Michaelmas; saving that he did pay unto Sir Christopher Raye tithe corn upon Weekeland whenas Branne did ear, plough and sow Weekeland. But if Branne did not ear Weekeland then he did not pay any tithes at all but only the tithes upon Stubcrofte Farm and Weekelands which are beforementioned; and all the farmers did always pay the like tithes. And that he hath seen the same tithes paid unto Sir Christopher Raye by Branne, for he hath been present at the payment thereof for 40 years ago and never heard nor knew any more tithes paid other than he hath formerly deposed. And that Weekelands hath for this 40 years been accounted by the parishioners of East Wittering to be part of Stubcrofte Farm and not as a thing proper of itself; for the occupiers of Stubcrofte Farm did scot and lot and pay all manner of taxations toward the reparation of the church and otherwise as well for Stubcrofte Farm and also for Weekeland jointly, as being but one thing; and also they did pay for all the time the fifteenths due to her late majesty as they do to his majesty as being but one farm. And that the farmers of Stubcrofte Farm have always paid their tithes upon Stubcrofte and Weekeland to the farmer of Shamblebarnes.

In 4. That he knoweth not, believeth not, neither hath heard that Weekeland was ever accounted to be a thing sole and entire of itself, but that for this 40 years Weekeland hath been commonly taken to be part of Stubcrofte Farm. ….

In 7. That he knoweth of no such purchase or division nor separation as is specified. ….

In 9. That he doth not know, believe, neither hath he heard it reported, that there was ever any seat in the parish church of East Wittering properly belonging to Weekeland.

* Unidentified; difficult reading.

In 10 & 11. That he cannot depose of any custom other than he hath already deposed: by the which he verily believeth Mr Todd hath no injury nor wrong offered. ···.

In 12. That he dwelleth in the parish of East Wittering; and if the like matter hereafter touch him he must defend the same as well as he can.

24/4 Thomas Holmes.[159] [*November 1605*]

Of Birdham, yeoman, where has lived about 4 years; before at East Wittering about 30 years; before at Chichester; born there; aged about 50. Signs with mark.

A1 That he hath known Weekeland for this 30 years amongst the parishioners of East Wittering to be commonly reputed as part of Stubcrofte Farm and not reputed to be a farm sole and entire of itself. For the occupiers of Weekeland did always use Weekeland and Stubcrofte Farm both together as one farm and not as two farms. And so the occupiers of Stubcrofte Farm and Weekeland of his own knowledge did always lot and scot as one thing with the occupiers of East Wittering towards the reparation of the church and all other duties; and also did always pay unto her late majesty, as now at the present John Newe doth to his Majesty our sovereign lord the King, all fifteenths due out of Stubcrofte Farm as being but one farm and not two. By reason of all which Weekelands is within the parish of East Wittering at this present and so hath been taken to be part of Stubcrofte Farm of his own knowledge. And that for all the time abovementioned he hath known of his certain knowledge no more tithes paid unto the parson of East Wittering out of Stubcrofte Farm and Weekeland save only one lamb at or after St Mark's tide, one fleece of wool at Sheartime, one cheese at Michaelmas every year in lieu of all tithes due unto the parson of East Wittering upon Stubcrofte and Weekeland and no more. And he hath seen the same tithes paid by Thomas Holmes his father who was farmer of Stubcrofte Farm and Weekeland divers times for ten years last past and upwards, saving that when Weekelands was eared, ploughed and sowed, then the parson of East Wittering always received of the occupier of Weekeland tithe corn in kind; but when Weekeland was not eared then the parsons never received any tithes of Stubcrofte Farm or Weekeland other than specified. ···.

In 1. *Satisfactory.* And as before to the preface of his examination and that he hath known Mr Todd this 7 or 8 years and John Newe 30 years.

In 8. That Cunnyes is no part of Stubcrofte Farm neither doth he know of any land within the parish of East Wittering that were part of Stubcrofte farm more than Weekeland . ···.

In 9. That he never heard of any seat in the parish church of East Wittering that ever belonged to the occupiers of Weekeland, but there belongeth seats to the farmers of Stubcrofte Farm and Weekeland as being joined together. ···.

In 11. *Cannot depose beyond what has already deposed* saving that he believeth Mr Todd hath no wrong or injury if he may have the tithes due out Stubcrofte Farm which are specified and deposed in his answer.

In 12. That if the like matter hereafter touch him he will defend the same as well as he can.

25/1 Mary Carden of Rustington v Nicholas Harber of Rustington. Defamation.[160]

Court acts: 13 July 1605 to 8 November 1606.

Mary Carden accused Nicholas Harber of announcing that he had lain with her. The defendant used a variety of devices to escape the suit. Initially he refused to appear and was excommunicated for contumacy. After absolution, he pleaded poverty and was represented 'in forma pauperis'. His final defence was that the couple had contracted to marry and were therefore held to be man and wife; but he failed to produce witnesses. After sentence he was ordered to pay costs and on failing to do so he was made to undergo penance in Rustington church. At time of divine service he had to confess his fault, to ask Mary Carden and the whole parish for forgiveness, and to hear a sermon against scandalous and defaming speeches.

Proctors: Scales for plaintiff; Cooke for defendant. Process: two depositions for plaintiff responding to libel of seven articles and interrogatories of six.

25/2 Sara Maister.[161] [*December 1605-January 1605/6*]

Wife of Edward Maister, tailor, of Rustington, where has lived six months; before at Rustington about 4 years; before at Preston about 7 years; before at Tortington in the parish of Lyminster; born there; aged about 25 years. Signs with mark.

To the libel

L1. *Refers to oath.*

L2. That in Lent last past a little before Easter, she, being at the house of one Campion at Arundel who keepeth a victualling house together with other of her friends, she heard Nicholas Harber say that he did lie with Mary Carden. But where he did not name; neither did he say that he had carnal knowledge of the body of Mary Carden. All which speeches were used and spoken by him against her in the presence of Agnes Mayne, the wife of Robert Mayne, Robert Mayne and one Thomas Hayle and Sara Maister. *For the rest does not know.*

L3. *Does not know beyond what has already deposed.*

L4. That the good name and fame of Mary Carden is much impaired and hurt in respect of the words of defamation.

L5. *Affirms.*

L6. *Refers to oath.*

L7. *Deposition is true.*

To the interrogatories

In 1. *Satisfactory,* and that her husband and John Carden father unto Mary Carden call one another cousin; but how near of kin they be or whether they be of kin or no she cannot depose.

In 2. *Does not know* because she is a married woman and worth nothing of her own proper goods.

In 3. That she came to testify at the request and charge of Mary Carden without compulsion.

In 4. *Negative.*

In 5. *Does not know beyond what has already deposed* for she never heard Mary Carden utter any words of defamation against Nicholas Harber, neither was she at that time then present.

In 6. *Does not know.*

25/3 Agnes Mayne.[162] *[December 1605-January 1605/6]*

Wife of Robert Mayne of Rustington, where has lived about 7 years; before at Tortington 2½ years; before at Steyning one year; before at Arundel; born there; aged about 24. Signs with mark.

L2. That in Lent last past a little before Easter she, Sara Maister the wife of Edward Maister, Robert Mayne her husband and one Thomas Hayle, being at the house of one Campion who keepeth a victualling house at Arundel drinking together, she heard Nicholas Harber say that he did lie with Mary Carden but he neither named the place nor time, neither did he say that he had carnal knowledge of the body of Mary Carden. All which speeches were used and spoken by Nicholas Harber against Mary Carden in the presence of Sara Maister, Robert Mayne, Thomas Hayle and Agnes Mayne.

In 2. That she is worth nothing of her own proper goods because she hath a husband.

In 3. That she came to testify at the request and charge of Mary Carden without compulsion.

In 5. *Does not know beyond what has already deposed,* for she heard Mary Carden utter no speeches of defamation against Nicholas Harber, neither was she as much as then at that time present.

26/1 Mr Samuel Todd, rector of East Wittering v Richard Rablis. Tithe. [163]

Court acts: 28 June 1605 to 22 March 1605/6.

The case is perhaps connected with no 24 above (see introductory note).

The plaintiff's claim involved hay from 'yockrooms' (hedgerows of arable fields) and 'long wood' (timber) and bushes from woodland. The proceedings followed a similar pattern to Todd's previous case.*

Proctors: Scales for plaintiff; Cooke for defendant. Examinations: two depositions for defendant responding to libel of eight articles, additional positions of seven, and interrogatories of twelve.

26/2 John Newton.[164] [*December 1605-January 1605/6*]

Of West Wittering, husbandman, where has lived about 25 years; before at East Wittering about 8 years; before at Hunston about 6 years; before at Bepton; born there; aged about 60. Is worth £10. Signs with mark.

To the libel

L1. *Affirms.*

L2. That for 25 years last past of John Newton's own knowledge the parsons of East Wittering have been, as their predecessors were for many years time out of mind, in quiet possession of both the great and small tithes within the parish of East Wittering, as Mr Todd now parson hath or ought to receive.

L3. *Affirms,* for either he receiveth or ought to receive the tithes in his own right.

L4 & 5. *Does not know beyond what has already deposed.*

L6 & 7. *Affirms from own certain knowledge.*

L8. *Deposition is true.*

To the additional positions

AP1. That he and one William Churcher, who worked together about two years ago, did mow and cut for Richard Rablis so much grass and hay as did grow upon certain yockrooms or hedgerows lying about the cornfields of Richard Rablis as was worth 3s 4d and no more. *For the rest does not know.*

AP2. *Does not know beyond what has already deposed.*

AP3. *Does not know.*

AP4. *Does not know,* saving that he and William Churcher did by the appointment of Richard Rablis cut and fell in the woods now in the occupation of Richard Rablis one day's work of long wood, bushes and thorns worth 6s 8d. *For the rest does not know.*

AP5. That the wood was, as he believeth in his own conscience, at the felling thereof at the growth of 24 years and worth 3s 4d the load, in toto 6s 8d. *For the rest does not know.*

---

* Neither term appears in the *OED.*

AP6. *Does not know beyond what has already deposed.*

AP7. *Deposition is true.*

To the interrogatories

In 1. *Satisfactory and responds in the negative.*

In 2. *Is worth £10;* and that he is a husbandman and thereby getteth his living.

In 3. That he came to testify at the request and charge of Richard Rablis without compulsion. *For the rest does not know.*

In 4. *Negative.*

In 5-11. *Does not know beyond what has already deposed.*

In 12. That he hath heard of such a piece of land called Weekeland as is specified in this article; but whether the same is part of Stubcrofte Farm also cannot depose. *For the rest does not know.*

26/3 William Churcher.[165] [*December 1605-January 1605/6*]

Of West Wittering, husbandman, where has lived about 15 years; before at Birdham about 5 years; before at East Wittering; born there; aged about 40. Is worth 40s. Signs with mark.

AP1. That he and one John Newton, who then did work together about two years ago, did mow and cut for Richard Rablis so much grass and hay upon certain yockroomes or hedgerows lying about the cornfields of Richard Rablis as was worth 3s 4d and no more. ···.

AP4. *Does not know,* saving that he and John Newton did by the appointment of Richard Rablis cut down and fell, in the woods now in the occupation of Richard Rablis, one day's work of long wood, bushes and thorns worth 6s 8d, which was not only for gates and reparations of the fences about the grounds but also for the reparation of the house of Richard Rablis situate within the parish of East Wittering. *For the rest does not know.*

In 3. That he came to testify at the request and charge of Richard Rablis without compulsion. ···.

In 12. *Does not know* because he doth not know the land called Weekeland.

27/1 John Reade, brother in law of Katherine Lenn of Up Waltham v William Lenn of Yapton. Testamentary: nuncupative will of Katherine Lenn. [166]

Court acts: 13 December 1605 to 15 March 1605/6.

A transaction to prove the will 'in form of law' * *rather than 'common form', as a means of protecting the executor against objections from members of kin, represented by William Lenn, junior. Katherine Lenn was a spinster who had died in September 1603, leaving a nuncupative will (proved in October 1603)*[167] *which included a legacy of £100 to her niece Margaret Reade, a minor. This represented a legacy which Katherine had received from her father William Lenn, senior. The depositions established that the will was properly executed. The defendant failed to appear after the initial hearing, did not appoint a proctor, and sentence was given for the plaintiff.*

The depositions' overall duplications with occasional variations in response to the main article are examples of a palimpsest which may reflect the phrasing of the allegation, the legal directions of the clerk and the witness's own recollections.

Proctors: Cooke for plaintiff. Examinations: four depositions for plaintiff responding to allegation of three articles with will annexed.

27/2 John Steele.[168] *Read over 20 January 1605/6.*

Of Brighthelmstone, husbandman, where has lived 6 months; before at Up Waltham about 4 years; before at Frensham, Surrey; born there; aged about 36. Signs with mark.

To the allegation and testament

A1. That in the year 1603 about the 24th day of September Katherine Lenn of the parish of Up Waltham, the testatrix, did make her last will and testament nuncupative, in the presence of Oliver Ide, Susan Warner, Joan Hamonde, Joan Russell the wife of Thomas Russell, Thomas Russell and John Steele; and did of her own accord give, will and bequeath every legacy in the same will nuncupative unto such person and persons and at such days and times and in such manner and form in all things, as in the same will exhibited and read unto John Steele at the time of his examination are specified, without the persuasion of any person whatsoever. And he further saith that at the time of making of the will Katherine Lenn was of perfect mind and memory, for she spoke well and sensibly in all things, in so much that he verily believeth that at that time she was of as perfect mind and memory as he at the time of his examination. All which legacies were given and bequeathed in the presence of the witnesses before recited.

A2. *Does not know beyond what has already deposed.*

A3. *Deposition is true.*

27/3 Oliver Ide.[169] *Read over 20 January 1605/6.*

Of Shawvud [Shalford?], Surrey, husbandman, where has lived 6 months; before at Up Waltham about 2 years; before at Compton, Surrey; born there; aged about 28 years. Signs with mark.

* See Introduction: Testamentary, Wills and Probate.

A1. That about the 28th day of September in the year 1603 Katherine Lenn of the parish of Up Waltham, the testatrix, did make her last will and testament nuncupative in the presence of John Steele, Susan Warner, Joan Hamonde, Joan Russell, the wife of Thomas Russell, Thomas Russell and Oliver Ide, and did, of her own accord without the persuasion of any person whatsoever, give will and bequeath every legacy in the same will nuncupative unto such person and persons as specified. And he further saith that Katherine Lenn was of perfect mind and memory at the making of her will, for she spoke sensibly and well and she knew everyone there present and gave no evil sign of light memory. In respect of all which he verily believeth that she was then of as perfect mind and memory as he is now at the time of his examination. All which legacies were given and bequeathed in the presence of the witnesses before mentioned.

27/4 Joan Russell.[170] *Read over 21 January 1605/6.*

Wife of Thomas Russell of Up Waltham, where has lived about 43 years; before at Bosham about 3 years; before at Up Waltham about 3 years; before at West Wittering; born there; aged about 70. Signs with mark.

A1. That about the 24th day of September in the year 1603 Katherine Lenn of the parish of Up Waltham, spinster, did make her last will and testament nuncupative being in perfect mind and memory although sick in body, in the presence of John Steele, Oliver Ide, Susan Warner, Joan Hamonde, Thomas Russell, Joan Russell's husband and Joan Russell, and did of her own voluntary accord and of her own mere motion without the persuasion of any person whatsoever, give will and bequeath every legacy in the same will as in the same will exhibited are specified. And she verily believeth that Katherine Lenn at the time of making of her will was of perfect mind and memory, for she spoke well and sensibly, and knew everyone there present, and made her prayers unto almighty God well and sensibly, and gave no evil sign of bad or evil memory. By reason of all which she verily believeth that Katherine Lenn at that time was of as perfect mind and memory as she is at the time of her examination. All which premises before mentioned was done in the presence of the witnesses before nominated.

27/5 Thomas Russell.[171] *Read over 21 January 1605/6.*

Of Up Waltham, husbandman, where has lived about 15 years; before at Woolavington about 6 years; before at Up Marden about 2 years; before at Funtington; born there; aged about 48. Signs with mark.

A1. That Katherine Lenn being of perfect mind and memory did make her will the 24th day of September 1603 of her own accord without the persuasion of any person whatsoever and did give will and bequeath every legacy as is specified; which will was exhibited into this court. And that Katherine Lenn was of perfect mind and memory for she spoke sensibly and well and knew everyone there present and gave no evil sign or token of bad memory; by reason of all which Thomas Russell verily believeth that she was of as perfect mind and memory as he is at the time of his examination. All which legacies were given and bequeathed in the presence of John Steele, Oliver Ide, Susan Warner, Joan Hamonde, Joan Russell, Thomas Russell's wife, and Thomas Russell.

28/1 Elizabeth Carpenter, relict and executrix of Laurence Carpenter of Chichester, deceased, v Matilda Robinson and Joan Kneller, sisters of deceased and John Robinson, son of Matilda Robinson. Testamentary: will of Laurence Carpenter. [172]

Court acts: 18 January 1605/6 to 15 March 1605/6.

A transaction to prove the will 'in form of law' * *rather than 'common form', as a means of protecting the executrix against objections from kinsfolk, represented by the testator's sisters and nephew. The depositions established that the will was properly prepared and executed. The defendants failed to appear, did not appoint a proctor, and sentence was given for the plaintiff. Before the start of the case Elizabeth Carpenter had been found contumacious in the court of the Dean's peculiar in November and December 1605 for failing to prove her husband's will.*[173] *The will has not been found among the records of the Chichester diocesan courts or Prerogative Court of Canterbury.*

Proctors: Scales for plaintiff. Examinations: three depositions for plaintiff responding to allegation of six articles with will annexed.

28/2 Thomas Martyn.[174] *Read over 30 January 1605/6.*

Of Steep, Hampshire, yeoman, where has lived about 3 years; before at Rogate about 12 years; before at Horsted Keynes about 5 years; before at Worth; born there; aged about 44. Signature.

To the allegation and testament

A1. That upon the 19th day of August in the year 1604, Laurence Carpenter of the city of Chichester citizen and merchant, being of perfect mind and memory did make his last will in writing, which is the very will now exhibited into this court; and by the will he did give every legacy of his own accord without the persuasion of any person whatsoever; and of the will he did appoint Elizabeth Carpenter his wife his sole executrix. And that Laurence Carpenter was at the making of his will of perfect mind and memory, for he spoke sensibly and well and walked up and down the chamber where he then lodged at his own house in Chichester, and knew everyone there present very well, and caused Henry Colbrooke and William Clapshewe, two other witnesses in this cause, to be sent for to be witnesses unto his will at the time when he did subscribe, seal and deliver the same. By reason of all which he verily believeth that Laurence Carpenter was at the time of as perfect mind and memory as Thomas Martyn is now. *For the rest does not know.*

A2. That the will was put in writing by the commandment of Laurence Carpenter for he gave him instructions how he would make his will and what and to whom he would give anything, and willed him to cause the same to be put in writing and be brought unto him to be ratified. Whereupon he procured one William Yalden scrivener in Petersfield to write the will; and after the writing thereof he brought the will unto Laurence Carpenter and did publicly read the same unto him, in the presence of Henry Colbrooke, William Clapshewe, witnesses thereunto specially called. And after he had read the will unto him, Laurence Carpenter requested Henry Colbrooke to read the will over again which he did accordingly in the presence of Thomas Martyn and William

---

* See Introduction: Testamentary, Wills and Probate.

Clapshewe. After all which Laurence Carpenter did acknowledge the same for his last will and testament in the presence of Henry Colbrooke, William Clapshewe and Thomas Martyn.

A3 & 4. *Affirms as it is alleged, from own knowledge.*

A5. *Does not know beyond what has already deposed.*

A6. *Deposition is true.*

28/3 Henry Colbrooke.[175] *Read over 4 February 1605/6.*

Of Chichester, chandler; born there; aged about 45. Signature.

A1-5. That he was sent for by Laurence Carpenter as he was informed by William Clapshewe, who came from Laurence Carpenter to request him to take the pains to come and speak with him to the intent that he should be a witness to his will. At whose request he went unto the house of Laurence Carpenter, at which his coming Laurence Carpenter and Elizabeth his now relict bid him welcome. And after some communication first had between Laurence Carpenter and Elizabeth, William Clapshewe and one Thomas Martyn who was also present, he told him that he made bold to send for him to be a witness unto his will, and presently tendered his will written in parchment which is the very will now exhibited. By which will he did give every legacy therein contained as is specified, and after the tendering of his last will presently caused the same to be publicly read by Thomas Martyn; and after, Laurence Carpenter did acknowledge the same for his last will in the presence of Thomas Martyn, William Clapshewe and Henry Colbrooke ···. And of the will he did appoint Elizabeth Carpenter his sole executrix.

And that Laurence Carpenter was of perfect mind and memory at the time when he acknowledged the will, for he walked up and down his chamber and spoke sensibly and well, and knew everyone there present well, and requested Henry Colbrooke to read it over again, and then answered it as well in all things and to his liking in all points, and thereupon set his hand and seal and requested him, Thomas Martyn and William Clapshewe to set their hands thereunto as witnesses. By reason of which he believeth that Laurence Carpenter was at the time of as perfect mind and memory as he ever see him in at any other time when he was more stronger of body.

28/4 William Clapshewe.[176] *Read over 4 February 1605/6.*

Of Chichester, yeoman; born there; aged about 51. Signature.

A1-5. That upon the 19th day of August last past Laurence Carpenter sent for him to be a witness unto his will; at which his coming Laurence Carpenter requested him to read the will, which he did accordingly. Then Laurence Carpenter requested him to call some other trusty friend to be a witness because there were only there present but Thomas Martyn and William Clapshewe. Then he asked whether he should call Henry Colbrooke, chandler, and Laurence Carpenter answered, 'Yes with a good will; I pray you request him to take the pains so to do'. And at the coming of Henry Colbrooke,

Laurence Carpenter first caused Thomas Martyn to read the will and afterwards caused Henry Colbrooke to read the same over again ···; and he did bequeath every legacy unto such person as is specified. And after the reading Laurence Carpenter did ratify the same and did constitute Elizabeth his wife his executrix. And for the better proof thereof, after the reading thereof so often, and the same being made and written by the appointment of Laurence Carpenter and with good deliberation, he set his mark and seal thereunto and did then again acknowledge the same for his last will, in the presence of Thomas Martyn, Henry Colbrooke and William Clapshewe. And he further deposeth that Laurence Carpenter at the ratifying of the will was of as perfect mind and memory as William Clapshewe is now, for he walked up and down in his the chamber and spoke sensibly and well and could repeat every legacy and gave no evil sign of light memory. And he requested Thomas Martyn, Henry Colbrooke and William Clapshewe to set their hands as witnesses, which they did. By reason of all which he certainly knoweth that at that time Laurence Carpenter was of perfect mind and memory.

29/1 Margaret West, widow of William West of Ford, deceased, v Anne Lane, niece of William West. Testamentary: Nuncupative will of William West.[177]

Court acts: 18 January 1605/6 to 5 July 1606.

*The initial stages of the case were aimed at establishing whether a deathbed promise by William West had the validity of a nuncupative will and could confirm his widow, Margaret, as inheritor of his estate. The couple had married in 1605 after complicated dowry arrangements had been set up; the depositions include references to a will made before the marriage. Shortly after the start of the case a licence was issued for the marriage of Margaret to Thomas Page. The will was opposed by Anne Lane, West's niece; but the main participant behind the opposition was Richard Mothe, one of West's debtors. The opposition focussed on whether West was too delirious to make a will, and moved on to exceptions made against the depositions of the plaintiff's witnesses, mainly on the grounds of their moral character. The office court records substantiate an accusation of adultery made in the exceptions against Joan Oliver. Just over a month after the publication of 14 depositions, a kinsman, Richard West, intervened in the case. Despite the opposition of the plaintiff, he presented an allegation and produced two new witnesses who provided remarkably extensive details of the earlier will, now lost. Shortly afterwards the plaintiff's proctor introduced letters of inhibition and the case was transferred to the Archbishop's Court of Audience.**

Proctors: Cooke for plaintiff; Scales for defendant; Freeman for Richard West, intervening. Examinations: five depositions for the plaintiff responding to allegation of five articles with will annexed with interrogatories of 22; nine depositions for the defendant responding to additional positions of 11 articles with interrogatories of 19; two depositions for Richard West, intervening, responding to allegation of 16 articles. Two witnesses deposed for both plaintiff and defendant.

29/2 Joan Oliver.[178] *Read over 31 January 1605/6.*

Wife of Thomas Oliver, husbandman, of Ford, where has lived about 40 years; before at Lyminster; born there; aged about 47. Signs with mark.

To the testament and allegation

A1. That Margaret West the relict of William West upon the 17th day of December last past about 8 of the clock in the morning sent for Joan Oliver being her neighbour to assist her to attend her husband who then was visited with sickness. Whereupon Joan Oliver came unto the house to visit him and found him sick in bed in a lower parlour or room; at which her coming she asked him how he did and he answered, 'Well, I thank you Goodwife Oliver', in the presence of Eden Wall who was present before she came. And after some communication first had betwixt William West and Eden Wall and Joan Oliver about 10 of the clock in the forenoon, seeing that Margaret West was not present and knowing that she was also sick and not well, he requested Joan Oliver to call her unto him, which she did accordingly. And when she came, seeing her husband very sick and herself also not being well, she could not choose but weep as she had done many times that day before; in so much that William West said unto her, in the presence of Eden Wall and Joan Oliver, taking her by the hand, 'Margaret, I pray thee be contented; weep not for I will give thee all'. And she verily believeth that William

* The relevant records of this court do not survive.

West at the uttering of these words was of perfect mind and memory, for he spoke sensibly and well and knew her very well and all others that came to visit him. And he lived twelve hours after, insomuch that when Magdalen Burt his maidservant came unto him about 6 of the clock in the afternoon to see how he did and asking him how he did, he knew her well and said, 'Magdalen, where hast thou been all this day that you wouldest not come before now to see how I did?' And she answering again that she had been about his business and he answered, 'It is well Magdalen.' By reason of all which speeches she verily believeth that William West was of perfect mind and memory. All which was spoken and done in the presence of Eden Wall and Joan Oliver

A2. *Does not know beyond what has already deposed.*

A3. *Affirms,* for anything that she ever heard to the contrary.

A4. *Does not know beyond what has already deposed.*

A5. *Deposition is true.*

To the interrogatories

In 1. *Satisfactory.*

In 2. *Negative.*

In 3. *Is indifferent to the parties and wishes victory for the party in the right; for the rest negative.*

In 4. That she is worth nothing of her own proper goods because she hath a husband. And she came to testify at the request of Margaret West and at her charge for her dinner and not otherwise. *For the rest negative.*

In 5. *Negative.*

In 6. *Cannot depose beyond what has already deposed.*

In 7. That the will was only made by word of mouth and not in writing and spoken from the testator's own mouth without the persuasion of any person whatsoever. *For the rest does not know.*

In 8. That William West did pronounce distinctly the words 'I will give thee all' with a disposing mind; for all that day being in perfect memory till his death he used no other words touching the disposing of his goods otherwise.

In 9. That there were nobody present at the uttering of the words but Eden Wall, Margaret West, and Joan Oliver. But after the uttering of the words there came to visit that day Mr John Ellis, clerk, John Madgeweeke, Nicholas Grenawaye [*sic*], John Drewitt and others. But Joan Oliver did not hear him repeat the words to any of them; neither can she depose why the words were not repeated.

In 10. *Cannot depose beyond what has already deposed.*

In 11. *Negative,* for she heard William West speak never an idle word all that day after any evil sort.

In 12. *Does not know* otherwise than that she see no such unruliness or outrageousness in William West all that day while she was with him as is contained in this article; for he was then well quiet and not troublesome to any. *For the rest does not know.*

In 13. *For self negative; for others does not know.*

In 14 & 15. *Does not know beyond what has already deposed.*

In 16 & 17. *Does not know beyond what has already deposed.*

In 18. That she heard no such words spoken by Mr Ellis as are contained in this article.

In 19. That she never heard Margaret West speak any such words as are contained in this article nor no such words in effect.

In 20. *Cannot depose beyond what has already deposed.*

In 21. That the day before William West, died she being with him, Mr Richard Harris came unto him and said, 'Goodman West, how do you?' Whereupon he answered, 'Well, I thank you Mr Harris.' Then Mr Harris said, 'I did hear you sent for me and therefore am come unto you. Wherefore did you sent for me: to make your will?' And William West answered, 'Yea, I sent for you therefore'. But what the reason was that Mr Harris did not make William West's will she cannot depose; but she further deposeth that she heard that William Costilove servant to William West was sent for Mr Harris by his master. *For the rest does not know.*

In 22. *Does not know beyond what has already deposed.*

29/3 Eden Wall.[179] *Read over 31 January 1605/6.*

Wife of John Wall, husbandman, of Ford, where has lived about one year; before at Bosham two months; before at Tortington about one year; before at Angmering; born there; aged about 20. Signs with mark. *

A1. That Margaret West sent for her upon the 17th day of December last past to come and speak with her, which she did accordingly. At which her coming, which was about 7 of the clock in the morning, Margaret West requested her to watch all that night with William West who did then lie sick in his bed, which she granted to do accordingly.† In so much that she continued with him till one Joan Oliver the wife of Thomas Oliver came to visit him and to see how he did; at which Joan Oliver asked him how he did and he answered 'Well, Goodwife Oliver,' and named her by her name. And after some distance of time and communication had betwixt William West, Joan Oliver and Eden Wall, he about 10 of the clock in the forenoon of the same day viz the 17th day of December last past, missing Margaret his wife in the parlour where he lay, requested Joan Oliver to bid his wife come. Which done Margaret West coming unto him and

* In other depositions her name appears in various forms: the most frequent is Edith Walles. Her husband is referred to as Henry in other depositions.

† *Deleted*: 'together with one Goodwife Dammer of Binsted and after that this night was past and the next day come which was the 17th day of December Margaret West requested her to stay a little longer and to help him in what she could in the extremity of his sickness and withal stayed all that day which William West …'

seeing in what extreme pains he lie [*sic*] and herself being not altogether well, she fell of weeping in so much that William West said unto her in the presence of Joan Oliver and Eden Wall, taking her by the hand, 'Why dost thou weep Margaret? Hold thyself content for I will give thee all', or the like words. And she verily believeth that William West at the uttering of the same words was of perfect mind and memory for he knew every person that came to visit him and named them by their names, and for he speak sensibly and well and lived twelve hours and upwards after the uttering of the speeches. Insomuch that when Magdalen Burt his maidservant came unto him about six of the clock in the afternoon to see how he did, her master knew her well and said, 'Magdalen, where hast thou been all this day that I could not see thee before now?' and she answered that she had been about his business, then he answered 'Then it is well Magdalen.' By reason of all which speeches she verily believeth that he was of perfect mind and memory. All which was done in the parlour or lower of room in the presence of John Wall, Margaret West and Eden Wall and no others.

A3. *Does not know* saving that she knoweth that William West at the making of his will nuncupative had never a child.

In 4. That she is worth nothing of her own proper goods because she hath a husband. And she came to testify at the request and charge of Margaret West but nothing given nor promised unto her save only her dinner paid for. ···.

In 8. That William West did pronounce distinctly the words 'I will give thee all' with a disposing mind, for all that day she did not hear him otherwise dispose of anything that he had. *For the rest does not know.*

In 9. That there were nobody present at the uttering of the words but Margaret West, Joan Oliver and Eden Wall. *For the rest does not know* because she was at some times absent from William West and did not note who came to visit after the uttering of the words.

In 10. That William West did use the words deposed unto his wife of his own accord. *For the rest does not know beyond what has already deposed.*

In 12. *Does not know,* saving that all the time that she watched with William West, he was quiet and meek and behaved himself in good order.

In 17 & 18. *Does not know,* for she never knew nor heard of any such matters as are specified in these two articles.

In 20. *Does not know* for she did not at that time see either Mr Ellis or Mr Harris.

29/4 Laurence Alcock.[180] *Read over 31 January 1605/6.*

Clerk, MA, rector of Tillington where has lived about 17 years; before at the City of Oxford about 10 years; before at the city of Worcester about 6 years; before at Tatenhill, Staffordshire; born there; aged about 50. Is worth £20. Signature.

A2. That about the beginning of Hilary term in 1604 Laurence Alcock, William West, John Thompson, brother of Margaret West, and John Madgeweeke met at Mr Bird's house at the sign of the Swan in Chichester to treat about a marriage to be had between

William West and Margaret Thompson, now the relict of William West, where William West alleged that the portion left by the father of Margaret was very small in regard to his estate, which he valued at £500 besides his free lands which he valued at £40 per annum, alleging further that what augmentation soever should be made of her portion should be for her own only benefit, considering that he had no other to leave either his own goods and lands or other portion unto. Whereupon it was concluded by Laurence Alcock, being for one of the brothers of Margaret West, and John Thompson, another of her brothers, with the consent of a third brother, that every one of the brothers should give a sum of money to make up the portion of Margaret, which sums should all be paid to William West at such time as he should make his estate of his free lands to her, the time appointed for that business being left to himself. And William West further requested at the same time that the money should be left in the brothers' hands till they could spy something to be bought to the use of Margaret, because his meaning was that she should have the benefit of all; and that matter rested for that time. And further William West received from the time of their marriage the whole portion left unto Margaret by her father; and the other augmentation which was made by her brothers was to be paid unto William West when the covenants on his part as is before mentioned were performed and not before. All which was done in the presence of the witnesses before recited.

29/5 John Madgeweeke.[181] *Read over 31 January 1605/6.*

Of Ford, husbandman, where has lived about 35 years; before at Harting; born there; aged about 60. Is worth £40. Signs with mark.

A2. That a little before Hilary term 1604, William West requested John Madgeweeke to accompany him to Chichester to meet with Mr Laurence Alcock and others who he had appointed to meet there to treat about a marriage which should be between William West and Margaret Thompson; which he did accordingly. At which time William West and John Madgeweeke met Laurence Alcock and John Thompson at one Mr Bird's house at the sign of the Swan in Chichester, where they had much treat together; but what they agreed upon John Madgeweeke cannot depose for he was many times absent and not in presence with them. But he well remembereth that William West said that he meant to leave her well after his decease, for he purposed to give but little of his goods from her for he had nobody else to give unto. And many other speeches he used to the like effect in the presence of Laurence Alcock, John Thompson and John Madgeweeke which he doth not now remember. *For the rest does not know.*

In 4. · He came to testify at the request of Margaret West and at her charges only for his diet and not otherwise.

In 18. *Negative,* for he did not hear Mr Ellis speak any such words as are contained in this article.

In 21. That Mr Harris was sent for by William West as John Madgeweeke hath heard to make his will. ···.

29/6 John Drewett.[182] *Read over 1 February 1605/6.*

Of Ford, husbandman, where has lived about two years; before at Strudland in Climping about one year; before at Ford about 10 years; before at Kingston in Ferring; born there; aged about 32. Is worth 40s. Signs with mark.

A2. That about Michaelmas last past he, being at that time at husbandry by the day and sometimes by the week or quarter of the year with William West, upon a day at the same time sitting at dinner with William West and Margaret West heard him ask her, who was then sick of an ague, 'Why art thou so sad Margaret; thou shalt have all my goods.' Then Margaret West answered, 'Yea but who shall have your free lands at Binsted; your cousin Fowler will have that.' Then William West answered, 'Fowler shall foul no lands of mine.' All which speeches were spoken in the presence of Margaret West and John Drewett and no more. *For the rest does not know.*

In 4. ···. He came at the request and charge of Margaret West to testify. But for rewards there is nothing neither given nor promised unto him. ···.

In 6-14. *Does not know,* because he knoweth nothing of the will.

In 15. That he hath heard that William West did make a will in writing and he named Anne Lane his sister's daughter his executrix. Which will was written by Mr Carus vicar of Arundel and there were witnesses thereunto, as he hath heard, John Mose of Binsted and Richard Gosden of the same place and Mr Carus the writer thereof. But what was given in the will formerly made he cannot depose. And that Richard Gosden told him at Christmas last past, but upon what day John Drewett cannot depose, that such a will was made and that Richard Gosden was a witness thereunto. All which Richard Gosden told him in the presence of Thomas Thompson at the kitchen door of Margaret West. *For the rest does not know.*

In 16-21. *Does not know.*

In 22. *Does not know beyond what has already deposed.*

29/7 Richard Harris.[183] *Read over 7 March 1605/6.*

Of Arundel, scrivener, where has lived about 5 years; before at Eastergate about 9 years; before at City of London about 18 years; before at Bramiston super montem [Braunston?], Northamptonshire; born there; aged about 49. Is worth £20. Signature.

*To the additional positions etc.**

AP1-9. That upon the 16th day of December last past one of the men servants of William West came unto his house at Arundel and told him that William West would request him to come the next morning, being Tuesday, and bring pen and ink and paper; which he did upon the 17th day of December accordingly. At which his coming which was about 9 of the clock in the forenoon, he found William West sick in his bed lying in a lower room of his house, and a woman whose name he knoweth not

* A general heading preceding this deposition indicates that it, and those following, are concerned with additional positions to exceptions against the witnesses.

attending upon him on one side of the bed and Thomas Stronge his man servant on the other to keep down the bedclothes and otherwise to help him. In whose presence he asked William West how he did, who answered, 'Well, I thank you Mr Harris'. Whereupon he said that he understood that William West did send for him, but about what business he could not then relate. But he said that he was come according to his request and asked William West wherefore he sent for him, whether it was to make his will or no. Then William West answered yes therefore he sent for him. Whereupon presently after he went out of the parlour where William West did lie into the hall of the house to Margaret West, William West's wife, and Mrs Thompson her mother, and asked Margaret West how long her husband had been sick; who answered that the day before, when her husband sent for him, he was sitting up by the fireside; and at his going to bed after his first sleep he changed and grew very sick and unquiet. By reason whereof Richard Harris compelled Margaret West to remove away Stronge her servant from the bedside out of his sight because William West until Thomas Stronge was removed would do nothing but rail at him as though he would have him go about his business, and would have stricken him if he could have come at him. And further Richard Harris asked Margaret West what she would have done and whether she would have any of her neighbours sent for; who answered she knew not what to do and she wished that her husband had sent for him one day sooner if it had been God's will, for he had promised many times before to make his will and did not. And she further said that Mr John Ellis was sent for and she looked for his coming; which John Ellis came unto the house about 10 of the clock in the forenoon upon the 17th day of December. And when John Ellis was come he went unto the bedside of William West and asked him how he did, but he answered nothing because he knew not John Ellis until he was told who he was, and then said 'Oh Mr Ellis'. Then John Ellis began to instruct William West touching his soul's health and afterwards John Ellis, the wife of John Madgeweeke, the wife of Nicholas Greenoe, Richard Knighte, John Drewett and Richard Harris went to pray with and for William West, and requested him to pray with them and to call upon God to help him in these his extremities of sickness; and at the end of the prayer William West said 'Lord help me', whereupon John Ellis was glad to hear him call upon God for help. After all which John Ellis and Richard Harris came forth of the parlour and went into the hall where John Ellis said that he did not know that William West was sick till that time and wished that he had come sooner that he might have drawn some good deeds of charity from him, the which then was too late for he was far past. And Richard Harris did not see any disposing mind in him, neither did he all the time that he was there, which was from nine of the clock in the forenoon until eleven, see him any way disposed or minded to dispose of anything that he had. Neither doth he believe in his conscience that William West was then of perfect mind and memory to dispose of anything he had any way in writing, or to any effect for Richard Harris's credit to write the same; for that all the while that he was at the house William West continually lay railing and talking out of one matter into another, and so inwardly that he could not understand one word out of six, with many idle speeches as: 'There is good sack at Forgooses,' and he said he would give an angel for a quart. And that William West called Margaret West unto him and whispered her in the ear; and she told John Ellis, the wife of John Madgeweeke, the wife of Nicholas Greenoe, Richard Harris and others, he asked her if her money was gone and said there was more in the bottles. By reason of all these things and many others he verily believeth that William

West, during all the time that he was with him, was not of perfect mind and memory to make his will in writing and set in order those things which God had lent him to dispose of in any good order or fashion to be put in writing by Richard Harris. And so about 11 of the clock upon the same day he departed and writ nothing. *For the rest does not know.*

AP10. *Does not know,* for he heard no such words spoken neither by William West nor Margaret West as are specified in this article all that time that he was at the house.

AP11. *Deposition is true.*

To the interrogatories

In 1. *Satisfactory for self; for the others does not know.*

In 2. That he came to testify at the request of Mr Richard Mothe who promised to bear his charges, but he was not compelled thereunto; because he understood otherwise he should have been compelled.

In 3. That he is a scrivener and thereby getteth his living; and that he is worth £20.

In 4 & 5. *Negative.*

In 6. *Negative for self; for the others does not know.*

In 7. *Does not know,* for he knoweth neither Joan Oliver nor Edith Wall.

In 8. That he very well knoweth Mr Laurence Alcock and John Madgeweeke to be very honest men and he verily believeth such men as will upon their oaths depose a truth; and for such men they are commonly reputed. And for Joan Oliver and Edith Wall he cannot depose.

In 9. That upon the 17th day of December last past William West, in the parlour of his house where he lay in bed, of his own accord without the instigation of any other did utter the words viz: 'There is good sack at Forgooses' and he said he would give an angel for a quart, in the presence of Mr Ellis, the wife of John Madgeweeke, the wife of Nicholas Greenoe and Richard Harris and Thomas Stronge, as he thinketh.

In 10. That he hath heard that Mr Richard Mothe hath and doth prosecute this suit for and in the behalf of Anne Lane; but what diligence he taketh to obtain the victory for her he cannot depose.

In 11. That he is very certain that Mr Mothe became in bond unto William West in his life time in £20 to pay unto him £11 in February last past: so as the same was due to William West in February last and not before; for he made the bond betwixt them.

In 12. *Does not know,* for he neither heard nor knew of any such matter.

In 13 &14. That he verily believeth William West was not of perfect mind and memory to make a will in writing all that time that he was with him, which was about two hours, for he speak [*sic*] weakly low and with a hollow voice and could not answer to questions in that he might understand him, save only here and there a word in six words he could speak plain that he could very well understand him although he speak without sense very weakly and with a hollow voice [*five lines deleted*]* for all the time [*eight lines deleted*];† neither did he know or name any there present save only Richard Harris at his first coming unto him. For he knew not Mr Ellis when he came unto him until he was named unto him, and then he said no more but 'Oh Mr Ellis'. And both at Mr Ellis's coming and after he ran out of one matter into another without any reason or sense, and in Richard Harris's judgement it was both in respect of his weakness in body and for want of memory in respect of his sickness, he being so far spent. *For the rest does not know beyond what has already deposed.*

In 15. *Deposes* as before to the 8th article; but whether they have testified the truth cannot depose because he cannot search into other men's consciences. But for such honest men they are credibly reported.

In 16. That William West had not any child of his body lawfully begotten, father nor mother, brother nor sister, alive at his death.

In 17. *Cannot depose beyond what has already deposed.*

In 18. *Does not know* because he knoweth no such thing as is contained in this article.

In 19. *Negative,* saving that he came premeditated what he could depose touching this suit.

29/8 Thomas Leaper.[184] *Read over 7 March 1605/6.*

Of Ford, husbandman; born there; aged about 22. Is worth £20. Signature.

AP1-4. There goeth report within the parish of Ford that Joan Oliver did steal a pig from John Drewett, but how long ago he cannot depose, neither whether it was so or no, but so the report now of late goeth. And that there is the like report within the parish of Ford that Joan Oliver did commit adultery or fornication with Stephen Starkye for a good while ago; but whether she did so he cannot depose. And he hath heard Joan Oliver did forswear herself in denying upon her oath the sale of a certain copyhold or other land unto Mr Ellis of Ford which she formerly bargained and sold unto him, as the report goeth. But by whom the reports were raised he cannot now remember saving that he heard John Drewett himself say that Joan Oliver did steal a pig from him. ⋯.

AP8. That William West sent for him upon Monday at night being the 16th day of December last past, which he did at about one or two of the clock in the morning that night. At which his coming William West complained unto him very idly and said that he was glad that he was come, for he thought that he would rid him of those fellows (pointing at Thomas Stronge and William Costilove, his menservants who stood beside his bedside) and said they kept him there against his will and bid them go about their

* *Deleted*: 'whether it was through insanity of mind or the weakness of his body he cannot depose. And for the distance of time betwixt the idle words and railing words uttered by William West and the time. But he.'

† *Deleted*: 'of two hours that he was with William West could not [*sic*] William West did talk out of one matter into another without any reason or sense for the understanding of Richard Harris and otherwise he cannot depose for he was there but two hours.'

business; and he bid him fetch the officer for he would lay them by the heels. Then he willed Thomas Stronge to stand aside; which he did and Thomas Leaper took his place for that time to attend upon him. Whereupon William West presently after raged against him and said that he was one of their company for all that he came in good will to visit and help him in his sickness. And he cried outrageously to call the constable and he scratched Thomas Leaper by the hand that it was seen plainly long after. All which seemed unto him that William West was not of perfect mind and memory; and so about six of the clock that morning he departed and left John Drewett and Thomas Stronge with William West.

In 2. That he came to testify at the request and charge of Mr Richard Mothe without compulsion.

In 7. *Does not know,* for he never had anything to do with Joan Oliver or Edith Wall.

In 8. That John Madgeweeke is a man of good life and conversation and such a one as will say nothing upon his oath but that which is true; and for such a one he is commonly reputed and taken within the parish of Ford. And for Mr Alcock he is unknown unto him and therefore touching him he can say nothing.

In 9-12. *Does not know* because he knoweth of nothing contained in them.

In 13 & 14. *Cannot depose beyond what has already deposed* saving that William West did all that time that he was with him call and rage as to the 8th article of the positiones additionales he hath deposed.

In 19. *Negative,* saving that he did premeditate what he could remember to depose before his examination.

29/9 Thomas Stronge.[185] *Read over 7 March 1605/6.*

Of Climping, husbandman, where has lived about 2 months; before at Ford about 4 months; before at Barnham about one year; before at Aldingbourne; born there; aged about 21 years and 4 months. Is worth 20s. Signs with mark.

AP8. That he upon Monday at night the 16th day of December last past, being servant unto William West, did watch with his master together with William Costilove, another of his servants. At which time William West was so unruly that neither William Costilove nor Thomas Stronge could scarce keep him in his bed for he would needs rise; in respect whereof we sent for Thomas Leaper in our master's name to help us. And when he came William West said, 'Thomas Leaper I am glad thou art come.' Then Thomas Leaper asked William West what he would have him do for he would do anything for him that he could. Then William West requested him to help him from those bad people, pointing at William Costilove and Thomas Stronge. Whereupon Thomas Leaper bid him depart which he did accordingly and Thomas Leaper took Thomas Stronge's place and helped him in what he could; yet notwithstanding although Thomas Leaper came in good will to help William West yet within a little while after he fell out with him and said that he was as bad as William Costilove and Thomas Stronge and scratched him, this examinate [*sic*], by the hand, and in outrageous sort called for the constable and cried for the constable, for he would have them all set by the heels;

and many other outrageous words he used without any sense or reason. And that a little before Thomas Leaper came, William West, in the presence of William Costilove railed at Thomas Stronge, and bid him saddle his horse for he must go to the visitation; and many other outrageous words he used all the night without any sense or reason, for he said if Thomas Stronge would not saddle and fetch his horse he would run him through with a prong. All which outrageous speeches he used almost all the night and many more as though he was out of his sense, in the presence of Thomas Stronge and William Costilove. *For the rest does not know.*

AP9. That he was present in the parlour when Mr Harris came upon Tuesday the 17th of December and asked William West how he did and also wherefore he sent for him: whether it was to make his will or no. And he answered yes it was; but what other words passed betwixt them he cannot depose because he was still running up and down to fetch wood and other things. *For the rest does not know.*

In 2. That he came to testify at the request and charge of Mr Richard Mothe without compulsion.

In 16. *Does not know,* saving that he believeth William West had never a child lawfully begotten at the time of his death.

In 19. *Does not know,* saving that he came premeditated what he could depose.

29/10 Nicholas Greenoe.[186] *Read over 12 March 1605/6.*

Of Ford, husbandman, where has lived about 8 years; before at Boxley Abbey, Kent, about 13 years; before at Bury, Lancashire; born there; aged about 52. Is worth 20s. Signs with mark.

AP1-8. That he upon the 17th day of December last past came to visit William West together with Joan Greenoe his wife, and at the first coming she asked him how he did, which was about 2 or 3 of the clock in the afternoon. Whereunto he answered 'Goodwife Greenoe, sick,' by reason whereof Nicholas Greenoe certainly knoweth that William West was of perfect mind and memory to know who came unto him, because he knew Nicholas Greenoe's wife and nobody did name her name unto him. And that he at about the hour before mentioned did speak unto William West and asked him also how he did in the presence of Joan Greenoe and John Drewett and others whose names he cannot now remember; whereunto William West answered nothing until Joan Greenoe spoke unto him and said it was her husband, then William West answered, 'Oh my neighbour Greenoe'. By reason of all which Nicholas Greenoe verily thinketh William West was then of perfect memory and understanding or else he could not have known this examinate's wife not being named unto him. And that William West did board with him three quarters of a year before he was married unto Margaret West; and afterwards that he was married he did board and diet with him one quarter of a year. In which quarter of a year after they were so married William West told him that he had made a will but if he did not alter the same will 'Woe be unto poor Meg'; but he said that he meant to lay that will he had already made low enough. And that there were nobody present with William West saving Nicholas Greenoe when he uttered the words. And touching Joan Oliver and Edith Wall he cannot depose. *For the rest does not know.*

In 2. That he came to testify at the request and charges of Mr Richard Mothe interrogated, being first compelled by process out of this court.

In 8. *Does not know,* saving that he very well knoweth John Madgwicke to be man of good name and fame and conversation and of good life, unto whose sayings credit always was and hath been given; and for such a one he is commonly reputed within the parish of Ford where he dwelleth. *For the rest does not know beyond what has already deposed* because he is not acquainted with Mr Alcock. ….

In 10. He verily believeth of himself, and also he hath heard from others, that Mr Richard Mothe hath used all the means that he can to make the will nuncupative interrogated void because he would have Anne Lane to prevail in this suit. ….

In 16. That he never heard that William West had either child of his body lawfully begotten, father or mother, brother or sister remaining alive at the time of his decease.

In 19. *Does not know* saving that he came premeditated what he could depose.

29/11 John Madgeweeke.[187] *Read over 12 March 1605/6.**

AP1-4. That Joan Oliver was presented for suspicion of incontinency with Steven Starkye about three or four years ago; but whether the same act was by her committed he cannot depose. But Steven Starkye upon the suspicion fled away out of Sussex. *For the rest does not know.*

AP7. *Does not know beyond what has already deposed to the allegation and testament exhibited ex parte Margaret West.*

In 2. That he came to testify at the request and charges of Mr Richard Mothe being first compelled by process out of this court.

In 7. *Does not know* otherwise than this. That as he believeth, Joan Oliver and Eden Wall have spoke the truth and no more but the truth.

In 8. *Affirms* for he never heard but Mr Laurence Alcock was always a man of good life and conversation, and so he is commonly reputed and taken within the parish of Tillington where he dwelleth and also in other places near. And touching himself he referreth to the world and they that be therein. *For the rest does not know.*

In 16. *Negative* for anything that he ever heard or knew.

In 19. *Negative* saving that he came premeditated to understand and think with himself what he could say touching this matter.

---

* The biographical details given are identical to those in Madgeweeke's's earlier deposition (**29/5**) except that his valuation falls from £40 to £20.

29/12 Richard Knighte.[188] *Read over 12 March 1605/6.*

Of Ford, husbandman; born there; aged about 30. Is worth £20. Signature.

AP1-4. That he hath heard that Joan Oliver was about four or five years ago suspected to have committed adultery with one Stephen Starkye, but whether Joan Oliver did commit the same fact he cannot depose; neither did he ever hear that the same was proved. And that he hath heard Mr John Ellis parson of Ford and John Drewett of Ford say that she did take a pig from the sow of John Drewett, being in the barn of Joan Oliver, and killed the same pig to her use. *For the rest does not know.*

AP5 & 6. *Does not know,* saving that Eden Wall's husband about two years ago asked him whether he could tell what was become of his wife and he answered he could not tell; then Eden Wall's husband answered that he had enquired for her two days and could not hear any news of her. *For the rest does not know.*

AP9. *Cannot depose beyond what has already deposed,* saving that Mr Richard Harris about 11 or 12 of the clock in the forenoon of the 17th day of December took his leave of William West and bid him adieu or farewell, whereunto William West answered nothing. *For the rest does not know.*

In 2. That he came to testify at the request and charge of Mr Richard Mothe being first compelled by process out of this court.

In 15. That John Madgeweeke is commonly reputed to be a man of good life and conversation and such a one as to whose words credit will be given. *For the others does not know beyond what has already deposed.*

In 16. *Does not know,* saving that he thinketh William West had never a child of his body lawfully begotten at the time of his decease.

In 17-19. *Does not know beyond what has already deposed,* saving that he came premeditated what he could depose.

29/13 John Drewett.[189] *Read over 14 March 1605/6.* *

AP1-4. That Joan Oliver about nine or ten years ago did convey a pig from him worth 16d and kept the same to her own use without any recompense; and denied the having thereof and swore divers and sundry times that she never had the pig. And afterwards she confessed and she was contented to pay 12d whereupon his wife, at the first unknown to him, took 12d for the pig; but so soon as he knew thereof he caused his wife to take the 12d to Joan Oliver again and told his wife that she should not be accessory to the taking away of the pig. So that Joan Oliver had the pig away from him, which as he verily believeth was felony. *For the rest does not know,* saving that he hath heard that Joan Oliver was suspected to have committed adultery or fornication with Stephen Starkye and thereof there was a common fame. ···.

* The biographical details given are identical to those in Drewett's earlier deposition (**29/6**).

AP5 & 6. *Does not know,* saving that Edith Wall was about two years ago absent from her husband some three weeks together in the wild of Sussex; but touching the manner of her living during the time of her absence he cannot depose.

AP7-10. *Cannot depose beyond what has already deposed to the other interrogatories ex parte Anne Lane against the witnesses produced ex parte Margaret West.*

In 2. That he came to testify at the request and charge of Mr Richard Mothe.

In 4. *Negative,* saving his charges and 12d for his horse hire and his day's labour.

In 7. *Negative* for anything he either knoweth or ever heard.

In 8. That he never knew nor heard but that Mr Laurence Alcock and John Madgeweeke were always accounted to be men of honest life and conversation and such men as to whose sayings credit always was to be given; and for such persons they are commonly reputed and taken.

In 10. *Affirms,* as he believeth. But what moveth him thereunto cannot depose.

In 19. That he did premeditate with himself before he came what he would depose. *For the rest does not know.*

29/14 John Ellis.[190] *Read over 18 March 1605/6.*

Bachelor of laws and rector of Ford, where has lived about 14 years; before at Broadwater about 2 years; before at Oxford about 5 years; before at Chichester about 5 years; before at Denbigh; born there; aged about 47. Is worth £20. Signature: John Elise*

AP1-4. That it was reported about eight or nine years ago that Joan Oliver was questioned about a pig which John Drewett laid to her charge to have stolen from him; but Joan Oliver denied the stealing. But what came further he cannot depose. And that Joan Oliver was about seven or eight years ago presented by the churchwardens of Ford upon the report of the wife of Thomas Bosworthe for committing fornication with Stephen Starkye; and otherwise he cannot depose. And that Joan Oliver did by her surrender in court make over her estate in a copyhold in Ford unto him; but he never remembereth that she was ever called unto any court of record upon her oath to justify or deny the surrender. *For the rest does not know.*

AP5. That about 2 or 3 years ago, the husband of Eden Wall told him that she was gone from him and that she dwelt at an honest man's house at Green.† In respect whereof Henry Wall requested his counsel over what he should do. Then he advised him to go down to Green and there to signify unto her master that she was a married woman and Henry Wall's wife; but before he went to Green, Eden Wall returned. And John Ellis, in respect that he was their minister, calling Henry Wall and Eden Wall together to know the cause of their living apart, Eden Wall alleged that her husband did

* The biography differs from Elise's earlier version (**6/3**). This later account adds short stays in Broadwater and Chichester and reduces the time spent at Oxford. The surname in his signature is 'Elise'; but in other depositions and elsewhere the more conventional 'Ellis' is frequently used.

† Wisborough Green

not provide sufficient victuals and other necessaries for her as a husband should provide for his wife; in respect whereof she thought it best as she then told John Ellis to live as a servant and take pains for her own living. In respect whereof John Ellis advising Henry Wall to have a greater respect to the maintenance of his wife and to live with her as man and wife ought to do, Henry Wall and Eden Wall have ever since that time lived together as man and wife ought to do without any spot of dishonesty of either part to his knowledge or hearsay. Neither did he ever hear that Eden Wall lived incontinently with any other person whatsoever. ···.

AP6. *Negative* for anything that he ever heard or knew.

AP7. That he was the 17th day of December at the house of William West from about eight of the clock in the forenoon till about eleven of the clock, during all which time he never heard William West speak those words articulated viz: 'Margaret be contented I will give thee all', nor no other words to the like effect; for he was betwixt the hours beforementioned many and most times absent from William West.* But touching the memory of William West, betwixt the hours above recited he did visit him several times within the space of three hours or thereabouts still exhorting him to pray and to enter into consideration of his salvation; he found him sometimes ready to join with him in prayer, repeating after him the greatest part of the Lord's Prayer and other prayers, until such time as his speech failed him as oftentimes it did, his violent fits coming upon him. But he verily thinketh that William West was of sufficient memory and utterance of speech divers times to deliver the few words articulate, for he remembereth that he often called for drink, for a warden [*sic*], and for his wife who coming to him he delighted in her presence, spoke to her, but what John Ellis could not well understand by reason he spoke so hollow; and he put out his hand in kind manner and stroked her face. *For the rest does not know.*

AP9. That he remembereth that he talked with Richard Harris saying that if the speech of William West did not mend he was not in case to declare his will in any good manner to be put in writing by reason of the infirmity of his speech, for so was his meaning; but never meant that William West was so void of memory but that he might utter his will by word of mouth in those few words viz: 'Margaret be contented, I will give thee all'. *For the rest does not know.*

In 2. That he came to testify at the request and charges of Mr Richard Mothe being first compelled by process out of this court.

In 3. That he is a minster and by his church living he liveth ···.

In 8. That Mr Laurence Alcock and John Madgeweeke were always accounted to be men of good reputation and worthy credit; and for such they are commonly reputed. And touching Joan Oliver and Edith Wall he cannot depose otherwise than he hath already.

In 10. That he verily believeth that Richard Mothe doth labour in what he may to infringe the will nuncupative and wisheth victory unto Anne Lane. *For the rest does not know.*

---

* *Deleted*: 'for every now and then he went out of the bed chamber.'

In 19. That he came premeditated what he could remember, because he was first requested to testify and afterwards called by the process out of this court.

29/15 Henry Ball.[191] *Read over 21 March 1605/6.*

Of Ford, husbandman, where has lived about 20 years; before at Singleton; born there; aged about 25. Is worth £60. Signature.

AP1-4. That Joan Oliver was suspected about six or seven years ago to have committed fornication or adultery with Stephen Starkye; for the which Joan Oliver was presented by the churchwardens into this court as the common fame of the parishioners went; and for such a woman he hath heard by report of others she was commonly reputed. *For the rest does not know.*

AP5 & 6. That he heard Henry Wall husband of Eden Wall say that she absented herself from him for the space of one fortnight but whether she in all that time lived incontinently and scandalously or no he cannot depose. Neither can he depose that she stole, purloined or conveyed anything from her husband. *For the rest does not know.*

In 2. That he came to testify being first compelled by process out of this court at the request and charges of Mr Richard Mothe.

In 8. That for John Madgeweeke he verily believeth he is an honest man and such a man as to whose sayings credit is to be given, and for such he is commonly reputed. And touching Mr Laurence Alcock he cannot depose for he knoweth him not. And for Joan Oliver and Edith Wall *cannot depose beyond what has already deposed.*

In 13 & 14. *Cannot depose beyond what has already deposed* because he was not present with William West at any time within one fortnight before his death. *For the rest does not know.*

In 19. That he came premeditated what he could remember to depose. ···.

29/16 William Carus.[192] *Read over 3 June 1606.*

Clerk, MA, vicar of Arundel, where has lived 9 years and more; before at the university of Oxford for 8 years or more; before at Kendal, Westmorland; born there; aged about 43. Signature: 'per me Guilielmum Carus'.

To [allegation ex parte Richard West]

A1. That William West about 5 years ago, being of perfect mind and memory, made his last will and testament in writing. And he gave unto Richard West of London, who is the said Richard West articulate, the sum of £20 or £10; and unto two of the sisters of Richard West (but which of them he cannot depose) £5 apiece; and he gave unto four of his servants, viz two men and two maids, every one of them a legacy either of 10s or 20s, but which of the sums he gave unto them he cannot depose; and he gave unto William Carus 40s. And he also gave divers other legacies to divers persons and divers charitable uses, as to the poor of Arundel, Pulborough and Binsted, which he cannot remember in respect the will, which is written with William Carus's own hand, is not extant. And the residue of his goods, cattles [*sic*], chattels and debts he gave unto Anne

Lane and made either her executrix, or Mr Thomas Bennett of Arundel (who is since departed) and Mr Richard Mothe of Arundel, gentleman, executors or overseers in trust to receive the residue of all his goods to the use of Anne Lane until she did accomplish the age of 21 years. And he is certain that William West was of perfect mind and memory for he spoke sensibly and well and delivered every legacy of his own accord, and he lived four or five years after; by reason of all which he deposeth he was of perfect mind and memory. And he is certain that the will was made and the legacies before deposed and many other legacies which he cannot now remember were given, for he writ the will himself; and one John Mose and another of his neighbours who he did not know were called to be witnesses thereunto, who set their marks thereunto as witnesses and*

A2. That the will was by the appointment of William West put in writing by William Carus and read unto William West and by him ratified and confirmed, in the presence of John Mose, William Carus and one other which he knoweth not nor cannot remember what his name was.

A3. That William West for the better proof of the will either set his hand by mark or otherwise by writing (but whether his mark or name he cannot depose), and he also set his seal thereunto in the presence of the witnesses.

A4-15. *Does not know.*

A16. *Deposition is true.*

29/17 Richard Gosden.[193] *Read over 4 June 1606.*

Of Binsted, weaver, where has lived about 20 years; before at Bignor; born there; aged about 50. Signs with mark.

To [allegation ex parte Richard West]

A1. That he was sent for by William West, and either William Costilove or William Barnes servants unto William West came for him, but whether of them he cannot depose. Whereupon he went unto William West's house at Binsted to know his mind what he would have with him; and William West answered that he sent for him to be a witness unto his will which Mr Carus of Arundel was then writing. And after the will was by the appointment of William West put in writing, the same was publicly read unto William West. And as he remembereth William West did give £20 or £10 unto Richard West of London his kinsman; but whether it was £20 or £10 he cannot depose. And he did also give unto two of the sisters of Richard West, whose names he remembereth not, £5 apiece. And he gave unto William Costilove and William Barnes his menservants 20s apiece, and to Elizabeth Etherton and Julian Browne his maidservants 20s apiece, and gave unto Mr William Carus vicar of Arundel 40s. He gave likewise unto William Browninge 40s, and he gave 40s to be divided amongst the children of William Browninge. And he gave to the children of Richard Holmes 40s apiece, and other legacies unto divers persons which he cannot now remember. And he did forgive William Farlowe, carpenter, all such debts as he did owe unto him. And he

* *Deleted*: 'this examinate writ his name thereunto as witness.'

constituted Anne Lane executrix, and he constituted Thomas Bennett and Richard Mothe of Arundel executors or overseers of trust for Anne Lane and to receive all things due unto her until she came unto the full age of 22 [*sic*] years, whether she was married before that time or not. And he gave unto Anne Lane all his goods, cattles [*sic*], chattels and debts not given nor bequeathed to any other, his debts and legacies first paid, to be employed by Thomas Bennett and Richard Mothe to her best use until she came to her age of 22 years. And he willed that if Anne Lane did die before she came to the age of 22 years then the children of Richard Holmes and William Browninge should be his full executors.* After all which William West being of perfect mind and memory did ratify the same will for his last will and testament. And otherwise he cannot depose because the will is not extant. But he verily believeth that William West was of perfect mind and memory for he spoke sensibly and well and delivered from his own mouth unto Mr Carus every legacy of his own accord without the persuasion of any person, and he lived four or five years after.

A2. That the testament by the appointment of William West was put in writing by Mr Carus and presently after publicly read unto William West in the presence of William Carus, John Mose who is since departed and Richard Gosden; and William West did ratify the same for his last will in the presence of the witnesses.

A3. That William West for the better proof of the will set his hand and seal thereunto and requested Richard Gosden and John Mose to set their hands thereunto as witnesses, which they did accordingly; but, as he remembereth, Mr Carus did not because he was a legatory [*sic*] named in the will.

* This sentence is inserted from the margin of f 231v.

30/1 Ex officio promoted by Thomas Baylye, executor, v William Soane and wife Cicily. Testamentary: re administration of goods of William Paye of West Marden. [194]

Court acts: 18 January 1605/6 to 31 May 1606.

In November 1601 William Paye, presumably a widower, had married Cicily Silvester. He made his nuncupative will on 1 May 1603, and was dead before 10 December 1603 when his widow was presented in the office court to exhibit it. On 15 December of the same year a licence was issued for the marriage of Cicily to William Soane. Cicily claimed that the will had been proved in the Prerogative Court of Canterbury, apparently on the grounds that Paye's property lay within two jurisdictions: the dioceses of Chichester and Winchester. His will does not survive among the PCC records; however, it was proved at Chichester on 2 November 1605, with administration granted to Thomas Baylye as trustee for Paye's son Robert, a minor. Baylye then instituted instance proceedings as executor of the will on 18 January 1605/6. The original will is accompanied by an allegation aimed at establishing that Paye was capable of making a valid will.*[195] *The first two depositions focussed on Paye's personal property, specifically crops in a barn owned by Mr Bannester of Idsworth and livestock on Warblington Common in Sussex and Hampshire; the later three added a debt due from John Bydinge of Catherington, Hampshire. On 10 May the Soanes were cited to appear to pay costs; the court act of 31 May 1606 bears the annotation 'Inhib'; and no further business was transacted. This suggests that case was removed from the bishop's jurisdiction; but the proceedings of neither the Archbishop's Prerogative Court nor the Court of Audience (the most likely destinations) have survived for the relevant period.*

Proctors: Scales for plaintiff; Cooke for defendant. Examinations: two depositions for the defendant responding to allegation of one article with interrogatories of nine; three further depositions for the defendant for responding to the allegation and interrogatories, with five additional interrogatories.

30/2 John Cooper.[196] *Read over 6 February 1605/6*

Of Harting, husbandman, where lived 4 months; before at West Marden about 6 years; before at Selsey about one year; before at Almodington about one year or more; before at Abbots Worthy, Hampshire; born there; aged about 33. Is worth £10. Signs with mark.

To the allegation.

A1 That in February in the year 1603 he began to thresh some certain wheat and barley for one William Paye late of West Marden, the testator deceased, which then remained in the barn of one Mr Edward Bannester of Idsworth, esquire; and made an end of threshing all the wheat and barley of William Paye remaining in the barn within one sevennight after the beginning of March in the same year. In so much that William Paye caused all the barley so threshed to be wymed† and carried thence to his own house at West Marden; but before all the wheat remaining in the barn and belonging unto him was either winnowed or carried away by William Paye or by another by his appointment, there happened a sow of Mr Bannester's to be killed by one mischance or other, whereupon Mr Bannester alleged that William Paye, John Cooper or some other that came about the threshing, winnowing and carrying away of his corn killed the sow.

* A William Paye married a Cicily Hackett at Compton in April 1571.

† Winnowed

In so much that Mr Bannester caused his barn doors to be locked and the wheat of William Paye to be stayed until satisfaction was made; which wheat was so detained from him till his dying day and long after, for he see the same wheat remaining in the barn a month after the decease of William Paye. He knowing the same wheat to be in controversy, every* now and then as he went by the barn about other business he took occasion to look into the barn, the same barn lying and adjoining to the king's highway, to see whether the wheat was there still or no. Which he might easily do for the barn doors stood sometime wide open and the wheat ready to be threshed was then in the barn, and sometimes doves and sometimes poultry eating thereof; so that he certainly knoweth that the same wheat was remaining in the barn both at William Paye's death and long after; but what became of the same wheat he cannot depose. And that both at the time when Mr Bannester caused the wheat to be stayed and also at the time of William Paye's decease there was not above 22 or 23 bushels at the most, every bushel worth 3s and no more. And at the same time William Paye had as much wheat straw in the barn as was worth 5s which Mr Bannester challenged to thatch the barn, which wheat and wheat straw was seen to be in the barn both before and after the decease of William Paye not only by John Cooper but also by John Perryn of Holte and Edward Clement, and also known to John Cooper and John Perryn and Edward Clement to be the proper goods of William Paye. And that William Paye had a mare running upon the common of Warblington in the county of Southampton about a year before his death, which mare he caused to be fetched home to his house to West Marden to go to work, and kept her at his home a while at work until such time that, by reason of her dullness at work, he himself struck out one of the eyes of the mare with a whip stub; and afterwards sent her to the Common to pasture again. Which Common is an entire common and a common part in Hampshire and part in Sussex; and for the most part the mare did use to pasture upon that part of the common that did lie in Hampshire as he hath heard. And the mare did pasture upon the common till after the decease of William Paye; but whether at the time of the death the mare was pasturing upon that part that lie in Hampshire or upon the other part that lie in Sussex he cannot depose, but saith that the mare was worth 30s or 33s 4d and not above. *For the rest does not know.*

To the interrogatories

In 1. *Satisfactory and deposes* as to the preface of his examination and that he hath known Cicily Soane this six years last past and William Soane her husband this two or three years; and for Thomas Baylye he hath but small acquaintance. *For the rest does not know.*

In 2. *Negative.*

In 3. *Negative* saving that since this suit began William Soane sent for him to come to his house at Stoughton to speak with him about some business which he did accordingly; and for his pains taking William Soane gave him home with him a piece of bacon worth 4d and no more. *For the rest negative.*

In 4. *Favours parties indifferently and wishes victory for the party in the right. For the rest negative.*

In 5. *Is worth £10. For the rest negative.*

In 6-9. *Cannot depose beyond what has already deposed.*

---

* ever *in MS.*

30/3 Edmund* Clement.[197] *Read over 6 February 1605/6*

Of Compton, yeoman, where lived about 20 years; before at East Marden; born there; aged about 38. Is worth £40. Signs with mark.

A1 That about a sevennight before Maytide was two years, William Paye told him that he was hardly dealt withall by Mr Edward Bannester of Idsworth: for he said that he had remaining in the barn of Edward Bannester ready threshed, of his own corn 20 bushels of wheat and something upwards, and as much wheat straw as was worth 5s, which Edward Bannester did detain from him because, when he and others were at the barn at Idsworth about the threshing of the wheat and other business, it happened Edward Bannester had a sow killed by one mischance or other near unto the barn. In so much that he alleged that either William Paye or some other that was then there did kill his sow and therefore he would stay the wheat and wheat straw from him unless he would make him satisfaction for his sow. And William Paye protested that for his own part he did no manner of hurt to the sow, neither did he know of any other that did her any hurt nor how she came by her death. All which wheat and wheat straw were due unto William Paye and remaining in the barn of Mr Bannester long before his death. For he and William Paye in his lifetime went to the barn divers times to see how the wheat did lie, which wheat they valued to be about 20 bushels; but William Paye could never receive the wheat nor the wheat straw from Mr Bannester because he would not pay for the sow. But he is sure that the wheat and wheat straw was belonging unto William Paye in his lifetime and at his death as his own proper goods, for one Edward Cowles, Mr Bannester's baylye [*sic*], told him that William Paye might fetch the wheat and wheat straw out of the barn when he would, making restitution for the sow. Which he would never do: in respect whereof the wheat and wheat straw remaineth in the hands of Mr Bannester still, as Cecily Soane told him since the death of William Paye. And that wheat at that time was worth 2s 10d a bushel and not above. *For the rest does not know.*

In 1. *Satisfactory and deposes* as before to the preface of his examination, and that he hath known Cicily Soane from her youth and so William Soane her husband and so Thomas Baylye.

In 2. That Cicily Soane and his wife are sisters. *For the rest negative*

30/4 Arthur Leger.[198] *Read over 10 March 1605/6*

Of Compton, husbandman, where lived about 8 years; before at West Marden in Up Marden; born there; aged about 43. Is worth £40. Signs with mark.

To the allegation upon the acts

A1 That about 2 years ago and as much as since Maytide, Edmund Clement of Compton told him that John Bydinge of Blendworth did owe unto William Paye at the time of his decease 45s for barley. And that he also reported that he had pasturing upon the common called Warblington Common one mare and a colt at the time of his decease, worth 55s one with the other. But whether he told the truth he cannot depose;

* 'Edward' *deleted in MS.*

neither can he depose anything at all touching the allegation whereupon he is examined. *For the rest does not know.*

To the interrogatories given in the first place

In 1. *Satisfactory and deposes* as before to the preface of his examination; and that he hath known Cicily Soane from her youth and so William Soane her husband and ever since he was of understanding; and so Thomas Baylye.

In 2. That he is somewhat kin to Cicily Soane but as he remembereth it is three or four degrees off. *For the rest does not know.*

To the interrogatories given in the second place

In (2) 1. *Cannot depose beyond what has already deposed.*

In (2) 2. That Warblington Common is an entire common and part in Hampshire and part in Sussex without any partition whereby to let and hinder cattle going from one part to the other. And the great part of the common called Warblington is in Sussex because he very well knoweth that Warblington Common of itself is not so much ground as the ground that lieth in Sussex.

In (2) 3-5. *Cannot depose beyond what has already deposed.*

30/5 Thomas Till.[199] *Read over 10 March 1605/6.*

Of Westbourne, husbandman, where lived about 3 years; before at West Thorney; born there; aged about 30. Is worth £20. Signs with mark.

A1 That about Maytide last past was two years, he being at the house of William Paye after the decease of William Paye as one of the prisers* of his goods, there came unto the house one John Bydinge of the parish of Catherington and asked the prisers whether they had done prising of all the goods. Whereupon answer was made that they had done all. Then John Bydinge said that they had put nothing into the inventory as due unto William Paye from him and they answered no because they knew not whether he was indebted unto him or no. In so much that John Bydinge said, 'Yes, I am indebted unto him upon the remainder of a bigger sum which I ought unto him for barley: the sum of 45s.' In respect whereof he said that he hoped that Cicily Paye his relict would not urge him to pay any more in regard that he had paid all that was due saving the 45s. Then Cicily and the prisers answered, 'No, God forbid.' All which was confessed to be due by John Bydinge in the presence of William Colpas, Edmund Clement and Thomas Till. But whether he did owe unto William Paye 45s at the time of his decease he cannot depose but by the relation of John Bydinge. And that he had a mare and a colt pasturing upon the entire common called Warblington Common, part whereof is in Hampshire and part in Sussex, as it is reported. But whether the mare and colt were at the time of decease in Hampshire or Sussex he cannot depose; but the mare and colt one with another were prised at 45s. *For the rest does not know.*

---

* Appraisers.

In 1. *Satisfactory and deposes* as before to the preface of his examination, and that he hath known Cicily Soane not above this two years, nor William Soane above this twelvemonth, Thomas Baylye above a twelvemonth.

In (2) 1. *Cannot depose beyond what has already deposed as to the allegation ex parte Mr Cooke concerning the acts.*

In (2) 2. That Warblington Common is an entire common and part in Hampshire and part in Sussex without any partition whereby to let and hinder cattle to go from one part to the other. And he cannot certainly tell whether the part belonging to Warblington or the part being in the county of Sussex is one greater than the other. *For the rest does not know.*

In (2) 4. That the mare was black with one eye and no more and of stature about 13 or 14 handfuls high, but what age he cannot depose; price 40s. *For the rest does not know.*

In (2) 5. *Affirms as he believes* for he never heard anything to the contrary.

30/6 Thomas Greene.[200] *Read over 12 March 1605/6*

Of Up Mmarden, yeoman, where lived about 20 years; before at Chichester about 3 years; before at Sidlesham about 12 years; before at Kingston; born there; aged about 80. Is worth £40. Signature.

A1 That he was one of the prisers of the goods of William Paye; and he neither heard nor knew of any goods that were due unto the testator at his death which were then remaining in any other diocese save the diocese of Chichester. *For the rest does not know.*

In 1. *Satisfactory and deposes* as before to the preface of his examination and that he hath known William Soane and Cicily his wife this 16 years. And he hath also known Thomas Baylye this 20 years.

In (2) 1. *Does not know,* saving that he thinketh William Paye died about three years ago.

31/1 Alice Collye alias Parson alias Slater, sister, v Joan Slater widow. Testamentary: re administration of goods of Michael Slater of Steyning.[201]

Court acts: 12 April 1606 to 21 March 1606/7; 16 January 1607/8 to 7 May 1608; 11 February 1608/9 to 8 April 1609.

Michael Slater died in November 1605. Administration was granted to his widow Joan on 19 January 1605/6, with his personal property valued at £469.[202] *His sister disputed the value of the probate inventory and the probate account.* The first two witnesses were called by Joan, the widow, to set out the difficulties caused by bad debts. Five months later the plaintiff called on the defendant to respond in justification of the property values given in her objections in the inventory, and then produced witnesses to give further valuations. The defendant sought judgement in the ensuing months; but the record of proceedings between March and October 1607 has not survived. The case resumed in January 1607/8 with the plaintiff seeking judgement, which she obtained on 19 March 1607/8. 1609 saw further proceedings between February and April aimed at getting the defendant to pay the costs. The final act book entry has a marginal note 'pax', to indicate that some kind of agreement had been reached.*

Proctors: Cooke for plaintiff; Scales for defendant. Examinations: two depositions for the defendant responding to one article concerning the account; personal response of the defendant responding to three articles; two depositions for the plaintiff responding to allegation of three articles and interrogatories of seven articles..

31/2 Henry Harriden.[203] *Read over 31 May 1606.*

Of Ashurst, husbandman, where lived about 5 years; before at Washington about 5 years; before at Burton about 1 year; before at West Grinstead where born; aged about 26.† Signature [crude]: 'Hindry Harydine'.

To the exhibited account

Ac. That John Skeate, mentioned in the account exhibited in this court on behalf of Joan Slater the relict and administratrix of Michael Slater the intestate deceased, was at the time of the decease a very poor man for, as he hath heard Thomas Arnold say who is his neighbour, he did pay £28 for him which John Skeate did owe to other men but he never had the same again of him. But it was in respect that the said Callingham was bound for John Skeate and for Thomas Arnold was executor or administrator of the goods of one Callingham, but which he cannot certainly depose, such a poor man he then was, as Thomas Arnold told him, reputed.‡ *For the rest does not know,* for he was never acquainted with John Skeate neither had he ever any conference with him. And that Thomas Smithier, also mentioned in the account and *additional positions,* was at the decease of Michael Slater a poor man; for he fled out of this country of Sussex in

* Neither document has survived, but in the defendant's objections (Ep I/15/1 (1606)) she claims that one lease valued at £30 is worth £500 and another valued at £66 13s 4d is worth £1000.

† *The following has been deleted at this point*: 'To the exhibited account. That John Skeate mentioned in the said account to owe by bond unto Michael Slater the sum of £7 by one bond and £10 by another bond was not able to pay any part for as Henry Harriden hath heard it reported by Thomas Arnold of Ashurst where he is a parishioner and a near neighbour Thomas Arnold did pay unto Michael Slater.'

‡ This portion is extremely confused and various additional phrases have been deleted.

respect he was not able to pay his debts, and his oxen was strained upon for rent by William Farnefolde of Steyning his landlord, and he was indebted to divers persons and not able to pay them; and for such a poor man he was then commonly reputed. And, touching Robert Munnerye, that, as he hath heard one [*blank*] Picknoll say, he had great hindrance by Robert Munnerye for he run away out of the country of Sussex in his debt, and that one of his children is kept by one [*blank*] Terrye of West Grinstead of alms because of his poverty. *For the rest does not know.* And he hath heard John Miller of Horsham say he did cast him the said [*sic*] Robert Durrante in Horsham goal for debt.* *For the rest does not know.* And for Charles Addames that he is commonly reputed within the parish of East Claiton† to be a poor man. *For the rest does not know.* And so is Charles Addames [*sic*] and Owen Powell also mentioned in the account accounted to be poor men and such as are not able to pay their debts. *For the rest does not know.*

31/3 George Linfeilde.[204] *Read over 30 May 1606.*

Of Ashurst, husbandman, where lived 10 about years; before at West Grinstead where born; aged about 42. Signs with mark.

To the exhibited account and additional positions

Ac. That he did hear Michael Slater say a little before his death that John Skeate, Thomas Smithier, Robert Munnerye, Robert Durrante, Charles Addames and Owen Powell did owe him the several sums mentioned in the account, and he deposeth that he verily believeth that they are very poor and not able to pay their debts. For John Skeate, as the common report went within the parish of Steyning and as George Linfeilde partly knoweth, ran away out of this country of Sussex for five years ago because he was so far in debt that he was not able to pay his creditors; and since he hath not been heard of; and he left his children being but young unprovided for in so much they are kept of alms. And touching Thomas Smithier, he ran away out of the parish of Steyning about 5 years ago for debts and was not able to pay Mr William Farnefolde of Steyning his landlord the rent due unto him; and in respect he was so far in debt to many several persons he left that small substance he had and so departed the country; but he never heard that Michael Slater his late master was paid any of his debts of £30 mentioned in the account. And, touching Robert Munnerye, that he took to rent a piece of land and some stock and cattle upon it of Thomas Picknoll of Ashurst about six years ago and afterwards sold the same stock of cattle, viz kine horses and swine, which were the proper goods of Thomas Picknoll, and stole away with the money and his wife and children with him, in respect he was more in debt than he could pay or procure to be paid. And touching Robert Durrante he was cast into Horsham gaol about 8 or 9 years ago at the suit of John Miller of Horsham gentleman; and afterwards lived not above a month or thereabouts but died and left little or nothing of his own goods to pay his debts, in so much that Michael Slater could not recover anything in his lifetime nor his wife since. And touching Charles Addames he is a poor man and hath nothing to live upon but his labour and hath a great charge of children. And touching Owen Powell, as he hath heard, he was a twelvemonth ago

---

* *Deleted*: 'and in respect that Robert Durrante was not able to pay his debts there he died in prison.'
† Unidentified. Perhaps East Clandon, Surrey?

burnt in the hand for felony and so fled away worth nothing, and left his wife and children at Shipley upon the alms of the parish. And the parties above named are for such poor people commonly reputed within the parish of Steyning. *For the rest does not know.*

31/4 Joan Slater.[205] *Read over 11 Oct 1606.*

Relict and administratrix of Michael Slater of Steyning.

Personal response. Signs with mark.

To material and schedule.

M1. *Believes locations stated as to life and death of Michael Slater. For rest does not believe article to be true in anything.*

M2 & 3. *Believes valuations given in inventory. For rest does not believe articles to be true in anything.*

31/5 Thomas Farnfolde.[206] *Read over 14 October 1606*

Of Steyning, gentleman; born there; aged about 30. Is worth £40. Signature.

To the allegation and schedule.

A1. That he doth know one of the leases mentioned in the schedule, of 4 acres of land with a house a barn and other edifices thereupon lying in Steyning for the term of one thousand years and by the rent of one couple of capons, did belong to Michael Slater late of Steyning deceased in his lifetime and at the time of his death; for Michael Slater did buy the premises of Thomas Farnfolde's father and he hath seen the lease set down in the inventory of Michael Slater and there prised at £66 13s 4d, which is a less sum than the lease is worth. And as concerning the other lease of 5 acres and a house of land [*sic*] mentioned in the schedule and inventory for two thousand years for the rent of one peppercorn by the year and prised in the inventory at £30, he can say nothing.

A2. That the lease of 4 acres with the house barn and other edifices is well worth by common estimation and in Thomas Farnfolde's judgement £100, and so much he will willingly give for the same. And as concerning the other lease of 5 acres and a house of land he can say nothing. But the same lease and 5 acres and a half of land demised by Thomas Farnfolde to Michael Slater for 2000 years for the rent of one peppercorn is worth by common estimation and in his judgement £40 and so he will willingly give for the same.

A3. *Deposition is true.*

To the interrogatories

In 1. *Satisfactory.*

In 2. *Favours neither party; for rest negative.*

In 3. *Is worth £40* and that he came to testify at the request of one Edward Godsmarke *and at his own expense. For the rest negative*

In 4. That Michael Slater had in possession at the time of his decease certain free lands in Broadwater worth by the year some £22. *For the rest negative.*

In 5. *Does not know.*

In 6. *Negative.*

In 7. *Deposes as before to the allegation and for the rest does not know.*

31/6 Richard Gater. *Read over 14 October 1606.*

Of Steyning, yeoman; born there; aged 30 or more. Is worth £20. Signature.

A1. That Michael Slater was in possession in his lifetime and at the time of his decease one lease of 4 acres of land and a house a barn and other edifices thereupon builded lying in Steyning of one thousand years for the yearly rent of one couple of capons, for he knoweth both the lands and other buildings. But as concerning the other lease of 5 acres and a house of land [*sic*] in the schedule mentioned for two thousand years at the rent of one peppercorn and prised in the inventory at £30 he cannot depose. But yet that Michael Slater had and was possessed of at the time of his decease one other lease of 5 acres and a half of land for 2000 years lying also in Steyning at the rent of one peppercorn by the year which he bought of Thomas Farnfolde of Steyning gentleman.

A2. That the lease of 4 acres with the house barn and other buildings is worth by common estimation and in his judgement £100 and so much he would willingly give for the same. And as concerning the other lease of 5 acres and a house of land he cannot say anything. But yet that the lease and 5 acres and a half of land before mentioned and which Michael Slater had and held in his own right and was possessed of at the time of his decease for the yearly rent of one peppercorn is worth by common estimation £40 and so much he would willingly give for the same.

In 3. ··· *Came to testify at the request of James Colley and Edward Godsmarke of Steyning and at their expense for travel. For the rest negative.*

A4. That Michael Slater died possessed of a certain farm or free lands in Broadwater which he bought with his money and is worth £20 for the year, *as he has heard. For the rest does not know.*

A5. That as he hath heard one Coortess son in law to Mr Francis Heiden, clerk parson of Broadwater, doth now enjoy the farm of the grant of Michael Slater, made as he hath heard him in his lifetime say, and so Coortess hath held the farm ever since.

32/1 Mary Robins, wife of William Robins of Shipley, v Edward Hayler of Shipley. Defamation.[207]

Court acts: 22 March 1605/6 to 5 July 1606.

In this short and inconclusive case, the details of the alleged defamation are not given. It may have involved an assertion that the plaintiff was not married (though the Horsham parish register records a marriage between William Robbins and Mary Bignall on 20 December 1599). The witnesses called by the plaintiff were not only reluctant to testify but professed no knowledge of the words of defamation. The plaintiff's intention to call further witnesses seems to have lapsed after the publication of the depositions and within weeks the proceedings ceased. The references to Peter Streeter suggest that there may be a connection with a later defamation case, between Joan Streater of Shipley and William Robins,[208] *where the depositions (made between September and November 1607) recorded that Robins had called Joan a whore and 'roged whore'.*

Proctors: Cooke for plaintiff; Scales for defendant. Examinations: two depositions for the plaintiff responding to libel of nine articles and interrogatories of six.

32/2 James Cappe.[209] *Read over 13 June 1606.*

Of [West] Tarring, yeoman, where lived about 2 years; before at Offington in Broadwater about 2 years; before at Rye about 3 years; before at Shipley where born; aged about 30. Is worth £20. Signs with mark.

To the libel

L1. *Refers to oath.*

L2. That about two months ago he being at the house of Edward Hayler at Shipley, which Edward Hayler keepeth a victualling house, he [James Cappe] being without doors there came in again, and seeing Mary Robins and William Robins her husband going by in the king's highway, he told Edward Hayler there went one by that he [James Cappe] should know. Whereunto he answered, 'It is William Robins and his wife'; whereupon Edward Hayler said unto Peter Streter who was present, 'Peter Streter, why do you not call in your tenant?' meaning William Robins or Mary Robins. Whereupon William Robins and Mary Robins were called into the house, but by whom he cannot depose, in the presence of John Henley and James Cappe and others. And *for the rest does not know* for he did not hear the words libellated at all nor the like in effect.

L3 & 4. *Cannot depose beyond what has already deposed.*

L5. That William Robins and Mary Robins were commonly reputed to be man and wife, as they are now, before the uttering of the words by this examinate formerly deposed to the second article of the libel.

L6. *Cannot depose beyond what has already deposed.*

L7. *Negative.*

L8. *Refers to oath.*

L9. *Deposition is true.*

To the interrogatories.

In 1. *Satisfactory.*

In 2. *Negative.*

In 3. *Is worth £20* and that he was compelled by process out of this court to testify. But he hath hitherto borne his own charges; and he hath come about this business, himself and his horse, three several times and received of William Robins for his charge 12d and no more neither for himself nor his horse.

L4. *Cannot depose beyond what has already deposed.*

L5. That the words by him formerly deposed unto the second article of the libel were spoken at the house of Edward Hayler about the time before by him deposed, but what day or hour of the day he cannot depose. All which words were spoken in the presence of Edward Hayler and James Cappe.

L6. *Cannot depose beyond what has already deposed.*

32/3 John Henley.[210] *Read over 13 June 1606.*

Of Shipley, husbandman; born there; aged about 24. Is worth £13 13s 4d. Signs with mark.

L2. That about 10 weeks ago he, being at the house of Edward Hayler who keepeth a victualling house at Shipley, Edward Hayler said unto Peter Streter, 'Peter Streter there goes thy tenant', meaning William Robins, 'call him in.' Upon which words Peter Streter called William Robins and Mary Robins into the house which William Robins and Mary Robins came into the house, there being present James Cappe, Peter Streter and John Henley with others. But touching the words libellated he cannot depose otherwise than he hath already deposed, nor any words to the like effect.

In 3. ··· that he came to testify the truth being first compelled by process out of this court. But hitherto he hath borne his own charges; and he hath come himself and his horse three times about this business and received 12d only for his charges and his horse and no more. But how otherwise he shall be recompensed he knoweth not.

33/1 Mr Ralph Earle vicar of Eartham v John Page. Tithe.[211]

*Court acts: 15 March 1605/6 to 21 March 1606/7[and perhaps later].**

The case concerned established local customs of tithing of livestock temporarily pastured outside the parish of Eartham. In response to the libel the defendant claimed that he had offered payment, and described in detail the parochial customs on which he based his defence. The plaintiff's witnesses provided a differing account of the customs. The defendant then produced an allegation, again setting out his version of the customs. Further witnesses were to be produced in support of the allegation but did not appear. In February the defendant sought to end the case, citing related proceedings in the common law court of Kings Bench (which had precedence over ecclesiastical courts in disputes over ancient customs). After the final surviving act there is a six month gap in the act book series. The records of the office court reveal how relations between the two men may have been exacerbated by friction over parish matters. Page was appointed churchwarden in 1605 and faced a number of charges in the ensuing year for failures in his duties. He was regularly presented for failing to receive communion, even when churchwarden. When, in 1607, he countered this by attributing it to 'controversies' between himself and the vicar, the court offered an unusual response in allowing him to receive in the adjacent parish of Aldingbourne. He was also accused of cohabiting with his wife's sister. Earle was also subject to charges of failing to repair the chancel of his church or to make parish perambulations.

Proctors: Scales for plaintiff; Cooke for defendant. Examinations: personal response by the defendant responding to libel of ten articles; three depositions for plaintiff responding to libel of ten articles and interrogatories of six. Statement from allegation of defendant describing customs.

Ralph Earle held the living of East Wittering from 1572 until his death in 1611.

33/2 John Page.[212] *Read over 28 May 1606.*

Personal response. Signature.

To the libel ex parte Ralph Earle vicar of Eartham.

L1. *Believes it to be true.*

L2 & 3. *Believes it to be true,* saving tithe milk of milch kine pasturing within Eartham otherwise than 1d yearly at Lammas for the white of every such cow in lieu of such tithe milk. And saving tithe lambs of ewes pastured from and out of the parish from the feast of St Thomas the Apostle in every year until the fall of their lambs and until the feast of the Annunciation of our blessed lady the Virgin Mary next following, otherwise than the whole tithe wool of the same ewes at shear time without defalcation in lieu of the part due unto the vicar of Eartham as well of the tithe of the same ewes so pastured from and out of the parish as of all such tithe lambs so fallen out of the parish, according to an ancient and laudable custom time out of mind used. And saving also that he doth not believe that any of the vicars of Eartham or their farmers did ever drive [*?*]† for any tithe calves, tithe lambs or tithe pigs fallen within Eartham, but believeth that time out of mind they have always used to receive yearly at Lammas of

* Court acts March-October 1607 do not survive.

† Difficult reading. Perhaps 'derive'?

every parishioner having under the number of seven calves of their kine, under the number of seven lambs, under the number of seven pigs, pastured within the parish ½d for the fall of every calf and lamb and every pig. And never did as he believeth drive [*?*] nor expect until every such person hath had or should have ten calves, ten lambs or ten pigs and then to take and accept their tithes thereof. To any of which tithes before excepted this respondent doth not believe that Mr Ralph Earle or his predecessors ever had or ought to have any other right or interest or ever were in lawful possession of having or receiving the same or any part in other manner than is by this respondent confessed.

L4. *Deposes as previously. Beyond this does not believe the article to be true in anything.*

L5 & 2nd schedule. Believes that he had pasturing within Eartham: in the year 1602 until about ten days after the feast of St Andrew in the same year, 22 ewes; and in every of the years 1603 and 1604 until about ten days after the feast in every of the years, 24 ewes; and in the year 1605 until about 14 days after the feast, 16 ewes. And he believeth that from and after ten days next following the feast in the years 1602, 1603 and 1604, and from 14 days following the feast in 1605, until the feast of the Annunciation of our Blessed Lady next in every of the years, he had all the ewes in manner and form by him confessed pasturing within the parish of Tangmere and out of Eartham. And he believeth that he had within Tangmere after the feast of St Thomas in 1602 and before the feast of the Annunciation, of his 22 ewes pasturing there, 20 lambs; and after the feast of St Thomas in every of the years 1603 and 1604 and before the feast of the Annunciation next following in every of the years, 23 lambs of his 24 ewes likewise pasturing there; and after the feast of St Thomas in 1605 and before the feast of the Annunciation, 15 lambs of his 16 ewes pasturing also within Tangmere, in manner and form as before by him confessed. Also he doth believe that in every of the years about one fortnight before St Mark's* day he had his ewes brought back again together with their lambs into Eartham and had them pastured there until St Mark's tide next following in every of the years.

L6 & 7 and 1st schedule, believes that he had pasturing within Eartham in the year 1603 four milch kine, and of them he had two calves; and in every of the years 1604 and 1605 three milch kine, and of them had in every of the years 1604 and 1605 three calves. And he believeth that every of the calves was worth 6s 8d. And he further believeth that he had pasturing within Eartham in 1602 and in all the months concurring in the same year eight ewes and of them had seven lambs; and likewise in every of the years 1603 and 1604, 16 ewes. And he believeth that in 1603 he had of his 16 ewes nine lambs, and in 1604 of his 16 ewes seven lambs. And he believeth that he had also pasturing there in 1605 33 ewes, and of them had 27 lambs. And he believeth that every of the lambs was worth 3s. *And for the customs set out in the first schedule responds that he believes them to be true,* except for lambs of ewes pastured out of Eartham from the feast of St Thomas in every one year until the feast of the Annunciation next following as is before confessed by him in his answers to the 2nd and 3rd articles. And touching the value of the lambs confessed by him to the 5th article and the 2nd schedule he doth believe that every of the lambs was worth 3s. *And does not believe 6th and 7th articles and their schedules to be true in anything beyond what he has stated in his response.*

---

* Difficult reading.

L8. *He is a layman and has no rights to tithe in Eartham. Believes he has paid to Mr Earle the tithe debts owed by law that he has admitted, or has been ready to pay in accordance with the laudable customs described, and to have released sums in accordance with acts of the court to Mr Earle as tithe duly owed and not paid.*

L9. *He is of Eartham and subject to jurisdiction of the court.*

L10. *Believes himself to be the party complained against on the part of Ralph Earle, however unlawfully. Believes what he has stated above that he believes, and denies what he has denied.*

33/3 Henry Browninge.[213] *Read over 26 June 1606*

Of Eartham, husbandman, where lived 30 years or more; before at Duncton where born; aged about 60. Is worth £20. Signs with mark.

To the libel

L1. *Affirms as he believes,* for so he is commonly reputed and taken within the parish.

L2. *Affirms from certain knowledge.*

L3. That Mr Earle for this 30 years and upwards, or his farmer, for this 30 years last past of Henry Browninge's own knowledge, hath quietly and peaceably received the tithes within the parish of Eartham. *For the rest does not know.*

L4. That he hath heard Thomas Peachye, a witness producted [*sic*] in this suit, say that he hath heard Gregory Peachye late of Eartham his father say, who is now deceased, that he did always pay to the vicar of Eartham or his farmer for the tithe lambs of his ewes sometime pasturing within the parish of Eartham and sometimes out of the parish, as of old it were always accustomed, the tithe lamb of such their ewes so pasturing, rateably and proportionably for the time that such their ewes did pasture within Eartham. And after that rate Henry Browninge, who hath ewes pasturing sometimes within the parish of Eartham and sometimes in other parishes near there unto, payeth and hath paid unto Mr Earle this 3 or 4 years last past.

L5. *To the article and schedule does not know,* saving that the parishioners of Eartham, or some of them, do for the most part in every year put out some of their ewes which they cannot keep in their own parish to pasture in some other parish adjoining, from the feast of St Thomas the Apostle until the feast of the Annunciation of Our Lady the blessed Virgin Mary in every year. *For the rest does not know,* because he knoweth not what number of ewes John Page had in any of the years libellate.

L6. *Cannot depose beyond what has already deposed.*

L7. *To the article and schedule does not know,* saving that it has always been accustomed within the parish ever since he dwelt there, which is about 30 years, for every inhabitant pasturing any milch kine within the parish to pay unto the vicar of Eartham for the milk or white of every one 1d, according to an ancient custom used time out of mind. And touching the number of ewes and lambs he cannot depose. But touching the tithe due to the vicar of Eartham, the custom always for this 30 years hath been that the vicar always had a lamb of seven lambs within the parish. But if any of the parishioners had of his ewes under the number of seven lambs in any one year, then the parishioner ought to pay for the fall of every lamb ½d. And for calves he cannot depose, save only for the fall of every calf ½d and for the milk or white of every cow 1d. *For the rest does not know.*

L8. That John Page is a mere layman and hath no right to the tithe within Eartham. *For the rest does not know.*

L9. *Affirms from certain knowledge*

L10. *Deposition is true.*

To the interrogatories

In 1. *Satisfactory; for self negative; for fellow witnesses does not know.*

In 2 & 3. *Is worth £20*; and that he is a husbandman and thereby getteth his living. And that he came to testify at the request and charge of Mr Earle without compulsion.

In 4 & 5. *Negative.*

In 6. *Does not know,* saving that he thinketh Mr Earle hath and ought to have the whole tithe wool also interrogated.

33/4 Thomas Peachie.[214] *Read over 26 June 1606*

Of Eartham, husbandman; born there; aged about 50. Is worth £20. Signs with mark.

To the libel

L1. That Mr Ralph Earle hath been vicar of Eartham for this 34 years and so he is commonly reputed. *For the rest does not know.*

L3. That Mr Earle for the space of 34 years did always peaceably and quietly enjoy all the tithes contained in this article, either by himself or his farmer in the right of his vicarage. *For the rest does not know.*

L4. That he hath not only heard Gregory Peachie his father, who is now deceased, say that he did for 23 years pay unto to the vicar of Eartham or his farmer the tithe of his lambs, pasturing at some times within every year within the parish of Eartham and at other times in every of the years pasturing in some other parish, rateably and proportionably for the time that such their ewes did pasture within Eartham, in such manner and sort as the parishioners of Eartham used and were accustomed to pay their whole tithe lambs for their ewes pasturing wholly and continually within the parish; but also Thomas Peachie himself for this 20 years hath paid the like unto the vicar of Eartham, and as he thinketh every parishioner having any ewes pasturing without the parish doth or ought to do the like. *For the rest does not know.*

L5. *Does not know* saving that the parishioners of Eartham for the most part useth to put out some part of their sheep to pasture in another parish about St Thomas's day in every year until Our Lady's day.

L6 & 7. *Does not know,* saving that the vicar always ought to have for this 30 years last past, as Mr Earle ought to have, of every parishioner having in any one year seven calves or seven lambs one calf and one lamb, and having under the amount of seven calves or seven lambs fallen in any one year then the vicar ought to have only ½d and for the white of every milch cow and for the fall of every lamb ½d. *For the rest does not know.*

In 6. That Mr Earle hath for this 30 years received the whole tithe wool of the sheep of every inhabitant of his parish pasturing as well within the parish as without at some times of the year and every year, but not in lieu of his tithe lambs, which was due of every man's ewes within the parish, pasturing sometimes within the parish and sometimes in other parishes, rateably for the time they pasture out of the parish.

33/5 William Pynham.[215] *Read over 1 July 1606*

Of Eartham, husbandman; born there; aged 50 or more. Is worth 40s. Signs with mark.

To the libel.

L2. That Mr Earle hath had right to have as well the great tithes as the small tithes of Eartham; and hath received the same of the inhabitants dwelling within Eartham this 30 years last past as being vicar. *For the rest does not know.*

L4.* That he hath heard the parishioners of Eartham for 20 years last past, having ewes pasturing in any one year sometimes within Eartham and sometimes in any other parish, have used to pay to the vicar of Eartham or his farmer rateably and proportionably for the time that such their ewes did pasture within Eartham, in such manner and sort as the parishioners of Eartham used, and were accustomed to pay their whole tithe lamb for their ewes pasturing wholly and continually within the parish. And that William Pynham for 17 years past did buy of Mr Ralph Earle certain lambs which did fall due unto him for tithes of the ewes of Edward Rassall deceased pasturing within the parish of Boxgrove, according to a custom used for all the time abovementioned, viz 17 years and upwards. *For the rest does not know.*

In 3. That he came to testify at the request and charge of Mr Ralph Earle without compulsion.

33/6 *Extract from allegation ex parte John Page.*[216] [*November 1606*]

A1. *For 60 years or more it has been established custom in Eartham* that every parishioner of Eartham having ewes pastured within the parish in any year until the feast of St Thomas, and afterwards having the ewes pastured out of Eartham from after the feast of St Thomas until the fall of their lambs and until the feast of the Annunciation, have been free from payment of every tithe lambs in kind; and in lieu of such portion of their tithe lambs due unto the vicar of Eartham as of such part of their tithe wool of the ewes, they have used to pay to the vicar of Eartham at shear time in every of the years

* '3' *in MS.*

the whole tithe wool from their ewes pastured from and out of Eartham in manner and form aforesaid.

A2. *Page has paid Earle tithes according to this custom.*

A3. *Page seeks justice in the light of this established custom.*

34/1 Agnes Nashe, wife of James Nashe of Middleton, v William Holden of Middleton. Defamation. [217]

Court acts: 28 June 1606 to 25 October 1606.

Agnes Nashe claimed that in March Holden had asserted on two occasions that she had been 'burned': infected by venereal disease. Holden made no significant defence and within a few sessions after the witnesses had deposed the brief final court act is annotated 'Pax', indicating that a settlement had been reached.

Proctors: Cooke for plaintiff; Scales for defendant. Extract from plaintiff's libel (article 2). Examinations: three depositions for the plaintiff responding to libel of seven articles and interrogatories of nine.

34/2 *Extract from libel of plaintiff [giving words of defamation.*[218] [*July 1606*]

L2. *Between August 1605 and June 1606, William Holden, within the parishes of Walberton, Yapton and Middleton defamed Agnes Nashe by the words:* Agnes Nashe hath committed or lived in adultery or fornication in London and was burned there and came home burned from London by committing the most foul act of adultery or fornication..

34/3 William Shorte.[219] [*July 1606*]

Of Middleton, husbandman, where lived about 30 years; before at Lyminster; born there; aged about 70. Signs with mark.

To the libel

L1. *Refers to oath.*

L2. That about Our Lady Day last past William Shorte and William Holden going into Madehurst Down driving of some certain sheep to pasture there, William Holden among other communication asked how Goodwife Nashe did, meaning how Agnes Nashe did. Then William Shorte answered she was sick; then William Holden answered that she was burned for he heard at Felpham mill before 20 people that she was burned. But there were nobody present at the uttering of the words before by him deposed save only William Holden and him. *For the rest does not know.*

L3. *Cannot depose beyond what has already deposed.*

L4. That the good name and fame of Agnes Nashe is much impaired and hindered by reason of the words of defamation amongst all the neighbours and friends of her.

L5. *Affirms.*

L6. *Refers to oath.*

L7. *Deposition is true.*

To the interrogatories

In 1 & 2. *Negative.*

In 3 & 4. *Cannot depose beyond what has already deposed.*

In 5. *Does not believe the words of defamation to be true.*

L6. That since William Holden did utter the words there hath been a fame thereof and not before, because it was never so much as heard of, nor in deed as yet there was never so much spoken of but by the relation of him. *For the rest does not know.*

L7. That he heard the words formerly deposed spoken by William Holden *directly and not by report.*

L8 & 9. *Cannot depose beyond what has already deposed.*

34/4 Margaret Cooke.[220] *Read over 24 July 1606*

Wife of Jerome Cooke, rector of Middleton, where lived about 10 years; before at Felpham about 3 years; before at Elmer Farm in Middleton about 7 years; before at Chichester where born; aged about 32. Signs with mark.

L2. That upon a Sunday happening upon or about Palm Sunday, William Holden, being at the house of Thomas Lenne of Middleton together with Hugh Launder and Margaret Cooke, Agnes Nashe being then also present and Thomas Lenne, William Holden, amongst other speeches said in the presence of the parties, that Agnes Nashe was burned for he did hear so before 20 people at Felpham mill. And so William Holden said he told unto William Shorte. *For the rest does not know.*

L4. That the good name and fame of Agnes Nashe is much impaired by reason of the words of defamation, and that she is the worse thought of by reason of the speeches amongst divers of her neighbours.

L5. *Does not believe the words of defamation to be true.*

L6. That since William Holden did utter the words there hath been a fame and a great speech within the parish, and never before.

34/5 Hugh Launder.[221] *Read over 25 July 1606.*

Of Middleton, sawyer, where lived for about 12 years; before at Chippenham, Wiltshire where born; aged about 55. Signs with mark.

L2. That upon one Sunday happening about Palm Sunday last, he being at the house of Thomas Lenne of Middleton together with Margaret Cooke the wife of Jeremy Cooke, clerk, William Holden and Agnes Nashe, she did challenge William Holden that he had reported unto William Shorte of Middleton that she was burned. Whereunto he said that indeed he spoke the words unto him and for his own part so he did hear it spoken at Felpham mill before 20. Then he requested William Holden to name one that said so besides himself and he said he could not remember any of them. All which speeches he spoke in the presence of Margaret Cooke, Agnes Nashe, and Hugh Launder. And touching his meaning in saying she was burned he verily believeth that William Nashe [*recte* Holden] meant that she had committed fornication or adultery with one man or other besides her husband and so came by that hurt. *For the rest does not know.*

L4. That the good name and fame of Agnes Nashe is much impaired amongst her neighbours by reason of the words of defamation. *For the rest does not know.*

In 5. *Does not believe the words of defamation to be true.*

In 6. That since William Holden did utter the words there hath been a great speech within the parish and never before.

35/1 Frances Tester v John Burdye alias Burdocke of Wisborough Green: Matrimonial (breach of betrothal contract).[222]

*Court acts: 12 July 1606 to 21 March 1606/7 [and perhaps later].**

Frances Tester claimed that the John Burdye had broken a contract to marry. Her witnesses recorded that between Easter and Christmas 1605 he had described the couple as man and wife in the sight of God; but it is significant that no mention was made of the normal betrothal ceremony, while the defendant's references to the need for a church ceremony (stipulated in the recent revision of the Canons, 1603) was dismissive. The office court records record involvement between Burdye and Joan Leigh (who in 1605 had been presented for 'making a drinking at the burial of her husband'). Later that year the couple were charged with incontinently living together; after Joan had produced compurgators in her defence the court ordered her not to consort with Burdye. In the later stages of the case, the defendant petitioned for sentence but there is no surviving record of the end of the case. The Wisborough Green register, however, records the marriage John Burdet and Joan Leygh, widow, on 26 November 1607.

Proctors: Cooke for plaintiff; Scales for defendant. Process: two depositions for plaintiff responding to libel and interrogatories, each of six articles.

35/2 John Scutt.[223] [*October 1606*]

Of Wisborough Green, husbandman, where lived about 14 years; before at Pulborough where born; aged about 40. Signature.

To the libel

L1. *Does not know.*

L2. That between Easter and Christmas last was 12 months, John Burdy alias Burdocke and Frances Tester were at his house in Wisborough Green at the churching of his wife; and John Burdy and Frances Tester talking of marriage between themselves, John Burdy did confess and acknowledge before the witnesses hereafter mentioned that he and Frances Tester had contracted matrimony together. And John Burdy and Frances Tester tarrying and staying until towards night, she taking care to repair home to her master's house, Richard Alderton in Wisborough Green, said, 'I must go home or else I shall be blamed or chidden.' Whereunto John Burdy said, 'Why? If thy master chide thee, come away from him hither to John Scutt's house again and lie here, and I will pay for thy board.' Whereunto John Scutt's wife then being present said that it was not fit for a bachelor to pay for a maid's board. Then John Burdy answered, 'I scorn to be a bachelor. I am a married man and we' (speaking of Frances Tester and himself) 'are man and wife before God. There wanteth but the asking of the same in the church and what is a little asking.' All which speeches were spoken in John Scutt's house in the presence of him and his wife and Alice Pittyll, wife of [*blank*] Pityll of Fittleworth. And that at another time since, John Burdy and Frances Tester and John Scutt being at a victualling house in Wisborough Green, John Burdy said he would buy a cow and requested John Scutt that he would keep the cow for him until he were married (meaning to Frances Tester). And he hath heard him oftentimes say that he and she

* Court acts March-October 1607 do not survive.

have contracted matrimony together and were man and wife before God. *For the rest does not know.*

L3. That by reason of the premises John Burdy and Frances Tester have been taken and reputed as man and wife within the parish of Wisborough Green and other parishes thereabout. *For the rest does not know.*

L4. *That John Burdy is of the parish of Wisborough Green and subject to jurisdiction of the court*

L5. *Affirms.*

L6. *Deposition is true.*

To the interrogatories

In 1. *Satisfactory.*

In 2-4. *Deposes as above to libel.*

In 5. That John Scutt married with Frances Tester's sister. *For the rest negative.*

In 6. *Favours parties indifferently and wishes victory for the party in the right.*

35/3 Alice Pyttell.[224] [*October 1606*]

Wife of William Pittell, husbandman, of Fittleworth where lived about 20 years; before at Poling 3 years; before at Angmering about 4 years; before at Easebourne where born; aged about 60. Signs with mark.*

L2. That about a year since, she being at the house of John Scutt in Wisborough Green together with John Burdy and Frances Tester at a child ale there, and at last night drawing on John Scutt asked Frances Tester when she would go home to her master's house. Then John Burdy answered, holding her in his arms, that he would bring or accompany her home; she said, 'No then my master will chide.' Then he said to her, 'If he chide thee or do not use thee well, I will have thee come hither to thy sister's (meaning John Scutt's wife) and I will pay for thy board here'. Then John Scutt's wife answered unto him that that were a simple motion, for a bachelor to pay for a maid's board, saying that she hoped Frances Tester should have no such need but would be able to pay for her own board; whereupon he replied that he scorned to be a bachelor for he was a married man before God, for there wanted nothing but asking in the church and marrying to make it known to the world, and what is that? All which words were uttered in the presence of John Scutt and his wife and Alice Pyttell. *For the rest does not know.*

L3. That by reason of the premises, John Burdy and Frances Tester have been (within the parishes of Wisborough Green and other parishes there about) commonly reputed to be man and wife; but of late the same report hath ceased by reason of some speeches of late raised† concerning a contract between John Burdy and widow Lee. *For the rest does not know.*

---

* The name appears in four different variant spellings in its five occurences.

† Difficult reading.

36/1 Joan Blaxton, widow of Henry Blaxton, canon residentiary of Chichester Cathedral v Henry Blaxton, junior, of Chichester, her son. Testamentary: will of Henry Blaxton, senior.[225]

Court acts: 25 October 1606 to 14 February 1606/7.

Henry Blaxton senior had been Chancellor of the Cathedral from 1573 to 1606, and had served as one of the senior surrogate judges in the office and instance courts for many years up to July 1606, only a month before his death in August. The proceedings are in some ways similar to other cases which attempted to prove a will 'in form of law', but it is not clear whether the dispute between mother and son goes beyond formalities. Henry junior, probably the eldest son, appeared only once, did not appoint a proctor and was pronounced contumacious throughout the proceedings. The main witness for the plaintiff, Richard Juxon, adds a puzzling element to the case. Through the initial stages he failed to depose and was pronounced contumacious; yet as the principal registrar of the court he continued to act at virtually all the court sessions, allowing his fellow notary Christopher Theker to substitute for him in specific proceedings concerning the Blaxton case. The final sequence of events is unexpected and puzzling. Sentence was given for the plaintiff on 14 February 1606/7; but it was not followed by the probate of the will in the Chichester courts (or in the Prerogative Court of Canterbury). Within a fortnight of the sentence Joan Blaxton made her will, on 28 February 1606/7; she was buried on 16 March 1606/7; and her will was proved the next day.[226] It contains no specific references to her husband's estate and was proved by her son and executor, Joshua; it includes a small bequest to her son Henry and a significant number of more substantial ones to other relations.*

Proctors: Cooke for plaintiff. Examinations: one deposition responding to allegation of two articles with will annexed; a second deposition responding to allegation of four articles with will annexed.

36/2 Richard Juxon.[227] [*December 1606*]

Of Chichester, gentleman, where lived about 30 years; before of London; born there; aged about 65. Signature.

To the allegation and exhibited will.

A1 & 2. That he in August last was sent for by Mr Doctor Blaxton, the testator, to come unto him, whereupon he went unto the testator where he found him lying in his bed in an upper chamber over the little parlour in his house. At which his coming Joan Blaxton by the appointment of Dr Blaxton fetched his will, now exhibited, and delivered the same unto him to be read; and Richard Juxon in the presence of Joan Blaxton, Henry Blaxton and Godfrey Blaxton, sons of Dr Blaxton, did read the same will containing four sheets of paper whereunto he had subscribed his hand to every of the four sheets and fixed them all together with a label and thereunto had fixed a piece of wax and set his seal. Which four sheets of paper were in many places interlined and many words blotted out before the reading thereof, in so much that Richard Juxon in reading did miss in many places because he could not perfectly read, wherein Dr Blaxton, in the presence of the witnesses, did help and direct him in those things wherein he missed, and especially in these legacies and places following: viz in the second leaf these words, 'To have and to hold the said indenture of lease' and the which words were stricken out before the reading, in respect whereof the other words

* See Introduction: Testamentary, Wills and Probate.

following were without sense, then he, by the appointment of Dr Blaxton and in the presence of the witnesses, read the same words and writ 'stet' over the head thereof in three several places. And likewise when he, in the end of the second leaf came to these legacies: first, 'That Joan my wife shall have the education and bringing up of Henry Peters, with all the profits and commodities of his portions and tenements and lands and other of the premises to him bequeathed, until the said Henry Peters shall accomplish the full age of 24 years', the testator said, 'It must be one and twenty'; whereupon he mended the same in two several places and made it 21 years, the testator liking well thereof. And further, in the legacy next following these words: viz 'Then I will that my son Joshua Blaxton shall have the education of the said Henry Peters and the rents and profits of his said lands tenements leases and portions before to him bequeathed for the maintenance and good education of the said Henry Peters until he shall come unto the age aforesaid. And if both my said wife and my son Joshua shall happen to decease before the said Henry Peters shall come to said age of 24 years' being strucken out with a pen, Richard Juxon did omit the reading of the words before written and read on unto the words following: viz 'Then I leave him to his free choice etc'; then either the testator or Joan his wife, but which of them he remembereth not, said, 'Woe it must be to my son Joshua'. Then he asked him whether the words before written which were stricken out should stand, whereunto Dr Blaxton said, 'Yes'. Then he writ 'stet' in seven several places and so read them although they were stricken out; and further, where it was written 'until he shall come unto the age aforesaid', he, to explain the said age, interlined 'of 21 years' and no more. All which was done by the appointment of the testator and in the presence of the witnesses. And in the beginning of the second line of the third leaf where it was written 'until he shall come unto the said age of 24 years etc.', he made the same 21 years and so afterwards read the same unto the testator. And so he proceeded afterwards through with the reading of the will with the interlineations of the testator's own hand, saving that, in the ninth line before the end of the last leaf, he did interline these words: viz 'and Henry Peters', and afterwards read the same words unto the testator and so finished the reading of the will verbatim as it is mentioned in the will exhibited, seen and perused by him, saving that in the 24th line of the first leaf underneath these words 'now apparent' there is a line drawn with a pen, and because it is not drawn through the words 'now apparent' but underneath them, whether he in the reading of the will did read them or omit them he doth not now remember. And that Dr Blaxton at the reading of his will was of perfect mind and memory, for as well besides the directing of him in reading of his will when he missed in anything, as also by altering and adding of divers words as before deposed, the testator did give this testator* thanks and appoint certain money to be given to him for his pains taken in coming unto him and reading of his will; which will now exhibited into this court was read unto the testator by him, wherein the testator named Joan his wife sole executrix. All which will was written by the testator himself in four leaves of paper with his own hand, and his name subscribed unto every leaf thereof and his seal put thereunto before the testament was delivered unto Richard Juxon to be read, as by the will now exhibited appeareth (except the interlineations and additions before interlined and added). And that after the reading of the testament the testator did acknowledge ratify and confirm the same for his last will. Then Richard Juxon asked

* Recte 'examinate'.

the testator whether it was his pleasure that he, Henry Blaxton, the younger, and Godfrey Blaxton his sons, being present, should be witnesses and the testator answered yes, whereupon Henry Blaxton, the younger, Godfrey Blaxton and Richard Juxon set their hands unto every of the four leaves as witnesses.

36/3 Godfrey Blaxton.[228] [*December 1606*]

Clerk, vicar choral of the Cathedral, Chichester, where lived about 30 years; before at Higham Ferrers, Northamptonshire; born there; aged about 36. Signature.

To the allegation and testament.

Al 1-3. That about the month of August last past Henry Blaxton, the testator, sent for him being his son to come and visit him, and withal to call Mr Richard Juxon to come along with him. Whereupon Richard Juxon and Godfrey Blaxton went along together to the house of Dr Blaxton, the testator, where they found him in the chamber over the little parlour. At which their coming the testator willed him to call his brother Henry Blaxton, also son of the testator, which he did accordingly; and when Richard Juxon, Mr Henry Blaxton, his brother, and Godfrey Blaxton were all together with the testator, the testator willed Joan Blaxton his wife who was also present to fetch his will, which she did accordingly, the same being ready written with the testator's own hand and his seal thereupon. Then the testator called to Richard Juxon to read the same unto him which he did accordingly, and in reading the same Richard Juxon did always ask the testator where there was any doubt or question to be made in anything, in respect the will was interlined and blotted out in many places, what his will and meaning was therein to avoid all controversies thereafter. Which the testator made plain in every point, in so much that Richard Juxon by the appointment of the testator writ 'stet' in divers and sundry places, in the presence of Henry Blaxton the younger and Godfrey Blaxton. And so Richard Juxon went still forward in reading the will till the end thereof and then he asked the testator whether this will was that (*sic*) (that will now exhibited into this court and then read unto the testator) was in all points as he would have it and whether it should stand, be and remain for his last will and testament, or the like words in effect. Whereupon the testator answered, 'Yes', in the presence of Henry Blaxton the younger, Richard Juxon, Godfrey Blaxton and Joan Blaxton the testator's relict. ···. And of the will the testator did nominate Joan Blaxton his sole executrix and the testator did give every legacy therein unto such persons as is specified. And that at the end of the reading of the will the same will was interlined and blotted out in such manner and form as now at the time of this examination. And that at the reading of the will the testator was of perfect mind and memory, for when Richard Juxon doubted of anything the testator was able of himself without the help of any other to direct him; and he did appoint Joan his wife to give unto him for his pains taken 5s; and further the testator requested Richard Juxon, Henry Blaxton the younger and Godfrey Blaxton after his will was read to write their names unto every sheet as witnesses, which they did accordingly. And afterwards the testator did acknowledge the same for his last will. By reason of all which he verily believeth the testator was at the reading of perfect mind and memory for he was of perfect mind and memory a fortnight afterwards and more.

A4. *Deposition is true.*

37/1 Margaret Tayler, wife of Matthew Tayler of Stoughton, v Richard Tillboroughe of North Marden. Defamation.[229]

Court acts: 27 September 1606 to 14 March 1606/7.

There is no obvious background to the defendant's accusations and he does not seem to have attempted a denial or explanation for calling Margaret Tayler a whore. Although he appointed a proctor to contest the suit, he failed to make a personal appearance during the first four months of the proceedings. When cited to make a personal response he avoided the searches of the apparitor but eventually made an appearance. After the judge gave sentence for the plaintiff, Tillboroughe's proctor gave notice of appeal; but there is no indication of further proceedings.

*The transcription has retained duplications within the depositions which suggest that the witnesses had compared their statements or have been 'guided' by the lawyers.**

Proctors: Scales for plaintiff; Cooke for defendant. Extract from plaintiff's libel (articles 2 and 4). Examinations: four depositions for the plaintiff responding to libel of eight articles and interrogatories of six; personal response of defendant responding to libel of eight articles.

Tillboroughe had been presented in the office court in 1604 for failing to receive communion at Up Marden.[230]

37/2 *Extract from libel.*[231] *[October 1606]*

L2. *Between October 1605 and September 1606, Richard Tillboroughe, within the parish of Stoughton defamed Margaret Tayler by the words:* Thou art a whore and an arrant whore as any in England.

L4. That Richard Tillboroughe is accustomed, and doth commonly and very often use publicly to malign, deprave and abuse many of his neighbours in calling them whoremasters and whores.

37/3 Nicholas Diggens.[232] *Read over 19 November 1606.*

Clerk, vicar of Stoughton, , where has lived for about 27 years; before at Elsted; born there; aged about 60. Is worth £13 13s 4d. Signature.†

To the libel

L1. *Refers to oath.*

L2. That in the month of July last Richard Tilboroughe was at the house of Nicholas Diggens to see how he did do, and by‡ Nicholas Diggens and Richard Tilboroughe talking together, amongst other things Richard Tilboroughe told him that Matthew Tayler had him in suit of law. Whereupon he asked the cause why; unto which question Richard Tilboroughe answered because he called Matthew Tayler's wife whore. 'And indeed' said he, 'I called her whore'. All which speeches were so used by Mr Richard

* See also **27/1-5.**

† There are some differences in the detail of this biography when compared with his earlier one (**23/3**).

‡ Difficult reading.

Tilboroughe against Margaret Tayler, wife of Matthew Tayler, in the presence of Nicholas Diggens and Mary Diggens his wife. *For the rest does not know.*

L3. That about six weeks ago he being at the house of Robert Soane of Stoughton upon some occasion together with others, Richard Tilboroughe said that Matthew Tayler did sue him in the law because he called Margaret Tayler whore. 'And indeed' said he, 'I did call her whore'. All which speeches were so spoken at the house of Robert Soane, in the presence of Mr Stephen Golden, clerk, Mary Soane, the wife of Robert Soane, and Nicholas Diggens. *For the rest does not know.*

L4. That Richard Tilboroughe called Nicholas Diggens at Nicholas Diggens's own house about three months ago, 'Civil* lecherer and whoremonger', in the presence of William Soane and Thomas Baylye of Stoughton, yeomen, and Mary Diggens, Nicholas Diggens's wife.

L5. *Affirms,* for whereas Margaret Tayler always was accounted to be a woman of good fame and honest reputation, now by reason of the words of defamation her name is in question, without desert as he verily believeth, to her great discredit† if her carriage and honesty were not well known to all the parishioners where she dwelleth. But she is well thought of in the parish and not accounted for any such woman, nor to any purpose tending her discredit in any way howsoever. *For the rest does not know.*

L6. *Affirms.*

L7. *Refers to oath.*

L8. *Deposition is true.*

To the interrogatories

In 1. *Negative.*

In 2. *Is worth £13 13s 4d.*

In 3. That he came to testify at the request of Matthew Tayler without compulsion.

In 4. *Favours parties indifferently and wishes victory for the party in the right.*

In 5. *Negative for self; for fellow witnesses does not know.*

In 6. *Cannot depose beyond what has already deposed.*

37/4 Mary Diggens.[233] [*November 1606*]

Wife of Nicholas Diggens, clerk, vicar of Stoughton, where lived about 7 years; before at Trotton about 16 years; before at Frensham, Surrey; born there; aged about 25. Signs with mark.

L2. That in the month of July last Richard Tilboroughe was at the house of Mary Diggens, and he falling in talk with Mary Diggens's husband about many things, he told her husband that Matthew Tayler did sue him in the law. Then her husband asked him wherefore Matthew Tayler sued him and he answered, 'Because I called his wife whore'.

---

* 'Sivell' *in MS.*

† 'Discrete' *in MS.*

'And indeed' said he, 'I called her whore'. All which speeches were used in the presence of Mary Diggens and Nicholas Diggens and no more. *For the rest does not know.*

L4. That Richard Tilboroughe did call her husband in her own house about three months ago, 'Civil lecherer and whoremonger.' But who were then present more than Mary Diggens and her husband she cannot now depose.

L5. *Negative,* for Margaret Tayler was always accounted amongst her neighbours to be an honest woman; yet the speeches by her deposed is not fitting any man to speak against an honest woman.

In 2. *Does not know,* because she hath a husband.

In 3. That she came to testify at the request and charges of Matthew Tayler without compulsion.

In 6. *Cannot depose beyond what has already deposed,* saving that those things that Richard Tilboroughe spoke, were spoken voluntarily in the presence of Nicholas Diggens and Mary Diggens. *For the rest does not know.*

37/5 Mary Hancocke.[234] [*November 1606*]

Of Stoughton, spinster, where lived about 3 years; before at Chichester about 6 months; before at Stoughton 1 year; before at Southwick, Hampshire; born there; aged about 30. Is worth £3. Signs with mark.

L2. That about this time twelvemonth last past, Mr Richard Tilboroughe came unto the house of Mr Matthew Tayler her master, and, finding Margaret Tayler her mistress sitting in her chair by the fire side he took her by the arm and said unto her, 'Rise you whore,' with many unseemly words which she is ashamed to rehearse. All which speeches were used by Richard Tilboroughe against Margaret Tayler in the presence of Mary Hancocke and Alice Martyn and no more. *For the rest does not know.*

L5. *Negative,* in respect Margaret Tayler is and always was accounted to be an honest woman.

In 1. *Satisfactory,* and that she is household servant to Matthew Tayler and Margaret Tayler his wife. *For the rest negative.*

In 3. That she came to testify at the request and charges of Matthew Tayler her master, without compulsion.

37/6 Alice Martyn.[235] [*November 1606*]

Of Stoughton, spinster, where lived about 2 years; before at Walberton where born; aged about 20. Is worth £6 13s 4d. Signs with mark.

L2. That about twelvemonth ago last past Richard Tilboroughe came to the house of Matthew Tayler her master, where he found Margaret Tayler her mistress sitting in a chair by the fire side. And he took her by the arm and said, 'Rise you whore' with many other unseemly words not fitting to be rehearsed. All which speeches were spoken in the presence of Alice Martyn and Mary Hancock and no more. *For the rest does not know.*

L5. *Negative,* saving that he hath very much abused Margaret Tayler in respect of the words deposed because she is an honest woman and always was so reputed.

In 1. *Satisfactory,* and that she is household servant to Matthew Tayler and Margaret Tayler his wife. *For the rest negative.*

In 3. That she came to testify at the request and charges of Matthew Tayler her master.

37/7 Richard Tillberow, gentleman. [236] [*February 1606/7.*]

Personal response. Signature. (Richard Tylber).

To libel ex parte Margaret Tayler.

L1 *Refers to oath.*

L2 & 3. *Does not believe articles to be true in anything.*

L4 *Responds that article is calumnious, irrelevant etc. and he has right not to be held to respond to it.*

L5. *Does not believe article to be true in anything.*

L6. *Is of the Archdeaconry of Chichester and subject to the court.*

L7. *Believes himself to be the party complained against on the part of Margaret Tayler however unlawfully.*

L8. *Believes what he has stated above that he believes, and denies what he has denied.*

38/1 Joan Johnson v Edward Woldridge* of Woolbeding, executor of Richard Shorter of Bepton. Testamentary: subtraction of legacy.[237]

Court acts: 6 July 1606 to 21 March 1606/7; 3 October 1607 to 28 May 1608.

When Richard Shorter married Margaret Rabnut in February 1592/3 she was already the grandmother of Joan Johnson. After his death Joan made a claim against his brother-in-law, the executor of his nuncupative will,[238] for 40s promised by her grandmother. After eight months of proceedings had produced depositions for the plaintiff, followed by depositions for the defendant, there is a gap in the court record due to the missing act book. The resumed record, however, consists of a long series of purely formal entries claiming sentence for the plaintiff – after which the proceedings lapse.

Proctors: Cooke for plaintiff; Scales for defendant. Extract from plaintiff's libel (article 2). Examinations: four depositions for the plaintiff responding to libel of eleven articles and interrogatories of nine; two for defendant responding to material of four articles and interrogatories of eight.

38/2 *Extract from libel.*[239] [*October 1606*]

L1. *Extract from nuncupative will of Richard Shorter made before witnesses (unspecified)* . Whereas before the solemnisation of marriage between me and Margaret my wife lately deceased, at her request I did promise unto Joan Johnson her grandchild the sum of 40s after the death of Margaret my wife if she should die before me. Which my promise I do now acknowledge before you, and my mind and will is that according to my promise the sum of 40s should be paid and satisfied to Joan Johnson.†

38/3 William Newton.[240] [*November 1606-February 1606/7*]

Of Midhurst, husbandman, where lived about 8 years; before at Bepton; born there; aged about 62. Is worth £5. Signs with mark.

To the libel.

L1. That about twelfthtide‡ last past, he being at the house of Richard Shorter, he then being of perfect mind and memory said, 'Here is Joan Johnson', meaning the party agent, 'come unto me for 40s which her grandmother', meaning Margaret Shorter his late wife, 'did give unto her' in the lifetime of Margaret Shorter. And Richard Shorter said, 'Whether I live or die she, Joan Johnson shall have the sum of 40s,' for it was his wife's request and her own mere gift and goodwill, Joan Johnson the party agent being then present. And he further added these words: rather than she should not be paid he would sell one of his kine to pay her. All which words were used by Richard Shorter in the presence of Margaret Newton, William Newton's wife and William Newton. *For the rest does not know.*

L2. *Cannot depose beyond what has already deposed.*

L3 &4. *Affirms from certain knowledge.*

---

* The name occurs in several variants. This form has been adopted throughout.

† These words do not appear in the registered will, which leaves Shorter's entire estate to his executor.

‡ Epiphany.

L5. *Affirms.*

L6. *Does not know.*

L7. That he verily believeth that Richard Shorter left goods enough to pay his debts and legacies, for he said that he ought only 2s 4d to one John Hall of Midhurst, ostler, and no more to any person whatsoever.

L8. *Does not know beyond what has already deposed.*

L9. *Affirms.*

L10. *Refers to oath.*

L11. *Deposition is true.*

To the Interrogatories

In 1. *Satisfactory.*

In 2. *Negative as concerning Joan Johnson.*

In 3. *Negative,* saving that he favoureth the parties indifferently and wisheth the law to take place.

In 4. *Is worth £5,* and that he came to testify at the request and charges of Edward Johnson, father of Joan Johnson, and for his pains taking herein and his wife's they are only allowed their ordinary expenses and no more.

In 5. *Cannot depose beyond what has already deposed,* saving that the words deposed to the first article were uttered by Richard Shorter about 8 of the clock in the forenoon in a low chamber of the house.

In 6. That the words were uttered by Richard Shorter voluntarily, without the motion of any other person whatsoever.

In 7. That the words were spoken by Richard Shorter all at one time and at one place, he then lying in his bed.

In 8. That he was not sent for by Richard Shorter to be a witness of the words, but his wife did attend him in his sickness three nights and four days, whereupon he went to visit him and stayed there about an hour. Neither were there any present all the while save only his wife and him. *For the rest does not know.*

In 9. *Does not know beyond what has already deposed.*

38/4 Margaret Newton.[241] [*November 1606-February 1606/7*]

Wife of William Newton of Midhurst, where lived about 38 years; before at Petersfield, Hampshire; born there; aged about 56. Signs with mark.

L1. That about a twelvemonth last past she, then attending upon Richard Shorter, heard him say that Joan Johnson was come unto him for 40s which her grandmother, the wife of Richard Shorter, gave unto her, and, said he, 'I have it not yet except I should sell one of my kine; but howsoever whether I live or die, she', meaning Joan Johnson, 'shall have the sum'. All which speeches were uttered in the presence of Margaret Newton and William Newton at the house of Richard Shorter.

L7. That she verily believeth Richard Shorter left goods sufficient to pay both his debts and legacies. *For the rest does not know.*

In 4. That she is worth nothing of her own goods because she hath a husband. And that she came to testify at the request and charge of Edward Johnson, father of Joan Johnson, which charges is [*sic*] only the ordinary charges of her diet and no more.

In 5. *Cannot depose beyond what has already deposed,* saving that the words deposed to the first article were uttered about 8 of the clock in the forenoon in a low chamber of the house.

In 8. That she was sent for to attend Richard Shorter in his sickness, with whom she continued four days and three nights. And for all that time there came unto him only John Aylewyn and Agnes his wife, Joan Aylewyn, the wife of William Aylewyn, Richard Woldridge and Joan his wife, and Joan Tayler the wife of John Tayler.

38/5 Joan Aylewyn.[242] * [*November 1606-February 1606/7*]

Wife of William Aylewyn of Bepton, where lived about 20 years; before at Bramshott [Hampshire]; born there; aged about 46. Signs with mark.

L1 That she, having occasion to go to the house of Richard Shorter upon Christmas Day last past, she heard Richard Shorter say that Margaret his wife was dead and she had given unto Joan Johnson the younger 40s; and, said he, 'By the grace of God she shall have it.' But there was nobody then present save only her.

In 4. That she is worth nothing of her own proper goods because she hath a husband; and that she came to testify at the request and charge of Edward Johnson father of Joan Johnson the younger, and she hath only her ordinary expenses allowed her.

In 7. That the words were uttered by Richard Shorter all at one time and at one place, viz at his own gate without doors.

38/6 John Aylewyn.[243] [*November 1606-February 1606/7*]

Of Bepton, brickmaker, where lived about 20 years; before at Elsted; born there; aged about 40. Is worth 20s. Signs with mark.

L1. That about 12 years ago, before the solemnisation of marriage between Richard Shorter and Margaret, he heard her say that she would not marry with him except he would give her leave (if she died before him) to dispose 40s to whom she list; whereunto he gave consent in the presence of one Thomas Tradd and John Aylewyn. And that upon Christmas Day last past early in the morning Margaret Shorter sent for

---

* 'Ayling' *deleted.* The form 'Aylewyn' seems to favoured by the scribes in this case and so has been adopted in transcription in place of the variants: Ayling(e), Alewi(y)n, Aylwyn.

him, she then being sick of body but in perfect mind and remembrance, whereupon he came unto her to Richard Shorter's house. Then Margaret Shorter called her husband unto her and said, 'Husband you remember the match that was betwixt you and I before we were married?' and he answered 'Yes'. Then Margaret Shorter said that she was to dispose 40s at her pleasure if it pleased God to take her out of this world before him; whereunto he answered with a good will. Then said she, being of perfect mind and memory, 'I give unto Joan Johnson daughter of Joan Johnson my daughter 40s'; and so afterwards died. Unto which speeches Richard Shorter answered that he was very well content therewith and said she should have the same by the grace of God. All which words were so spoken upon Christmas Day last in the presence of him only, save only that after the death of Margaret Shorter there came unto the house that very day Richard Woldridge and Joan his wife and [*blank*] Sherfolde the wife of William Sherfolde, unto whom Richard Shorter said God had taken away his wife and she had given 40s unto Joan Johnson, her daughter's daughter, which, by the grace of God, he would see paid unto her rather with the better than the worse, in the presence of John Aylewyn and the parties above named.

In 4. ··· he came to testify at the request and charge of Edward Johnson, father of Joan Johnson the younger, which is only his ordinary charge for his diet.

In 7. *Deposes as previously to the first article of the libel* and that Richard Shorter was then standing.

In 8. That he was sent for by Margaret Shorter to come unto her to witness that which he hath formerly deposed, and stayed there about 2 hours. ···.

38/7 Edward Woldridge.[244] [*March 1606/7*]

Of Bepton, husbandman; born there; aged about 53. Is worth £40. Signs with mark.

To the material articulated.

M1. That in January was 12 months, Richard Shorter then being of perfect mind and memory, Edward Woldridge coming to visit him asked him how he did; and he answered 'Sick.' Then Richard Woldridge said, 'It is reported that Joan Johnson lays claim to 40s'; but by whom it should be due he cannot depose because Richard Woldridge named nobody. Then Richard Shorter answered that Joan Johnson had more than his good will was that she should have already, and that she should have no more. But upon what occasion he spoke or what she ever had of him he cannot depose, nor whether there was ever any such legacy of 40s. All which speeches were spoken in the presence of Edward Woldridge and Richard Woldridge. *For the rest does not know.*

M2. *Cannot depose beyond what has already deposed.*

M3. That that day he was with Richard Shorter, which was in January was twelvemonth, he did not live above three or four hours after. *For the rest does not know.*

M4. *Deposition is true.*

To the interrogatories.

In 1. *To the danger of perjury deposes* that he is brother unto Richard Woldridge. *For the rest negative.*

In 2. That he is a husbandman and thereby getteth his living and that he is worth £40.

In 3. *For self negative; for fellow witnesses does not know.*

In 4. *Favours parties indifferently and wishes victory for the party in the right. For the rest does not know.*

In 5. *Negative.*

In 6. That he came to testify at the request of Richard Woldridge and at his own charges.

In 7 & 8. *Cannot depose beyond what has already deposed.*

38/8 Joan Tayler.[245] [*March 1606/7*]

Wife of Richard Tayler, husbandman, of Bepton, where lived about 15 years; before at Petersfield, Hampshire; born there; aged about 48. Signs with mark.

M1. That about Shrovetide was twelvemonth, she being at the house of Richard Shorter to visit him he then being sick and not well, she heard Richard Woldridge say unto him, 'What is your will and meaning touching forty shillings that was demanded to be due unto Joan Johnson?' Whereunto he answered that she had as much and more than his good will was already. All which speeches were spoken in the presence of Edward Woldridge and Joan Tayler. *For the rest does not know.*

M3. That, that day that she was with Richard Shorter, which was about Shrovetide was twelvemonth, he did not live above two hours or three at the most. *For the rest does not know.*

In 2. That she is another man's wife and therefore worth nothing.

In 6. That she came to testify at the request and charges of Richard Woldridge and without compulsion.

39/1 Rose Harris wife of William Harris of Tortington, v Edward Graye of Tortington. Defamation. [246]

*Court acts: 31 January 1606/7 to 21 March 1606/7 [and perhaps later].**

Too little of the proceedings have survived to provide a clear understanding of the case. Graye called Harris a whore at a Christmas dinner provided for the parishioners of Tortington given by Sir William Gratwicke, the principal landowner, probably at Tortington Place. The case moved relatively quickly, with the plaintiff delivering the libel by the end of January, the depositions being published by the end of February, and the plaintiff pressing for sentence by the end of March (when the break in the act book series begins).

Proctors: Scales for plaintiff; Cooke for defendant. Extract from plaintiff's libel (article 2). Examinations: three depositions for the plaintiff responding to libel of seven articles.

39/2 *Extract from libel.*[247] [*January 1606/7*]

L2 *Between October 1606 and January 1606/7 Edward Graye said in Tortington*: Thou art a whore and an arrant whore.

39/3 John Baylye.[248] [*February 1606/7*]

Of Tortington, husbandman, where lived about 9 years; before at Maresfield about 12 years; before at Withyham; born there; aged about 48. Signs with mark.

To the libel

L1. *Refers to oath.*

L2. That he at Christmas last, the certain day he cannot now remember, he together with other of his poor neighbours being invited to the house of Sir William Gratwicke within Tortington to dinner, he heard Edward Graye call Rose Harris whore; but upon what occasion or speech he cannot depose because he was not present at the beginning of their speeches or falling out. All which speeches were uttered in the presence of William Blaber, William Tupper, John Baylye and others whose names he cannot now remember. *For the rest does not know.*

L3. *Cannot depose beyond what has already deposed.*

L4. *Affirms,* for it is no credit for an honest woman to be called whore before such an auditory as were present.

L5. *Affirms.*

L6. *Refers to oath.*

L7. *Deposition is true.*

---

* Court acts March-October 1607 do not survive.

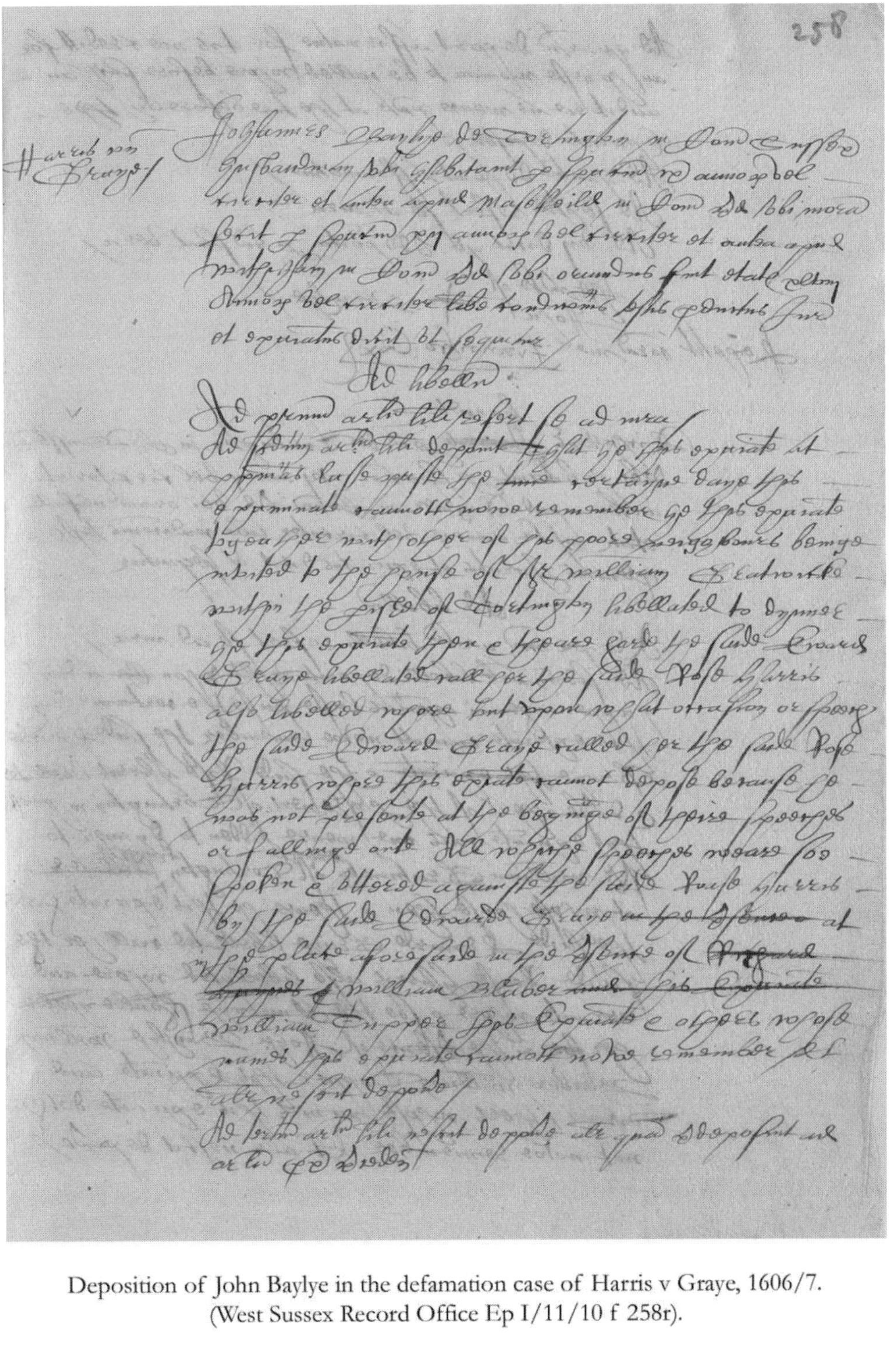

Deposition of John Baylye in the defamation case of Harris v Graye, 1606/7.
(West Sussex Record Office Ep I/11/10 f 258r).

39/4 Richard Haynes.[249] *[February 1606/7]*

Of Tortington [occupation not given] where lived about 16 years; before at Ringmer; born there; aged about 50. Signature.

L2. That upon a day happening in Christmas last past, the certain day he cannot now remember, Edward Graye and Rose Harris and divers others of Tortington were bidden to dinner to Sir William Gratwicke of Tortington, knight. At whose house he heard Edward Graye call Rose Harris whore and arrant whore and so the country should yield her, in the presence of John Baylye, William Blaber, William Tupper, Richard Haynes and divers others whose names he doth not now remember. ···.

39/5 William Blaber.[250] *[February 1606/7]*

Of Tortington, husbandman, where lived about 23 years; before at Tarring about 28 years; before at Broadwater; born there; aged about 60. Signs with mark.

L2. That upon St John's Day* in Christmas last past or some other day happening thereabouts, he and divers others of Tortington were bidden to dinner to Sir William Gratwicke's house, amongst whom were Rose Harris and Edward Graye; and Edward Graye called Rose Harris whore and arrant whore and for a whore the country should yield her. All which speeches were so used in the house of Sir William Gratwicke in the presence of John Baylye, Richard Haynes, William Tupper and William Blaber and divers others whose names he doth not now remember. ···.

L4. *Affirms,* for it is a great discredit for an honest woman to be called an arrant whore before a multitude of people.

* 27 December.

40-42 Mr Michael Birkeheade, vicar of Warnham: Tithe (three cases):
v Richard Barttelot;
v William Perkyn;
v John Pancrasse (and Thomas Rapley and Thomas Somersall).

At an early stage in his incumbency as vicar of Warnham, Birkeheade began a series of tithe cases. The main purpose seems to have been to claim rights to the great tithes (from corn and other growing crops) which were normally paid to the lay rector rather than the vicar. The proceedings are confusing because the properties on which the plaintiff claims tithe are not accurately identified. In the libels for all three cases, the plaintiff refers to Denne or Denne Lands and Blunde or Blunde Lands. The depositions make it clear that Denne is occupied by the defendant in the first case, Richard Barttelot, while the property occupied by the defendant in the second case, William Perkyn, is Knells or Gills Land (unmentioned in the libels). For the third case the deponents do not identify a specific property occupied by the defendant, John Pancrasse. The same four witnesses† were called to depose in the first two cases, all produced by the plaintiff; and two of them provided the depositions in the third - but this time called by the defendants. When appearing as the plaintiff's witnesses, they do not seem to have given his case full endorsement, as their corrections to the properties demonstrate. They also appeared only after compulsion; and while confirming that the vicarial tithe was paid in cash rather than kind, they implied that it followed the usual pattern in being confined to small tithe (which excluded growing crops) while the great tithe should be paid to the lay rector. This practice they confirmed when appearing in the third case.*

It would appear that at a late stage, in March 1606/7, Birkeheade initiated a fourth case, combining as defendants Barttelot and Perkyn from the first two cases, together with the two farmers of the rectorial tithe, Somersall and Rapley, who had intervened in the third case. The deposition book contains no examinations for this latter case.

The conclusion of all the cases is unknown because the acts which would have recorded the final stages, during the period between March and October 1607, have not survived.

Michael Birkeheade was instituted as vicar of Warnham 27 July 1605 and held the living until his resignation in 1615. He appears to have been something of a vexatious litigant, determined to increase his tithe income; but the depositions of the witnesses he compelled to appear do not fully endorse his claims. Other aspects of his ministry reflect controversy within his parish. Early in 1607 three men (one of them the son of the deponent Thomas Lucas) were presented in the office court for attending service outside the parish; but they claimed that there were no sermons given in their church. He was presented in the office court between June and October 1607 for failing 'to instruct the youth nor say service on Wednesdays and Fridays'[251] and briefly excommunicated. A year later he complained of a rival teacher in his parish and accused the court apparitor of taking bribes.[252]

---

* The libels survive for all three cases but that for the first case is incomplete and lacks the schedule listing the crops grown.

† The depositions which each witness gave in the separate cases are entered in sequence *en bloc* in the deposition book; biographical details are given only in the first deposition.

40/1 Michael Birkeheade, vicar of Warnham v Richard Barttelot,* esq. Tithe.[253]

Court acts: 27 September 1606 to 14 March 1606/7 [and perhaps later]

This case and the following one (41) against separate defendants proceeded through a series of virtually identical court acts. The third case (42), concerned with the tithe of flax and hemp, initially followed an almost identical course but was then complicated by the intervention of additional parties in January 1606/7.

Richard Barttelot was the occupier of property called Denne or Denne Lands, on which vicarial tithe had been compounded for a money payment instead of payment in kind. Late in the proceedings, Birkeheade's proctor produced a document from the Bishop's registry dated 1247; but neither side appeared to have accepted it as the solution to the dispute.† The conclusion of the case is uncertain due to the gap in the act book series between March and October 1607 – and is further complicated by the appearance of Barttelot as a party in a new case which commences on 4 March 1606/7.

Proctors: Cooke for plaintiff; Scales for defendant. Examinations: personal response of the defendant responding to libel of eleven articles; four depositions for plaintiff responding to libel of eleven articles.

40/2 Richard Barttelot, esquire.[254] *Read over 16 Jan 1606/7.*

Signature: 'Richard Barttelot'.

Personal response to libel ex parte Mr Michael Birkeheade.

L1. *Believes it to be true.*

L2 & 3. *Does not believe articles to be true in anything.*

L4 & 5 & schedule. *That, concerning* Denne Lands or the lands of Denne, Blunde Lands or the land of Blunde, *does not believe articles or schedule to be true in anything.*

L6. *Refers to statute and believes what it contains.*

L7. *Is a layman; for the rest does not believe article to be true in anything.*

L8. *Accepts that he refused, justly as he believes, to pay the tithes.*

L9. *Is of the Archdeaconry of Chichester and subject to the court.*

L10. *Believes he is the party complained against on the part of Mr Michael Birkeheade in this case, though unlawfully.*

L11. *Believes what he has stated above that he believes, and denies what he has denied.*

---

* This spelling is used in the signature of the personal response. Several variants (including Bartlett) are used elsewhere.

† No document of appropriate date associated with Warnham has been found in W.D. Peckham's *Chichester Cathedral Chartulary* (Sussex Record Society vol. 46) or A.M. Edwards's *Calendar of the Ancient Charters of Dean and Chapter of Chichester* (WSRO, Cap I/51/6).

40/3 John Tayler. [255] [*February 1606/7*]

Of Warnham, yeoman; born there; aged about 60. Signs with mark.

To the libel.

L1. That Mr Michael Birkeheade hath been vicar of Warnham for 2 years, as he is at this present and so was commonly reputed.

L2. That Mr Michael Birkeheade hath right to receive a certain sum of money in respect of his vicarage of all the occupiers of the lands of Denne or Denne Lands in lieu of the small tithes in or upon the said lands, and sometimes called by the name of Pynese Lands; for, as he hath heard, Sir John Shorte, who was vicar of Warnham for 50 years ago or thereabouts, did compound and agree with John Worsfolde who then did occupy the same lands for his tithes; but for how much he cannot depose. And in like manner did Sir John Hunter, Sir Henry Patcheinge and one Mr Swinderton and one Sir Graye and Mr Allen, who were all vicars of Warnham since that time, compound with the occupiers of the said lands for a certain sum of money by the year as they could agree. But he cannot depose how much any of the occupiers of the lands paid unto the vicars of Warnham, but he hath heard John Thornden and John Maye say divers times, who were then occupiers of the said lands, that they paid unto Sir John Shorte always a certain sum for their tithes upon the said lands and never paid any tithes to the vicar of Warnham in kind, neither did they ever hear that there was any tithes paid in kind unto the vicars of Warnham out of the lands. And that he hath heard Thomas Lucas say that about 40 years ago he did gather the tithes for Sir Graye upon the lands and he never received any tithes in kind upon the lands but only money. And as he hath also heard by Thomas Rapley the elder and Thomas Somersall, Mr Allen late vicar of Warnham did receive money in lieu of the tithes and never received any in kind, for they received of the occupiers of the lands the money due unto Mr Allen for his tithes themselves and paid it to Mr Allen, but how much he cannot depose. Neither did he ever hear anything to the contrary but that the occupiers of the lands did always pay a certain sum of money in lieu of their tithes due to the vicar of Warnham and no tithes in kind. Neither did he ever hear that any parishioner did ever pay any tithes in kind to any of the vicars but always did agree for money with the vicars, sometimes for more and sometimes for less according as they could agree. And that the lands is not always called by the name of Denne or Denne Lands for he hath heard John Thornden and John Maye the elder say that it was called by the name of Pynesse.* But touching the lands of Blunde or Blunde Lands he cannot depose.

L3. The predecessors of Mr Michael Birkeheade for this 50 years last past have been in quiet possession of the tithes before by him deposed, as Mr Birkeheade ought to be. *For the rest does not know.*

L4 & 5. *Does not know beyond what has already deposed.*

L6. *Refers to statute.*

L7. That Mr Barttelot is a mere layman and in respect thereof hath no right to the tithes. *For the rest does not know.*

---

* Difficult reading.

L8. *Does not know.*

L9. *Affirms.*

L10. *Refers to oath.*

L11. *Deposition is true.*

40/4 Thomas Lucas, senior.[256] [*February 1606/7*]

Of Warnham, yeoman; born there; aged about 73. Signature.

To the libel

L2. That Mr Michael Birkeheade hath no right to have any tithes in kind out of the lands called Denne or Denne Lands but only a sum of money in lieu. For Thomas Lucas hath known Sir John Shorte, who was vicar of Warnham for threescore years ago, receive a sum of money for all the tithes upon Denne and Denne Lands for 10 years together at the hands of one John Worsfolde who then did occupy the said land, and no tithes in kind; but he cannot depose how much money. And that Sir John Hunter, who was vicar of Warnham for three years together next after Sir John Shorte, did likewise receive a certain sum of money of John Worsfolde; Sir Henry Patcheinge, vicar for the space of five years received of Worsfolde a certain sum of money in lieu in like manner; Mr John Fowler, Mr John Swinderton and Mr John Graye, vicars, did receive likewise a certain sum of money of Worsfolde in lieu and never any tithes in kind. And this much he knoweth of his own knowledge for he dwelt with John Worsfolde in his house eight years together about 60 years ago and afterwards dwelt near adjoining unto him, in so much that he did deal about much business for him till his dying day. But he cannot depose how much money John Worsfolde did pay six several vicars of Warnham before recited, for some of them at their first coming did not only raise the sum of money which his predecessor had compounded for with him, but did also raise the sums of money which some of his predecessors had compounded for before with all the parishioners or the most of them, so that at the coming of every new incumbent vicar or most of them they did make a new composition with every one of their parishioners for all their tithes as they could agree. For he hath heard of divers, whose names he cannot now remember, that at the first coming of Sir John Shorte he had in all but only £18 a year for all the small tithes within the parish; and he of his own knowledge knoweth that Mr John Graye when he was vicar raised the same rents among the parishioners to £38, for Thomas Lucas gathered the same himself; and after that Mr Allen raised the sum to £40. So that he is sure that the vicars did agree with the parishioners for money for their tithes in such sort as they could agree and not otherwise, since which time he never heard that there were any tithes in kind at all paid to the vicars of Warnham but only composition. And touching the Lands of Blunde or Blunde Lands he cannot depose because he never knew of any such lands.

L3. *Does not know beyond what has already deposed,* saving that he never heard of any man that was sued for his tithes within Warnham before this suit began.

40/5 John Bowton.[257] [*February 1606/7*]

Of Rudgwick, yeoman, where lived 1 year; before at Warnham about 18 years; before at Ockley, Surrey; born there; aged about 44.

L2-5. That Mr Michael Birkeheade hath right to receive a certain sum of money in lieu of his small tithes in such manner and sort as Mr Birkeheade and every of his parishioners can agree, but that he hath heard Thomas Lucas say that he never heard to the contrary for this 60 years last past but that the vicars did always compound with all the inhabitants for a certain sum of money; but for how much he cannot depose. And they nor any of them ever received any tithes in kind, by reason of which he doth not believe that Mr Birkeheade ought to have any tithes in kind. And that he hath heard divers others affirm to the like, and that he for 12 years ago did compound with Mr Matthew Allen then vicar of Warnham for all the tithe due from him for a certain sum of money so that he never paid any tithes in kind. After whose departure John Bowton had only one half year to come in the lands which he then occupied, for which half year whereas he paid before unto Mr Allen by the year only 20s Mr Birkeheade had of him for the half year 13s 4d. And that he never heard of any tithes in kind paid unto any vicar of Warnham but only a sum of money in lieu according to the number of acres they did occupy and as the parishioners and the vicar could agree at their first coming and not otherwise. And touching the lands libellated and the grain thereupon or the tithes occurring or the valuation thereof due unto Mr Birkeheade, he cannot depose because he knoweth not what was sown upon the lands.

40/6 John Charman.[258] [*February 1606/7*]

Of Warnham, husbandman; born there; aged about 50. Signs with mark.

L2-5. That he never heard that any vicars of Warnham had any right to receive any tithes in kind upon the lands called Denne or Denne Lands, for he hath heard Thomas Lucas and John Tayler say many times that the vicars of Warnham for this 40 years last past and upwards never received any tithes in kind, neither of the said lands now in the occupation of Mr Barttelot nor of any other lands, but that all the vicars did always compound with all the parishioners for all their small tithes for a certain sum of money as every one of the vicars and parishioners could agree and not otherwise, but they did always agree for their tithes for a certain sum of money in lieu. So that, as he hath heard by Thomas Lucas and John Tayler, the vicars did never receive any tithes in kind of any the parishioners but only a certain sum of money as the vicars and parishioners could agree; but for how much or how little he cannot depose. And John Charman did compound with Mr Matthew Allen for his own small tithes for six years together in his lifetime for 8s by the year; and since the death of Mr Allen he hath compounded with Mr Birkeheade for 12s by the year; so he payeth the more by 4s the year. And touching the lands called Blunde or Blundlands he cannot depose because he knoweth no such lands. Neither doth he know what grain of corn Mr Barttelot had growing; nor what tithe out of the same or the valuation thereof by Mr Barttelot he cannot depose, because he taketh no notice thereof but followeth his own business, save only he see [*sic*] a close of the same land sown with wheat of some four acres in the years libellated. *For the rest does not know.*

41/1 Mr Michael Birkeheade, vicar of Warnham v William Perkyn. Tithe. [259]

Court acts: 27 September 1606 to 14 March 1606/7 [and perhaps later].

The second case in the series parallels the case against Richard Barttelot (40). The court acts for each session normally duplicate those of the first case, and of course lack any conclusion. William Perkyn was the occupier of the land called Knells or Gills. Like Barttelot, Perkyn was subsequently cited as a defendant in the new case commencing on 4 March 1606/7.

Proctors: Cooke for plaintiff; Scales for defendant. Examinations: four depositions for plaintiff responding to libel of eleven articles.

41/2 Extract from libel.[260] [*October 1606*]

Schedule.

William Perkyn in the years and months specified had in his occupation of the lands of Denne or Denne lands: 40 acres sown with wheat, 40 acres sown with barley, 20 acres sown with rye, 15 acres sown with oats, 8 acres sown with pease, 10 acres sown with fatches and 4 acres sown with beans. And on every acre sown with wheat he had as much wheat as was worth £3. On every acre sown with barley he had as much barley as was worth 40s. On every acre sown with rye he had as much rye as was worth 40s. On every acre sown with oats he had as many oats as were worth 30s. On every acre sown with pease he had as many pease as were worth 26s 8d. On every acre sown with fatches he had as many fatches as were worth 20s. And on every acre sown with beans he had as many beans as were worth 40s.

41/3 John Tayler.[261] [*February 1606/7*]

To the libel.

L1. That Mr Michael Birkeheade hath been vicar of Warnham for 2 years as he is at this present and so was commonly reputed.

L2. That Mr Birkeheade hath right to receive a certain sum of money in respect of his small tithes upon a certain piece of land called Knells and Gills now in the occupation of William Perkyn, but he never heard that William Perkyn nor any of his predecessors farmers or occupiers did ever pay any tithe corn nor money in lieu. Neither did he ever hear that William Perkyn nor any of his predecessors did ever call the same lands by the name of Blunde or Blunde Lands and the lands of Denne and Denne Lands but always by the name of Knells and Gills Lands. And, as he hath heard Thomas Lucas the elder say, that about 40 years ago he did gather the tithes due to Sir Graye out of the lands called Knells and Gills but he never received any tithes in kind but only a sum of money; but how much he cannot depose. Neither did he ever hear that any parishioners did ever pay any tithes in kind to any of the vicars of Warnham, but always did agree with the vicars sometimes for more sometimes for less money as they could agree. And he also heard Thomas Lucas say that the occupiers did always pay their tithe corn upon the said lands unto the farmers of the parsonage of Warnham and never unto the vicars; and he hath heard divers others affirm the like, as namely John Thornden and John Maye the elder, John Bowton and divers others.

L3. That the predecessors of Mr Michael Birkeheade for this 50 years last past have been in quiet possession of the tithes before by him deposed, as Mr Birkeheade ought to be.

L4 & 5. That some part of Knells and Gills were sown with corn, but how much or of what kind he cannot depose nor the valuation thereof.

L6. *Refers to statute.*

L7. That William Perkyn is a mere layman and in respect thereof hath no right to the tithes. *For the rest does not know.*

L8. *Does not know.*

L9. *Affirms.*

L10. *Refers to oath.*

L11. *Deposition is true.*

41/4 Thomas Lucas.[262] [*February 1606/7*]

L2. That Mr Michael Birkeheade hath no right to have any tithes in kind out of the lands called the Lands of Blunde or Blunde Lands and the Lands of Denne or Denne Lands of William Perkyn, because he occupieth no such lands; but he occupieth the lands called Knells and Gills and other lands within Warnham, out of which lands Thomas Lucas thinketh Mr Birkeheade hath no right to have any tithes in kind but only a sum of money in lieu. For he hath known Sir John Shorte, vicar of Warnham threescore years ago for 10 years together, Sir John Hunter who was also vicar of Warnham for three years together next after Sir John Shorte, Sir Henry Patcheinge who was also vicar about five years, Mr John Fowler who was also vicar of Warnham, Mr John Swinderton and Mr John Graye also vicars, to have and receive a certain sum of money one after the other successively of John Worsfolde, who then did occupy Knells and Gills and other lands now in the occupation of William Perkyn, in lieu of all the tithes; and never any tithes in kind. And this much he knoweth for he dwelt with John Worsfolde in his house eight years together about 60 years ago and afterwards dwelt near adjoining unto him, in so much that he did deal about much business for him till his dying day. But he cannot depose how much money John Worsfolde did pay unto the six vicars of Warnham because every several vicar or most of them did rear the rate of the rent for all their tithes as they and every one of them successively could agree with him. And that every one of the vicars beforementioned at their first coming did rear the rate of the rent for all their tithes as they could agree with every one of their parishioners. So that he never knew any tithes this 60 years or thereabouts to be paid in kind but only a certain sum of money.

L3. *Cannot depose beyond what has already deposed,* saving that he never heard of any suit betwixt the vicar of Warnham and any of his parishioners for any tithes till this suit began.

L4 & 5. *Does not know,* because he hath not seen the said grounds since Mr Birkeheade was vicar.

41/5 John Bowton.[263] [*February 1606/7*]

L2-5. That Mr Michael Birkeheade hath right to receive a certain sum of money in lieu of his small tithes in such sort as Mr Birkeheade and every of his parishioners can agree; but that he hath heard Thomas Lucas say that he never heard to the contrary for this 60 years last past but that the vicars did always compound with all the inhabitants for a certain sum of money, but for how much he cannot depose. And that they never received any tithes in kind but only a certain sum of money, by reason whereof he doth not believe that Mr Birkeheade ought to have any tithes in kind; and that he hath heard divers others affirm to the like. And that he for 12 years ago did compound with Mr Matthew Allen then vicar of Warnham for all the tithes upon certain lands then in the occupation of John Bowton called Knells and Gills, which lands are now in the occupation of William Perkyn; and he did compound with Mr Allen for 20s by the year which he paid unto Mr Allen during his life. And after the departure of Mr Allen, John Bowton having but one half year to come in the lands, was glad to compound with Mr Birkeheade for the half year and give him 13s 4d. And that he never heard that any vicar of Warnham did ever receive any tithes in kind but only a sum of money in lieu as the vicar and every parishioner could agree at their first coming. And touching the lands libellated and the grain thereupon, or the tithes occurring, or the valuation thereof, due unto Mr Birkeheade by William Perkyn, he cannot depose because he knoweth no such lands now in the occupation of William Perkyn as are specified in the libel save only William Perkyn doth occupy the lands called Knells and Gills. But what number of acres were sown with any kind of grain or what value every acre was worth he cannot depose, because he now dwelleth out of the parish and taketh no notice or regard of any such thing. *For the rest does not know.*

41/6 John Charman.[264] [*February 1606/7*]

L2-5. That he never heard that the vicars had any right to have any tithes in kind upon any lands in Warnham, as he hath heard Thomas Lucas and John Tayler say that the vicars of Warnham for this 40 years last past and upwards did never receive any tithes in kind of any occupier or farmer but that all the vicars did always compound with all the parishioners for all their small tithes for a certain sum of money as every one of the vicars and parishioners could agree and not otherwise. But they did always agree for the tithes for a certain sum of money in lieu, so that, as he hath heard by Thomas Lucas and John Tayler, the vicars did never receive any tithes in kind of any the parishioners but only a certain sum of money as the vicars and parishioners could agree; but for how much or how little he cannot depose, saving that he for his own part did compound with Mr Matthew Allen for his own tithes for six years together in his lifetime upon his lands for 8s by the year, and since the death of Mr Allen he hath compounded with Mr Birkeheade for 12s by the year; so he payeth more by 4s the year. And touching the lands called Blunde or Blundlands and the lands of Denne or Denne Lands which should be in the occupation of William Perkyn, he cannot depose because he never heard that he ever occupied any such lands. But he must needs say that William Perkyn occupieth certain lands called Knells and Guilles [*sic*]; but what grain or corn he had in the years libellated, or what tithes thereof did accrue, or what the value thereof was, he cannot depose because he taketh no notice thereof but followeth his own business. *For the rest does not know.*

42/1 Mr Michael Birkeheade, vicar of Warnham v John Pancrasse with, later, Thomas Somersall and Thomas Rapley, farmers of the rectory of Warnham, intervening. Tithe. [265]

Court acts: 27 September 1606 to 21 February 1606/7 and 31 January 1606/7 to 14 March 1606/7 [and perhaps later].

In the third case of the series, the vicar of Warnham sued for tithe on flax grown by John Pancrasse, claiming the right to tithe flax and hemp throughout the parish. The claim is unusual as these crops would normally be considered great tithes and therefore due to the lay rector. Up to 21 February, the proceedings are almost identical with two previous cases (40 and 41), but the case appears thereafter to have merged with a new one, commenced on 31 January 1606/7, with the farmers of the lay rectory of Warnham, Thomas Somersall and Thomas Rapley intervening to join Pancrasse as defendants. The intervening defendants produced an allegation against the plaintiff, calling two of Birkeheade's witnesses from the previous cases. No conclusion had been reached when the gap in the court acts begins. An undated draft sentence, submitted by the defendants, survives among the court papers for 1607.[266] *In it they sought that Birkeheade's claims against all three be rejected and that he be ordered to pay the costs. Somersall and Rapley subsequently appeared as defendants in the new case commencing 14 March 1606/7.*

Proctors: Cooke for plaintiff; Scales for defendant; Freeman for Somersall and Rapley intervening. Examinations: two depositions for defendant responding to allegation of five articles and interrogatories of six.

42/2 Extract from libel.[267] [*October 1606*]

Schedule.

S John Pancrasse in the years and months specified had growing as much flax as was worth the sum of £4.

42/3 John Tayler.[268] [*February 1606/7*]

To the allegation

A1-3. That all the inhabitants of Warnham for this 40 years last past did ever pay their tithe flax and hemp upon any of the lands in their occupation unto the proprietaries farmers and occupiers of the parsonage, as of right belonging unto them and not to the vicars of Warnham, nor anything in lieu as due unto the vicars. For he hath himself compounded with the proprietaries or farmers for tithe flax upon certain lands in his possession for 32 years: as namely he did compound with one Mrs Welche for tithe flax and hemp due by him, which Mrs Welche was the farmer of the parsonage; and he did likewise compound with one John Michell of Coxe which was farmer of the parsonage 20 years ago for the like tithe of flax and hemp; and so consequently he did agree with every farmer of the parsonage since that time, as he hath done for this 10 years last past with Thomas Somersall and Thomas Rapley now farmers of the parsonage. And he hath heard John Clowser of Sheremarke, who soweth much flax and hemp within the parish of Warnham, say that he did always compound with the proprietaries or farmers of the parsonage of Warnham for his tithe flax and hemp and that he never paid anything in lieu to the vicars of Warnham. And he hath also heard Richard Clowser of Warnham, who sowed much flax and hemp in his lifetime, affirm the like for 20 years ago, and Henry Roffye of Warnham, who married Richard Clowser's widow, who doth likewise sow much flax and hemp at this present, that he always compounded with the proprietaries or farmers of the parsonage of Warnham for the tithe of his flax and hemp as he now hath done with Thomas Somersall and Thomas Rapley, and never paid anything to the vicars of Warnham. And that he never heard nor knew to the contrary but that the proprietaries, farmers or occupiers of the parsonage did always receive the tithe flax and hemp, as also of all other kind of grain, as Thomas Somersall and Thomas Rapley doth at this present.

A4. *Does not know,* saving that he verily thinketh John Pancrasse hath satisfied the tithes to Somersall and Rapley.

A5. *Deposition is true.*

To the interrogatories

In 1. *Satisfactory and for self responds in the negative.*

In 2. *Favours parties indifferently and wishes victory for the party in the right.*

In 3. *Cannot depose beyond what has already deposed.*

In 4. *Cannot depose beyond what has already deposed* for he never heard that the tithe of flax was accounted to be small tithes.

In 5. *Cannot depose beyond what has already deposed* for he never knew any vicar of Warnham receive any tithes in kind but only money.

In 6. *Does not know.*

42/4 Thomas Lucas.[269] [*February 1606/7*]

A1-3. That for this 60 years he never heard that any parishioner ever pay [*sic*] any tithe flax or hemp upon their lands unto the vicar but always to the proprietaries or farmers of the parsonage as of right due unto them, and not unto the vicars nor anything else in lieu. For he himself hath compounded with Thomas Somersall and Thomas Rapley for tithe flax and hemp due unto them as farmers of the parsonage any time this 10 years last past. And he is certain that he never knew nor heard that any vicar this threescore years ever had any tithe flax or hemp nor no other agreement for the same, and that for 25 years ago he heard a question asked of Mr John Graye whether tithe flax and hemp was due unto the vicar or the proprietaries of the parsonage, whereunto he answered that he had nothing to do with tithe hemp and flax for the tithe thereof belonged to the proprietaries of the parsonage. And so he hath heard divers others say, whose names he cannot now remember. And that he never heard nor knew to the contrary but that the proprietaries farmers or occupiers of the parsonage did always receive the tithe flax and hemp, as also the tithe of all other kind of grain, as Thomas Somersall and Thomas Rapley doth at this present.

A4. *Does not know,* saving that he verily thinketh John Pancrasse hath satisfied the tithes to Somerley [*sic*] and Rapley.

In 1. That his wife is aunt to Thomas Rapley but nothing of kin to Thomas Somersall. *For the rest negative for self; for fellow witnesses does not know.*

In 4. *Cannot depose beyond what has already deposed,* for he never heard that the tithe of flax was accounted to be small tithes.

43/1 Mr Hugh Roberts, vicar of Yapton v Henry Standen of Felpham. Tithe.[270]

Court acts: 8 November 1606 to 14 March 1606/7, 3 September 1607 to 4 June 1608, 21 January 1608/9 to 22 April 1609.*

In the initial sessions of this protracted case the vicar of Yapton sought to get a significant increase in his tithes, as set out in the libel and backed up by the depositions of his witnesses. The court acts for the months following March 1606/7 have not survived, but in October 1607 the defendant produced an allegation claiming that he should continue to pay tithe at the rate (30s per year) agreed in a previous composition. After the depositions of the defendant's witnesses the plaintiff pressed for sentence throughout the period between December 1607 and April 1608. The judge ruled that the defendant must pay costs of £7 by Michaelmas but Standen notified his intention to appeal. Further proceedings in January and February 1608/9 led to his excommunication – from which he sought absolution in April 1609.

The case is unusual in setting out the precise claims of each party and the attempts at compromise. The statements of the witnesses for both sides appear to confirm that the vicar's claim was substantially exaggerated while Standen's claimed size of holding and rates of payment were a fair reflection of an earlier composition. Up to 1605 he had compounded for the sum of 30s per year. Thereafter the vicar attempted to arrange a new composition which demanded 8d in the noble (6s 8d) for every acre of pasture. After an attempt to agree a new composition failed, Standen refused to pay tithe.

On the day the case started a parallel case, Roberts v Duke, had commenced; but the proceedings lapsed after five weeks without witnesses having been called.

Roberts was vicar of Yapton from 1582 t0 1622. During the years 1600-1606 the office court records include a series of presentments against him for failures in his parochial duties. One recorded a brawl in the chancel with Thomas Knight, the previous occupier of Standen's land.. In 1603 Standen was also presented, for failing to pay for the repair of church pews.

Proctors: Cooke for plaintiff; Scales for defendant. Schedule of six articles from plaintiff's libel. Allegation (eight articles) of defendant. Examinations: personal response of the defendant responding to libel of eleven articles; three depositions for plaintiff responding to libel and interrogatories of seven articles; two depositions for the defendant responding to the allegation and fourteen interrogatories; one deposition for the defendant responding to the libel and interrogatories and the allegation and interrogatories.

43/2 Extract from libel ex parte Roberts.[271] [*October 1606*]

Schedule.

In primis: Henry Standen in the months and years specified in the first article had in his occupation within Yapton 20 acres of meadow; and of every acre he had mowed and made three loads of hay worth 20s.

Item: he had in his occupation 40 acres of pasture ground every acre worth 13s 4d by the year.

* The act book recording proceedings between March and September 1607 is missing.

Item: he had pasturing upon pasture grounds and the Ruens [*sic*] or after pasture of the meadow grounds 100 head of barren or idle cattle, as fatting oxen, bullocks, ….ts,* steers, horse beasts, three yearings, two yearings, twelvemonthings and such like barren and idle cattle, the pasturing of each worth by the week 12d.

Item: he had pasturing 20 milch kine and of them he had 20 calves, every calf worth 13s 4d. And of the milk he had of his milch kine he had made 20 cheeses, every cheese worth 2s 6d.

Item: he had pasturing and couching 100 wethers and 100 ewes; and of his ewes he had 100 lambs, every lamb worth 5s. And of his wethers and ewes he had 400 pound of wool, every pound worth 12d.

Item: he had pasturing 100 fatting sheep which he sold away before shear time, the pasturing of them being worth 40s.

43/3 Henry Standen[272] [*January-February 1606/7*]

Personal response. Signs with mark [*'H'*].

To the libel

L1. *Believes it to be true.*

L2 & 3. *Does not believe articles to be true in anything.*

L4 & 5. That he had in every of the years and months mentioned in the libel within Yapton 12 acres of meadow ground; and on every of the acres he had in 1606 one load of hay, every load worth 12s. Also he believeth that in every of the years he had 18 acres of pasture ground. And he believeth that he had feeding upon the pasture ground and upon the ruen [*sic*]† or after pasture of the meadow in the months of October, November and December in 1605, 40 wethers. And he believeth the pasturing of every of the wethers was worth for the time of their pasturing 6d apiece. And he believeth that he had for three weeks in the months libellated in 1605 10 other beasts and 4 horses feeding upon the pasture and the ruen or after pasture. And he believeth the pasturing of every of the beasts and horses was worth by the week 3d apiece. And he believeth he had 12 milch kine feeding upon the ruen of the meadow and on the pasture by the space of three weeks between the first day of October and the first of November in 1605. And he believeth he had of the milk of the kine, 9 cheeses, every cheese worth 6d apiece. Also he believeth that he had pasturing upon the ruen and pasture grounds by the space of two months between the midst of May and the midst of July libellated, 6 fatting oxen and 4 barren heifers. The pasturing of every of the beasts for the time that they pastured there worth every month 2s apiece. Likewise he believeth that he had feeding upon the ruen and pasture grounds from a week inclusive before the beginning of July until the first day of November last past 40 wethers which he sold away. The feeding of every such wether worth 12d apiece. Also he believeth that he had pasturing upon the ruen and pasture grounds by the space of three weeks

* Difficult reading: perhaps 'runts'..

† Rues, hedgerows.

between the feast of St Michael the Archangel and the feast of All Saints in the year 1606, 12 milch kine. And he believeth that of the milk of the kine he had 9 cheeses, every cheese worth 6d apiece. And he believeth that he had pasturing during the foresaid 3 weeks 10 other idle beasts. The pasturing of every such idle beast worth by the week 3d apiece. And further he believeth that the pasture of the 18 acres of pasture was worth for the time libellated £7 and no more, because he could make no more of the pasturing of his cattle in the time by him confessed, as he believeth. *For rest does not believe articles to be true in anything.*

L6. *Refers to the statute libellated and believes as is contained therein. Does not believe the rest.*

L7. *Believes he took away the tithes he acknowledged from the places where they grew in the years and months libellate before he divided the 10th part from the rest of the 9 parts; but not before he compounded. For rest does not believe article to be true in anything.*

L8. *Believes he has paid debt to Hugh Roberts of the tithes he admitted by law, or to have been prepared to pay as court should direct.*

L9. *Is of the Archdeaconry of Chichester and subject to the court*

L10. *Believes himself to be the party complained against however unlawfully..*

L11. *Believes what he has stated above that he believes and denies what he has denied.*

43/4 Anthony Nashe.[273] [*February – March 1606/7*]

Of Yapton, yeoman; born there; aged about 40. Signature

To the libel.

L1. *Affirms from certain knowledge.*

L2. That all the small tithes within Yapton have always ever since Anthony Nashe hath been of remembrance been paid unto the vicar of Yapton, as now they are due unto Mr Hugh Roberts. And that he himself hath paid, and seen paid by his friends, tithe calf, tithe lamb, tithe wool, tithe hay, tithe pigs and all other small tithes any time this 20 years last past. *For the rest does not know.*

L3. That the vicars of Yapton did always quietly and peaceably have the tithes to his knowledge until this suit began.

L4 & 5. That Henry Standen had in his own occupation four acres of meadow and of every of those acres he mowed and made one load or carriage of hay worth 6s 8d or thereabouts. And that he had 26 acres of pasture ground, every acre worth by the year 6s 8d. And that upon the pasture and the Rueus [*sic*] or after pasture of the meadow he had pasturing certain labouring cattle as oxen, horses and mares and such like, but how many and how long they did pasture there together he cannot depose. And he had some certain idle cattle pasturing upon the pasture grounds as kine and other small beasts, but how many or what kind or for what time they did pasture he cannot depose because he took no great notice thereof; but such idle cattle he hath seen. And touching the number of milch kine, the number of calves, the number of cheeses, the number of wethers, ewes and lambs, or the number of pounds of wool and fatting sheep, he cannot depose nor the value of them for the reasons above mentioned. *For the rest does not know.*

L6. *Refers to statute.*

L7. That Henry Standen is a mere layman. *For the rest does not know.*

L8. *Does not know.*

L9. *Affirms.*

L10. *Refers to oath.*

L11. *Deposition is true.*

To the interrogatories

In 1. *Satisfactory and deposes* as to the preface of the examination, and that he hath known Henry Standen from his childhood and Mr Roberts for this 10 or 12 years last past.

In 2. *Favours parties indifferently and wishes victory for the party in the right; for the rest negative.*

In 3. That he thinketh Mr John Curtys, who was vicar of Yapton 14 or 15 years ago, did quietly and peaceably have all small tithes of Thomas Knighte of Shripney and Thomas Knighte of Yapton who were then occupiers of the land now in the occupation of Henry Standen, or money in lieu; for he never knew any suit for the same tithes till this suit began. *For the rest does not know.*

In 4. *Cannot depose beyond what has already deposed.*

In 5 &6. *Cannot depose beyond what has already deposed* because he never took any notice thereof.

In 7. *Cannot depose beyond what has already deposed.*

43/5 William Stamer.[274] *[February – March 1606/7]*

Of Yapton, husbandman; born there; aged about 36. Signs with mark.

L2. That all the small tithes within Yapton have always since William Stamer's remembrance been due unto the vicar of Yapton, as they are unto Mr Hugh Roberts. And that he himself hath paid for five years ago last past a certain sum of money as Mr Roberts and he could agree in lieu. *For the rest does not know.*

L4 & 5. That Henry Standen had in his own occupation, as he hath at this present, four acres of meadow; and William Stamer hath heard Anthony Nashe say Henry Standen had mowed and made one load of hay of every acre, every load worth 6s 8d. He had also 24 or 25 acres of pasture every acre worth by the year 6s 8d. And touching barren and idle cattle, milch kine, cheeses, wethers, ewes, wool and fatting sheep he cannot depose, because he neither knoweth of any number nor value of any of them pasturing in Yapton in the occupation of Henry Standen, in respect he never took any notice thereof. *For the rest does not know.*

In 1. Deposes as before to the preface of his examination and that he hath known Henry Standen from his childhood and Mr Hugh Roberts for this 10 or 12 years last past.

In 3. That he never heard but that Mr John Curtysse, who was vicar of Yapton next before Mr Roberts, was always for 13 or 14 years in quiet possession of all the small tithes or money in lieu, as Mr Curtysse and every parishioner could agree, and as Mr Roberts ought to have; for he never heard of any suit commenced by the vicar of Yapton for any tithes before this suit began.

In 5 & 6. *Cannot depose beyond what has already deposed* because he never took any notice thereof.

43/6 John Peachie.[275] [*February – March 1606/7*]

Of Aldingbourne, yeoman, where lived about 4 years; before at Yapton about 4 years; before at Eartham; born there; aged about 35. Signature.

L2. That for all the time that he dwelt within Yapton, which was about four years, he did compound with Mr Hugh Roberts for all his small tithes as Mr Roberts and he could agree.

L4 &5. *Does not know* saving that Henry Standen had 4 acres of meadow ground and 25 acres of pasture ground; but what hay he had growing thereon or what cattle he had pasturing thereon he cannot depose because he hath not been remaining within the parish this four years last past. *For the rest does not know.*

In 1. Deposes as before to the preface of his examination and that he hath known Henry Standen this 12 years last past and Mr Hugh Roberts for this 10 years.

In 3. That he never knew any vicar of Yapton ever sue any man that occupied any lands within the parish of Yapton for any tithes before this time. …

43/7 *Extract from allegation ex parte Henry Standen.*[276] [*October 1607*]

A1. *Henry Standen denies all the tithes of Yapton in years and months mentioned except those accepted in his personal response. Mr Roberts appointed John Winton alias Winston and Richard Winton alias Winston of Yapton collectors for tithes.*

A2. That Hugh Roberts before beginning of this suit, or since the month of October 1605, did covenant with John and Richard Winton that they should collect all tithes mentioned, and should pay him for all such tithes collected a certain sum of money, or otherwise make an account unto him.

A3. That Mr Roberts before or since the month of October mentioned did give authority unto John and Richard Winton to dispose of all the tithes and did promise to ratify whatsoever they should do touching the sale .

A4. That Mr Roberts before October did compound with Henry Standen that he should pay unto him yearly during the three or two years next at the feast of St John the

Baptist the sum of 30s for all his tithes and by him in his personal answers unto the libel confessed.

A5. That Mr Roberts according to the agreement did for one year of the two or three years mentioned receive 30s of Henry Standen in manner following: viz so much hay as was worth 7s and the rest 23s in money, in payment of all his tithes by Henry Standen in his personal answers unto the libel confessed.

A6. That the years and time for which the composition was made is not expired.

A7. That Henry Standen, at the feast of St John Baptist last and especially before the beginning of this suit, did really tender unto Mr Roberts, John or Richard Winton 30s for all the tithes according to the composition, or at least in full discharge of all the tithes by him in his personal answers confessed in the point provided.

43/8 Daniel Hartley.[277] [*November 1607*]

Of Yapton, husbandman; born there and lived all his time; aged about 45. Is worth 40s. Signs with mark.

To the material articulated

A1-4. That, as he hath heard, John and Richard Winton are farmers of all the small tithes of Yapton or at the least of the most part of them; for he heard them say so, and divers others whose names he doth not now remember. And it seemeth it is so for they did sell unto him certain tithe grass growing upon certain ground in the occupation of Henry Standen within Yapton, which ground Henry Standen took to farm of Mr John Ellis clerk; and Daniel Hartley bought the same at St James tide was two years last past and paid unto John Winton and Richard Winton for the same as true owners and farmers 7s, after which time Mr Hugh Roberts, nor any other for him, demanded anything for the grass tithe. In respect whereof he verily believeth that they had compounded and agreed with Mr Roberts for the small tithes of his vicarage and rented the same of him as farmers. And otherwise he cannot depose touching one thing or other contained in this article.

A5-7. *Does not know.*

A8. *Deposition is true.*

To the interrogatories

In 1. *Satisfactory for self; for the others does not know.*

In 2. *Is worth 40s* and that he came to testify at the request and charge of Henry Standen without compulsion.

In 3. *For self negative; for the others does not know.*

In 4. *Negative.*

In 5 & 6. *Cannot depose beyond what has already deposed.*

In 7. That the vicars of Yapton have always had all the tithes mentioned (tithe crue excepted)* and they have been in quiet possession for anything he ever heard until this suit began. And that he himself hath paid unto Mr Roberts vicar of Yapton, for this three years last past, for the fall of every calf 4d, tithe cheese, and for the white of every milch cow 4d, and tithe lamb and tithe wool. *For the rest does not know.*

In 8-11. *Does not know.*

In 12-14. *Does not know.*

43/9 John Ellis.[278] [*November 1607*]

Clerk, vicar of Ford, where lived about 22 years; before at university of Oxford for about 6 years; before at Denbigh, Denbighshire; born there; aged about 50. Is worth 40s. Signature.

A1-3. That in the year 1605 Mr Hugh Roberts did covenant with John and Richard Winton that they should collect the vicar's tithes due unto him, for they as farmers or collectors of the same tithes received of John Ellis divers tithes due unto Mr Roberts, some in kind and other some he compounded with them for a certain sum of money as divers others of Yapton did the like. By reason of all which he verily believeth that they were appointed collectors and gatherers of the same tithes by Mr Roberts, for they received the same in his name, he agreeing thereunto for what they did. He never contradicted the same and John Ellis talking with him about the paying of his tithes, Mr Roberts acknowledged John and Richard Winton collectors or rather farmers of his tithes, for he said he had sold the same unto them.

A 4. That before the month October 1605 Mr Roberts spoke to him to persuade Henry Standen to compound with John and Richard Winton for his tithes upon certain lands called the hams situate within Yapton. He meeting with Mr Roberts and Henry Standen at Arundel, he endeavoured to cause them to agree and compound for the tithes according to his request but could not prevail with them, for Henry Standen would give but 23s for the same tithes that year 1605 over and above 7s which John and Richard Winton had made of hay growing upon the said lands. And withal Henry Standen would not yield to give the 23s unless he might have all the tithes growing upon the same lands at 30s by the year for two years longer, which Mr Roberts would not grant at that time.

In 1. *Satisfactory for self; for the others negative* saving that Henry Standen doth rent the lands called hams of him; *and for the others does not know.*

In 2. … That he came to testify at the request and charge of Henry Standen without compulsion.

In 7. *Does not know* saving that he knoweth the vicar of Yapton for this two years last past have [*sic*] been in quiet possession of tithe hay, calves, cheese, wool and lambs. But for tithe of pasture ground, tithe pasture of barren and idle cattle, tithe pasturing of fatting sheep, he cannot depose for himself never paid nor knew any paid.

* Unidentified.

In 8. That Henry Standen had in his occupation in the year articulate within the parish of Yapton about 28 or 30 acres of pasture ground and meadow, every acre worth by the year 10s or thereabouts. …

43/10 John Winton alias Winston.[279] [*November 1607*]

Of Yapton, blacksmith, where lived about 12 years; before at Merston where born; aged about 33. Is worth £40. Signature ('Winston'). *

To the libel

L4 & 5. That Henry Standen in the month and years libellate did mow† 12 acres of meadow ground within Yapton then and now in his own occupation. And of the same 12 acres of meadow he had about 12 loads or carriages of hay, every load worth about 10s. And in the months and year also libellate Henry Standen had about 18 acres of pasture in his occupation within Yapton, every acre worth 13s 4d by the year. But touching the number of barren and idle cattle that he had pasturing upon the pasture grounds and the Rewens and after pasture of the meadow ground, he cannot depose because he never took any view or notice thereof. Neither can he depose of any thing mentioned in the 4th and 5th articles further than he hath already deposed.

L7. That Henry Standen is a mere layman and hath no right to the tithes libellate; neither did he leave the tenth part of his hay due unto Mr Roberts in the year 1606 for his Mr Roberts his tithes, as John Winton hath heard by Richard Winton his uncle. For as Richard Winton told him, who‡ was then collector and gatherer up of the said tithes together with John Winton, who rented the tithes of Mr Roberts and employed them to their own uses according to a composition made betwixt John Winton, his uncle and Mr Roberts, Henry Standen denied the payment thereof or otherwise to compound with him and his uncle to the value of the tithes. …

In 1. *Satisfactory and deposes* as before to the preface of his examination and that he hath known the parties interrogated both of them this ten years.

In 2. That he favoureth the parties indifferently and wisheth the law to take place. …

Read over before Mr Francis Cox.

To the material articulate§

A1-3. That in the months and years not only libellated but also of the adverse party Henry Standen, John and Richard Winton his uncle were collectors or gatherers of the small tithes within Yapton according to an agreement made betwixt Mr Roberts, John Winton and Richard Winton; and did collect, gather and receive the tithes of every parishioner and did employ the same to their own proper uses. Saving that in the year

* Throughout the depositions the surname is spelt inconsistently, with 'Wilson' often used in place of 'Winton'.

† 'Move' in MS.

‡ i.e. Richard Winton.

§ A continuation of John Winton's deposition.

1606 Henry Standen did not nor would not pay any tithes upon any of his lands unto John nor Richard Winton as being collectors; neither did he pay the same unto Mr Roberts that ever he heard; and Mr Roberts did certify and confirm whatsoever they did by reason of his agreement formerly made with them.

A5. *Does not know,* saving that he and Richard Winton did receive in the year 1605 7s of Daniel Farley for the tithe of hay or grass of four acres of meadow then in the occupation of Henry Standen, which they as collectors sold unto him. And touching the 23s articulate over and above the 7s also articulate, John Winton by the appointment of Mr Roberts received the sum in payment of all and singular his tithes in that one year. But that the agreement betwixt Mr Roberts and John and Richard Winton was that if one or two parishioners refused to pay unto them after the rate of 8d in the noble for every acre of pasture wherein they did fat any beasts or breed any young cattle, then they should give leave unto Mr Roberts to sue for the tithes due. …

In 7. That all the tithes or the most part of them have been paid unto Mr Roberts or his lawful receiver for this three or four years last past; for within the time John Winton hath known Thomas [*sic*] Standen late of Yapton pay unto him, as farmer unto Mr Roberts, tithe lambs, one tithe calf, cheese and wool; and, as he thinketh, every other parishioner doth or ought to do the like. And touching tithe pasture of fatting sheep sold away from Yapton before shear time he cannot depose.

In 8. That Henry Standen had 18 acres of pasture in the months and years libellated, every acre worth 13s 4d. …

In 9. That Henry Standen had in his occupation in every of the months and years 12 acres of meadow and ground mowed; and of the same he had about 12 loads or carriages of hay worth 10s the load.

44/1 Thomas Herold* of Pulborough v Elizabeth Hitchcock. Defamation.[280]

Court acts: 7 June 1606 to 14 March 1606/7; 31 October 1607 to 14 May 1608.†

The plaintiff claimed to have been defamed by having been accused of witchcraft. The case made little progress in the first six months, which the plaintiff attributed to hopes of agreement between the parties. After the defendant had been excommunicated for contumacy and subsequently absolved, the plaintiff's witnesses were examined. During the six months following (a period for which the court acts are lost) the defendant called two witnesses (one of them her husband) to make exceptions to discredit the plaintiff's witnesses and deny that any defamatory words had been spoken. By the time the next court act book commences, sentence had been given in favour of the plaintiff, condemning the defendant to pay costs. Proceedings were further delayed by the defendant's attempts to appeal – which lapsed in early 1607/8. On 9 April 1608 the defendant was condemned to do penance in Pulborough church; and after further delay leading to the threat of excommunication, the case ended in May 1608.

Proctors: Cooke for plaintiff; Scales for defendant. Extract from plaintiff's libel. Examinations: four depositions for plaintiff responding to libel of seven articles and interrogatories of eight; two for defendant responding to exceptions of six articles and interrogatories of nine. Extract from act book giving sentence of penance.

44/2 *Extract from libel of plaintiff giving words of defamation.*[281] [*June 1606*]

L2 *Between July 1605 and June 1606 Elizabeth Hitchcock, then of Lewes defamed Thomas Herold with the words* 'Thomas Herold is a witch and he hath practised or exercised witchcraft'.

44/3 Edward Talmye.[282] *Read over 9 March 1606/7*

Of Pulborough, husbandman; lived there 40 years; before at Fittleworth; born there; aged about 45. Signs with mark.

To the libel

L1. *Refers to oath.*

L2. In the month of February last past was a twelvemonth, Elizabeth Hitchcock said at the barn door of William Hitchcock her husband in Pulborough unto Edward Talmye that Thomas Herold was a witch and did bewitch her husband's cattle that they could not prosper for him. And whosoever dealt with Thomas Herold they should not prosper for they, William Hitchcock and Elizabeth Hitchcock, did never prosper since he did deal or meddle any manner of ways with [them].‡ All which was spoken to Edward Talmye himself alone save only that Simon Talmye his brother might hear some of the words in respect that he was winning§ of some tares or fatches at the place. *For the rest he does not know.*

L3 & 4. *Cannot depose beyond what as already deposed.*

---

* The name appears in various spellings, including 'Harold'.

† The act book covering the intermediate months does not survive.

‡ MS names Thomas Herold here, apparently in error.

§ Wyninge in MS.

L5. *Affirmative.*

L6. *Refers to oath.*

L7. *Deposition is true.*

To the interrogatories

In 1. *Deposes as to the 2nd article of the libel; beyond that does not know.*

In 2. *Cannot depose beyond what has already deposed.*

In 3. *Does not believe the article true in any respect.*

In 4. *Deposes as to the 2nd article of the libel.*

In 5. *Cannot depose beyond what has already deposed.*

In 6. That he came to testify what he doth know in this matter at the request of Thomas Herold, being first compelled by process out of this court; and that he favoureth the parties indifferently and wisheth the law to take place.

In 7 & 8 *Negative.*

44/4 Simon Talmye.[283] *Read over 9 March 1606/7*

Of Pulborough, husbandman; born there; aged about 40. Signs with mark.

L2. That in the month of February last past was twelvemonth Elizabeth Hitchcocke said, at the barn door of William Hitchcocke her husband situate within the parish of Pulborough, that Thomas Herold was a witch and did bewitch her, her husband's cattle and her children that nothing they had could prosper with them. All which speeches were spoken in the presence and hearing of Edward Talmye, Simon Talmye's brother, and Simon Talmye. *For the rest does not know*

In 3. *Does not believe the article.*

In 6. That he came to testify at the request of Thomas Herold, being first compelled by process out of this court …

44/5 Margery Fivian.[284] [*March 1606/7*]

Wife of William Fivian, husbandman of Pulborough, where lived for about 13 years; before at Iping for about 10 years; before at Houghton for about 6 years; before at Wisborough Green; born there; aged about 60. Signs with mark.

L2. That betwixt Maytide and Whitsuntide was two years last past, Elizabeth Hitchcocke came to Margery Fivian's house in Pulborough and amongst other words said that she could have nothing that she had about her thrive. Whereupon Margery Fivian answered and said, 'What is the reason thereof?' Then Elizabeth Hitchcock answered that Thomas Herold was a witch and had bewitched her and hers, and that whosoever did ever deal anything with him should never prosper. Which speeches were so spoken unto her only and no other; neither was there any other persons then present. *For the rest does not know.*

In 3. *Does not believe the words of defamation are true.*

In 6. That she came to testify at the request of Thomas Herold, being first compelled by process out of this court …

44/6 Alice Talmye.[285] [*March 1606/7*]

Wife of Simon Talmye, husbandman, of Pulborough, where lived about 12 years; before at Madehurst; born there; aged about 40. Signs with mark.

L2. That about hay harvest was two years last past, Elizabeth Hitchcock in her own house in Pulborough said unto Alice Talmye that Thomas Herold was a witch and had bewitched her and hers that nothing could prosper with her, and whosoever had anything to do with him they should never prosper, in the presence of William Hitchcocke, son of Elizabeth Hitchcock, and Alice Talmye and no others.

In 3. That that the words before by her deposed is [*sic*] true touching the speech of Elizabeth Hitchcock; but touching Thomas Herold she doth not believe him to be any such manner of man as Elizabeth Hitchcock hath deposed.

In 6. That she came to testify at the request of Thomas Herold, being first compelled by process of court. …

44/7 William Hitchcocke.[286] *Read over 7 June 1607.*

Of Pulborough, husbandman, where lived 30 years or more; born at Stonstrete in the county of Surrey; aged about 61. Is worth little. Signs with mark.*

To the exceptions.

E1 & 2. That true it is Edward Talmye, Simon Talmye, Alice Talmye and Margery Fivian are capital enemies to Elizabeth Hitchcocke defendant in this cause, and are the especial good friends and favourites of Thomas Herold and have not deposed a truth, but lies falsehood and things to truth altogether contrary. And especially Edward Talmye, a pretended witness on behalf of Thomas Herold producted sworn and examined, for whereas he deposeth that in the month of February last past before his examination that Elizabeth Hitchcock did say at the barn door of William Hitchcock in Pulborough unto him that Thomas Herold party agent in this cause was a witch and did bewitch her husband's cattle that they could not prosper and so as in this second article is declared, she did not speak with, had any talk or communication with Talmye at any time during that time at which the words articulated were [pretended]† to be spoken, which was at the winning of tares. But that she came unto the barn and only asked the wife of Edward Talmye, who was then winnowing of tares in the barn, how she could so hardily endure the cold weather, and asked him how many tares he had, who

* Parish not indentified. Perhaps Stane Street.

† Difficult reading.

answered he had ten bushels; and did not speak any one word to him or anybody else concerning Thomas Herold. *For the rest does not know*

E3. That in truth there is no credit to be given or reposed in Simon Talmye or his words, for he hath deposed falsely in his depositions to the libel on the behalf of Thomas Herold and lies and things altogether contrary to truth. And especially in the words articulate, for although Elizabeth Hitchcock were at the barn and barn door of William Hitchcock, yet she did neither see hear or talk with Simon Talmye that time any word concerning Thomas Herold; neither was he at the barn all that time until night, at which time she was at her own house and not at the said barn, neither in the sight, [presence]* or hearing of Simon Talmye; neither was he in the [presence] or sight of Elizabeth Hitchcock nor hearing of any [of] the articulate's words. All which he knoweth to be true for he was that day often going between his house and his barn and servicing of his cattle then being at the barn. *For the rest does not know.*

E4. *Does not know.*

E5. *Deposes as to the 3rd article; for the rest does not know.*

E6. *Deposition is true.*

To the interrogatories

In 1. That he is husband unto Elizabeth Hitchcock; *for the rest negative.*

In 2. *Deposes as to the 1st.*

In 3. That he is a tailor by his occupation but now useth husbandry and thereby getteth his living

In 4. That he is worth little his debts paid.

In 5. *He came at the request of his wife and at his own expense.*

In 6. That of the two parties litigant he favoureth his wife best yet he wisheth right to take place.

In 7. That this cause doth somewhat concern him because he is husband to the party defendant; *for the rest negative.*

In 8. *Negative*

In 9. That Elizabeth Hitchcock did never speak the words interrogate nor the like in effect as he verily thinketh. *For the rest does not know.*

44/8 George Snellinge.[287] *Read over 8 June 1607.*

Of Pulborough, husbandman, where has lived about 20 years; born in Clanand† in Surrey; aged about 50. Is worth 20s. Signs with mark.

---

* Difficult reading (abbreviated).

† Unidentified. Perhaps East or West Clandon, parishes near Guildford. The name Snelling appears in Guildford parish registers of this period.

E1 & 2. That true it is that Edward Talmye, Simon Talmye, Alice Talmye and Margery Fivian, pretended witnesses on the behalf of Thomas Herold produced against Elizabeth Hitchcock, are capital and mortal enemies to her and especial friends and well-willers unto Thomas Herold and have not deposed the truth but lies false tales and things altogether contrary to truth. And further this deponent saith that there is no truth or credit to be put or reposed in Edward Talmye and Simon Talmye for that they depose that, in February was 12 months before their examination, Elizabeth Hitchcock did speak and utter against Thomas Herold at the barn or barn door of William Hitchcock the words articulate in the aforesaid month at the winning of tares; whereas in truth she did not speak any such words either to Edward Talmye concerning Thomas Herold but only came unto the barn and asked Edward Talmye's wife, who was then winning of tares, if she were not acold [*sic*] and whether she had made an end of winning; and never uttered any of the pretended words. All which he knoweth to a .. true* because he was present all that day at the barn working from sun rising until sunset of the same day and did not see Elizabeth Hitchcock stay any long time there, but as soon as she had asked her question and talked a word or two more she went away presently to her house and there did abide, which is about a cast from the barn; and came not again all the time that Edward Talmye, or his wife, Simon Talmye or George Snellinge were there .

E3. That there is not any truth or credit to be put in the words of Simon Talmye, and especially that he hath deposed in this cause that Elizabeth Hitchcock did speak the words concerning Thomas Herold in the presence of him, Simon Talmye, whereas in truth he, Simon Talmye, was not at the barn when Elizabeth was there but he was carrying of a load of vetches from the barn to his own house far from the place where the words were pretended to be spoken, where he could neither hear nor see her. All which he knoweth to be true for the reasons specified. *For the rest does not know.*

E5. *That he came voluntarily and at the request and expense of Elizabeth Hitchcock.*

44/9 *Extract from act book, 9 April 1608.*[288]

[*Instruction for confession by Elizabeth Hitchcocke as public penance in Pulborough church*].

That she is sorry for having uttered words of defamation against Thomas Herold and then and there shall desire Thomas Herold if he be there present to forgive her.

* Perhaps error for 'to be true'.

45/1 Joan Elliott alias Tapper of Bramshott, Hampshire v Richard Coote of Charlton in Singleton, with, later, Robert Baxter intervening. Matrimonial (breach of betrothal contract).[289]

*Court acts: 21 February 1606/7 to 14 March 1606/7; 3 October 1607 to 29 October 1608.**

In the initial proceedings up to March 1606/7, the plaintiff sought to establish that there was a contract to marry with the defendant. During the months following (when the court acts do not survive) a new party, Robert Baxter, intervened in support of the defendant. Additional witnesses were called in June and September to be questioned about an earlier relationship between Elliott and Baxter. From November 1607 onwards the plaintiff sought sentence, with some opposing process from the defendants during the next three months. Thereafter the plaintiff continued to press for sentence but the case lapsed at the end of October 1608.

No marriage records for Joan Elliott, Richard Coote or Robert Baxter have been found.

There may be a connection between the parties in this case and an earlier one, also matrimonial. The defendant in this case was Richard Coote of Charlton in Singleton; the plaintiff in the earlier case (11) was Mary Coote, also of Charlton in Singleton. The Singleton registers record the baptisms of Richard, son of John Coote, in October 1576 and of Mary Coote, daughter of John, in April 1583.

Proctors: Cooke for plaintiff; Scales for defendant; Freeman for Baxter intervening. Examinations: four depositions for plaintiff responding to libel of six articles and interrogatories of four; one deposition for Baxter responding to material of four articles and interrogatories of eleven; three depositions for Baxter responding to the material and interrogatories, with additional interrogatories of six articles; two depositions [probably for Baxter] responding to the material and both interrogatories with additional interrogatories of six articles.

45/2 George Skinner.[290] *[March 1606/7]*

Of Midhurst, MA, where lived about 5 months; before at Hempnall, Norfolk; before at the university of Cambridge; before at Norwich; aged about 35. Signature.†

To the libel

L1. That either in the latter end of November or the beginning of December last past he, being sent for unto the house of Nicholas Bishoppe, was by Robert Billingshurst requested to make a contract of lawful matrimony between Richard Coote and Joan Elliott, both then being present. Upon which request made he saith [*sic*] that he gladly would do it, but first he would examine the parties whether there was consent of parents on both parties and whether there was not any precontract by every or either of them before made; whereupon they both answered that they knew not of any. Then asking them severally whether they would then be contented to be contracted they yielded their consents. Whereupon he proceeded unto the contract and in the contract used the very words specified in the Book of Common Prayer and thereupon a ring was

* The act book covering the intermediate months does not survive.

† Only the first length of residence is given. Skinner does not appear as an incumbent or curate in the Clergy of the Church of England Database; but he is cited in office court on a number of occasions from February 1607/8 onwards to provide proof of ordination (Ep I/17/12 ff 168, 181, 215, 226).

given and taken. All which was done at the house of Nicholas Bishoppe in the presence of Robert Billingshurst, Nicholas Bishoppe and Elis Hames and divers others. *For the rest does not know.*

L2 & 3. *Cannot depose beyond what has already deposed.*

L4. *Affirms as he believes.*

L5. *Refers to oath.*

L6. *Deposition is true.*

To the interrogatories

In 1. *Satisfactory*

In 2. *Cannot depose beyond what has already deposed,* saving that the contract was made in a little parlour of the house of Nicholas Bishoppe.

In 3. *Cannot depose beyond what has already deposed,* saving that the contract was made the parties standing and not sitting, Richard Coote being uncovered.

In 4. *Cannot depose beyond what has already deposed.*

45/3 Nicholas Bishoppe.[291] [*March 1606/7*]

Of Midhurst, innkeeper, where lived about 12 years; before at Gatcombe, Hampshire, about 2 years; before at Horwell, * *Hampshire; born there; aged about 50. Signature.*

L1. That a month before Christmas last Mr George Skynner, curate of Midhurst, was sent for unto Nicholas Bishoppe's house where was Richard Coote and Joan Elliott and Robert Billingshurst and Nicholas Bishoppe; and afterwards Ellis Hames was sent for. And after some communication had amongst them Richard Coote requested to be contracted unto Joan Elliott, at whose request Robert Billingshurst said unto Mr Skynner 'Then Mr Skynner I pray you contract them together.' Which he with the consent of both the parties did accordingly and in all points according to the Book of Common Prayer, whereupon a ring was given and received in the presence of Robert Billingshurst, George Skynner, Ellis Hames and Nicholas Bishoppe in a little parlour of the house. …..

In 3. *Cannot depose beyond what has already deposed,* saving that the contract was made the parties standing and Richard Coote uncovered.

In 4. That there is a fame all over Midhurst of the contract, for he hath heard Henry Gates, William Tate and divers others speak thereof; and the day for the marriage upon the contract was appointed; and Ellis Hames was spoken unto to procure a licence out of this court to marry them by Richard Coote himself. ….

---

* Unidentified; perhaps Hordle?

45/4 Ellis Hames.[292] [*March 1606/7*]

Of Midhurst, apparitor, where lived 12 about years; before at Chichester; born there; aged about 40. Signature.

L1. That about a month before Christmas last he was sent for by Richard Coote and Robert Billingshurst unto the house of Nicholas Bishoppe of Midhurst; and there he found George Skynner, curate of Midhurst, Robert Billingshurst, Richard Coote, Joan Elliott and Nicholas Bishoppe, one Gregory of Lipacke* and Richard Gardyner, in a little parlour of Nicholas Bishoppe's house. Then Richard Coote, George Skynner and Robert Billingshurst said, 'Ellis we sent for you to know what the fee is for a licence for marriage,' whereunto Ellis Hames said 11s 4d. Then upon further communication betwixt them they agreed that the parties should first be contracted because they were then present and afterwards to be married. Whereupon Mr Skynner asked Richard Coote and Joan Elliott whether they were contented to contract themselves together and whether there were any let or impediment why they might not be contracted together; and they both answered 'No.' Then he asked them severally whether they had consent of parents to contract themselves together. Whereunto Richard Coote answered that he had a mother alive, but he needed not her consent for he was of years sufficient to dispose of himself; and she answered that she had neither father nor mother alive but requested Robert Billingshurst, who was then present and her guardian, to give his consent thereunto, which he did accordingly. Then Mr Skynner bid them stand together which they did, Richard Coote and every one present putting off their hats; then he used the very words contained in the Book of Common Prayer by joining of the hands of Richard and Joan together and using the ring which was given by Richard and received by Joan. All which was done in all things according to the Book of Common Prayer in so much that they were fully contracted together in the presence of the parties beforenamed with free assent and consent. And that Richard Coote did appoint Ellis Hames to meet him here at Chichester the next morning to procure a licence for the marriage.

In 4. *Cannot depose beyond what has already deposed* because he taketh no notice of thing [*sic*] past.

45/5 Robert Billingshurst.[293] [*March 1606/7*]

Of Midhurst, yeoman, where lived about 26 years; before at Chiddingfold, Surrey; born there; aged about 58. Signature.

L1. That about a month before Christmas last, he being at the house of Nicholas Bishoppe in Midhurst and motion being made of a marriage to be had and solemnised between Richard Coote and Joan Elliott by Nicholas Bishoppe saying that it was a fit match for them to be married together, he, Robert Billingshurst, being guardian unto Joan Elliott said if she thought it fit and convenient, he did consent thereunto. In so much that upon further communication betwixt Richard Coote and Joan Elliott it was agreed upon that they should be married together, whereupon he, thinking with himself

* Liphook.

how the same should be effected with the least charge they could, he caused Mr Skynner curate of Midhurst to be sent for to know his advice, therein thinking that he would tell what the fee of a licence was to be married at Chichester to save charges in respect it was winter,* time for at that time they would not trouble many of their friends. Then Mr Skynner answered he could not tell what the fee was here, but the fee of such a licence at the place from whence he came was 13s 4d or thereabouts, and further said 'If you send for Ellis Hames he can tell you what the fees are here.' Whereupon he was sent for and came presently and said the fees here at Chichester was 11s 4d or thereabouts. Then upon further communication it was agreed upon that Richard Coote and Joan Elliott should be contracted together and afterwards to procure a licence. Whereupon Mr Skynner at† the request of Robert Billingshurst demanded of Richard and Joan whether there was not any let or impediment but that they might be contracted together and afterwards solemnise matrimony; and both of them answered no. Then he asked them and either of them whether they were contented to be contracted together or no, who answered yes and gave their free assents and consents thereunto. Then he asked them whether they had their parents' consents thereunto; then Joan Elliott answered that she had neither father nor mother but Robert Billingshurst as her guardian, whose consent thereunto she requested which he granted; and Richard Coote was some 28 years of age and therefore needed no consent of parents. Then Robert Billingshurst requested Mr Skynner to contract Richard and Joan together seeing they both were agreed, which he, at Robert Billingshurst's request and with both their consents and good liking, did in such manner and form as is prescribed in the Book of Common Prayer in all things by giving of hands and receiving of a ring, which Richard gave unto Joan in token and pledge according to their contract. All which was done in a little parlour of the house of Nicholas Bishoppe, Richard Coote then standing barehead and Joan Elliott stood by him, and all the parties present also standing barehead, viz Mr George Skynner curate of Midhurst, Nicholas Bishoppe, Ellis Hames, John Gregory, Richard Gardyner, Robert Billingshurst and others whose names he doth not now remember.

In 2. *Cannot depose beyond what has already deposed,* saving that the contract was about 8 or 9 of the clock in the morning

In 4. *Cannot depose beyond what has already deposed,* because he giveth no regard thereunto but expected when the marriage should be solemnised .

45/6‡ Robert Billingshurst.[294] [*June 1607*]

Of Midhurst, yeoman, where lived about 26 years; before at Chiddingfold, Surrey, about 30 years; born there; aged about 58. Signature.

To the material ex parte Robert Baxter.

---

* 'Witter' in MS.

† 'And' in MS.

‡ Depositions **45/6-9** are entered under the heading *Examinations ex parte Robert Baxter v Joan Elliott alias Tapper*

M1. That long before the contract of matrimony between Richard Coote and Joan Elliott alias Tapper, there was once talk of marriage between Robert Baxter and Joan Elliott at one Gregory's house at Liphook, being father in law* to Joan Elliott, in the presence of Robert Billingshurst. And sometimes the mother of Joan, going up and down about the house in her business, did hear some of the talk between Robert Baxter and Joan Elliott. And Robert Billingshurst heard all the said talk which was nothing touching any contract at all but that Joan Elliott said unto Robert Baxter she was content to marry him if he was worth three score pounds, as he then and there said he was, and if also she might have her father in law's, mother's and his goodwill and liking, being guardian unto Joan Elliott. *For the rest does not know.*

M2. *Does not know,* saving that Robert Baxter hath said sometimes unto Robert Billingshurst that he and Joan Elliott were lawfully contracted together by the words before by him deposed in the precedent article. *For the rest does not know.*

M3. *Does not know.*

M4. *Deposition is true.*

To the interrogatories

In 1. *Satisfactory.*

In 2. That he married Joan Elliott's mother's sister. *For the rest does not know.*

In 3. *Negative.*

In 4. That of the two parties he favoureth Richard Coote best and to him wisheth the victory, yet according to truth and equity notwithstanding. *For the rest does not know.*

In 5. *Cannot depose beyond what has already deposed.*

In 6. *Does not know.*

In 7. *Negative.*

In 8. That he did say unto Robert Baxter at the time of the communication before deposed that Joan Elliott's portion was £20, and asked him whether he could maintain her by the same and his own portion if the marriage did proceed; and that if it did he must put in bond to pay unto Joan Elliott's mother 40s a year during her life. *For the rest does not know.*

In 9. That the mother of Joan Elliott, being sick at the time of the matrimonial communication, departed this life about two months or upwards after. *For the rest does not know.*

In 10. *Does not know.*

In 11. *Negative,* saving he was willing Joan Elliott should be contracted to Richard Coote for so much as he knew of no let or impediment to hinder the contract.

45/7 John Parkes.[295] *Read over 30 June 1607.*

* The term throughout this case appears to be used to denote stepfather.

Of Liphook in Bramshott, Hampshire, sawyer, where lived about 6 years; before at Rogate about 1 year; before at Up Marden; born there; aged about 47. Signs with mark.

M1. That by the confession of Joan Elliott made before Richard Chase and his wife of Liphook, John Waterman and Anthony Dunn, Joan Elliott said that she was contracted unto Robert Baxter as man and wife in the way of matrimony before God, as he hath heard by Richard Chase and his wife, John Waterman and Anthony Dunn, a quarter of a year before she was thought to be contracted to Richard Coote. And further he cannot depose for the time he doth not remember.

M2. *Does not know,* saving that he heard Richard Chase and [*blank*] Chase his wife, John Waterman and Anthony Dunn examine Joan Elliott at the house of John Gregory of Liphook by way of communication whether she and Robert Baxter were not man and wife lawfully contracted. Whereunto she answered if she was wife unto him she was his wife still. Then Robert Baxter took a glass of beer and drunk unto her and said, 'Joan you know you are my wife and so pledge me,' and she took the glass and so pledged him thereupon. But touching the time he cannot now remember; but it was at the place before mentioned and in the presence of the parties before named.

In 5. That he was sent unto Richard Coote from Robert Baxter to signify that Joan Elliott was contracted in matrimony unto him before she was contracted unto him. Then Richard Coote sent for John Parkes to accompany him to Chichester to speak with Mr Scales his counsel, unto whom he said that Robert Baxter said that Joan Elliott and he was contracted together and that she and he did accompany together and walked about the country two days and two nights together.

In 6. *Does not know,* saving that he hath heard the wife of Robert Chase and Eleanor and Elizabeth Chase her daughters affirm that they heard the father in law of Joan Elliott and her own mother give their consent that Robert Baxter and she should marry together as man and wife.

In 10. *Affirms,* for all or the most part of the inhabitants of Liphook report that Robert Baxter and Joan Elliott are man and wife before God, as namely Richard Chase and his wife, John Waterman, Anthony Dunn and divers others.

To the interrogatories given in the last place

In (2) 1. *Cannot depose beyond what has already deposed.*

In (2) 2. That he heard Richard Coote say that Robert Billingshurst was the occasion of the contracting of Joan Elliott and him. *For the rest does not know.*

In (2) 3. That Joan Elliott, as it was reported, did about the time interrogated secretly and privately depart and go away alone with Robert Baxter from her father Gregory's house by night unto one Mose's house of Haslemere, being three miles from Liphook, and there they continued all that night together.

In (2) 4. *Does not know.*

In (2) 5. That he hath heard of such a matter as is contained in this article by Anthony Dunn, Richard Chase, John Waterman and others. *For the rest does not know.*

In (2) 6. *Does not know.*

45/8 Margaret Ball.[296] *Read over 30 June 1607.*

Of Midhurst, spinster; born there; aged about 30. Signs with mark.

M1 & 2. That she, being household servant unto John Gregory of Liphook father in law unto Joan Elliott, about Christmas last amongst other communication had betwixt Robert Baxter and Joan heard him say unto her, 'Joan are not you my wife before God, by God you are my wife'. Whereunto she answered, 'If I were your wife I am your wife still'. Whereupon he said, 'Upon that I will drink unto you,' and thereupon drunk unto her; and she pledged him in the presence of Richard Chase and [*blank*] Chase his wife, John Waterman, Anthony Dunn, John Parkes, Elizabeth Elliott widow and Margaret Ball. But she did not hear Joan Elliott say that she was his wife. ⋯.

In 10. *Does not know* because she never took any heed or regard thereunto.

In (2) 3. That Joan Elliott, upon a Sunday at night lying with Margaret Ball and Elizabeth Elliott widow at the house of John Gregory father in law of Joan, did rise out her bed at dead time of the night all unready unto Robert Baxter, he then lying in her father's house, and departed alone with him secretly and privately from her father's house. But whither they went or whereabouts she cannot depose.

45/9 Elizabeth Elliott als Tapper.[297] *Read over 30 June 1607.*

Of Midhurst, widow, where lived about 10 years; before at Stedham; born there; aged about 37. Signs with mark.

M1 & 2. That about Christmas last, Elizabeth Elliott having occasion to visit John Gregory her father in law at his house at Liphook, she amongst other words had betwixt Robert Baxter and Joan Elliott heard him say unto her, 'Joan can you deny before these parties now present but that you are my wife? By God you are my wife'. Whereunto she answered, 'If I were your wife I am your wife still'. Whereupon he drunk unto her and said, 'I drink unto you'; and so she pledged him in the presence of Richard Chase and [*blank*] Chase his wife, John Waterman, Anthony Dunn, John Parkes, Margaret Ball and Elizabeth Elliott. But she did not in express words say she was his wife. *For the rest does not know.*

In 2. That she married the natural brother of Joan Elliott. ⋯.

In 10. *Does not know* because she never heard of any such common fame.

In (2) 3. That Joan Elliott, upon a Sunday at night happening about Christmas last lying in bed with her and Margaret Ball at the house of John Gregory father in law of Joan, did rise out of her bed about midnight all unready and undressed and went down into the hall unto Robert Baxter, the said Robert then lying in the house and first calling unto her to come unto him very suspiciously. And that night went away with him secretly and privately alone to Haslemere three miles from her father's house by night. ⋯.

In (2) 5. That afterwards in the morning they went together towards Guildford all alone, till they were pursued and taken by John Gregory brother in law of Joan Elliott who stayed them.

45/10 Richard Chase.[298] *Read over 11 September 1607.*

Of Liphook, Hampshire, yeoman, where lived about 10 years; before at Trotton about 3 years; before at Liss, Hampshire; born there; aged about 47. Is worth £100. Signature.

M1 & 2. That he hath divers times heard Robert Baxter say that Joan Elliott was his wife before God, and they were contracted together as man and wife before Mr Robert Billingshurst, John Gregory and his wife and others before this suit began; and heard him say unto Joan Elliott, 'Art not thou my wife?' and she answered, 'If I was your wife I am your wife still', in the presence of John Gregory, Anthony Dunn, Margaret Ball, Elizabeth Elliott and Richard Coote. And that at the time and place above mentioned and in the presence of the witnesses above mentioned, John Gregory and Joan Elliott did both say unto Robert Baxter that if he was worth £40 according to promise they were man and wife and she would marry him, otherwise not; and he replied that if he was worth but forty pence he was worthy to have as good a woman as she. *For the rest does not know.*

To the interrogatories given in the first place ex parte Coote.

In 10. That he hath heard of many in Liphook that Robert Baxter and Joan Elliott should be married together.

To the interrogatories in the 2nd place ex parte Richard Coote

In (2) 3. That he hath heard it commonly reported within the parish of Liphook that Joan Elliott did rise out her bed at dead of the night since this suit began, and went away with Robert Baxter towards Haslemere very suspiciously and in an undecent manner all alone from her father John Gregory his house. And thereof there goeth a common fame within the parish for they were away together two nights.

In (2) 5. *Affirms* as he hath heard John Gregory say. ···.

To the interrogatories ex parte Joan Elliott.

In (3) 1. *Satisfactory and responds in the negative.*

In (3) 2. Deposes as to the preface of this examination.

In (3) 3. That he is worth of his own proper goods £100.

In (3) 4. That he came to testify at the request and charge of Robert Baxter and Richard Smithe. *For the rest negative.*

In (3) 5. *Negative.*

In (3) 6. *For the rest does not know beyond what has already deposed.*

45/11 Anthony Dunn.[299] *Read over 11 September 1607.*

Of Liphook, Hampshire, butcher, where lived about 13 years; before at Tratlitt, Wiltshire; born there; aged about 50. Is worth 20s. Signs with mark.*

---

* Unidentified

M1 & 2. That about Michaelmas last he being at the house of Richard Chase of Liphook about business amongst other communication heard Robert Baxter say unto Joan Elliott 'Joan art not you my wife before God?' and she answered that if she were she was his wife still whereupon he drunk unto her and she pledged him in the presence of Richard Chase and Agnes, his wife John Gregory, Margaret Ball, Elizabeth Elliott Anthony Dunn and others. And at the time and place above mentioned and in the presence of the witnesses above mentioned Joan Elliott did say unto Robert Baxter that if he was worth £40 according to promise she would marry him. And he answered that if he was not worth forty pence he was worthy to have as good a woman as she. *For the rest does not know.*

In 10. That there was a common fame within the parish of Liphook that Robert Baxter and Joan Elliott should be married.

To the interrogatories in the 2nd place ex parte Richard Coote

In (2) 3. That about a fortnight after Michaelmas last, Joan Elliott being in bed together with Elizabeth Elliott als Tapper widow and Margaret Ball, she about the dead time of night did arise out her bed in her father John Gregory's house and went unto Robert Baxter, who then did likewise lie in her father's house, and the same night went secretly away alone with him towards Haslemere.

In (2) 5. That Robert Baxter and Joan Elliott did depart by night from Haslemere towards Guildford all alone very suspiciously and undecently, and [were] pursued by John Gregory and forced to return back again.

To the interrogatories ex parte Joan Elliott.

In (3) 4. That he came to testify at the request and charge of Robert Baxter and Richard Smithe without compulsion. ···.

46/1 William Chatfeilde, gentleman, farmer of Oving rectorial tithe v John Whatley, and v Richard Knighte (with later Raphael Widdowson, vicar of Oving intervening), and v Richard Aylinge. Tithe in Oving. Three parallel cases.[300]

*Court acts: 19 July 1606 to 21 March 1606/7; 3 October 1607 to 3 June 1609.**

William Chatfeilde was the farmer for the prebendary of Oving (the precentor of the Cathedral) and claimed for the tithe of hay, particularly on copyhold land held by tenants of the manor. He brought separate cases against three of the copyholders, and at a later stage the vicar of Oving, Raphael Widdowson intervened as a party on behalf of a defendant Richard Knighte. The complicated procedures were paralleled by a further case brought separately by Widdowson against Chatfeilde, claiming vicarial tithes. The depositions all respond to material arising in the cases Chatfeilde promoted and do not arise from Widdowson's separate case. As in other cases over the central period of 1607, the court acts between March and September have not survived.

Only two depositions were given on behalf of the plaintiff; and they are relatively technical: they aimed to establish that Chatfeilde had been legally appointed as farmer. All the others were given on behalf of the defendants; several deponents respond in sequence to the different cases, often producing repetitive material.

The first five of the defendants' depositions were taken in May 1607 and record the manorial customs under which the tenants of copyholds performed agricultural tasks for the prebendary or parson,† who was lord of the manor of Oving. On 4 June came four more, specifically on behalf of Knighte and Aylinge, including one from Widdowson. They record the custom under which certain copyholders paid tithe hay to the vicar from certain plots called 'doales'.

Almost a year of inconclusive proceedings followed, but Widdowson's intervention increased activity, particularly from Knighte's case. This may reflect increasing hostility between Chatfeilde and Widdowson, which is recorded in the proceedings of the office court. In 1605 Chatfeilde had been presented for failure to repair the chancel, endangering the safety of the minister. After the vicar had commenced his instance case in January 1607/8, the office acts in May and June record a clash between the two men, initially over rights to seats in the church. This was followed by a presentment, filed by Widdowson, in which he accuses Chatfeilde of publicly proclaiming that the vicar's wife was mad.

Activity was renewed in June 1608 with a third batch of depositions: four more, this time on behalf of Widdowson's intervention, which record that the hay plots were within the manor of Colworth but were tithed to the vicar. They also include references to the inclosure of common meadows at Colworth.

In July 1608 there followed the fourth and final batch: two depositions emphasising that hay as small tithe was payable to the vicar rather than the prebendary – and also providing information about attempts to control, by the creation of sluices, damage from incursion of seawater.

For most of 1608 the defendants pressed for sentence, and from July so did the plaintiff. On 11 March 1608/9 the verdict was given in favour of the three original defendants.‡ In the next two months the court acts record that Chatfeilde failed to pay the costs and failed to appear. He was also sued by his proctor for failing to pay his fees.

---

* The act book covering the intermediate months does not survive.

† The terms prebendary and parson are used interchangeably throughout all the depositions in this case.

‡ In December 1608 the court also gave sentence in favour of Widdowson in his counter-case.

In editing the depositions of this case it was particularly necessary to take account of the repetition or near repetition between the statements of different witnesses: this was particularly striking in the accounts of the customs. The nearly identical phraseology produced in certain articles suggests that the witnesses were accepting statements set out by the lawyers or officials rather than recounting their personal recollections.

Proctors: Cooke for plaintiff; Scales for defendant. Examinations: one deposition for plaintiff responding to allegation of one article; five depositions for defendant responding to material of eight articles and interrogatories of twelve, and material ex parte Aylinge of seven articles with interrogatories of twelve and thirteen articles; four depositions for defendant responding to material of eight articles and interrogatories of twelve and three articles; one deposition for plaintiff responding to exceptions and allegation of one article; extract from court act book concerning customs; four depositions for defendant responding to allegations of Widdowson in five articles and one interrogatory of eight articles; one deposition for defendants Knighte and Widdowson responding to additional positions of nine articles and interrogatories of ten and eight articles; one deposition for defendant Widdowson responding to material of five articles, additional positions of eight articles and interrogatories of seven and ten articles.

Deposition ex parte William Chatfeilde.

46/2 Robert Langrishe.[301] *Read over 24 April 1607*

Of Chichester, yeoman, where lived 3 years and more; before at Havant, Hampshire; born there; aged about 22. Signature.

To the allegation and exhibit

A1. That upon the 27th day of July in the year of the reign of James king of England the third, and of Scotland the 38th,* he did engross the lease mentioned in the allegation, by the appointment of Mr Anthony Smith who was then his master. And after the writing thereof he did see Mr George Chatfeilde subscribe his name unto the lease and set his seal thereunto; and afterwards GC did deliver the lease as his act and deed unto Mr William Chatfeilde. And this he knoweth to be true because all the indenture of lease is written with his own hand and he was present at the sealing and delivery thereof and writ his name thereunto at the request of Mr William Chatfeilde as a witness. And Mr Richard Chatfeilde mentioned upon the backside of the indenture did likewise set his hand as a witness and see the sealing and delivering of the indenture in the presence of Robert Langrishe. *For the rest does not know.* †

Depositions ex parte John Whatley and Richard Aylinge

46/3 John Graye.[302] *13 May 1607*

Of Chichester St Pancras, husbandman, where lived about eight years; before at Oving; born there; aged about 68. Is worth £6 13s 4d. Signs with mark.

To the material.

---

* 1605

† Two versions, in a different hand, follow on f 290 r & v.

M1. That there hath been and is an ancient custom within the parish of Oving that every tenant or occupier of land pertaining to the prebend or parsonage of Oving did do and perform the work and service in this article mentioned, viz: he that had two yardland belonging to the prebend or parsonage of Oving was wont and accustomed to do, and yet doth, upon 24 hours warning given by the prebendary, parson or his farmer (and for meat and drink provided for the tenant or his servants at the charge of the prebendary on their working days) to help on four days every year to make his hay; and also to work two days in every year at harvest to the harvesting of his corn and grain; and to carry or cause to be carried four loads or carriages of his hay to the barn or hay house of the prebendary (when as the hay was ready to be carried). And likewise to plough or cause to be ploughed four acres of the land of the prebendary, viz: two acres at wheat season for wheat and two acres for pease and fatches. And he of the said tenants of the prebendary which had but one yardland of the prebendary's hold was wont to do, and did and yet doth and performeth, the moiety or half of the works and service, viz: two haying days or meading* days, one harvest day, and to carry two loads or carriages of hay when the same was fit to be carried, and to plough two acres of the land of the prebendary, viz: one acre at wheat season for wheat and one other acre for pease or fatches.† All which was done for the use and behoof of the prebendary by his tenants and hath been so accustomed to be done in manner and form above declared and so continued from time to time these forty years, to this examinate's own knowledge. For he hath been heretofore a tenant to the prebendary by the space of these forty years last past and upwards, and holding of the prebend or parsonage hold one yardland and three cottages did either by himself or his servant yearly perform and do the work and service before recited, viz: two meading days or haying days, two harvest days and carried two loads or carriages of hay with his team or cart, and also ploughed or caused to be ploughed two acres of the prebendary, viz: one acre for wheat and one other acre for pease or fatches at their usual and accustomed seasons for his yardland; and three haying days or meading days and three harvest days for his three cottages, that is to say for every cottage one haying day and one harvest day. For every tenant having one cotland did do and perform one meading day and one harvest day as well as he that had one yardland did. All which was done and performed by this examinate for forty years ago as aforesaid and so hath been declared‡ and continued ever since by all other the tenants of the prebend; and never heard the contrary until now this suit begun by Mr William Chatfeilde. And further he saith that he hath heard his grandfather John Afeild say, who was farmer of the prebend for three score years ago, that he had and did take, accept and receive the accustomed services and works as due and accustomed to be done for him as farmer of the prebend. For he did dwell with John Afeild at that time and for so long ago. *For the rest does not know.*

M2. That every such tenant as had two yardland of the parsonage or prebend hold, doing and yearly performing the works labours and services in the first article declared, hath been heretofore, is and ought to be, quite freed, discharged and disburdened from the payment of any tithe hay upon his meadow ground. And so likewise he that had one yardland and he which had less. And never paid any such tithe hay in kind of their

---

* Difficult reading.

† Seven lines deleted.

‡ Difficult reading.

meadow grounds unto the parsons. For this examinate, for the work aforesaid, hath been ever free from payment for his yardland for any tithe hay. And so hath all other tenants from payment of tithe hay in consideration of the works aforesaid, as he hath ever heard said and never heard anything to the contrary.

M3. That the prebendaries have, yearly and from year to year during the space of these 40 years, taken and accepted the labours, works and services of their tenants and occupiers of the lands in full satisfaction, payment and discharge of their tithe hay growing upon their meadow grounds belonging to the prebends, as he hath heard John Afeild (his grandfather) and Mr Stapleton (with which Mr Stapleton he did dwell by the space of seven years) say that they did accept these works for their tithe hay. And also that Mr Robert Harrison and Mr George Chatfeilde the elder, being farmers of the prebend successively one after the other, did likewise accept these works for their tithe hay without any denial that ever he heard.

M4. That John Whatley hath in his tenure and occupation two copyholds, being one yardland apiece, belonging to the prebendary *from this deponent's knowledge. For the rest does not know.*

M5. That during the time that he was dwelling in Oving, which was for 40 years and above, he never knew nor heard but that John Whatley did willingly do and perform the works and accustomed services for the prebendaries, and that in payment satisfaction and discharge of his tithe hay growing upon his meadow grounds appertaining to the parson or prebendary, having warning thereof. But what he hath done or not done or otherwise neglected to do since this examinate hath been dwelling from Oving, which hath been about eight years, he cannot say. *For the rest does not know.*

M6. That the works labours and accustomed services doing and yearly performing by John Whatley for his two yardland is yearly worth 10s or upwards; and that his hay in his meadow is yearly worth 6s or scarce so much, in this examinate's judgement. *For the rest does not know.*

M7. *Deposes as in second article. For the rest does not know.*

M8. *Deposition is true.*

To the interrogatories given in the first place.

In (1) 1. *To the danger of perjury – denies.*

In (1) 2. That he is a husbandman *and is worth £6 13s 4d.*

In (1) 3. *That he came at the request and expense of John Whatley, and of his own volition without compulsion.*

In (1) 4-6. *Negative.*

In (1) 7 & 8. *Deposes as to the second article of the material. For the rest does not know.*

In (1) 9. That William Chatfeilde in the years interrogate, or some of them or one at least and especially in the year 1606, was farmer of the tithes belonging to the parsonage, and so is at this time commonly reputed for ought he knoweth. And hath in some of the years, and especially in 1606, either by himself or others for him, peaceably collected all manner of tithes belonging to the prebend (except the tithe hay now in question) without the gainsaying of any pretending any title or property therein. For this examinate hath been often present with Mr Chatfeilde and his servants when they had come to Shopweeke within the parish of Oving and tithed the wheat and other grain and carried the same away. *For the rest does not know.*

In (1) 10. That George Chatfeilde brother to William Chatfeilde was, next and immediately before William, farmer of all the tithes belonging to the parsonage for the space of two or three years; and was in quiet and peaceable possession of tithes (except the tithe hay now in question). And that George Chatfeilde was commonly reputed and taken for the farmer of all the tithes. *For the rest does not know.*

In (1) 11. That John Whatley had in every of the years 1605 and 1606 five acres of meadow ground, upon the which he might have yearly ([when]* he mowed the same) about four little loads of hay, every load thereof worth about 9s or 10s. *For the rest does not know.*

In (1) 12. *Negative.*

To the material given ex parte Richard Aylinge.

MRA 1-3. That there hath been and is at this present an ancient custom within the parish of Oving that every tenant or occupier of land pertaining to the prebend did do and perform, and doth do and perform, the works, labours and services mentioned, viz: he that had half a yardland, upon 24 hours warning and for meat and drink provided upon the accustomed working days by the prebendary parson or his farmer for the tenant or his servant, was wont and accustomed to do yearly, and so doth at this present, one haying day or meading day and one harvest day, and also plough or cause to be ploughed one acre of the ground, viz: half an acre for wheat and half an acre for fatches or pease at the accustomed times and seasons of the year. All which works and accustomed services hath been done and performed by such tenants of half yardlands for the space and term of these six and fifty years of this examinate's own knowledge and remembrance. And so he hath heard the works have been done for 60 years and upwards. And further that every such tenant performing and yearly doing the works and accustomed services have been from time to time, during the terms of years above by this examinate set down and expressed, freed, acquitted and discharged from payment of his tithe hay growing upon his meadow grounds, and never paid any tithe hay in kind of any of his meadow ground that he ever knew or heard for this 60 years and upwards. And that the parson did always accept and take the accustomed services and labours in lieu and in discharge of payment of such tithe hay as the tenants had yearly growing upon his meadow grounds. And so he hath known John Afeild his grandfather take and accept the same for 56 years ago last past, who was then farmer of the parsonage; and as he hath heard, so have other farmers of the parsonage for 60 years ago last past. And further that he never heard that any of the parsons did ever demand or ask any tithe hay of any their tenants for by [*sic*] and during all the term by this examinate set down. *For the rest does not know.*

---

* 'when' deleted in MS.

MRA4. That Richard Aylinge hath had during the time and years libellated, and so hath at this present, in his occupation half a yardland of the tenure and holding of the parsonage of this examinate's own knowledge. *For the rest does not know.*

MRA5. That he verily believeth that Richard Aylinge hath yearly by himself or his servants done and performed the accustomed services in such manner as this examinate hath declared. *For the rest does not know beyond what he has deposed.*

MRA6. *For the rest does not know beyond what he has deposed.*

MRA 7. *Deposition is true.*

To the interrogatories given in the first place.

MRA In (1) 1. *To the danger of perjury – denies.*

MRA In (1) 2. That he is a husbandman and thereby getteth his living and is worth *£6 13s 4d.*

MRA In (1) 3. *That he came to testify of his own volition without compulsion and at the request and expense of Richard Aylinge and John Whatley as he believes.*

MRA In (1) 4-6. *Negative.*

MRA In (1) 7 & 8. *Deposes as to previous material. For the rest does not know.*

MRA In (1) 9. That William Chatfeilde in the years interrogated, and especially in the year 1606, was farmer of the tithes; and so is at this time commonly reputed for ought this examinate knoweth. And hath especially in 1606, by himself or others for him, quietly collected the tithes for ought this examinate hath heard (except the tithe hay now in question) without contradiction of any claiming or pretending any title or property therein. For this respondent hath been often present with the servants of William Chatfeilde, and sometimes with Mr Chatfeilde himself, when they have come to Shopweeke and tithed the wheat and other grain of the tenants and carried the same away with their carts. *For the rest does not know.*

MRA In (1) 10. That George Chatfeilde, brother to William Chatfeilde, was the next farmer before William Chatfeilde of all the tithes belonging to the parsonage for the space of two or three years, and was in quiet possession of same for ought he ever heard (except the tithe hay in question); and so was commonly reputed and taken. *For the rest does not know beyond what has already deposed.*

MRA In (1) 11. That Richard Aylinge had in the years interrogated in his tenure and occupation about one acre and a half of meadow ground; and might have yearly upon the same, in this respondent's judgement, two loads of hay, every load worth 7s. *For the rest does not know.*

MRA In (2) *To the three interrogatories given in the second place deposes* that every the interrogated persons hath a cottage of the parsonage or prebend hold but no meadow ground to any of them belonging, or any hay growing. *For the rest does not know.*

46/4 John Park.[303] [*May 1607*]

Of Merston, husbandman, where lived for 40 years and more; before at Oving for about three years; before at Battle for about three years; before at Merston; born there; aged about 80. Is worth 40s. Signs with mark.

To the material.

M1. That for 40 years ago he, dwelling with one John Barttlett in Oving, was sent by Barttlett, his master, to Mr Stapleton, who was then farmer of the prebend, to do and perform certain custom days for Mr Stapleton due and accustomed to be done by John Barttlett by reason that he was tenant unto the prebendary and held one yardland; and for that cause did, or caused to be done, such works and services as in this article is declared, viz: that, upon warning given by Mr Stapleton to John Barttlett, he did perform, or caused to be performed by this examinate, two days work at meading or haymaking and one day at harvest for the harvesting of his corn and grain; and did carry or cause to be carried two loads of hay from the meadows or fields of Mr Stapleton to his barn or hay house; and did also plough or cause to be ploughed two acres of the ground or land of Mr Stapleton, viz: one acre for wheat and one other for pease or fatches, which of them happened first at their accustomed seasons. All which works were done for Mr Stapleton by such tenants as held of the parsonage hold by an ancient custom long time before used, as he did hear say among the tenants. And after that he departed from his master's service he was hired often by the tenants of the parson to do and perform their custom days, as sometimes at hay making, sometimes at harvesting of corn and other sometimes at plough, as the times and seasons of the year fell out. But what the names of the tenants were that hired him to do their custom days, or how much every one of them was charged, or how many days, or what their lands were (for which they did such custom), being so long ago he cannot now remember. And further that he never heard to the contrary but the custom hath been so kept and still continued from time to time until this suit began by William Chatfeilde now farmer of the parsonage. And more to this article he cannot say, saving that he thinketh by his own reason such of the tenants which have two yardland apiece should do and perform twice so much custom as he that hath but one yardland. *For the rest does not know.*

M2. That, as he hath heard, all such of the tenants of the prebendary which did and do their accustomed services were and have been freed from paying any tithe hay in kind of their meadow grounds to the prebendary by and during all the time before by this examinate set down. And further that he never heard that any tithe hay was demanded by the prebendary of any tenant performing his accustomed services these 60 years last past. *For the rest does not know.*

M5. That John Whatley, in consideration of his two yardlands, doth do and perform the works and services in this article mentioned … *For the rest does not know.*

To the interrogatories given in the first place.

In (1) 3. *That he came to testify of his own volition without compulsion and at the request and expense of John Whatley.*

In (1) 7. That the accustomed services and works have been done and performed and are yearly done by the tenants of the prebendary or parson for no other duty or consideration but only being in lieu and discharge of their tithe hay, as he hath heard. *For the rest does not know.*

To the interrogatories given in the second place

In (2) 1-3. *Does not know.*

To the material given ex parte Richard Aylinge.

MRA1. That as he hath heard there is, and hath been for these 40 years, a custom in Oving that such of the tenants as doth hold half a yardland of the prebendary have usually done and performed some of the services for the prebendaries for his or their half yardland, as making of hay and harvesting the corn and such like. But how many days or in what sort (concerning half yardlands) he cannot say. *For the rest does not know.*

MRA2. As he hath heard, every such one of the tenants holding of the prebendary half a yardland and doing such works as was and is required was and is freed from payment of any tithe hay growing upon his meadow ground. And further that he never knew nor heard that any tithe hay was demanded by the parson of any tenant of the said holding which did perform his accustomed services, for these 60 years last past. *For the rest does not know.*

To the interrogatories given in the first place.

MRA In (1) 3. *That he came to testify of his own volition without compulsion and at the request and expense of Richard Aylinge.*

MRA In (1) 7. That the accustomed services and works have been done and are yearly done by the tenants of the prebendary for no other duty or consideration but in lieu and in discharge of their tithe hay growing on their meadow grounds, as he hath heard. *For the rest does not know.*

MRA In (1) 12. *Negative for self; for fellow witnesses does not know.*

46/5 Joan Benham,[304] [*May 1607*]

Of Oving, wife of John Benham, husbandman; born there, aged 60 or more. Signs with mark.*

To the material ex parte John Whatley

M1. [*Corroborates detail for tenants of two yardlands*]… All which works are at this present and so have been done for the prebendary yearly by and during the space of 40 years, for she hath dwelled within Oving these 40 years and upward and known the accustomed works to be done. And, as she hath heard by her parents and other her friends, the accustomed works were done in such manner as she hath before deposed for threescore years ago. *For the rest does not know.*

M2 & 3. … And further that she never heard or knew that any of these men hereafter named (who were farmers of the prebend) [did] ask or demand any tithe hay of any of the tenants as: John Afeild, Mr Stapleton, Thomas Rose, Mr Ryman (with which Mr Stapleton and Mr Ryman she dwelled and did belong and retain ten years together), Mr

* The name appears in a number of variants, including Beneham and Beanham.

Robert Harrison, Mr George Chatfeilde the elder and George Chatfeilde the younger; but always from time to time and yearly did accept and take the accustomed services of the tenants in full satisfaction and discharge of their tithe hay growing upon their meadow grounds. *For the rest does not know.*

M5. That John Whatley, in every of the years libellated, by himself or his servants hath according to the custom done the works, and that in full satisfaction and payment of his tithe hay of his meadow ground, to this examinate's knowledge; for she and her husband hath been present with John Whatley or his servants when they did do the accustomed works (saving only at ploughing). *For the rest does not know.*

To the interrogatories given in the first place.

In (1) 2. That she is worth nothing of her proper goods because she hath a husband.

In (1) 3. *That she came to testify of her own volition without compulsion and at the request and expense of John Whatley and of other parishioners of Oving.*

In (1) 8. That she knoweth not any one tenant holding any grounds belonging to the prebend but also hath some meadow ground, more or less, belonging thereunto. *For the rest does not know.*

In (1) 9. That William Chatfeilde hath been farmer of all the tithes by the space of these three years …

To the material ex parte Richard Aylinge

MRA2. That for this 40 years and upwards she never knew nor heard that any the tenants of the parson, whether they held two yardland, one yardland or half a yardland, yearly doing their accustomed works, did ever pay any tithe hay of their meadow grounds to the prebendary. *For the rest does not know.*

MRA3. That for the space and time mentioned she never heard nor knew that any tithe hay was ever demanded by any the prebendaries of any their tenants but they did yearly accept the accustomed works of their tenants in full satisfaction and discharge of such tithe hay as their tenants had yearly growing upon their meadow ground. And so did John Afeild, Mr Stapleton, Thomas Rose Mr Ryman, Mr Robert Harrison, Mr George Chatfeilde the elder, farmers of the parsonage, accept and take the same. All which she knoweth to be true, for she dwelled with Mr Stapleton and Mr Ryman and was retaining unto them for the space of ten years, in which time she knew many of the accustomed services accepted and taken so as aforesaid, and so have done* long time before as she hath heard.

To the interrogatories.

MRA In (1) 3. That she came to testify without compulsion and that at the request of Richard Aylinge, John Whatley and other [*sic*] of the parish of Oving, and† at the charges of these John Whatley and Richard Aylinge only for her diet and no [*sic*] otherwise.

* Difficult reading.

† Deleted: 'for her charges she hath not so much as her dinner for her labour'.

MRA In (1) 7. That the accustomed works have been and are yearly performed by the tenants of the prebendary for no other consideration, cause or duty but only in satisfaction and discharge of such tithe hay as they have yearly grown upon their meadow grounds, for ought that ever she heard to the contrary. *For the rest does not know.*

MRA In (1) 8. That she knoweth not any one tenant holding any grounds of the prebend but hath likewise some meadow ground much or little to the same belonging. *For the rest does not know.*

46/6 John Benham.[305] [*May 1607*]

Of Oving, husband [sic], where lived about 40 years; before at Sherborne, Hampshire; born there; aged about 70. Is worth little or nothing. Signs with mark.

To the material ex parte John Whatley

M1. That there is at this present, and so there hath been to his own knowledge for 50 years last past, an old and ancient custom within the parish of Oving [*corroborates detail for tenants of two yardlands*]... All which he knoweth to be true for he hath dwelled within the parish of Oving all this time before by him deposed and seen and known the same to be done. *For the rest does not know.*

M2 & 3. ...that the farmers of the prebend have yearly accepted and taken the accustomed works in full satisfaction of their tithe hay growing upon their meadow ground. For so did Mr William Ryman and Mr Thomas Rose, farmers of the parsonage, take and accept the said works; and so have divers others before them, as John Afeild and Mr Stapleton, as he hath credibly heard, who then were farmers. And since Mr Ryman and Thomas Rose he hath known Mr Harrison and Mr George Chatfeilde the elder, farmers, so take and accept the same. For he hath wrought and worked with divers of the farmers and seen and known the services done and accepted in [payment].* *For the rest does not know.*

M4. That John Whatley hath at this present, and so hath had in his occupation for this six years to this examinate's knowledge, two yardland of the said tenure and holding. *For the rest does not know.*

To the interrogatories given in the first place.

In (1) 2. That he is a husband [*sic*] and liveth by his labours and is worth little or nothing his debts being paid.

In (1) 3. That he came without compulsion at the request of John Whatley and Richard Aylinge and, as he thinketh, at their charge for his diet and not otherwise.

To the interrogatories given in the second place.

In (2) 1. That this examinate, Thomas Mares, Robert Horscroft, William Len, Arthur Dunynge, John Man, Richard Faggater and David Dubberley hath every of them a cottage appertaining to the prebend.

---

* Difficult reading

In (2) 2. That he and the other cottagers do every one of them yearly, by himself or some other, two meading days or haying days and one harvest day at reaping for the farmer of the parsonage of the manor.* But he thinketh they have the more wrong. *For the rest does not know.*

In (2) 3. That neither he nor any of the cottagers mentioned hath either meadow ground or hay appertaining to their cottages and yet every of them doth do and perform the customs and services. *For the rest does not know.*

To the material ex parte Richard Aylinge

MRA1. That there is, and so always hath been for the space of 50 years last past to his own knowledge, an old and ancient custom within the parish that every tenant holding one half yardland belonging to the prebend was and is wont and accustomed to do, upon 24 hours warning and for meat and drink, two haying or meading days for the prebendary yearly, and also to work one harvest day, and to plough or cause to be ploughed one acre of land, viz half an acre for wheat and half an acre for pease or fatches, at the accustomed time and seasons of the year. All which was and is done by every such tenant as had one half yardland for the use of the prebendary. *For the rest does not know.*

MRA2 &3. That every such tenant of one half yardland doing and performing the accustomed services, for the space of these 50 years to this examinate's knowledge, hath been and is freed from payment of his tithe hay upon his meadow ground and did never pay any tithe hay in kind of any their meadow grounds that ever he heard or knew. And that the farmers of the parsonage did and have accepted the accustomed services of their tenants in full satisfaction and discharge of their tithe hay growing upon their meadow grounds. For so did Mr William Ryman and Thomas Rose, farmers of the prebend, to his own knowledge and remembrance, accept the accustomed works in lieu of their tithe hay. And so did John Afeild and Mr Stapleton, farmers of the parsonage before Mr William Ryman and Thomas Rose, as he hath credibly heard. And since, he hath known Mr Robert Harrison and George Chatfeilde the elder, gentleman, who were farmers also do the like. And never heard that any such tithe hay was ever demanded. *For the rest does not know.*

46/7 William Moorye.†[306] [*May 1607*]

Of Oving, husbandman, where lived about 44 years; before at Eartham eight years; before at Mundham about two years; before at Aldingbourne about three years; born at Eartham; aged 60 or more. Is worth 40s. Signs with mark.

To the material

M1. That he hath known for the space of these 43 years an ancient custom within the parish of Oving duly observed [*corroborates detail for tenants of two yardlands*]... All which is done for the use and behoof of the prebendary, and as he hath heard, hath been done for this 40 years. *For the rest does not know.*

---

* Deleted: 'for so this examinate and the rest of the cottagers are bound by their custom'.

† The name occurs in a number of variants, including Morye and Morie.

M2 & 3. That, during the time by this deponent set down, every tenant holding two yardlands and doing the accustomed services was and is freed from payment of any tithe hay upon their meadows. And never during the term of these 44 years did pay to the prebendary any tithe hay in kind of any their meadow ground. And that for 40 years ago Mr William Ryman and Thomas Rose, being joint farmers of the prebend, and after them Mr Robert Harrison and Mr George Chatfeilde the elder and George Chatfeilde the younger, of this examinate's own knowledge, have accepted the accustomed services in full satisfaction of their tithe hay. And further he hath heard that John Afeild who was farmer of the prebend did for three score years ago accept of the tenants the accustomed services in lieu of their tithe hay; and so did Mr Stapleton the like for 50 years ago. *For the rest does not know.*

M6. That the doing of the accustomed services by John Whatley for the prebend is yearly worth 10s by common estimation and that his hay yearly growing on his meadow grounds is worth 6s.
To the interrogatories given in the first place.

In (1) 3. *That he came of his own volition without compulsion at the request and expense of John Whatley and Richard Aylinge. And otherwise he denies.*

To the interrogatories given in the second place.

To the material given ex parte Richard Aylinge.

MRA1-3. [*Corroborates detail for tenants of half yardlands*]… And further he hath heard that the works have been so done for this three score years last past. And that every such tenant performing the accustomed services hath been freed acquitted and discharged from payment of any tithe hay … for this 60 years that he knew. And that the parson hath always accepted the accustomed services in full satisfaction of their tithe hay. For so he heard that John Afeild did accept the services for three score years ago last past, being then farmer of the parsonage. And so did Mr Stapleton after him. And further that he hath known Mr William Ryman and Thomas Rose accept the services for 40 years ago last past being then joint farmers of the parsonage. And consequently Mr Robert Harrison and others. And that there was not any tithe hay asked by any parson of any tenants during all the time above that ever he knew. *For the rest does not know.*

Examinations re material ex parte Richard Knighte.

46/8 John Oliver.[307] *Read over 4 June 1607*

Of Colworth in Oving, husbandman; born at Drayton in Oving parish; aged 50 and more. Is worth 40s. Signs with mark.

To the material.

M1-3. That there is at this present and so hath been for the space of these 40 years certain meadow grounds lying in Colworth belonging to the copyholds and copyholders, viz: to the copyhold of Agnes Moorye widow; Richard Martin; one hold late one Lambe's; one other late one Peter's (both in the tenure of William Sandham the elder); one other Elizabeth Spurnell's, widow; one other of Richard Strong's; one other late of one Bartlett's, late Thomas Poat's; and th'other late one Hooker's, late in the tenure of William Sandham the younger. And in the meadows certain parcels of meadow ground called doales* have been yearly staked, bounded and measured out by the tenants and occupiers of the copyholds and copyhold lands in Colworth, and by the tenants used and accustomed yearly to be cut and mowed, raked and set up in grass cocks at haying time to the use of the vicar of Oving in full payment of the tithe hay. And this deponent saith of his own knowledge, for he hath seen John Duckle, sometimes a tenant of the manor of Colworth, take, set and bound one doale of grass at the time of cutting thereof for his copyhold lying within the manor of Colworth for 40 years ago and upwards, for the use of the vicar of Oving (which was one Sir Bond as he remembereth). And since, this deponent himself working and mowing in the meadows of Colworth for one John Goble (who married Duckle's widow and by that means was afterward tenant to Duckle's copyhold) do the like for the use of Mr Martis the vicar, which is, as he remembereth, almost 40 years since. And further that he hath heard his father and other his ancestors say that the bounding, setting out and cutting of the doales of grass for the use of the vicars have been used and accustomed for these 40 years and upward. *For the rest does not know.*

M4. That Richard Knighte is farmer unto mead grounds in Colworth which he holdeth and farmeth of one widow Moorye, and also in his occupation a copyhold of his own and meadow grounds thereunto belonging of the manor of Colworth (but lieth in Oving). *For the rest does not know.*

M5. That as he hath heard, Richard Knighte hath, either by himself or some other for him, cut, raked or set up in grass cocks the grass of the doales belonging to the meadow ground of Agnes Moorye in his possession, in full payment of the tithe hay upon the rest of the meadow grounds belonging to the copyhold of Agnes Moorye for all the years libellated; or otherwise compounded with the vicar. *For the rest does not know.*

M6. That all the copyholders, in consideration of the cutting raking and cocking of the doales of grass yearly or otherwise compounding with the vicar, have been acquitted from payment of any other tithe hay upon their meadow grounds. And their copyholders never paid any tithe hay of their meadows during the term before by this deponent expressed to his knowledge or hearsay. *For the rest does not know.*

M7. *Does not know.*

M8. *Deposition is true.*

To the interrogatories given in the first place.

In (1) 1. *To the danger of perjury, negative.*

In (1) 2. That he is a husband [*sic*] and thereby getteth his living† and is worth 40s.

In (1) 3. *That he came of his own volition without compulsion at the request and expense of Richard Aylinge.*

---

* Not in *OED*

† Deleted: 'and hath dwelled all his lifetime in the parish of Oving saving only at Felpham for the space of three years or thereabouts which is about four years since'.

In (1) 4-6. *Negative.*

In (1) 7-11. *Does not know.*

In (1) 12. *Negative.*

To the interrogatories given in the second place.

In (2) 1-3. *Does not know.*

46/9 Richard Napcrofte.[308] *Read over 4 June 1607*

Of Oving, husbandman where lived about 50 years; born at Fishbourne in Bosham; aged about 60. Is worth 40s. Signs with mark.

To the material.

M1-7. That there are certain meadows which lie within the manor of Colworth belonging only to the copyholds or copyhold lands of the manor, viz: to the copyhold late one Lambe's; one other sometimes Mercholl's,* now in the tenure of William Sandham the elder; one other sometimes Hooker's; one other of Richard Martin's; one other of Elizabeth Spurnell's, widow; one other of Agnes Moorye's, widow; one other of Richard Strong's; one other in the tenure of Henry Mackerell; and th'other in the occupation of John Bartlett. In the which meadows are also certain plots or parcel of ground called doales, which are set out, marked, measured and bounded from the rest of the meadow grounds, and are plainly and distinctly known in what place they lie by their metes† and bounds; and are four doales in number. Which four doales of meadow or grass have been yearly, for the space of 49 years to his knowledge, cut, mowed, raked and the grass thereof set up in grass cocks for the use of the vicar by the tenants and copyholders, in full satisfaction of the tithe hay upon the rest of the meadow grounds of the tenants. Or else the tenants have compounded with the vicar by buying the doales of meadow or grass so bounded set out and meted to the use of the vicar. For he hath known one Mr Williams, Mr Bone otherwise called Smyth, vicar of Oving for 40 years ago or thereabouts, take and accept the doales of grass so set out, cut, raked and cocked in lieu of the tithe hay. And so have divers others which have been vicars of Oving since done the like: as Mr Martis, Mr Richardson, Mr Roades and Mr Widdowson. And further that the copyholders, in consideration of their yearly mowing, cutting, raking and cocking their doales of meadow or grass or otherwise compounding with the vicar, have been freely acquitted from payment of any tithe hay upon any their meadows, and never paid any tithe hay, to this deponent's own knowledge these 40 years last past and upwards; and they never paid any tithes of their meadows this 60 years and upwards. *For the rest does not know*, saving that Richard Knighte doth hire and farm a copyhold of one widow Moorye, and also is a copyholder in his own right of the manor of Colworth, but the copyhold and lands thereunto belonging lie in Oving. *For the rest does not know.*

To the interrogatories given in the first place.

---

* Difficult reading

† Boundaries

In (1) 3. *That he came of his own volition without compulsion at the request and expense of Richard Aylinge.*

In (1) 4-6. That this cause doth concern Mr Widdowson now vicar of Oving. *For the rest negative.*

In (1) 9. That William Chatfeilde hath received tithe corn as wheat and barley, pease, beans and fatches for these two years or thereabouts. *For the rest does not know.*

In (1) 10. *Concerning George Chatfeilde deposes as above. For the rest does not know.*

In (1) 12. *For self negative; for others does not know.*

46/10 Thomas Spurnell.[309] *Read over 4 June 1607*

Of Colworth in Oving husbandman where lived about 15 years; before at Hunston about two years; before at Colworth about 11 years; before at Bersted for one year; before at Felpham for one year; before at Colworth; born there; aged about 60. Is worth £3. Signs with mark.

To the material.

M1. That there are and have been for these 42 years and upwards (to this deponent's knowledge for he hath dwelled in Colworth the most part of these times) and so hath been, as he hath heard before, certain meadow grounds in Colworth belonging only to eight [*sic*] copyholds lying in Colworth village, viz: one Lambe's hold and one Nercholl's [?] hold both in the tenure of William Sandham the elder; one other hold sometimes one Hooker's in his tenure also; one other of Richard Martin's; one other of Elizabeth Spurnell's, his mother; one other of Agnes Mooryе's, widow; one other Richard Strong's; one other in the tenure of Henry Mackerell; and th'other in the tenure of John Bartlett.

M2-7* That there are certain of these meadow grounds called doales, staked, bounded and set out from the rest of the meadow ground and plainly known by their stakes and bounds from the rest; which doales or plots of meadows or grass have been used to be mowed yearly at grass cutting, and the grass raked and set up in grass cocks by the copyholders in whose meadows the same doales do lie, for the use of the vicar of Oving in payment of the tithe hay upon the rest of the meadow ground belonging to every of the eight copyholds. All which he hath known to be done the space and term of this 42 years last past, for he hath dwelled in Colworth these 40 years except four years. He saith that he hath been hired to mow and cut some of the meadows by some of the copyholders, and by reason thereof did mow and cut some of the doales of grass for 30 years ago for the use of Mr Martis then vicar of Oving, and since for Mr Roades and Mr Widdowson now vicar of Oving. *To the 4th article* he saith that Richard Knighte is a copyholder and hath one copyhold and certain meadow grounds and is tenant and farmeth also certain meadow ground appertaining to the copyhold of Agnes Moorye.... *To the 5th article does not know. To the 6th* he saith that every of the eight copyholders yearly cutting, raking and cocking of the doales of meadow or grass, or otherwise compounding with the vicar, have been freely acquitted from payment of any tithe hay

* Recte 1-6.

of the rest of their meadows, and never paid any tithe hay this 42 years for ought he ever heard or knew. And further that he hath heard his father say, which was about 80 years of age at his death, they never paid any tithes these 60 years and upwards to the parson of Oving or his farmer. *For the rest does not know.*

To the interrogatories given in the first place.

In (1) 3. *That he came of his own volition without compulsion at the request and expense of Richard Aylinge, as he believes.*

In (1) 10. That George Chatfeilde was in possession of the tithes next before William Chatfeilde for the space of three years or thereabouts. *For the rest does not know.*

46/11 Raphael Widdowson.[310] *Read over 4 June 1607.*

Of Oving, clerk, where has served as vicar six years and more; before at Preston next Brighton nine years; born at Thrumpton, Nottinghamshire; aged about 45. Is worth £20. Signature.

To the material.

M1. That there are and hath been to his knowledge all the time of his being vicar of Oving, which hath been for the space of six years and upwards, and so hath been as he hath heard for this 50 or 60 years, certain meadow grounds lying within the manor of Colworth belonging to every copyhold of the manor. *For the rest does not know.*

M2. That there are six yardlands of the manor lying near unto Oving church which pay to the vicar of Oving, time out of mind as he hath heard, and do pay to him being now vicar of Oving, 4s yearly that is to say 16d [*sic*] apiece whether the meadow be mowed or not mowed by the copyholders. And further that there have been for the time aforesaid, as he hath heard and so are at this present, certain meadows in Colworth near or about the chapel which belong to eight yardlands within the manor wherein are four doales of meadow or grass staked, measured and bounded out to the use of the vicar. *For the rest does not know.*

M3. That there hath been … and so are at this present time in the meadows belonging to the eight yardlands near unto the place there where the chapel of Colworth sometimes did stand, four doales of meadow or grass so as aforesaid marked and bounded out from the residue of the meadow grounds belonging to the eight yardlands, which have been and are yearly mowed, raked and cocked up in grass cocks at the time of grass cutting by the tenants for the use commodity and benefit of the vicar in lieu of the tithe hay upon the rest of the meadow grounds. *For the rest does not know.*

M4. That Richard Knighte is a copyholder of the manor of Colworth of the third part of the six yardlands near Oving church and of the meadow grounds belonging unto the copyhold, and also doth farm one of the meadows of the eight yardland [*sic*] (near unto the place where the chapel was) belonging to the copyhold of one widow Moorye. *For the rest does not know.*

M6. That for all the time as he hath heard and for these six years of his knowledge, all the copyholders of the eight yardland in Colworth village, in regard of their yearly cutting, raking and setting up into grass cocks at hay harvest time the grass growing upon such doales and parcels of their meadow grounds, or otherwise compounding with the vicars, have been acquitted from paying any other tithe hay upon their meadow grounds; and never paid any other tithe hay of their meadows for ought that he hath heard. *For the rest does not know.*

To the interrogatories given in the first place.

In (1) 2. That he is a minister and liveth by his function and is worth £20.

In (1) 3. *That he came of his own volition without compulsion at the request and expense of Richard Aylinge.*

In (1) 4. That this matter doth somewhat concern him because the tithes in question do by right belong unto him by reason of his vicarage. *For the rest negative.*

To the interrogatories given in the second place.

In (2) 1. *Affirms (as he believes). For the rest does not know.*

In (2) 2 & 3. *Negative.*

[*Deposition ex parte plaintiff*]

46/12 Richard Chatfeilde.[311] *Read over 9 June 1607.*

Of Chichester, gentleman, where lived about 8 years; born in city of London, county of Middlesex [sic]; aged about 45. Signature.

To the exceptions and allegation.

E1 That upon 27 July in the year of James of England the third and of Scotland the 38th the lease whereupon he is now examined made between George Chatfeilde and William Chatfeilde was subscribed, sealed and delivered by George Chatfeilde as [his] very act and deed. All which Richard Chatfeilde knoweth to be true for he was present and did see George Chatfeilde seal and deliver the same lease mentioned in the allegation as the only act and deed of George Chatfeilde unto William Chatfeilde. And after the sealing Richard Chatfeilde at the request of George Chatfeilde or William Chatfeilde did set his hand as a witness and so did Robert Langrishe, being also present at the sealing, set his hand as a witness. *For the rest does not know.*

Statement by the plaintiff concerning custom at Colworth:

46/13 *Extract from act book,* 30 January 1607/8.[312]

The copyholders or occupiers of meadow ground within the prebend of Colworth have used and accustomed to cut, rake and set up into grass cocks the grass of all such plots, parcels or doales of meadow ground belonging unto any of the copyholds or meadow grounds in any of their possessions for the use of the vicar of Oving …

Yet did the copyholders and occupiers of meadow ground cut, rake and set up into grass cocks the grass of all such plots of meadow ground in consideration that the vicar of Oving should keep a horse for his riding from Oving to Colworth chapel on Sundays and holy days, to the end that he might say divine service in the chapel there in convenient and due time: that at his coming thither he might have hay or the feeding of his horse, and not in lieu and discharge of the tithe hay grown within the prebend of Colworth due unto the parson, prebendary or farmer of the tithes belonging to the prebend of Oving.

Depositions ex parte Mr Widdowson

46/14 Henry Mackerell.[313] [*June 1608*]

Of Colworth in Oving, husbandman where lived about 24 years; before at Ford; born there; aged about 72. Signs with mark,

To the allegation

A1. That Mr Raphael Widdowson was, long before the beginning of the suit and especially in the years and months libellate, as he is now, vicar of Oving; and for lawful vicar there he was and is commonly reputed. *For the rest does not know.*

A2-4. [That] for the space of 23 or 24 years last past, during which time this examinate hath dwelt at Colworth, the vicar of Oving or his farmer hath had all the small tithes and namely of the hay of four doales or plots of meadow ground lying within the prebend, manor or village of Colworth. Which doales, as he hath heard, have been in times past and now are assigned and allotted unto the vicar in lieu and recompense of all his tithe hay of Colworth. And do lie within the meadows belonging to four copyholds in Colworth, namely: the copyhold now in the tenure and occupation of this examinate and William Sandham; a copyhold wholly in the tenure of William Sandham; the copyhold of widow Moorye; and the copyhold of Richard Martin. For he hath known Mr William Ryman, Mr Robert Harrison and Mr George Chatfeilde the elder, farmers successively to Mr William Roades then vicar and next predecessor to Mr Widdowson, to have received the hay of the four doales. And further that he hath heard by divers old men about Colworth that the vicars or their farmers have had the hay of the doales, or of four doales lying in the common mead of Colworth before the division thereof, in manner and form as ne hath deposed time out of mind and exceeding the memory of man. *For the rest does not know.*

46/15 Richard Stronge.[314] [*June 1608*]

*Of Colworth in Oving, husbandman, where lived for about 10 years; before at Slindon about 14 years; before at Climping; born there; aged about 35. Signature.**

A2 & 3. That during the time that he hath dwelt within the village of Colworth the vicar hath had the small tithes and especially tithe hay within the village or hamlet of Colworth …. For he hath known Mr Robert Harrison (farmer to Mr William Roades, vicar of Oving, of the small tithes) or servants by his appointment, to have come and demanded, taken, received and carried away all the hay of the doales in full recompense

* Stronge was a churchwarden and made a statement in the office court supporting Widdowson's presentment of Chatfeilde.(Ep I/15/3/16/98).

of all such tithe hay of the meadows and hay grounds within Colworth. And so is Mr Widdowson in like possession of receiving all the hay of the doales. And further that he hath heard that the vicar of Oving hath had the hay of the doales, or of four doales lying in the common meadows of Colworth before the division thereof, for this the three score years and time out of mind. *For the rest does not know.*

A4. *Affirms from what he has heard.*

46/16 John Warde.[315] *[June 1608]*

Of Bersted, husband [sic] where lived all his life; born there; aged about 30. Signature.

A2 & 3. That the vicar of Oving for the space of these twelve years to this examinate's knowledge hath been in possession of the hay of four doales in Colworth … which have been yearly cut, raked and set up in grass cocks for the vicar and so are now for Mr Raphael Widdowson. Which doales did lie in the common mead of Colworth before the inclosing thereof and were mowed raked and cocked for the vicar, being in lieu of all such tithe hay within the hamlet of Colworth. And further that the vicar of Oving hath received the hay before the inclosing in lieu of all the tithe hay yearly growing within the hamlet of Colworth for these 50 years last past. And so doth Mr Widdowson now receive the same at this present. *For the rest does not know.*

A4. *Affirms from his knowledge.*

46/17 William Sandham, senior.[316] *[June 1608]*

Of All Saints in the Pallant, Chichester, yeoman, where lived about 16 years; before in the Subdeanery, Chichester about 14 years; before at Colworth in Oving about 12 years; born there; aged about 68 [sic]. Signature: William Sandam.

To the allegation.

A2 & 3. That he hath known the vicar of Oving these 50 years last past to have had the tithe hay within Colworth, namely the tithe hay of four doales of meadow lying within the common meads of Colworth called hoe meads before the dividing thereof. And now since the inclosing, the plots or doales do lie in four distinct places of the meadows, the tithe whereof hath been and is yearly paid unto the vicars. For he hath known one Mr Richardson, Mr Smyth and Mr Williams, Mr Martis and Mr Roads vicars of Oving, predecessors of Mr Widdowson to have had the tithe hay; and so doth Mr Widdowson, and hath done for the time of his incumbency there, receive the same hay. And never knew any other to have or receive or make any claim or challenge thereunto for all the time aforesaid. *For the rest does not know.*

A4. *Affirms from what he has heard and from the relation of Mr Widdowson. For the rest does not know.*

To the interrogatories

In 1. *To the danger of perjury, negative.*

In 2. *Negative within his own knowledge.*

In 3. *Negative beyond what already deposed*, saving that since the dividing of the common mead of Colworth the tithe hay of the doales hath been paid by four copyholders, viz: by this examinate, Richard Knighte, and one Mackerell, and one Richard Martyn, and their predecessors. Because at the division of the meadows the doales did fall out to lie in four meads belonging to their copyholds. *For the rest does not know.*

In 4. That he hath meadow grounds lying within Colworth meadow whereof, if the party producent should prevail in this suit, he doth not think he should pay any more tithe. Because he payeth the whole tithe hay of one doale in lieu of all the tithe of his said meadows. *For the rest does not know.*

In 5. *That he comes at the request of Mr Widdowson* and as for his charges he hath requested none, neither doth he expect any from him. *For the rest does not know.*

In 6. That of the two he favoureth Mr Widdowson best and could wish that he might prevail because of his right.

In 7 & 8. *Negative.*

Depositions ex parte Knighte and Widdowson

46/18 Henry Mackerell.[317] *Read over 13 July 1608*

Of Colworth husband [sic]. Signs with mark.

To the additional positions

AP1. That for the space of this 23 or 24 years, which time he hath dwelled at Colworth, he never heard that the parsons of Oving ever received any tithe hay of any the meadow grounds in Colworth belonging to any copyhold of the manor. And further that he hath heard by his ancestors and divers old men of the parish of Oving and other parishes thereabouts that the parsons nor their farmers ever received any tithe hay of the meadow grounds during the memory of man and especially for these 60 years last past. *For the rest does not know.*

AP2. That for the space of this 24 years to his knowledge, and so for all the space of time aforesaid as he hath heard, the vicars have been in possession of tithe hay upon the meadow grounds belonging unto the copyholds of the manor. And so is Mr Widdowson and so hath been for all the time of his incumbency there, viz of the hay of four doales or plots of meadow ground which have been yearly at hay harvest time staked, bounded and marked out from the residue of the meadow, and mowed and set up in grass cocks by the copyholders within whose meadows the plots do lie, for the use of the vicars of Oving in payment of all their tithe hay. For he hath known William Moorye now deceased and William Sandham pay for the hay of their doales unto the farmers of the vicarage, Mr William Rymber,* Mr Robert Harrison and others; and so hath this examinate done the like unto Mr Widdowson. *For the rest does not know.*

---

* Presumably scribal error for Ryman.

AP3. That in the years libellated Richard Knight was tenant unto one of the copyholders and the meadow ground thereunto belonging, namely for the copyhold of widow Moorye. *For the rest does not know.*

AP4. That Richard Knight did cut, rake and set up into grass cocks the grass of the doale in his occupation in the years, or did otherwise agree with Mr Widdowson. *For the rest does not know.*

AP5. That he never knew for all the time mentioned but that all the copyholders staking, bounding, cutting, raking and cocking the hay, or compounding with vicars of Oving, were ever acquitted from payment of any other tithe hay. And further that they never paid any tithe hay of their meadows unto the parsons for all the time mentioned as he hath heard. *For the rest does not know.*

AP6. *Does not know.*

AP7. That he hath heard say by divers old and ancient men that the tithe hay of the brooks and meads within the prebend hath been paid unto the vicars by the name of small tithes, and were esteemed little worth because, as he hath heard, the brooks or meads have been in times past (before the sluices were made for the conveying away of the water) overflowen with water, as in this article is declared. And so they are and have been every year for the most part since the making of the sluices, but not so much nor so often as they were before, whereby the grass of these brooks or meads did and do yearly for the most part lie many months under water in the winter time; and by reason thereof the grass hath been very full of rushes, flags and reeds, and so is at this present in many places. *For the rest does not know.*

AP9. *Deposition is true.*

*To the interrogatories given in the first place.**

In (1) 1. *To the danger of perjury, for himself negative.*

In (1) 2. *Negative.*

In (1) 3. *Deposes as to the previous articles. For the rest does not know.*

In (1) 4. That he hath two acres of meadow ground in Colworth. *For the rest negative.*

In (1) 5. *That he came to testify of his own volition without compulsion and at the request of Mr Widdowson. As for expenses, he has not yet sought any.*

In (1) 6 *Favours parties indifferently and wishes victory for the party in the right.*

In (1) 7 & 8. *Negative.*

To the interrogatories [in the second place]†

In (2) 1 & 2. *Does not know beyond what has deposed to the second article of the additional positions.*

---

* Inserted later in the volume at f 119v.

† Entered in the volume immediately following the additional positions.

In (2) 3. That the brooks or meadows have been good meadow and hay grounds this 14 or 15 years. *For the rest does not know.*

In (2) 4. That he never knew but that tithe hay was always accounted small tithes, as is lamb wool and pig and such small things, and not in the number of great tithes as wheat and barley and such like; and that the parsons never had or received any tithe hay but that the same doth belong unto the vicar of Oving and so doth the tithe corn and hay growing upon the demesne lands. *For the rest does not know.*

In (2) 5. Affirms.

In (2) 6. That when the chapel was standing it was distant from the parish church of Oving about a mile. *For the rest does not know.*

In (2) 7-9. *Does not know.*

In (2) 10. *Does not know beyond what has deposed to the second article of the additional positions.*

46/19 John Oliver.[318] [*July 1608*]

Of Colworth in Oving, husband [sic]; born there; aged about 48. Signs with mark.

To the material

M1. That Mr Raphael Widdowson was and is now vicar of Oving long before this suit began; and so is commonly reputed. *For the rest does not know.*

M2 & 3. That for the space of these 34 years last past the vicars of Oving have been in quiet possession of the tithe hay upon the meadow grounds belonging to the copyholds within the manor or prebend of Colworth, viz the hay of four doales or plots of meadow ground which have been yearly staked, bounded and divided from the residue of the meadow grounds and cut, raked and set up into grass cocks at hay harvest time for the use of the vicars by the copyholders in whose meadow grounds the same doales do lie. For this examinate saith that he hath mowed, cut, raked and cocked the grass of some of the doales, and namely the doales belonging to the copyhold sometimes William Moorye's and John Gobles (now deceased) many times, for the use of Sir Boane, Mr Richardson, Mr Martis and Mr Roades, vicars of Oving and predecessors to Mr Widdowson. And further that the vicars have been in possession of the tithe hay for these 60 years as he hath heard his father related [*sic*] unto him, who died about 30 years ago and was at his death 70 years old. And so is Mr Widdowson in possession of the tithe hay or of money in consideration thereof. *For the rest does not know.*

M4. *Does not know.*

M5. *Deposition is true.*

To the additional positions to the material

AP1. That for the space of these 34 years last past he never heard that any the parsons of Oving ever received any tithe hay of the meadow grounds of Colworth. And further that he hath heard his father say that he never heard that any of the parsons were ever in possession of the same tithes for 60 years before his death. And so this deponent hath heard of divers others. *For the rest does not know.*

AP7. That he hath heard by divers old and ancient men about Colworth that the tithe hay of the brooks and meads … is accounted small tithes and little worth because in times past the brooks or meadows have been (before the making of the sluices) drowned with water from the sea, which breaking in did cause the fresh water to return and overflow the same which caused the grass to be full of flags, rushes and reeds and so little or nothing worth. *For the rest does not know.*

To the interrogatories given in the first place

In (1) 4. That Henry Mackerell hath in his occupation some part of the meadows but this examinate hath not any. *For the rest does not know.*

In (1) 5. *That he came without compulsion at the request of Mr Widdowson and at his expense.*

In (1) 6 *Favours parties indifferently and wishes victory for the party in the right.*

To the interrogatories given in the second place.

In (2) 3. That in times past when the brooks and meads were wont to be overflowen with water as in the *additional positions* is declared, they were not all mowed and the grass cut for hay but eat [*sic*] up with cattle because of the water standing in the same and the badness of the grass being full of rushes, flags and reeds. And the sea hath ceased from overflowing the same about these 30 years in such abundant sort and measure as it did before the making of the sluices, although continually every winter the brooks or meadows be somewhat overflowen. And further that the brooks or meads have been cut and mowed for the most and greatest part thereof ever since the sluices were made. *For the rest does not know.*

APPENDIX 1

Deposition of Alice Dash concerning John Lilliatt and Alice Smyth, 26 March 1607.[319]

No acts relating to a case which could have produced this deposition have been found in the records of the Bishop's consistory, or of the Dean's or Archbishop's peculiar courts It has not been entered in the Deposition Books and has survived as a single document among the Miscellaneous Court Papers (Ep I/15). It has the all the indications of having been produced for normal court proceedings: the handwriting is probably that of the notary George Stent; the deposition provides responses to a formal allegation; and it bears the customary endorsement of having been read over before a judge.

Although it bears no case title, it seems likely to arise from a claim of defamation between Alice Smith and a clergyman, John Lilliatt, whose career over 40 years is documented in the episcopal and cathedral records. Ordained in 1590, he held posts in Chichester parishes from 1593 onward, principally serving as rector of St Pancras until his death in 1629. He was also a vicar choral in the cathedral and was their Principal from 1618 onwards. He and his wife were buried in the cathedral. A John Lilliatt married Grace Hellier at Birdham in 1602; but by 1622 his wife was Mary. In that year she introduced an element of scandal by being charged with adultery with John Rose;[320] and concurrently she initiated a case against the composer, Thomas Weelkes, who was one of the cathedral singing men. Frustratingly, the act books give no indication of the nature of this case. Both cases ended by an agreement after six months. Lilliatt's career was equally tainted by scandal. In 1604, three years before Alice Dash's deposition, he was involved in a case in the Dean's court[321] over the mother of a bastard child – a case in which none of the main participants admitted knowledge of the child's father. In this case he voiced the same fears as those recounted in the deposition: that the publicity might lead to the loss of his incumbency of St Pancras.

Biographical information on Alice Smith is more sparse. In April 1599 John Smith of Chichester was cited in the Dean's court for fornication, having got Alice Horscroft with child;[322] the couple married in the same month. A year later an Alice Smith was cited for fornication with James Went of West Wittering and subsequently delivered of a child.[323] It is certainly possible that she bore a child to John Lilliatt, as alleged in the deposition: the Binsted Bishop's Transcripts record a baptism on 6 January 1606/7 of John, son of John Smith. In 1613 Christopher May of Rumboldswhyke was cited for harbouring an Alice Smith who had borne a child (which she claimed was begotten by her husband John).[324]

Information about Alice Dash is even more thin. A woman of that name, wife of Richard, was presented in the Dean's court in 1603 as a 'lewd woman'.[325] In 1604 the couple were presented for not receiving communion at St Martin's, Chichester.[326]

It remains difficult to attempt an evaluation of this document, in the absence of any supporting evidence of court proceedings. One can only guess that it represents some kind of preliminary draft, despite its legal formalities. It is worth noting that it lacks the interrogatories which would be supplied by an opposing party – and perhaps it is even more significant that it is not accompanied by a statement from a second witness, as the court would not normally proceed on the evidence of a single deponent. Perhaps it proved difficult to find further witnesses: the only other people mentioned in the deposition, Alice and John Smith, might well have felt reluctant to expose themselves to examination. This lack of corroboration may have led to the case being dropped; and it is easy to believe that the clerical establishment of the cathedral might have been happy to avoid some potential embarrassment.

Plaintiffs and proctors: not named. Examination: one deposition responding to allegation of 13 articles.

Deposition of Alice Dash *Read over before Mr Francis Cox 26 March 1607.*

Wife of Richard Dash, husbandman, of Chichester, where lived about 16 years; before at Chailey[?] in [Sussex] about 8 years; before at Brickhurst [?]† in the parish of Gilstoke[?]‡ in Hampshire, where lived for major part of childhood; born at Romsey, Hampshire; aged about 30.*

To the allegations

A1. That Alice Smyth dwelt and had her abode in the house of widow Boane, without the north gate of the city of Chichester and near unto the city, the space of one quarter of a year which was about the feast of St James the Apostle last. And this saith of her own knowledge because she dwelt there with Alice Smyth all the time in the house of widow Boane. And afterwards Alice Smyth dwelt at one [*blank*] Whittington's in Binsted one quarter of a year, where she was delivered of a man child, *from the knowledge of the deponent. For the rest does not know.*

A2. *Does not know.*

A3. That Alice was delivered of a child in Whittington's house in Binsted. *For the rest does not know.*

A4. That she hath heard Alice Smyth say both before and after the time of her delivery that John Lilliatt had carnal knowledge of her and had begotten her with child. *For the rest does not know.*

A5-9. That about 14 days or three weeks before the delivery of Alice Smyth, which is about 16 weeks since she sent [Alice Dash] to Mr John Lilliatt for money, and so she coming to him declaring her message to him,§ said that he would come unto Alice Smyth himself; and so did about 7 of the clock at night of the said day that Alice Dash was sent unto him. And meeting with her about the Friars Gate within the city of Chichester, which was a place appointed by John Lilliatt to meet with her, came with her unto the house of widow Bone [*sic*] and he caused her to call Alice Smyth unto him into a field called the Sloe Fair Field near unto the widow Bone's house, which she did accordingly. And then he said unto her, 'Alice Smyth, this woman, meaning [Alice Dash], saith that you say I am father of your child which you now go withal'. And then Alice Smyth said, 'So you are'. Then he denied it and said 'You know that I cannot be father of your child for it cometh too soon for me to be father thereof and I had not to do with you before,' and named the time thereof which [Alice Dash] hath utterly forgotten. And then and there much speech being spoken and used to the purpose, which she doth not now remember, John Lilliatt at the conclusion thereof gave unto Alice Smyth a piece of money, but how much [she] cannot depose (but as Alice Smyth told her the morrow after it was 13½d). And he moreover said unto her, 'If you should

---

* Difficult reading: probably Cheyleigh.

† Difficult reading.

‡ Difficult reading.

§ *Deleted*: 'sent unto Alice Smyth 12d for this [*illegible*]'.

bring my name in question concerning this matter I should lose my living and be undone', (or the like words). And if she would not bring his name in question, his purse should be as open to her as her husband's, and that she should not lack anything. *For the rest does not know* saving that John Lilliatt said unto her, 'I hope you will not charge me to be father of your child; and if you do or shall charge me withal I will forswear it.' And also that he did earnestly entreat her and Alice Smyth to conceal him and not to charge him to be the father of her child or to have carnal knowledge of her body, and promised as before she hath deposed (or the same or like in effect). *For the rest concerning articles 5-9 does not know beyond what has already deposed.*

A10. That Alice Dash at the request of Alice Smyth went unto John Lilliatt for money to relieve her in that her need, by whom he sent unto her 12d. And did then confess unto her that he had carnal knowledge of Alice Smyth's body, but that was too long ago to be father of the child of the which she did go withal. *For the rest does not know beyond what has already deposed.*

A11. That John Lilliatt came to [Alice Dash's] house at another time and left 2s with her to be paid* to Alice Smyth from him which she did to her accordingly. And withal he desired her to commend him unto her (who was at that time from [Alice Dash's] house) and to tell her that she should keep all things close and secret and not to bring his name in question by any means. *For the rest does not know.*

A12. That there hath been and is a common and public fame and report in and about the places mentioned that John Lilliatt hath begotten Alice Smyth with child or at least hath had carnal knowledge of her body. *For the rest does not know.*

A13. *Deposition is true.*

[Mark]

---

* Difficult reading.

APPENDIX 2

Account for the case of Coote v Brydye

A full account of the costs charged in the case of Coote v Brydye has survived among the Miscellaneous Court papers.[327] It provides a good example of the process of a case as well as the fees charged. At the end of the proceedings taxed costs amounting to £5 11s 8d were awarded against Brydye. A summarised version of the account is given below

Costs calculated on behalf of Mary Coote in a matrimonial case against John Brydye	
Citation with inhibitions	3s 4d
Execution of citation	2s
1st fee of proctor	2s
28 July 1604	
Making of return and act	1s 2d
Fee of proctor	2s
Summary of petition	5s
For its admission and act	1s
Decree on behalf of principal party, and act	2s 4d
22 Sept 1604	
Fee of proctor	1s
28 Sept 1604	
Fee of proctor	1s
Execution of decree	2s
For return of decree and act	8d
Production of Brydye and act	1s 10d
Copy of personal response of Brydye	8d
6 Oct 1604	
Fee of proctor	1s
Act	4d

13 Oct 1604	
Fee of proctor	1s
20 Oct 1604	
Examination of two witnesses concerning summmary petition	2s 4d
Expenses of the two witnesses twice journeying to Chichester for production and examination	4s
Act	4d
Fee of proctor	1s
Copy of articulate material on behalf of Brydye	3s 4d
27 Oct 1604	
Fee of proctor	1s
3 Nov 1604	
Fee of proctor	1s
10 Nov 1604	
Fee of proctor	1s
17 Nov 1604	
Fee of proctor	1s
24 Nov 1604	
Fee of proctor	1s
Preparation of interrogatories administered to witnesses on behalf of Brydye concerning his articulated material produced and examined.	3s 4d
For examination of witnesses re interrogatories	1s 8d
1 Dec 1604	
Fee of proctor	1s
8 Dec 1604	
Fee of proctor	1s
15 Dec 1604	
Fee of proctor	1s
Two acts	8d
19 Jan 1604/5	
Fee of proctor	1s
Copies of examinations of two witnesses on behalf of party Mary Coote	2s 4d
Act	4d
26 Jan 1604/5	
Fee of proctor	1s

Preparation of response of Coote concerning material submitted by Brydye	2s 6d
9 Feb 1604/5	
Fee of proctor	1s
Copies of depositions of two witnesses on behalf of Brydye	2s 4d
16 Feb 1604/5	
Fee of proctor	1s
23 Feb 1604/5	
Fee of proctor	1s
Act	4d
2 Mar 1604/5	
Fee of proctor	1s
Two acts	8d
9 Mar 1604/5	
Fee of proctor	1s
Act	4d
16 Mar 1604/5	
Fee of proctor	1s
Act	4d
23 Mar 1604/5	
Fee of proctor	1s
Act	4d
25 May 1605	
Fee of proctor	1s
Act	4d
8 Jun 1605	
Fee of proctor	1s
Act	4d
15 Jun 1605	
Fee of proctor	1s
Act	4d
22 Jun 1605	
Fee of proctor	1s

28 Jun 1605	
Fee of proctor	1s
Fee of proctor	1s
Act	4d
6 Jul 1605	
Fee of proctor	1s
Act	4d
13 Jul 1605	
Fee of proctor	1s
20 Jul 1605	
Fee of proctor	1s
27 Jul 1605	
Fee of proctor	1s
Fee for sentence	£1
21 Jun 1606	
Fee of proctor	1s
Decree concerning sentence	2s
Act	4d
13 Dec 1606	
Fee of proctor	1s
Execution of decree	2s
Return of decree and act	8d
Decree enforcing by viis et modis and act*	2s 4d
17 Jan 1606/7	
Fee of proctor	1s
Return of decree for viis et modis and act.	8d
24 Jan 1606/7	
Fee of proctor	1s
28 Feb 1606/7	
Fee of proctor	1s
Act	4d

* If a defendant failed to appear after being cited, the court could follow up with a citation 'viis et modis' (by all ways and means). This would normally be posted prominently in the place where the defendant lived, and if he failed to appear he could be declared contumacious and excommunicated.

7 Mar 1606/7	
Fee of proctor	1s
Act	4d
14 Mar 1606/7	
Fee of proctor	1s
Preparation of this account	3s
Admission of same and act	1s
Monition for paying expenses	2s
Execution of the same	2s
Monition for solemnisation of marriage and act	2s 4d
Execution of the same	2s
	£6 11s 8d
Taxation of the account	£5 11s 8d

APPENDIX 3

EXAMPLE OF THE TRANSCRIPTION METHOD

SILENT OMISSIONS IN TRANSCRIPTION

The repeated and formulaic phrases used by the scribes who wrote out the depositions can make reading confusing and tedious. Fortunately a large amount of this phrasing can be omitted without affecting the sense. Initially I feared that making such omissions could introduce a subjective element into transcription; but I discovered that omitable phraseology can be defined into quite specific categories.

The following principles have been adopted:-

Insignificant formulaic phrases are silently omitted if they fall into the following clearly definable categories:

1. Identifying:

   Certain specific words or phrases: "aforesaid"; "before mentioned"; "the said"; "articulate"; "examinate"; "libellate".

2. Tautological/redundant:

   e.g. "answered *and said*"; "*then and there*"; "*last past*"; "all *and singular*"; "*verily* believeth".

3. Specifying:

   e.g. "at the time and place aforesaid"; "and titheable places therein"; "coming growing and renewing". There are many similar phrases which set out matter which has already been stated or is implicit.

4. Locating:

   e.g. "in the county of Sussex"; "in the parish of"

5. Qualifying, excepting or confirming:

   e.g. "as he remembereth"; "he cannot remember"; "as he hath previously deposed".

The following examples illustrate the transcription method.

1. Literal transcript of the English text of the original deposition, retaining the original spelling. Abbreviations and contractions (especially in the Latin) are expanded. English words and phrases suitable for omission are set out in bold type. All Latin is in bold italic; some of the Latin reflects later rather than classical forms (e.g. testes for testis; parochie for parochiae, etates for aetatis).

2. Edited transcript using modern spelling, minimal punctuation and omitting words and phrases identified in version 1.

FULL TRANSCRIPT

[Ep I/11/10 f 133v]

Robertus Slater p[ar]o[chi]e de Ashengton cum Buncton in Com[itatu] Sussex husbandman ubi habitavit p[er] spaciu[m] duor[um] annor[um] vel circiter et antea apud Warminghurste in Com[itatu] p[re]d[ictu] ubi mora[m] fecit p[er] spaciu[m] xij annor[um] vel circiter et antea apud Wiston in Com[itatu] p[re]d[ictu] ubi mora[m] egit p[er] spaciu[m] ix annor[um] vel circiter et antea apud Westegreenesteade in Com[itatu] p[re]d[ictu] ubi oriundus fuit etates xlvij annor[um] vel circiter lib[er]e condic[i]onis testes p[ro]ductus iuratus et exa[mi]natus dicit ut sequitur

Ad allegac[i]o[n]em

Ad primu[m] ar[ticu]lum deponit that Mr Peter Waters **articulate** is **and hathe beene** parson of Wiston **articulate** before the beginninge of this suite **as this examinate verilye believethe** for he **this examinate** was present when he tooke possession of the churche **aforesaide accordinge to order** which was aboute November last paste and **this examinate** further saithe that Mr John Woodcocke, clerke, was **then and theare** also present and did **accordinge to order** deliver him possession; ***et al[ite]r nescit.***

Ad s[e]c[un]dum that aboute Michaelmas in the yeare **of our Lorde god** 1603 he **this examinate** beinge then receiver unto Sr Thomas Sherley, knight, of all his rentes and tithes **cominge growing and renewing unto him** within **the parishe of** Wiston **articulate** for that yeare **the saide Sr Thomas Sherley** willed **this examinate** to geather the tithes due unto the parson of Wiston **articulate** accordinge to a scrowle whiche he gave unto **this examinate** whiche was onely to receive of everye man whose name was therein contained suche **some and** somes of money as weare also therein contained and **the saide Sr Thomas Sherley** willed **this examinate** to paye unto **the saide** Mr Waters **articulate** fortye poundes soe soone as he **this examinate** could gather upp the money specified in the scrowle **before mentioned** for tithes due unto Mr Waters for the yeare 1603 in soe muche that he **this examinate** gathered upp **by virtue of the saide scrowle** soe muche money as **this examinate** could gather [and made it upp [*deleted*] accordinge to his **mr** Sr Thomas Sherleye's command which he did make upp and pay unto **the saide** Mr Waters **articulate** xxxviij li some parte whereof he **this examinate** paid unto **the saide** Mr Waters before the beginninge of this suite and the residue **or other parte thereof this examinate** hath paid unto **the said** Mr Waters since the beginninge of this suite **as he remembrethe**; And he **this examinate** further saithe that he hath knowne **the said** Sr Thomas Sherley **articulate** to have received some tithe in kinde as wheate, Barley, Pease, Beanes, Oates, Fatches or Teares, haye and suche like of Phillipe Bennett, John Darkeinge and John Bennett for theire tithe Corne sand hay **growinge and renewinge** within the parish of Wiston **articulate**

wheare they occupied lande for sixteene years agoe and both they and some other hath paid the like tithe in kynde ever since who have occupied the **saide** landes unto **the saide** Sr Thomas Sherley for **this examinate** dwelling with **ye said** Sr Thomas Sherley hath received the same tithes in kynde to the use of **the said** Sr Tho: Sherley. And **this examinate** further saithe that one Thomas Willett of Wiston upon some composition **or other concluded and agreed upon betwixte the saide Sr Thomas Sherley and the said Thomas Willett** did receive some tithes in kynde namely haye of one Wm Whitebreade of Ashehurste **in the Countye of Sussex** who occupied one meadowe or two aboute some five or sixe years agoe last past. And **the saide** Thomas Willett's father by vertue of the like agreemente **from the saide Sr Thomas Sherley** received the like tithe hay **cominge and growing and renewing of the saide one or two meadowes situate and beinge within the parishe of Wiston aforesaide** for **twentye** years agoe last paste or **theare aboutes of this examinate's knowledge; *et al[ite]r nescit.***

Ad tertiu[m] nescit depon[er]e.

Ad quartu[m] nescit depon[er]e al[ite]r qua[m] p[re]deposuit.

Ad quintu[m] nescit depon[er]e saving that **the saide** John Willett in the year 1603 paid unto **this examinate** tithe oates in kynde viz two quarters **of oates or theareabouts to the use of Sr Thomas Sherley articulate** and in the same year **this examinate** received of William Foster **articulate** about some xijs for all his tithes **due unto the saide Sr Thomas Sherley articulate cominge growing and renewinge within the saide parishe of Wiston or due unto the parson of Wiston for anything this examinate knowethe**; ***et al[ite]r nescit.***

Ad vj dicit q[uo]d p[re]depo[s]ita p[er] eu[m] sunt vera.

Ad posic[i]ones add[itiona]les

Ad primu[m] ar[ticu]lu[m] deponit that **the saide** Mr Byngham **articulate** in his lifetime did covenante **and graunte** that **the said** Sr Thomas Sherley **articulate** should enioye **all and singular** the tithes of Wiston **comeinge growing and renewing within the parishe of Wiston articulate and titheable places thereof** soe longe as **the said Sr Thomas Sherley** did pay **unto the saide Mr Byngham** yearely aboute sixteen or twenty days after everye quarter **in everye yeare v li by the quarter** and everye yeare a quarter of wheate and a quarter of barley aboute Candlemas **in everye yeare** and also that **the said Sr Thomas Sherley** shoulde **and myghte upon the covenaunte aforesaid** dispose of the tithes **aforesaid for the time aforesaid in manner and forme aforesaide** at his will and pleasure; ***et al[ite]r nescit.***

Ad s[e]c[un]dum nescit depon[er]e al[ite]r qua[m] p[re]deposuit.

Ad tertiu[m] et quartu[m] nescit depon[er]e al[ite]r qua[m] p[re]deposuit.

Ad **quartu[m]** [*recte quintum*] that he **this examinate** received all the tithes due unto **the saide Sr Thomas Sherley** [of the saide John *crossed through but reinstated*] Willett and Wm Foster **also articulate** due unto him at **and untill** the feaste of All Saints **in the yeare of our lorde god** 1603 **articulate to the use of the saide Sr Thomas Sherley and by his appointement.**

Ad vj nescit depon[er]e.

Ad vij nescit depon[er]e al[ite]r qua[m] p[re]deposuit saving yt he **verilye** believeth **the saide** Mr Waters **articulate** dothe or maye enioye the parsonage house of Wiston **articulate** if he liste **at such time and when he liste either by himself or any other** .

Ad viij nescit depon[er]e al[ite]r qua[m] p[re]deposuit.

Ad ix dicit q[uo]d p[re]depo[s]ita p[er] eu[m] sunt vera.

Roberte Slater [signature].

EDITED TRANSCRIPT

15/4 Robert Slater. *[January 1604/5]*

Of Ashington cum Buncton, husbandman, where has lived about 2 years; before at Warminghurst about 12 years; before at Wiston about 9 years; before at West Grinstead; born there; aged about 47. Signature.

To the allegation

A1. That Mr Peter Waters is parson of Wiston before the beginning of this suit for he was present when he took possession of the church, which was about November last past. And Robert Slater further saith that Mr John Woodcocke, clerk, was also present and did deliver him possession. *For the rest does not know.*

A2. That about Michaelmas in the year 1603, he being then receiver unto Sir Thomas Sherley, knight, of all his rents and tithes within Wiston for that year, Sir Thomas willed him to gather the tithes due unto the parson of Wiston according to a scroll which he gave unto him; which was only to receive of every man whose name was therein contained such sums of money as were also therein contained. And he willed him to pay unto Mr Waters £40 so soon as he could gather up the money specified in the scroll for tithes due for the year 1603. In so much that he gathered up so much money as he could gather* according to his master's command, which he did make up and pay unto Mr Waters £38; some part whereof he paid unto Mr Waters before the beginning of this suit and the residue hath paid unto Mr Waters since the beginning of this suit. And further saith that he hath known Sir Thomas Sherley to have received some tithe in kind as wheat, barley, peas, beans, oats, fatches [*sic*] or tares, hay and such like of Phillip Bennett, John Darkeing and John Bennett for their tithe corn and hay within the parish of Wiston where they occupied land for 16 years ago. And both they and some other [*sic*] hath paid the like tithe in kind ever since who have occupied the lands unto Sir Thomas; for Robert Slater dwelling with Sir Thomas hath received the same tithes in kind to the use of him. And he further saith that one Thomas Willett of Wiston, upon some composition, did receive some tithes in kind, namely hay of one William Whitebreade of Ashurst who occupied one meadow or two about some 5 or 6 years ago. And Thomas Willett's father by virtue of the like agreement received the like tithe hay for 20 years ago last past. *For the rest does not know.*

---

* *Deleted*: 'and made it up.'

A3. *Does not know.*

A4. *Does not know beyond what has already deposed.*

A5. *Does not know,* saving that John Willett in the year 1603 paid unto him tithe oats in kind viz two quarters, and in the same year he received of William Foster about some 12s for all his tithes. *For the rest does not know.*

A6. *Deposition is true.*

To the additional positions.

AP1. That Mr Byngham in his lifetime did covenant that Sir Thomas Sherley should enjoy the tithes of Wiston so long as he did pay yearly about 16 or 20 days after every quarter £5, and every year a quarter of wheat and a quarter of barley about Candlemas; and also that Sir Thomas should and might dispose of the tithes at his will and pleasure. *For the rest does not know.*

AP2-4. *Cannot depose beyond what has already deposed.*

AP4 [*recte* 5]. That he received all the tithes due unto Sir Thomas Sherley [of the said John]* Willett and William Foster due unto him at the feast of All Saints 1603.

AP6. *Does not know.*

AP7. *Does not know,* saving that he believeth Mr Waters doth or may enjoy the parsonage house of Wiston if he list.

AP8. *Cannot depose beyond what has already deposed.*

AP9. *Deposition is true.*

---

* Crossed through but reinstated.

ENDNOTES

With one exception all references cited in the notes are to documents in the West Sussex Record Office in the following collections and classes:

Ep I/10/	Chichester Episcopal records: Chichester Archdeaconry instance court act books;
Ep I/11/	Chichester Episcopal records: Chichester Archdeaconry instance court deposition books;
Ep I/15/	Chichester Episcopal records: Chichester Archdeaconry miscellaneous court papers;
Ep I/17/	Chichester Episcopal records: Chichester Archdeaconry office court act books;
Ep III/4/	Chichester Episcopal records: Dean of Chichester Peculiar act books;
Ep III/6/	Chichester Episcopal records: Dean of Chichester Peculiar miscellaneous court papers;
Ep IV/4/	Chichester Episcopal records: Archbishop's Peculiar of Pagham and Tarring court act books;
STC/I	Sussex Testamentary Records: Archdeaconry of Chichester registered wills;
STC/II	Sussex Testamentary Records: Archdeaconry of Chichester original wills;
STC/III	Sussex Testamentary Records: Archdeaconry of Chichester probate act books;
STD/I	Sussex Testamentary Records: Dean of Chichester's Peculiar wills.

TNA PROB refers to the National Archives Prerogative Court of Canterbury wills.

---

1 Ep I/11/9 f 213v-215r, 257r-259r; Ep I/11/10 ff 34v, 46r & v; Ep I/15/1 (1603).
2 Ep I/11/9 f 213v.
3 Ep I/11/9 f 214r.
4 Ep I/11/9 f 214v.
5 Ep I/15/1 (1603).
6 Ep I/15/1 (1603).
7 Ep I/11/9 f 257r.
8 Ep I/11/9 f 258r.
9 Ep I/11/10 f 34v.
10 Ep I/11/10 f 45v.
11 Ep I/11/10 ff 1r-12r, 25v-34r.
12 Ep I/11/10 f 1r.
13 Ep I/11/10 f 3r.
14 Ep I/11/10 f 5r.
15 Ep I/11/10 f 7r.
16 Ep I/11/10 f 8v.
17 Ep I/11/10 f 25v.
18 Ep I/11/10 f 26v.
19 Ep I/11/10 f 29r.
20 Ep I/11/10 f 30r.
21 Ep I/11/10 f 32r.
22 Ep I/11/10 f 33r.
23 Ep I/11/10 f 35r.
24 Ep I/11/10 ff 12v-14v, 85v-95v, 97r-100r, 112r-118v, 119v-129r, 138v-140v, 145v-146v; Ep I/15/1 (1603, 1604); Ep I/10/24 f 52v.
25 Ep I/11/10 f 12v.
26 Ep I/11/10 f 14r.
27 Ep I/11/10 f 85v.
28 Ep I/11/10 f 88r.
29 Ep I/11/10 f 89r.
30 Ep I/11/10 f 90r.

31 Ep I/11/10 f 91r.
32 Ep I/11/10 f 92r.
33 Ep I/11/10 f 93r.
34 Ep I/11/10 f 94r.
35 Ep I/11/10 f 94v.
36 Ep I/11/10 f 97r.
37 Ep I/11/10 f 99r.
38 Ep I/15/1 (1604).
39 Ep I/15/1 (1604).
40 Ep I/11/10 f 112r.
41 Ep I/11/10 f 114r.
42 Ep I/11/10 f 115v.
43 Ep I/11/10 f 117r.
44 Ep I/11/10 f 119v.
45 Ep I/11/10 f 122r.
46 Ep I/11/10 f 124r.
47 Ep I/11/10 f 126r.
48 Ep I/11/10 f 128r.
49 Ep I/11/10 f 138r.
50 Ep I/11/10 f 145v.
51 Ep I/15/1 (1604).
52 Ep I/10/24 f 52v.
53 Ep I/11/10 ff 14v-17r.
54 Ep I/11/10 f 14v.
55 EpI /11/10 f 16r.
56 Ep I/11/10 ff 17v-25v, 37r-45r.
57 Ep I/11/10 f 17v.
58 Ep I/11/10 f 20r.
59 Ep I/11/10 f 22v.
60 Ep I/11/10 f 37r.
61 Ep I/11/10 f 40r.
62 Ep I/11/10 f 42v.
63 Ep I/11/10 ff 46v-51v.
64 Ep I/11/10 f 46v.
65 Ep I/11/10 f 47v.
66 Ep I/11/10 f 45a r.
67 Ep I/11/10 f 49r.
68 Ep I/11/10 f 50r.
69 Ep I/11/10 ff 52r-58v.
70 Ep I/11/10 f 52r.
71 Ep I/11/10 f 54v.
72 Ep I/11/10 f 56v.
73 Ep I/11/10 ff 59r-79r.
74 Ep I/11/10 f 59r.
75 Ep I/11/10 f 61v.
76 Ep I/11/10 f 64v.
77 Ep I/11/10 f 67r.
78 Ep I/11/10 f 70v.
79 Ep I/11/10 f 73v.
80 Ep I/11/10 f 76v.
81 Ep I/11/10 ff 79r-81v.
82 Ep I/17/12 f 195v.
83 Ep I/11/10 f 79r.

84 Ep I/11/10 f 80r.
85 Ep I/11/10 ff 81v-85r.
86 Ep I/11/10 f 81v.
87 Ep I/11/10 f 84r.
88 Ep I/11/10 f 84v.
89 Ep I/11/10 ff 95v-97r, 100r-101r, 130r-133r.
90 Ep I/11/10 f 95v.
91 Ep I/11/10 f 100r.
92 Ep I/11/10 f 130r.
93 Ep I/11/10 f 131v.
94 Ep I/11/10 ff 101v-104r.
95 Ep I/11/10 ff 101v.
96 Ep I/11/10 ff 102v.
97 Ep I/11/10 ff 103r.
98 Ep I/15/1 (1604).
99 Ep I/11/10 ff 105v-107v, 110r-111v.
100 Ep I/11/10 ff 105v.
101 Ep I/11/10 ff 106v.
102 Ep I/11/10 ff 110r.
103 Ep I/11/10 ff 110v.
104 Ep I/11/10 ff 108r-109v, 118v-119r.
105 Ep I/11/10 f 108r.
106 Ep I/11/10 f 109r.
107 Ep I/11/10 f 118v.
108 Ep I/15/1 (1605).
109 Ep I/11/10 ff 133v-135r, 136v, 138r, 142v-143v, 144r, 145r.
110 Ep I/15/1 (1604).
111 Ep I/15/1 (1604).
112 Ep I/11/10 f 133v.
113 Ep I/11/10 f 142v.
114 Ep I/15/1 (1604); Ep I/11/10 ff 141r-142v.
115 Ep I/15/1 (1604).
116 Ep I/15/1 (1604).
117 Ep I/11/10 f 141r.
118 Ep I/15/1 (1604); Ep I/11/10 ff 147r-149v.
119 Ep I/15/1 (1604).
120 Ep I/11/10 f 147r.
121 Ep I/11/10 f 148v.
122 Ep I/15/1 (1604); Ep I/11/10 ff 150r-152v, 156r-157v.
123 Ep I/15/1 (1604).
124 Ep I/11/10 f 150r.
125 Ep I/11/10 f 150v.
126 Ep I/11/10 f 151v.
127 Ep I/11/10 f 156r.
128 Ep I/11/10 f 156v.
129 Ep I/10/24 ff 48v, 53r-v; Ep I/11/10 ff 152v-155v, 158r-159v.
130 Ep I/10/24 f 48v.
131 Ep I/11/10 f 152v.
132 Ep I/11/10 f 154r.
133 Ep I/11/10 f 155r.
134 Ep I/11/10 f 158r.
135 Ep I/11/10 f 158v.
136 Ep I/10/24 f 53r.

137 Ep I/11/10 ff 162v-165v.
138 STC I/15/239.
139 Ep I/11/10 f 162r.
140 Ep I/11/10 f 164r.
141 Ep I/11/10 ff 165v-169r.
142 STC I/15/219.
143 Ep I/11/10 f 165r.
144 Ep I/11/10 f 166v.
145 Ep I/11/10 f 167v.
146 Ep I/11/10 f 168r.
147 Ep I/11/10 ff 169v-173r.
148 Ep I/11/10 f 169v.
149 Ep I/11/10 f 170v.
150 Ep I/11/10 f 171r.
151 Ep I/11/10 ff 173v-179r.
152 TNA PROB 11/107 f 61.
153 Ep I/11/10 f 173v.
154 Ep I/11/10 f 175r.
155 Ep I/11/10 f 177v.
156 Ep I/11/10 ff 179v-184r, 185v-188r.
157 Ep I/11/10 f 179v.
158 Ep I/11/10 f 182v.
159 Ep I/11/10 f 186r.
160 Ep I/11/10 ff 188r-189v.
161 Ep I/11/10 f 188r.
162 Ep I/11/10 f 189r.
163 Ep I/11/10 ff 190r-192r.
164 Ep I/11/10 f 190r.
165 Ep I/11/10 f 191r.
166 Ep I/11/10 ff 192v-195r.
167 STC I/15/167.
168 Ep I/11/10 f 192v.
169 Ep I/11/10 f 193r.
170 Ep I/11/10 f 193v.
171 Ep I/11/10 f 194v.
172 Ep I/11/10 ff 195r-198r.
173 Ep III/4/7 f3r, 4r.
174 Ep I/11/10 f 195r.
175 Ep I/11/10 f 197r.
176 Ep I/11/10 f 198r.
177 Ep I/11/10 ff 198v-205v; 209r-215r; 217v-219v; 220v-226v, 229r-232r.
178 Ep I/11/10 f 198v.
179 Ep I/11/10 f 200v.
180 Ep I/11/10 f 202v.
181 Ep I/11/10 f 203v.
182 Ep I/11/10 f 204v.
183 Ep I/11/10 f 209r.
184 Ep I/11/10 f 212v.
185 Ep I/11/10 f 213v.
186 Ep I/11/10 f 217v.
187 Ep I/11/10 f 219v.
188 Ep I/11/10 f 220v.
189 Ep I/11/10 f 221v.

190 Ep I/11/10 f 223r.
191 Ep I/11/10 f 225v.
192 Ep I/11/10 f 229r.
193 Ep I/11/10 f 230v.
194 Ep I/11/10 ff 205v-208v, 215r-217r, 220r-220v.
195 STC I/15/220v; STC II 1605 Boxgrove deanery.
196 Ep I/11/10 f 205v.
197 Ep I/11/10 f 207v.
198 Ep I/11/10 f 215r.
199 Ep I/11/10 f 216r.
200 Ep I/11/10 f 220r.
201 Ep I/11/10 ff 226v-228v, 241r-242v; Ep I/15/1 (1606).
202 STC III/E f 87.
203 Ep I/11/10 f 226v.
204 Ep I/11/10 f 227v.
205 Ep I/15/1 (1606).
206 Ep I/11/10 f 241r.
207 Ep I/11/10 ff 232r-233v.
208 Ep I/11/11 ff 65-67.
209 Ep I/11/10 f 232r.
210 Ep I/11/10 f 233r.
211 Ep I/11/10 ff 234r-238r; Ep I/15/1 (1606).
212 Ep I/15/1 (1606).
213 Ep I/11/10 f 234r.
214 Ep I/11/10 f 235v.
215 Ep I/11/10 f 237r.
216 Ep I/15/1 (1606).
217 Ep I/11/10 ff 238r-240v; Ep I/15/1 (1606).
218 Ep I/15/1 (1606).
219 Ep I/11/10 f 238r.
220 Ep I/11/10 f 239r.
221 Ep I/11/10 f 239v.
222 Ep I/11/10 ff 242v-244v.
223 Ep I/11/10 f 242v.
224 Ep I/11/10 f 243v.
225 Ep I/11/10 ff 244v-247r , 256v-257v.
226 STD I/3/73.
227 Ep I/11/10 f 244v.
228 Ep I/11/10 f 256v.
229 Ep I/11/10 ff 248r-251r, Ep I/15/1 (1606).
230 Ep I/17/11 f 64v, 66v, 79.
231 Ep I/15/1 (1606).
232 Ep I/11/10 f 248r.
233 Ep I/11/10 f 249r.
234 Ep I/11/10 f 250r.
235 Ep I/11/10 f 250v.
236 Ep I/15/1/ (1606).
237 Ep I/11/10 ff 252r-256r, 283r-284v.
238 STC I/15/232.
239 Ep I/15/1 (1606).
240 Ep I/11/10 f 252r.
241 Ep I/11/10 f 253r.
242 Ep I/11/10 f 254r.

[243] Ep I/11/10 f 255r.
[244] Ep I/11/10 f 283r.
[245] Ep I/11/10 f 284r.
[246] Ep I/11/10 ff 258r-259v.
[247] Ep I/15/1 (1606).
[248] Ep I/11/10 f 258r.
[249] Ep I/11/10 f 258v.
[250] Ep I/11/10 f 259r.
[251] Ep I/17/12 ff 99-139.
[252] Ep I/15/3/16/122.
[253] Ep I/15/1 (1606), Ep I/11/10 ff 260r-261r, 264v-265v, 269v-270v, 272r-273r.
[254] Ep I/15/1 (1606).
[255] Ep I/11/10 f 260r.
[256] Ep I/11/10 f 264v.
[257] Ep I/11/10 f 269v.
[258] Ep I/11/10 f 272r.
[259] Ep I/15/1 (1606), Ep I/11/10 ff 261v-262r, 265v-267r, 270v-271v, 273r-274v.
[260] Ep I/15/1 (1606).
[261] Ep I/11/10 f 261r.
[262] Ep I/11/10 f 265v.
[263] Ep I/11/10 f 270v.
[264] Ep I/11/10 f 273r.
[265] Ep I/15/1 (1606), Ep I/11/10 ff 262v-263v, 267r-268r.
[266] Ep I/15/1 (1607).
[267] Ep I/15/1 (1606).
[268] Ep I/11/10 f 262v.
[269] Ep I/11/10 f 267r.
[270] Ep I/15/1 (1606, 1607), Ep I/11/10 ff 274v-279r, Ep I/11/11 ff 60v-65r.
[271] Ep I/15/1 (1606).
[272] Ep I/15/1 (1606).
[273] Ep I/11/10 f 274v.
[274] Ep I/11/10 f 276r.
[275] Ep I/11/10 f 277v.
[276] Ep I/15/1 (1607).
[277] Ep I/11/11 f 60v.
[278] Ep I/11/11 f 61v.
[279] Ep I/11/11 f 63r.
[280] Ep I/15/1 (1606), Ep I/11/10 ff 279v-282v, Ep I/11/11 ff 28v-30v; Ep I/10/28 f 65v.
[281] Ep I/15/1 (1606).
[282] Ep I/11/10 f 279v.
[283] Ep I/11/10 f 280v.
[284] Ep I/11/10 f 281r.
[285] Ep I/11/10 f 282r.
[286] Ep I/11/11 f 28v.
[287] Ep I/11/11 f 29v.
[288] Ep I/10/28 f 65v.
[289] Ep I/11/10 ff 285r-289v, Ep I/11/11 41r-45r, 58r-60v.
[290] Ep I/11/10 f 285r.
[291] Ep I/11/10 f 285v.
[292] Ep I/11/10 f 286v.
[293] Ep I/11/10 f 287v.
[294] Ep I/11/11 f 41r.
[295] Ep I/11/11 f 42r.

296 Ep I/11/11 f 43v.
297 Ep I/11/11 f 44v.
298 Ep I/11/11 f 58r.
299 Ep I/11/11 f 59v.
300 Ep I/11/10 f 289v, Ep I/11/11 f 2r-20r, 23r-28v, 31r, 105v-109r, 115v-119v; Ep I/10/28 f 41v, 43v.
301 Ep I/11/10 f 289v.
302 Ep I/11/11 f 2r.
303 Ep I/11/11 f 7r.
304 Ep I/11/11 f 10v.
305 Ep I/11/11 f 13v.
306 Ep I/11/11 f 17r.
307 Ep I/11/11 f 23r.
308 Ep I/11/11 f 24v.
309 Ep I/11/11 f 25v.
310 Ep I/11/11 f 27r.
311 Ep I/11/11 f 31r.
312 Ep I/10/28 f.41v, 43v.
313 Ep I/11/11 f 105v.
314 Ep I/11/11 f 106v.
315 Ep I/11/11 f 107r.
316 Ep I/11/11 f 108r.
317 Ep I/11/11 f 115v.
318 Ep I/11/11 f 117v.
319 Ep I/15/1 (1607).
320 Ep III/4/10 f 153 ff.
321 Ep III/6 Box 407, folder 3.
322 Ep III/4/5 f 111 ff.
323 Ep IV/2/7 ff 71, 75.
324 Ep III/4/8 f 72.
325 Ep III/4/6 f 41.
326 Ep I/17/11 f 40 ff.
327 Ep I/15/1 (1605).

Indexes

General notes

The reference numbers cited in the indexes are the numbers allotted to the individual cases or the sub numbers (e.g. 3/5) allotted to individual depositions. References to the Introduction are given to page numbers in Roman numerals.

Index of Persons

It is likely that readers will find it helpful to identify plaintiffs, defendants and deponents (with references to their depositions); two short separate indexes have been made in order to do this. The third index contains all persons mentioned in the depositions in any context.

To avoid confusion the title "Sir" has been included only when it refers to a knight and not when used as the courtesy title for a clergyman.

Index of Plaintiffs (P) and Defendants (D)

Ayling(e) *see* Aylewyn
Aylewyn, Richard D 46/1
Barttelot, Richard D 40/1
Baxter, Robert D 45/1
Baylye, Thomas P 30/1
Betsworth, Peter P 17/1
Birkeheade, Michael P 40/1; 41/1; 42/1
Bishoppe, Robert D 1/1
Blaxton, Henry D 36/1
Blaxton, Joan P 36/1
Browne, James P 4/1
Brydye, John D 11/1
Burdocke, John D 35/1
Burdye, John D 35/1
Butcher, Eleanor P 14/1
Carden, Mary P 25/1
Carpenter, Elizabeth P 28/1
Chandler, Charity P 21/1
Chandler, Ralph D 21/1
Chandler, William D 21/1
Chatfeilde, William P 46/1
Collye, Alice P 31/1
Coote, Mary P 11/1
Coote, Richard D 45/1
Coxe, Richard D 5/1
Daniell, Agnes P 1/1
Deare, Ralph P 8/1
Diggens, Nicholas P 18/1
Duffeild, Edward D 22/1
Earle, Ralph P 33/1
Elliott, Joan P 45/1
Farnden, Julian D 13/1
Foster, William D 15/1
French, John D 2/1
Goodwyn, Thomas P 16/1; D 19/1
Gradell, Joan P 20/1
Gradell, William D 20/1
Graye, Edward D 39/1
Greene, Alice P 10/1

Harber, Nicholas D 25/1
Harold *see* Herold
Harris, Rose P 39/1
Hatfeild, John D 15/1
Hawsted, Thomas D 8/1
Hayler, Edward D 32/1
Herold, Thomas P 44/1
Hitchcocke, Elizabeth D 44/1
Hitchcocke, Robert P 19/1
Hitchcocke, Thomas P 19/1
Hitchecocke *see* Hitchcocke
Hobb(e)s, Richard D 3/1
Holden, William D 34/1
Humfrey, William D 4/1
Hunt(e), Susan D 7/1
Hunt, Thomas P 7/1
Hunt, William D 7/1
Johnson, Henry D 9/1
Johnson, Joan P 38/1
Johnson, Robert P 9/1
Kneller, Joan D 28/1
Knighte, Richard D 46/1
Lacker, James P 3/1
Laker *see* Lacker
Lane, Anne D 29/1
Len [Lenn, Lenne], Richard D 14/1
Legate, Julian D 13/1
Legate, Mary P 13/1
Lenn, William D 27/1
Lodger, Arthur D 23/1
Lodger, Margaret P 23/1
Nashe, Agnes P 34/1
Newe, John D 24/1
Northe, Edward D 17/1
Page, John D 33/1
Palmer, John D 18/1
Palmer, Margaret P 23/1
Pancrasse, John D 42/1
Parker, John D 15/1
Parson, Allice P 31/1
Pellett, James P 5/1
Perkyn, William D 41/1
Pyper, Eleanor P 14/1
Rablis, Richard D 26/1
Racton, Mary P 13/1
Rapley, Thomas D 42/1
Reade, John P 27/1
Roberts, Hugh P 43/1
Robins, Mary P 32/1
Robinson, Matilda D 28/1
Rose, Agnes D 12/1
Rose, Edward D 12/1
Slater, Alice P 31/1
Slater, Joan D 31/1
Soane, Cicily D 30/1
Soane, William D 30/1
Somersall, Thomas D 42/1
Squier, Katheryn P 22/1
Stamer, Alice P 10/1
Standen, Alice P 6/1
Standen, Henry D 6/1; D 43/1
Standen, John D 6/1
Tapper, Joan P 45/1
Tayler, Margaret P 37/1
Tester, Frances P 35/1
Tickenor, John D 10/1
Tillboroughe, Richard D 37/1
Todd, Samuel P 24/1; P 26/1
Walters, Peter P 15/1
Warde, Richard P 2/1
Waters *see* Walters
West, Margaret P 29/1
Westemill, Rose D 12/1
Whatley, John D 46/1
Widdowson, Raphael P 12/1; D 46/1
Willett, John D 15/1
Woldridge, Edward D 16/1; D 38/1

Index of Deponents and Depositions

Alcock, Laurence 29/4
Alewyn *see* Aylewyn
Andrewe, John 19/7
Apitt, Margaret 23/4
Apitt, Mark 23/2
Arcoll, Thomas 2/6
Arnold, Robert 17/4
Austyn, John 3/8, 3/10
Aylewyn, Joan 38/5
Aylewyn, John 38/6
Ayling(e) *see* Aylewyn
Aylwyn *see* Aylewyn
Ball, Henry 29/15
Ball, Margaret 45/8
Barttelot, Richard 40/2
Baylye, John 39/3
Baylye, Thomas 18/6
Beache, Nicholas 3/14
Beake, Edward 3/22
Beake, William 3/21
Beanham [Ben(e)ham] Joan 46/5
Beanham [Ben(e)ham], John 46/6
Belchamber, William 6/4
Beneham *see* Beanham
Benham *see* Beanham
Billing(s)hurst, Robert 21/5; 45/5
Bishoppe, Nicholas 45/3
Bishoppe, Robert 1/5
Blaber, William 39/5
Blaxton, Godfrey 36/3
Bowton, John 40/5, 41/5
Bradfolde, William 8/6
Brooker, John 2/4
Browninge, Henry 33/3
Butcher, John 14/2
Cappe, James 32/2
Carus, William 29/16
Catcheler, Thomas 18/5
Cayger, Lambert 2/3
Charman, John 40/6; 41/6
Chase, Richard 45/10
Chatfeilde, Richard 46/12
Churcher, William 26/3
Clapshewe, William 28/4
Clement, Edmund 30/3
Cobby(e), Francis 7/4
Cobby(e), Oliver 3/6
Colbrooke, Henry 28/3
Comber, John 2/11
Combes, Robert 1/2
Cooke, Margaret 34/4
Cooke, Thomas 4/2
Cooper, John 30/2
Coote, John 5/3
Court, Daniel 11/4
Cradell, Stephen 2/7
Crowcher, John 18/7
Daniell, Agnes 1/6
Darkenall(e), Edward 3/17; 7/2
Diggens, Mary 37/4
Diggens, Nicholas 23/3; 37/3
Dowce [Dowse], John 22/2
Drewett, John 29/6, 13
Drewett, Thomas 10/2
Dunn, Anthony 45/11
Eglie, Richard 1/4
Elise *see* Ellis
Elliott, Elizabeth 45/9
Ellis, John 6/3; 29/14; 43/9
Esteade, John 10/3
Etherton, John 3/19
Farnfolde, Thomas 31/5
Finch, Robert 3/7
Fivian, Margery 44/5
Floate, Richard 17/3
Floate, Thomas 22/3
Furlonger, Thomas 6/5
Gardener [Gardyner], Edward 3/13

Gardener [Gardyner], Richard 11/2
Gardener [Gardyner], William 3/5
Gater, Richard 31/6
Goodwyn, Thomas 16/3; 19/2, 8
Gosden, Richard 29/17
Graye, John 10/4; 46/3
Greene, Thomas 30/6
Greenefeild, John 9/3
Greenefeild, Richard 12/2
Greenoe, Nicholas 29/10
Hames, Ellis 21/4, 45/4
Hancocke, Mary 37/5
Harman, Constantine 21/3
Harriden, Henry 31/2
Harris, Richard 29/7
Harrison, Henry 1/8, 10
Hartley, Daniel 43/8
Hawarde *see* Haywarde
Haynes, Richard 39/4
Haywarde, John 2/10
Haywarde, Thomas 2/12
Henley, John 32/3
Hitchcocke, Robert 16/4
Hitchcocke, William 44/7
Hitchecocke *see* Hitchcocke
Holmes, Thomas 24/4
Horne, Edmund 11/5
Howcrofte, Joan 18/4
Hull, John 19/3
Hunt(e), Thomas 3/25
Ide, Oliver 27/3
Jaxon, Daniell 7/3
Juxon, Richard 36/2
Knighte, Richard 29/12
Kyne, John 3/27
Lacker, James 3/15, 28
Langrishe, Robert 46/2
Launder, Hugh 34/5
Lawrence, John 6/6
Leaper, Thomas 29/8
Lee, Richard 14/5
Leger, Arthur 30/4
Linfeilde, George 31/3
Longe, Edward 13/3
Lucas, Thomas 40/4; 41/4; 42/4
Mackerell, Henry 46/14, 18
Madgeweeke, John 29/5, 11
Maister, Sarah 25/2
Markes, Oliver 3/9
Marner, Thomas 8/3
Martyn, Alice 37/6
Martyn, Thomas 28/2
Mason, Edward 21/2
Mayne, Agnes 25/3
Moorye [Morie, Morye], William 46/7
Napcrofte, Richard 46/9
Nashe, Anthony 43/4
Newton, John 26/2
Newton, Margaret 38/4
Newton, William 19/5; 38/3
Northe, Edward 17/2
Northe, John 3/2, 26
Northe, Thomas 3/3; 5/6
Oliver, Joan 29/2
Oliver, John 46/8, 19
Page, Henry 20/3
Page, John 5/4; 33/2
Page, Thomas 13/2
Palmer, John 18/2
Park, John 46/4
Parson, Edward 14/3
Peachie [Peachye], Henry 12/3
Peachie [Peachye], John 43/6
Peachie [Peachye], Thomas 33/4
Pellett, James 3/4
Penn, John 8/5
Perley, John 3/23; 5/2
Pitt, Mark 8/2
Prichard, David 20/2
Pynham, William 33/5
Pyper, John 14/2
Pyttell, Alice 35/3

Rasoll, John 18/3
Reames, William 6/2
Rooke, Richard 4/3
Rose, Edward 12/5
Rumbridger, William 24/2
Russell, Joan 27/4
Russell, Thomas 27/5
Sandam *see* Sandham
Sandham, William 46/17
Scutt, John 35/2
Shorte, William 34/3
Skinner [Skynner], Barbara 13/5
Skinner [Skynner], George 45/2
Slater, Joan 31/4
Slater, Robert 15/4
Smith(e), Richard 11/3
Smith(e), Robert 2/9
Snellinge, George 44/8
Sole, Christopher 2/8
Sole, Daniel 2/5
Somer, Nicholas 8/7
Stamer, William 43/5
Standen, Henry 43/3
Steele, John 27/2
Stempe, John 3/12
Stiant, Thomas 3/20
Stradlinge, Anthony 3/24; 5/7
Stradlinge, Edward 5/5
Stronge, Richard 12/4; 46/15
Stronge, Thomas 29/9
Styler, John 15/5
Sutton, William 24/3
Talmye, Alice 44/6
Talmye, Edward 44/3
Talmye, Simon 44/4
Tapper, Elizabeth 45/9
Tayler, Joan 38/8
Tayler, John 40/3; 41/3; 42/3
Thorneden, John 3/11
Till, Thomas 30/5
Tilboroughe (Tillberow, Tillboroughe) Richard 37/7
Turner, Richard 8/4
Upfull, William 22/4
Voake, Henry 19/4
Wady *see* Wadye
Wadye, Thomas 2/13; 9/2
Wall, Eden (Edith) 29/3
Walles *see* Wall
Walters, Peter 15/2-3
Warde, John 46/16
Ware, Anthony 8/8
Warner, Winifred 1/3
Waters *see* Walters
Wells, John 14/4
White, Gideon 3/18
Widdowson, Raphael 46/11
Win(s)ton, John 43/10
Woldridge, Edward 16/2; 19/6; 38/7
Woodland(e), Thomas 1/7, 9
Woodyer, Thomas 2/2

Consolidated Index of Persons

-, Joseph 20/2
Addames, Charles 31/2-3
Afeild, John 46/3, 5-7
Alcock, Laurence 29/4-5, 7-8, 10-11, 13-15
Alewin *see* Aylewyn
Alewyn *see* Aylewyn
Allen, Matthew 40/3, 5-6; 41/5-6
Andrewe, Joan 19/5, 7
Andrewe, John 19/2, 5, 7
Apitt, Margaret 23/2, 4
Apitt, Mark 23/1-4
Apsley, Susan 7/1
Arcoll, John 2/6
Arcoll, Thomas 2/2, 6, 8, 10, 13
Arnold, Robert 17/4
Arnold, Thomas 31/2
Arnolde, John 5/4-5
Austyn, John 3/1, 4-5, 8, 10, 16, 20-24, 26
Averell, - 5/7
Avery(e), - 5/2, 4
Aylewyn, Agnes 38/4
Aylewyn, Joan 38/4-5
Aylewyn, John 38/4, 6
Aylewyn, William 38/4-5
Aylinge *see also* Aylewyn
Aylinge, John 19/3
Aylinge, Nicholas 5/4
Aylinge, Richard 46/1-9, 11
Aylwyn *see* Aylewyn
Badcocke, - 5/4
Ball, Henry 29/15
Ball, Margaret 45/8-11
Bancombe, John 2/8
Bancroft, Richard (Archbishop of Canterbury) xiii
Bannester, Edward 30/1-3
Barden, Ann 11/1, 5
Barden, Charles 11/2
Barker, Hugh (Proctor) xvii, xxxiv, xxxv
Barlow, Thomas xix
Barnard, Robert 9/2-3
Barnes, William 29/17
Bart(t)lett, - 3/23-24
Bart(t)lett, John 46/4, 8-10
Barttelot, Richard 40/1-3, 6
Barttelot, Richard 41/1
Base, Mary xxxvi
Baxter, Robert 45/1, 6-11
Baylye, John 39/3-5
Baylye, Thomas 18/6; 30/1-6; 37/3
Beache, Nicholas 3/1, 14, 16, 20-24, 26
Beake, Edward 3/1, 22, 26
Beake, William 3/1, 21, 25
Beanham [Ben(e)ham], Joan 46/5
Beanham [Ben(e)ham], John 46/5-6
Beeke, John 3/13
Beeke, Susan 3/13
Beeke, Thomas 3/13
Belchamber, William 6/2-4
Bennet, William 2/3-4
Bennett, John 15/4
Bennett, Phillip 15/4
Bennett, Thomas 29/16-17
Bennett, Thomas 29/17
Bennett, William 2/3-4
Betsworth, Peter 17/1-4
Bignall, Mary 32/1
Billing(s)hurst, Robert 21/5; 45/2-6, 10
Bingham, John 15/2, 5
Bird, - 29/4-5
Birkeheade, Michael xxxvi, 40/1-6; 41/1, 3-5; 42/1
Bishoppe, Alice 1/8
Bishoppe, Nicholas 45/2-5
Bishoppe, Robert 1/1-10

Blaber, William 39/3-5
Blaxton, Godfrey 36/2-3
Blaxton, [Henry] 1/7
Blaxton, Henry xxxiv, 36/1-3
Blaxton, Joan 36/1-3
Blaxton, Joshua 36/1-2
Blencowe, Anthony xxxii
Blewett, John 11/2-3, 5
Blundell, William 4/2-3
Bo(a)ne, - 46/9, 19; App 1
Bolsham, - 11/2
Bond, - 46/8
Bosworthe, Thomas 29/14
Bowton, John 40/5; 41/3, 5
Bradfolde, William 8/6
Branne, - 24/3
Braye, Richard 8/2
Bridger, Giles 16/4
Brighte, - 18/7
Brooker, John 2/2-4, 13
Browne, James 4/1-3
Browne, Jane 3/5
Browne, Julian 29/17
Browne, Thomas 11/5
Browneing, Jane 3/5
Browninge, Henry 33/3
Browninge, William 29/17
Brydye, Blaise 11/2-3, 5
Brydye, John xxxix, 11/1-5; App 2
Brydye, Rachel 11/5
Bunche, Nicholas 3/13
Burdet, John 35/1
Burdocke, John 35/1-2
Burdye, John 35/1-3
Burrowe, Francis 18/4
Burt, Magdalen 29/2-3
Burton, - 19/5
Bushoppe, Richard 2/2
Butcher, Eleanor 14/1-4
Butcher, John 14/2-4
Butcher, Richard 14/1-4
Byckley, Henry 19/5
Bydinge, John 30/1, 4-5
Byngham, John 15/1, 4
Callingham, - 31/2
Campion, - 25/2-3
Campion, Thomas 8/3
Capp, Bernard xxiii
Cappe, James 32/2-3
Carden, John 25/2
Carden, Mary 25/1-3
Carpenter, Elizabeth 28/1-4
Carpenter, Laurence 28/1-4
Carrel, Sir Edward 8/2, 5, 8
Carrel, Sir Thomas 8/2
Carus, - 29/6
Carus, William 29/16-17
Catcheler, Edward 18/5
Catcheler, Thomas 18/5
Catcheler, William 18/5
Cathelove, Julian 18/5
Cayger, Lambert 2/3-4
Chalcrofte, Joan 13/2
Chalcrofte, Thomas 13/2
Champion, Thomas 8/3
Chandler, Charity 21/1-3
Chandler, Ralph 21/1
Chandler, William 21/1-5
Charman, John 40/6; 41/6
Chase, Agnes 45/11
Chase, Eleanor 45/7
Chase, Elizabeth 45/7
Chase, Richard 45/7-11
Chatfeilde, George 46/2-3, 5-7, 9-10, 12, 14
Chatfeilde, Richard 46/2, 12
Chatfeilde, William 46/1-3, 5, 9-10, 12
Chaundler, - 5/5
Chaundler, Edward 5/7
Churcher, William 26/2-3
Clapshewe, William 28/2-4
Clare, Robert 19/3-4

Clark, Peter xii, xxxix
Clement, Edmund 30/3-5
Clement, Edward 30/2
Clerke, Francis xix
Clerke, John 2/6
Clowser, John 42/3
Clowser, Richard 42/3
Cobby(e), Francis 7/2-4
Cobbye, Mary 3/14
Cobbye, Oliver 3/4, 6, 16, 21-23
Cockes, Richard 5/1
Colbrooke, Henry 28/2-4
Colley, James 31/6
Collye, Alice 31/1
Colpas, John 8/3-4
Colpas, William 30/5
Comber, John 2/11
Combes, Robert 1/2
Cooke, - 3/4
Cooke, Edward (Proctor) xxxiv, xxxv
Cooke, Jeremy (Jerome) 34/4-5
Cooke, Margaret 34/4-5
Cooke, Thomas 4/2-3
Cooles, Richard 11/4
Cooper, John 30/2
Coortess, - 31/6
Coote, Jane 11/3-4
Coote, John 5/3; 45/1
Coote, Mary xxxix, 11/1-5; 45/1; App 2
Coote, Richard 11/5; 45/1-7, 10
Costilove, William 29/2, 8-9, 17
Court, Daniel 11/4-5
Courte, Richard 11/5
Cowles, Edward 30/3
Coxe, Francis xxxiv
Coxe, Richard 3/1; 5/1-2, 4-5, 7
Cradell, Stephen 2/7
Crowcher, - 19/4
Crowcher, John 18/7
Crowcher, Thomas 18/7
Crowcher, William 19/7
Curteys, Richard (Bishop) xxxiv
Curtys(se), John 43/4-5
Dammer, - 29/3
Dammer, John 6/1-2, 6
Daniell, Agnes 1/1-10
Daniell, Richard 1/1, 7-8, 10
Darkeing, John 15/4
Darkenall(e), Edward xxxviii, 3/16-17, 25-26; 7/1-4
Dash, Alice App 1
Dash, Richard App 1
Deare, Ralph 8/1-8
Diggens, Mary 37/3-4
Diggens, Nicholas 18/1-7
Diggens, Nicholas 23/1-4
Diggens, Nicholas 37/3-4
Doell, Francis 5/5
Dowce [Dowse], John 11/2-3, 5; 22/2-4
Drewett, John 29/6-8, 10, 12-14
Drewett, Thomas 10/2
Drewitt, John 29/2
Drury, John xxxiv
Dubberley, David 46/6
Duckle, John 46/8
Duffeild, Edward 22/1-4
Duke, - 5/4, 7
Dunn, Anthony 45/7-11
Dunynge, Arthur 46/6
Durrante, Robert 31/2-3
Earle, Ralph 33/1-3, 5-6
Earle, Richard 33/4
Edens, Robert 2/4
Eglie, Richard 1/2-4
Elise, John *see also* Ellis 6/2-6
Elliott, Elizabeth 45/8-11
Elliott, Joan 45/1-11
Ellis, John xxxviii, 29/2-3, 5, 7-8, 12, 14; 43/8-9

Elson, - 5/5, 7
Esteade, John 10/3
Etherton, Elizabeth 29/17
Etherton, John 3/19
Faggater, Richard 46/6
Faller, Richard 8/7-8
Faller, Robert 8/6
Farley, Daniel 43/10
Farlowe, William 29/17
Farnden, Julian 13/1
Farn(e)folde, William 31/2-3, 5-6
Feilde [Field], Thomas 2/6, 13
Finch, Robert 3/4, 7, 16-17, 20-28
Fivian, Margery 44/5, 7-8
Fivian, William 44/5
Floate, Richard 17/3
Floate, Thomas 22/2-4
Foake, Richard 22/2-4
Ford, Edmund 8/2
Forder, John 2/6
Foster, William 15/1, 4
Fowler, - 29/6
Fowler, John 40/4; 41/4
Franckewelle, - 18/7
Freeman, Benjamin xxxvi
French, John xli, 2/1-2, 6, 8, 10, 13
Fuller, William 5/2, 4, 7
Furlonger, Thomas 6/2-3, 5
Furnivall, Frederick J xi, xxxvi
Gardener *see* Gardyner
Gardyner [Gardener], Anthony 3/13
Gardyner [Gardener], Denise 3/13
Gardyner [Gardener], Edward 3/13, 16, 21-23
Gardyner [Gardener], Joan 3/5
Gardyner [Gardener], Richard 11/2, 4-5; 45/4-5
Gardyner [Gardener], William 3/1, 4-5, 8, 16-17, 19-26
Gater, Richard 31/6
Gates, Henry 45/3
Giberidge, Thomas 3/13
Giese, Loren L xli
Glaciter [Glacister, Glociter] Robert 5/2-5
Goble, John 46/8, 19
Goble, William 5/5, 7
Godsmarke, Edward 31/5-6
Golden, Stephen 37/3
Goodwyn, Thomas 16/1-4; 19/1-5, 8
Goring(e), William 3/22, 26
Gosden, Richard 29/6, 17
Gowing, Laura xii, xxiii, xlii
Gradell, Fortunatus 20/1
Gradell, Joan 20/1-3
Gradell, William 20/1-3
Gratwicke, Sir William 39/1, 3-5
Graye, Edward 39/1-5
Graye, John *see also* Graye, John 10/4; 46/3
Graye, John 40/3-4; 41/3-4; 42/4
Greene, - 5/2
Greene, Alice 10/1-4
Greene, John 10/2-4
Greene, Richard 5/5
Greene, Thomas 30/6
Greenefeild, John 9/2-3
Greenefeild, Richard 12/2
Greenoe, Joan 29/10
Greenoe, Nicholas 29/7, 10
Gregory, John 45/4-11
Grenawaye, Nicholas 29/2
Hackett, Cicily 30/1
Hall, John 38/3
Hames, Ellis xxxvi, 21/2, 4; 45/2-5
Hames, John xxxvi
Hamon, Nicholas 11/5
Hamonde, Joan 27/2-5
Hancock(e), Mary 37/5-6
Harber, Nicholas 25/1-3
Harman, Constantine 21/2-3, 5
Harold *see* Herold

Harriden, Henry 31/2
Harris, Richard 29/2-3, 7, 12, 14
Harris, Rose 39/1, 3-5
Harris, William 39/1
Harrison, Henry 1/7-10
Harrison, Joseph 1/8
Harrison, Robert 46/3, 5-7, 14-15, 18
Harsnett, Samuel (Bishop) xxxii
Hartley, Daniel 43/8
Hatfeild, John 15/1-2
Hawarde *see* Haywarde
Hawsted, Thomas 8/1-6
Hayle, Thomas 25/2-3
Hayler, Edward 32/1-3
Haynes, Richard 39/4-5
Haywarde, John 2/10
Haywarde, Thomas 2/12
Heiden, Francis 31/6
Hellier, Grace App 1
Henley, John 32/2-3
Herold, Thomas 44/1-9
Hitcham, Christopher 2/2, 5
Hitchcock, Hitchecock, Hitchecocke *see* Hitchcocke
Hitchcocke, Elizabeth 44/1-7
Hitchcocke, William 44/3-4, 6-8
Hitchcocke, Katheryn 19/3-4, 7
Hitchcocke, Martha 19/3-4, 7
Hitchcocke, Robert 16/1-4; 19/1, 3-4, 7
Hitchcocke, Thomas 16/1; 19/1, 3-4, 7-8
Hobb(e)s, Francis (Frauncis) 3/1, 4-5, 7, 13; 5/2, 4-5, 7
Hobb(e)s, Richard xxx, xxxi, xxxv, xxxvii, xl, 3/1-8, 10, 13, 15-17, 21, 25-29; 5/1
Holden, William 34/1-5
Holmes, Richard 29/17
Holmes, Thomas 24/4
Hooker, - 46/8-10
Horne, - 11/4
Horne, Edmund *see* Horne, Edward
Horne, Edward 11/2-3, 5
Horscroft, Alice App 1
Horscroft, Robert 46/6
Hover, Andrew 13/2, 5
Howard-Drake, Jack xli
Howcrofte, Joan 18/4
Howcrofte, John 18/4
Hubbard, Eleanor xxiii
Hubberde, - 22/2-4
Hull, - 11/5
Hull, John 19/3, 5
Humfrey, William 4/1-3
Hunt(e), George 7/1-4
Hunt(e), Susan 7/1-4
Hunt(e), William 7/1-4
Hunt(e), Thomas xxxi, 3/16-17, 25-26; 7/1-4
Hunter, John 40/3-4; 41/4
Ide, Oliver 27/2-5
Jackett, Thomas 2/2
Jackson (Jaxon), Daniell 7/2-4
James, - 19/5
Johnson, - 9/2
Johnson, Edward 38/3-6
Johnson, Henry 9/1-3
Johnson, Joan xxiii, 9/1-3; 38/1-8
Johnson, Robert 9/1-3
Johnston, Hilda xii
Juxon, Richard xxxiv, xxxv, xxxvi, xl, 18/1; 36/1-3
Juxon, William xxxv
Kempe, - 3/2-3
Keynishe, - 8/4
Keyse, William 8/8
Kneller, Joan 28/1
Knighte, Richard 29/7, 12; 46/1, 8-11, 17-18
Knighte, Thomas 43/1, 4
Kyne, John 3/1, 27

Lacker, Elizabeth 3/4, 7
Lacker, James xxx, xxxi, xxxvii, xl, 3/1-8, 11, 13, 15-16, 21-22, 25-26, 28-29; 5/1
Lacker, John 17/3
Lacye, William 11/2, 5
Laker *see* Lacker
Lambe, - 46/8-10
Lanciter, Robert 5/3
Lane, Anne xxxv, 29/1, 6-7, 10, 13-14, 16-17
Langrishe, Robert 46/2, 12
Larkyn, Joan 9/2-3
Launder, Hugh 34/4-5
Lawrence, John 6/2-3, 6
Leaper, Thomas 29/8-9
Lee, Joan 35/3
Lee, Richard 14/1-5
Leigh *see* Leygh
Legate, Edward 13/1-3
Legate, Everit 13/4
Legate, Julian 13/1-5
Legate, Mary 13/1-5
Legate, Robert 13/4-5
Legate, William 13/4
Leger, Arthur 30/4
Len [Lenn, Lenne], John 3/23-24
Len [Lenn, Lenne], Katherine 27/1-5
Len [Lenn, Lenne], Thomas 34/4-5
Len [Lenn, Lenne], William 27/1; 46/6
Lewar, John 4/2
Leygh, Joan 35/1
Lilliatt, John App 1
Lilliatt, Mary App 1
Linfeilde, George 31/3
Lipscombe, Richard 8/8
Lodger, Arthur 23/1-4
Lodger, Margaret 23/1, 4
Lodger, Richard 23/1-4
Lodger, William 23/1-4
Long(e), Edward 13/2-3, 5
Lucas, Thomas 40/1, 3-6; 41/3-6; 42/4
Ludgate, William 5/5
Ludgater, - 5/4-5, 7
Lushar, - 2/2
Mackerell, Henry 46/9-10, 14, 17-19
Madgeweeke (Madgwicke), John 29/2, 4-5, 7-8, 10-15
Maister, Edward 25/2-3
Maister, Sara 25/2-3
Man, John 46/6
Mares, Thomas 46/6
Markes, Oliver 3/1, 4, 9, 16, 18-26
Marner, Thomas 8/3
Martin *see also* Martyn
Martin, Mary xxxvi
Martis,- 46/8-10, 17, 19
Martyn, - 19/3, 5
Martyn, Alice 37/5-6
Martyn, Richard 16/4; 46/8-10, 14, 17
Martyn, Thomas 28/2-4
Mason, Edward 21/2
May, Christopher App 1
Maye, John 40/3; 41/3
Mayne, Agnes 25/2-3
Mayne, Robert 25/2-3
Mercholl, - 46/9
Mersher, John 8/2
Michell, John 42/3
Miles, - 5/5
Miller, John 31/2-3
Mills, John 17/3
Monke, John 2/13
Moone, Thomas 3/12
Moorye [Morie, Morye], Agnes 46/8-11, 14, 18
Moorye [Morie, Morye], William 46/7, 18-19
Mose, - 45/7
Mose, John 29/6, 16-17
Mothe, Richard 29/1, 7-17
Munnerye, Robert 31/2-3

Napcrofte, Richard 46/9
Nashe, Agnes 34/1-5
Nashe, Anthony 43/4-5
Nashe, James 34/1
Nercholl, - 46/10
Newe, John 24/1-2, 4
Newton, Edward 16/4
Newton, John 26/2-3
Newton, Margaret 38/3-4
Newton, William 19/3, 5; 38/3-4
Northe, Edward 17/1-4
Northe, John xxx, xxxi, 3/1-16, 18-28
Northe, Thomas xxx, xxxi, 3/1, 3-14, 16, 18-29; 5/6
O'Hara, Diana xxiii
Oliver, Joan 29/1-3, 7-8, 10-15
Oliver, John 46/8, 19
Oliver, Thomas 29/2-3
Orgalles, - 5/5
Orgalls, William 5/7
Packe, - 8/4, 6
Packer, Henry 16/4
Page, Henry 20/2-3
Page, John xxiv, 5/4-5
Page, John 33/1-3, 6
Page, Thomas 13/2, 5; 29/1
Palmer, John 18/1-5
Palmer, Margaret 23/1-4
Pancrasse, John 40/1; 42/1-4
Park, John 46/4
Parke, Richard 8/8
Parker, John 15/1, 3
Parkes, John 45/7-9
Parson, Allice 31/1
Parson, Edward 14/2-4
Patcheinge, Henry 40/3-4; 41/4
Paye, Cicily 30/1, 5
Paye, Robert 30/1
Paye, William 19/5; 30/1-6
Peachie [Peachye], Gregory 33/3-4
Peachie [Peachye], Henry 12/3
Peachie [Peachye], John 43/6
Peachie [Peachye], Thomas 33/3-4
Pellett, James xxx, xxxi, 3/1, 4-5, 7, 13, 15-28; 5/1-6
Penn, John 8/5
Perkyn, William 40/1
Perkyn, William 41/1-6
Perley, John 3/1, 23-24; 5/2, 5
Perley, Thomas 3/23-24
Perryn, John 30/2
Peters, - 46/8
Peters, Henry 36/2
Picknoll, - 31/2
Picknoll, Thomas 31/3
Pitt, Mark 8/2, 7
Pittell [Pittyll], Alice 35/2-3
Pittell [Pittyll], William 35/2-3
Poat, Thomas 46/8
Powell, Owen 31/2-3
Prichard, David 20/2-3
Prior, Ralph 8/3, 5-6
Pynham, William 33/5
Pyper, Eleanor 14/1-4
Pyper, John 14/2, 4
Pyper, Richard 14/1-4
Pyper, Thomas 4/3
Pyttell *see* Pittyll
Rablis, Richard 26/1-3
Rabnut, Margaret 38/1
Racton, Adam 5/5
Racton, Mary 13/1
Rapley, Thomas 40/1, 3; 42/1-4
Rasoll, John 18/3
Rasoll, Julian 18/3
Rassall, Edward 33/5
Raye, Christopher 24/2-3
Reade, John 27/1
Reade, Margaret 27/1
Reames, William 6/2-3
Richardson, - 46/9, 17, 19

Road(e)s, William 46/9-10, 14-15, 17, 19
Robbins, William 32/1
Roberts, Hugh 43/1-10
Robins, Mary 32/1-3
Robins, William 32/1-3
Robinson, John 28/1
Robinson, Matilda 28/1
Roffye, Henry 42/3
Roman, Jane 3/26
Rooke, Richard 4/2-3
Rose, Agnes 12/1
Rose, Edward 12/1, 5
Rose, George 7/3
Rose, John App 1
Rose, Thomas 46/5-7
Rumbridger, William 24/2
Russell, Joan 27/2-5
Russell, Thomas 27/2-5
Ryman, William 46/5-7, 14, 18
Rymber, William 46/18
Salsbery(e), Thomas 8/4
Sand(h)am, William 46/8-10, 14, 17-18
Sayer, John 16/4
Scales, Thomas (Proctor) xxxiv, xxxv, 45/7
Scutt, John 2/13; 35/2-3
Selden, John xvii, xxxv
Shepard, Alexandra xiii, xxxix
Shepparde, Thomas 5/4
Sherfolde, William 38/6
Sherley, Sir Thomas 15/1-2, 4-5
Shorte, Simon 5/5
Shorte, John 40/3-4; 41/4
Shorte, William 34/3-5
Shorter, - 8/2, 5
Shorter, Margaret 38/2-3, 5-6
Shorter, Richard 38/1-8
Silvester, Cicily 30/1
Skeate, John 31/2-3
Skerle, John 22/2-4
Skinner [Skynner], Barbara 13/5
Skinner [Skynner], George 45/2-5
Skinner [Skynner], Richard 5/4
Skinner [Skynner], William 13/5
Slater, Alice 31/1
Slater, Henry 2/13
Slater, Joan 31/1-2, 4
Slater, Michael 31/1-6
Slater, Robert 15/4
Smith *see also* Smyth
Smith(e), Alice App 1
Smith(e), Anthony 46/2
Smith(e), John 23/1; App 1
Smith(e), Robert 2/9
Smith(e), Richard 11/2-3, 5; 45/11
Smithier, Thomas 31/2-3
Smyth, - 46/9, 17
Smyth, Alice App 1
Snellinge, George 44/8
Soane, Cicily 30/1-6
Soane, Mary 37/3
Soane, Robert 37/3
Soane, William 30/1-6; 37/3
Sole, Christopher 2/5-6, 8
Sole, Daniel 2/5, 8
Sole, Richard 2/5, 8
Somer, Nicholas 8/7
Somerley, Thomas 42/4
Somersall, Thomas 40/1, 3; 42/1-3, 4
Spurnell, Elizabeth 46/8-10
Spurnell, Thomas 46/10
Squier, Katheryn 22/1-4
Squier, Richard 22/1-4
Squier, William 22/2-4
Stakers, - 3/4
Stamer, Agnes 10/1-4
Stamer, Alice 10/1-2
Stamer, John 10/1
Stamer, William 43/5
Standen, Alice 6/1-6
Standen, Henry 6/1-6; 43/1-8, 10

Standen, John 6/1-6
Standen, Thomas 6/1-6; 43/10
Stanney, Mrs 24/2
Stapleton, - 46/3-7
Starkye, Stephen 29/8, 11-15
Steele, John 27/2-5
Stempe, John 3/4-5, 11-12, 16, 21-23
Stent, George App 1
Stiant, Thomas 3/20
Stiles, - 1/2-4
Stradlinge, Anthony 3/1, 23-24; 5/5, 7
Stradlinge, Edward 5/4-5
Streater, Joan 32/1
Stre(e)ter, Peter 32/1-3
Stronge, Richard 12/4; 46/8-10, 15
Stronge, Thomas 29/7-9
Styler, John 15/5
Sutton, William 24/3
Swayne, Thomas 22/2-4
Swinderton, John 40/3-4; 41/4
Talmye, Alice 44/6-8
Talmye, Edward 44/3-4, 7-8
Talmye, Simon 44/3-4, 6-8
Tapper, Elizabeth 45/9, 11
Tapper, Joan 45/1, 6
Tate, William 45/3
Tayler, Joan 38/4, 8
Tayler, John 38/4; 40/3, 6; 41/3, 6; 42/3
Tayler, Margaret 37/1-7
Tayler, Matthew 37/1, 3-6
Tayler, Richard 38/8
Terrye, - 31/2
Tester, Frances 35/1-3
Theker, Christopher xxxv, 36/1
Thompson, John 29/4-5
Thompson, Margaret 29/4-5, 7
Thompson, Thomas 29/6
Thorn(e)den, John 3/4; 40/3; 41/3
Thorneden, John 3/11-12, 16, 21-23, 25
Tickenor, Agnes 10/3
Tickenor, John 10/1-4
Tilboroughe, (Tillberow, Tillboroughe) Richard 37/1-7
Till, Thomas 30/5
Tillberow *see* Tilboroughe
Tillboroughe *see* Tilboroughe
Todd, Samuel 24/1-2, 4; 26/1-2
Tolpott, Richard 4/2-3
Tradd, Thomas 38/6
Tupper, William 39/3-5
Turner, Richard 8/4
Tylber *see* Tilboroughe
Upfull, William 22/2-4
Vaffin, - 5/5
Vallor, Robert 8/2
Voake, Henry 19/4
Wady(e), Thomas xxvi, 2/13; 9/2-3
Wall, Eden (Edith) 29/2-3, 7-8, 10-15
Wall, Henry 29/3, 14-15
Wall, John 29/3
Walles *see* Wall
Walters, Peter 15/1-5
Warde, John 46/16
Warde, Michael 2/1, 5
Warde, Mrs 2/3
Warde, Richard xli, 2/1-4, 6, 8-10, 12-13
Ware, Anthony 8/8
Warner, Susan 27/2-5
Warner, Thomas 1/3
Warner, Winifred 1/2-3
Wassher, - 5/5
Waterman, John 45/7-9
Waters *see* Walters
Weaver, Edward 16/3
Weelkes, Thomas App 1
Welche, Mrs - 42/3
Weller, Agnes 19/3-4, 7
Wells, John 14/2-4
Went, James App 1

West, Margaret xxxv, 29/1-4, 6-7, 10-11, 13
West, Richard 29/1, 16-17
West, William 29/1-10, 12, 14-17
Westemill, Rose 12/1
Whalley [Whallye], Randall 5/2, 4-5, 7
Whatley, John 46/1-7
Whitbreade, William 15/4
White, Gideon 3/18
White, William 19/3-4, 7
Whittington, - App 1
Widdowson, Raphael 12/1-5; 46/1, 9-11, 13-14, 16-19
Wilbye, - 5/2, 6
Willett, John 15/1, 4
Willett, Thomas 15/4
Williams, - 46/9, 17
Winsomme, Elizabeth 3/4, 14
Win(s)ton, John 43/7-10
Win(s)ton, Richard 43/7-10
Woldridge, Edward 16/1-4; 19/1, 6; 38/1, 7-8
Woldridge, Joan 38/4, 6
Woldridge, Richard 38/4, 6-8
Woldridge, William 19/6
Wood, Richard 2/6, 13
Woodcocke, John 15/4
Woode, Richard 11/1
Woodland(e), Thomas 1/7-10
Woodyer, Thomas 2/2
Worsfolde, John 40/3-4; 41/4
Wright, Richard 16/2
Wynnsome *see* Winsomme
Yalden, William 28/2

Index of places

Notes

The majority of places named in the text occur in the witnesses' biographies which precede their depositions: almost all are parish names, as the parish was normally the area used to identify a deponent's residence. The names of specific farms, lanes, fields etc have generally been omitted; however, where names of smaller units, usually farms, have been significant enough to occur in the introductory note for each case, these have also been included.

Places are in Sussex except where indicated.

Abbots Worthy (Hants) 30/2
Aldingbourne 3/1; 10/4; 12/3; 22/1; 29/9; 43/6-7
Almodington 30/2
Alsnill (Hants) 24/3
Amberley 3/13; 4/1-2; 7/3-4; 10/3; 11/3
Anglesey (Anglesey) 20/2
Angmering 6/4, 14/4; 29/3; 35/3
Arundel xxxvi, 3/5, 12; 25/2-3; 29/6-7, 16-17; 43/9
Ashington 2/13; 15/4
Ashurst 14/3; 15/4; 31/2-3
Barnham 1/8; 2/3; 3/18-19; 29/9
Battle 46/4
Bepton 16/1-4; 19/1-8; 26/2; 38/1, 3, 5-8
Bersted 46/10
Bignor 5/3, 6; 29/17
Billingshurst 2/11; 3/7, 17, 25; 7/1-2
Binsted 20/1-3; 29/3, 6, 16-17; App 1
Birdham 23/3; 24/1-2, 4; 26/3; App 1
Bishopshurst xxxiv
Blatchington 6/2
Blendworth (Hants) 2/9; 30/4
Blunde (Lands) in Warnham 40/1-4, 6; 41/3-4, 6
Bosham 12/3; 27/4; 29/3; 46/9
Boxgrove 11/1-5; 19/3, 5; 22/2-3; 33/5
Boxley Abbey (Kent) 29/10
Brahurste 17/3
Bramiston super montem [Braunston?] (Northants) 29/7
Bramley 7/3
Bramshott (Hants) 38/5; 45/1, 7
Brickhurst App 1
Brighthelmstone xxxiv, 27/2
Brighton xxxiv, 27/2
Broadwater 29/14; 31/6; 39/5
Burpham 2/11
Burton 31/2
Burton on Trent (Staffs) 21/3
Bury 3/2, 10, 13, 21, 26-7; 5/6
Bury (Lancs) 29/10
Cambridge (University) 45/2
Catherington (Hants) 30/1, 5
Chailey App 1
Charlton in Singleton 11/2, 4-5; 45/1
Chichester 3/2, 4, 6-7, 9, 13; 8/2; 12/2; 21/4; 24/4; 28/1-4; 29/4-5, 14; 30/1, 6; 34/4; 36/1-3; 37/5; 45/4-5, 7; 46/2-3, 12, 17; App 1
Chiddingfold (Surrey) 21/5; 45/5-6
Chiltington 3/14; 9/2, 9/3
Chippenham (Wilts) 34/5
Clanand [Clandon?] (Surrey) 44/8

Clandon (Surrey) 44/8
Climping 12/4; 14/3; 29/9; 46/15
Coates 4/3
Cocking 11/3; 19/5
Coldwaltham 7/3-4
Colworth in Oving 46/1, 8-11, 13-19
Compton 23/1; 30/3-4
Cranleigh (Surrey) 3/14
Crundall (Hants) 13/5
Cuckfield 3/1
Cunny's in East Wittering 24/1-2, 4
Denbigh (Denbighshire) 6/3; 29/14; 43/9
Denford 8/2
Denne (Lands) in Warnham 40/1-4, 6; 41/2-4, 6
Didling 2/9
Drayton in Oving 46/8
Duncton 33/3
Durford in Rogate 11/3
Eartham xxiv, 5/3; 12/3; 33/1-6; 43/6-7
Easebourne 35/3
East Claiton [East Clandon?] 31/2
East Dean 22/2
East Harting 8/1-7
East Marden 8/4; 19/3; 30/3
East Wittering 24/1-4; 26/1-3; 33/1
Eastergate 11/2; 22/1-4; 29/7
Elsted 16/2; 23/3; 37/3; 38/6
Falmer 3/10
Farnham 21/2
Farnham (Surrey) 16/4
Felpham 5/3; 7/4; 34/3-5; 43/1; 46/8, 10
Ferring 10/1
Fishbourne 6/4; 46/9
Fittleworth 4/1-2; 35/2-3; 44/3
Flansham 6/4
Ford 6/3-4; 11/2; 29/1-3, 5-6, 8-10, 12, 14-15; 43/9; 46/14
Frensham (Surrey) 27/2; 37/4
Funtington 27/5
Gatcombe (Hants) 45/3
Gills Land in Warnham *see* Knells Land
Gilstoke (Hants) App 1
Greatham 3/10
Guildford (Surrey) 45/9, 11
Harting 8/1-8; 11/2-3, 5; 19/4; 23/2; 29/5; 30/2
Haslemere (Surrey) 13/5; 45/7, 9-11
Havant (Hants) 46/2
Hawkley (Hants) 3/9
Hempnall (Norfolk) 45/2
Higham Ferrers (Northants) 36/3
Horsham 31/2-3; 32/1
Horsted Keynes 28/2
Horwell (Hants) 45/3
Houghton xxx, 3/1-18, 21-22, 25-29; 7/1, 3-5; 44/5
Hunston 26/2; 46/10
Idsworth 30/1-3
Iping 44/5
Kendal (Westmorland) 29/16
Kingston by Ferring 10/1-4
Kingston by Ferring 29/6; 30/6
Kirdford xxiv, 6/5; 17/1-4
Knells Land in Warnham 40/1; 41/1, 3-6
Lancing xvi
Lewes xvi
Linch 19/1-8
Linchmere 8/3; 11/1-2, 5
Liphook (Hants) 45/6-11
Liss (Hants) 45/10
Litlington 3/7
Littlehampton 3/7
Littleton 3/7, 16-17
Lodsworth 13/1-5
London (City) 29/7; 46/12
Lower Fittleworth 4/2
Lurgashall 13/5

Lyminster 3/23-24; 25/2; 29/2; 34/3
Madehurst xxiv, xxx, 3/1, 4, 8, 10, 16, 23-24; 5/1-7; 20/3; 34/3; 44/6
Maresfield 39/3
Merston 43/10; 46/4
Middleton 34/1-5
Midhurst xxxvi, 11/2-3, 5; 19/5; 21/1, 3-5; 38/3-4; 45/2-6, 8-9
Mundham 46/7
Musgrave (Westmorland) 21/2
New Wood in East Harting 8/1-8
Newton (Hants) 19/3
North Marden 2/9; 37/1
North Stoke 3/22; 5/6
Northchapel 17/4
Norwich 45/2
Nuthurst 3/1
Ockley (Surrey) 3/17; 7/2; 40/5
Odiham (Hants) 7/3
Offington in Broadwater 32/2
Ore 3/25
Oving 12/1-4; 22/3; 46/1, 3-11, 13-19
Oxford (Oxon) 2/1; 29/4, 14
Oxford (University) 3/4; 6/3; 8/1; 20/2; 29/16; 43/9
Pagham xvi, 1/8
Petersfield (Hants) 28/2; 38/4, 8
Petworth 3/7; 4/1
Poling 6/3; 35/3
Preston 25/2; 46/11
Preston Candover (Hants) 7/3
Pulborough xxxiv, 2/7; 7/1; 9/2-3; 12/2; 29/16; 35/2; 44/1, 3-9
Racton 18/7
Rewell (the) in Madehurst 3/1; 5/1-7
Rewell Lodge *see* Rewell
Rewell Wood *see* Rewell
Ringmer 39/4
Rogate 8/1-6, 8; 11/3; 19/4; 28/2; 45/7
Romsey (Hants) App 1
Rudgwick 40/5
Rumboldwyke App 1
Rusper xvi, 15/5
Rustington 25/1-3
Rye 32/2
Saffron Walden (Essex) 2/13
Selham 13/1
Selsey 1/1-5, 7-8; 3/25; 30/2
Shalford (Surrey) 7/3; 27/3
Shamblebarne in Birdham 24/2-3
Shawvud [Shalford?] (Surrey) 27/3
Sherborne (Hants) 46/6
Sheremarke 42/3
Shipley 31/3; 32/1-3
Shottermill 11/3
Shripney 43/4
Sidlesham 11/3; 30/6
Singleton 5/5; 11/1-2, 4; 29/15; 45/1
Slaughter (Glos) 4/2
Sleaford (Lincs) 21/2
Slindon 3/2; 12/4; 46/15
Slinfold 3/17; 7/2
South Bersted 10/4
Southwick (Hants) 37/5
Stane Street (Surrey) 44/7
Stedham 45/9
Steep (Hants) 28/2
Steyning 3/4; 10/4; 15/1, 5; 25/3; 31/1-6
Stonstrete [Stane Street?] (Surrey) 44/7
Stopham 3/23-24; 6/6
Storrington 2/10, 12; 6/6; 14/4; 22/3
Stoughton 18/1, 3-7; 23/1-4; 30/2; 37/1-6
Strudland in Climping 29/6
Stubcrofte Farm in East Wittering 24/1-4
Sullington xxv, 2/4; 6/6
Tangmere 11/2; 22/2-4; 33/2
Tarring xvi, 39/5
Tatenhill (Staffs) 29/4

Thakeham xxxvi, 2/1-13; 4/2; 9/2
Thrumpton (Notts) 46/11
Tillington 29/4, 11
Tortington 5/7; 20/2-3; 25/2-3; 29/3; 39/1-5
Tratlitt (Wilts) 45/11
Trotton 37/4; 45/10
Up Marden 23/1-2, 4; 27/5; 30/4, 6; 45/7
Up Waltham 27/1-5
Walberton 3/9, 18-20; 6/2, 4-6; 13/1; 34/2; 37/6
Warblington 30/1-2, 4-5
Warminghurst 2/9; 3/17; 7/2; 15/4
Warminster (Wilts) 21/3
Warnham xxxvi, 3/11; 40/1, 3-6; 41/1, 3-6; 42/1, 3
Warningcamp 2/11
Washington 2/9; 14/1-5; 31/2
Weekelands in East Wittering 24/1-4
Wells (Somerset) 3/14
Wepham 6/4
West Burton 4/2
West Chiltington 9/1
West Dean 19/3
West Grinstead 15/4; 31/2-3
West Harting 8/8
West Marden 6/5; 30/1-2, 4
West Tarring 32/2
West Thorney 30/5
West Wittering 26/2-3; 27/4; App 1
Westbourne 23/4; 30/5
Westhampnett 11/3; 12/1
Whetstoane 24/2
Wiggonholt 6/6; 9/3
Wimbledon (Surrey) 21/3
Winnall (Hants) 7/3
Wisborough Green 17/3; 29/14; 35/1-3; 44/5
Wiston 15/1-5
Withyham 39/3
Wittering xxxiv
Wolsey 7/3
Wonersh (Surrey) 3/27; 10/3
Woodmans Green in Linch 19/1, 3-8
Woolavington 27/5
Woolbeding 38/1
Worcester (Worcs) 29/4
Worth 28/2
Yapton 3/4, 20; 6/1-2, 4-6, 20/2-3; 27/1; 34/2; 43/1-10

Index of subjects

Notes

This index is necessarily selective. It is hoped that the content of tithe cases will be of interest to agricultural historians; similarly, procedural material may prove helpful to the understanding of the context of the cases.

References in **bold** indicate the primary subject of a complete case.

accounts 3/21; 8/2; 31/1-3; 43/7; App 2
act books xi-xii, xiv, xix-xxi
administration (probate) 3/13; 10/1; 30/1; 31/1-2
adultery *see also* baggage
xv, xviii, xxiii, xxxi, 1/2; 3/1, 16, 21, 26; 4/2; 9/2-3; 13/1-5; 22/2-4; 24/1; 29/1, 8, 11-13, 15; 34/2, 5; App 1
allegations *see under* Court procedure
alms 31/2-3
apparitor *see under* Court procedure
apples *see under* crops
backgammon 4/1-3
baggage *see also* adultery
1/3; 13/1-5
bailiff *see* bayley
banns 11/1-2, 4-5
barley *see under* crops
bastardy xxx, xxxvi, 3/1, 5; 9/2-3; App 1
'Bawdy Court' xvi
see also office court
bayley 8/2; 30/3
beans *see under* crops
bees *see under* livestock
betrothal xv, xxiv, 11/1-3, 5; 35/1-3; 45/1-11
Bible *see under* Church
bishop, role as judge xxxii
bishop's chancellor xxxii, xxxiv
bishop's commissary xxxii, xxxiv
bishop's registrar xxxiv
blasphemy xxix, 3/15, 17, 21, 25-26, 28
Book of Common Prayer *see under* Church
bounds (parish) xxiv, 5/2-3, 5-7; 8/2-8; 46/9-10
brawl 43/1
breach of promise xxiv, **3**, **35**, **45**
bullocks *see under* livestock
burning (venereal disease) 34/1-5
calves *see under* livestock
Catholicism *see under* Church
cattle *see under* livestock
cheese *see under* produce
chrisom *see under* Church
christening *see under* Church
Christmas dinner 39/3-5
Church
Bible 3/21
Book of Common Prayer 3/17, 21; 45/2-5
Catholicism xiii, xvi
christening 5/2-3, 6-7; 19/2-6
chrisom 18/1-2, 4-7
church court records xii
church rights **18**, **19**
churching 5/7; 18/1-2, 4-5; 19/3-6; 35/2
Communion xxiv, 3/21; 5/2-3, 6-7; 18/1, 19/3-5; 33/1; 37/1; App 1
hollybread 5/6

Church *(cont)*
holy water 5/2, 4, 6
offering (church) 5/2, 5; 19/3
psalms 3/25-26
Puritanism xiii, xvi
rights to services and sacraments **19**
sacraments 19/2-6, 8
seat (church) 1/1-2; 5/2-7; 24/2-4; 46/1
services xv, 3/26; 5/2-3, 5-7; 13/2; 19/2-6; 25/1
church rights *see under* Church
churching *see under* Church
churchwarden xii, xvi, xxiv, xl, 2/6, 9; 3/4-5, 8, 10, 16-18, 21-22, 26, 28; 5/2-7; 19/1, 7; 29/14-15; 33/1; 46/15
claret 11/2
clothing 10/4
colts *see under* livestock
common 5/1, 3-7; 8/2-5; 30/2, 4-5; 46/1, 17
commoner 8/2-5
Communion *see under* Church
composition (agreement) 1/7-10
composition (tithes) xxvi, 15/2, 4-5; 40/3-5; 41/3-6; 42/3-4; 43/1, 6-7, 9; 46/8, 10
consistory court xvi, xvii, xxxi
see also instance court, office court
constable 3/16, 20-22, 26-28; 5/2-4, 6-7; 29/8-9
coppice wood *see under* woodland
copyhold 10/2-3; 11/3; 29/8, 14; 46/1, 3, 8-11, 13, 17-19
corn *see under* crops
costs (court) *see under* Court procedure
Court procedure xv-xxi, xxvi, xxxi-xxxii
allegations xiv, xviii, xxi, xxviii, xxxii, 1/1, 6-10; 3/1-3; 6/1-2; 7/1-2; 11/1-5; 14/1; 15/1-4; 16/1, 3; 17/1, 3; 20/1-2; 21/1-2; 23/1-2; 24/1-2; 27/1-2; 28/1-2; 29/1-2, 11, 16-17; 30/1-2, 4-5; 31/1-5; 33/1, 6; 36/1-3; 42/1-3; 43/1, 7; 46/12, 12, 14; App 1
apparitors xxxvi, 2/13; 9/2; 21/4; 37/1; 45/4
costs (Court) xviii, xxiii, xxix, xxxix, 1/1; 3/1, 29; 11/1; 12/1; 18/1; 25/1; 30/1; 31/1; 42/1; 43/1; 44/1; 46/1
exceptions xviii, xxviii, 3/1, 4, 16-17; 29/1; 44/1
fees (Court) 1/7-8; 45/4-5; 46/1
inhibition, letter of xxviii, xxxi, 3/1; 29/1; 30/1
interrogatories xiii, xvii-xviii, xx-xxi, xxxvii
judge xvi, xviii-xx, xxii, xxiv, xxvii-xxix, xxxiii-xxxiv
libels xiii-xiv, xviii-xix, xxi, xxvii
location xxxi, xxxii
notaries xvi, xix, xxxv
probate xxii, xxvi, xxviii, 6/1; 21/1; 31/1
proctors xvi-xxii, xxvii, xxxii, xxxiv-xxxv
publication xviii-xx, xxii, xxvii-xxix, xxxviii
sentence xiii, xvii-xix, xxii, xxvi-xxvii, xxxii, xxxvii, 4/1; 5/1; 6/1; 7/1; 17/1; 18/1; 19/1; 20/1; 22/1; 23/1; 25/1; 27/1; 28/1; 35/1; 36/1; 37/1; 42/1; 43/1; 44/1; 45/1; 46/1
crops
apples 8/6
barley 3/22; 10/2-4; 15/4; 30/2, 4-5; 41/2; 46/9

crops (*cont)*
corn 2/1, 4; 3/25, 8/2-3, 6-7; 10/1-2; 15/4; 16/3; 17/2; 24/2-4; 46/4
beans 15/4; 41/2; 46/9
fatches 15/4; 41/2; 44/8; 46/3-4, 6, 9
flax 42/1-4
furze 17/3
grain 16/3; 17/3-4; 46/4
grass 24/2; 26/2-3; 43/8, 10; 46/8-9, 11, 13
hay 2/2, 5, 13; 8/3, 6-7; 15/4; 17/3-4; 24/1-2; 26/1-3; 43/2-7, 9-10; 46/1, 3-11, 14-19
hemp 8/6; 42/1, 3-4
herbage 12/2-4
oats 2/2-4, 6-10, 12-13; 15/4; 17/2-4; 41/2
peas 15/4; 41/2; 46/3-4, 6, 9
rye 17/2-4; 41/2
straw 30/2-3
tares 15/4; 44/3, 7-8
vetch *see also* fatches 44/8
wheat 2/2-4, 6-10, 12-13; 3/18-20, 22; 8/2; 10/2-4; 11/2-3; 15/4; 17/2-4; 30/2-3; 41/2; 46/3-4, 6, 9
crue 43/8
cuckoldry xv, xxiii, 3/5; 4/2-3; 14/2-4; 22/1-4
customs (parish) xxiv, xxvi-xxvii, xxix, 2/1, 2, 6-8; 3/2; 5/1; 12/2, 4; 17/3; 19/3-5; 24/2-3; 33/1-3, 6; 46/1, 3-8, 13, 18-19
debt 31/2-3
deer *see under* livestock
defamation cases xviii, xxi, xxiii, xxvi, xl, **1**, **4**, **9**, **13**, **14**, **22**, **25**, **32**, **34**, **37**, **39**, **44**, **App 1**
depositions xi-xxii, xxix
language xxxvi
preservation xx
purpose and role xxvii
devonshiring xxiv, 17/1-4
diocesan records, value and accessibility xi-xii, xiv
divine service *see under* Church
doale 46/1, 8-11, 14-19
earing *see also* ploughing 24/2-4, 46/3-6
education, clerical and legal xix
enclosure *see* inclosure
exceptions *see under* Court procedure
executor, executrix xxii-xxiii, 6/1-5; 7/2-4; 20/2; 21/1-3; 23/1-4; 27/1; 28/1-4; 29/16-17; 30/1; 31/2; 36/1-3; 38/1
farming *see* crops; livestock; produce; woodland
fatches *see under* crops
fees (Court) *see under* Court procedure
fifteenth (tax) 24/2-4
fivings 2/1-13
flax *see under* crops
fornication xxiii, 1/1; 3/16, 21, 26; 4/2; 13/3, 5; 22/2-4; 25/1-3; 29/8, 11, 13-15; 34/2, 5; App 1
furze *see under* crops
gangemonday 5/6
geese *see under* livestock
grain *see under* crops
grass *see under* crops
harvest 2/9; 46/3-4
hay *see under* crops
hazel *see under* woodland
healings, heals 2/1-10, 12-13
heath 17/1, 3-4
hedgerow 26/1-3, 43/3
hemp *see under* crops
herbage *see under* crops

historical context xiii, xv-xvii
hives 16/1-3
hollybread *see under* Church
holy water *see under* Church
honey *see under* produce
hornbeam *see under* woodland
horses *see under* livestock
improvement (land) xxiv, 17/1
'in form of law' (*in forma iuris*)
  see will, proof in form of law
inclosure xxiv, 5/5; 8/2; 46/1, 16-17
inhibition, letter *see under* Court
  procedure
instance court xii-xiii, xvii
interrogatories *see under* Court
  procedure
intestacy 10/2; 31/2
jacitation 8/1
judge *see under* Court procedure
Justice of the Peace 3/22, 24, 26
kine *see under* livestock
lambs *see under* livestock
landscot *see* tax
Latin xi-xii
lease 31/1, 5-6; 36/2; 46/2, 12
libels *see under* Court procedure
livestock
  bees 16/2-4
  bullocks 17/3-4; 43/2 calves 8/3-4,
    7; 33/2, 4; 43/2, 4, 8-10
  cattle 3/13; 5/3, 5-7; 8/2-6; 12/2-4;
    43/2-3, 5-6, 9-10
  colts 2/2-4, 6, 11; 5/2-4, 7; 8/2-3,
    5-7
  deer 17/4
  geese 3/1, 22, 26; 8/2-3, 5-6
  horses 12/2; 43/2-4
  kine 12/2; 17/3-4
  lambs 5/3-4, 7; 8/3-4, 7; 24/2-4;
    33/2-6; 43/44, 8-10; 46/18
  mares 5/2-4
  milch kine 5/2-4, 7; 8/4, 7; 12/3;
    33/2-3; 43/2-3, 5, 8
  oxen 12/2; 43/2-4
  pigs 3/3, 29; 5/2; 8/2-7; 33/2;
    43/4; 46/18
  sheep 3/1-2, 13, 23-24;5/3-7; 12/2;
    17/3-4; 33/4-6; 43/2-3, 5, 9
  steers 43/2
  yearings 43/2
long wood *see under* woodland
lying xxx, xl, 3/4-14, 16, 21
malt *see under* produce
mares *see under* livestock
marriage licence 45/3-5
matrimonial cases xviii, xxi, xxiv, xxvi-
  xxvii, xl, **11**, **35**, **45**
meadow 15/4; 17/3; 43/2-6, 10; 46/1,
  3-11, 13-15, 17-19
milch kine *see under* livestock
mortuary payments 18/1-7
notaries *see under* Court procedure
oats *see under* crops
offering (church) *see under* Church
office court xii, xvi-xvii
oxen *see under* livestock
park 17/4
pasture 5/2-7; 8/2-6; 12/1-4; 17/3-4;
  30/2, 4-5; 33/1-5; 43/2-6, 9-10
peas *see under* crops
perambulations 5/1-7; 8/2-8; 33/1
pigs *see under* livestock
pigeons 3/29
ploughing 17/4; 24/2-4; 46/3-6
prison 31/2-3
probate *see under* Court procedure
proctors *see under* Court procedure
produce
  cheese 24/2-4; 43/2-3, 5, 8-10
  honey 16/1, 3-4
  malt 3/27; 11/2-3
  wax 16/3-4

produce (*cont*)
  wool 3/1-3, 29; 5/3-4, 7; 8/3-4, 7, 24/2-4; 33/2, 4, 6; 43/4, 8-10, 46/18
property, leasehold 7/1
property, real 6/1; 7/1
psalms *see under* Church
publication *see under* Court procedure
Puritanism *see under* Church
registrar xvi, xxxii, xxxv-xxxvi
reputation xv, xviii, xxi, xxiii, xxviii, xxix, 1/3, 4; 3/1, 4-14, 16, 21-22, 26; 4/2-3; 9/3; 22/1; 25/2; 29/15; 34/3-5; 37/3-6
rights to services and sacraments *see under* Church
rye *see under* crops
sacraments *see under* Church
scot *see* tax
seat (church) *see under* Church
secretary hand xi-xii
sentence *see under* Court procedure
sheep *see under* livestock
shoe-mending 3/12
side(s)man 5/2-4, 6-7
silver (money) 8/2-3
slander 3/22
sluice xxiv, 46/1, 18-19
source material xiv
steers *see under* livestock
straw *see under* crops
tale-telling xxx, xl, 3/4-16, 21
tares *see under* crops
tax 5/2, 4-7; 24/2-4
testamentary cases xvii-xviii, xxi-xxii, xxvi, xl, **6**, **7**, **10**, **20**, **21**, **23**, **27**, **28**, **29**, **30**, **31**, **36**, **38**
thatch 30/2
theft xxxi, 3/1, 23-24, 26; 13/2-5; 29/8, 12-14
thorns 24/2
tithe cases xv, xvii-xviii, xxi, xxiv, xxvi-xxviii, **2**, **3**, **5**, **8**, **12**, **15**, **16**, **17**, **24**, **26**, **33**, **40**, **41**, **42**, **43**, **46**
tithe collector 2/6, 9, 13; 15/4; 40/3; 41/3; 43/7, 9-10; 46/3
tithes (great) 24/1; 33/5; **40-42**; 46/18
tithes (small) 3/29; 5/2-6; 8/2-7; 12/4; 16/3; 18/4-7; 26/2; 33/5; 40/3-6; 41/3, 5-6; 42/3-5, 8, 10; 46/1, 14-15, 18-19
venereal disease *see* burning
vetch *see under* crops
waste 17/1-4
wax *see under* produce
wheat *see under* crops
whore (accusation) xviii, xxiii, 1/1-5; 14/1-4; 22/1-4; 32/1; 37/1-6; 39/1-5
whoremonger (accusation) xxiii, 4/1-3; 37/2-4
will *see* testamentary cases
will, proof in form of law xxii, xxiii, xxvi, xl, xlii, 6/1; 7/1; 21/1; 23/1; 27/1; 28/1; 36/1
willow *see under* woodland
winning, winnowing 44/3, 7-8
witchcraft xvi, xxiii, 44/1-7
woodland
  coppice wood 24/1-2
  hazel 24/2
  hornbeam 24/2
  long wood 26/1-3
  timber see long wood
  willow 24/2
wool *see under* produce
yearings *see under* livestock
yockroom *see* hedgerow 26/1